INSIGHT GUIDES

ROME

APA PUBLICATIONS
L
Part of the Langenscheidt Publishing Group

INSIGHT GUIDES
ROME

Project Editor
Catherine Dreghorn
Picture Manager
Steven Lawrence
Cartography Manager
Zoe Goodwin
Series Editor
Rachel Lawrence
Publishing Manager
Rachel Fox

Distribution

UK & Ireland
GeoCenter International Ltd
Meridian House, Churchill Way West
Basingstoke, Hampshire RG21 6YR
sales@geocenter.co.uk

United States
Ingram Publisher Services
One Ingram Blvd, PO Box 3006
La Vergne, TN 37086-1986
customer.service@ingrampublisher services.com

Australia
Universal Publishers
1 Waterloo Road
Macquarie Park, NSW 2113
sales@universalpublishers.com.au

New Zealand
Hema Maps New Zealand Ltd (HNZ)
Unit 2, 10 Cryers Road,
East Tamaki, Auckland 2013
sales.hema@clear.net.nz

Worldwide
Apa Publications GmbH & Co. Verlag KG (Singapore branch)
7030 Ang Mo Kio Ave 5
08-65 Northstar @ AMK
Singapore 569880
apasin@singnet.com.sg

Printing

CTPS – China

First Edition 1991
Seventh Edition 2011

www.insightguides.com

About This Book

What makes an Insight Guide different? Since our first book pioneered the use of creative full-colour photography in travel guides in 1970, we have aimed to provide not only reliable information but also the key to a real understanding of a destination and its people.

Now, when the internet can supply inexhaustible (but not always reliable) facts, our books marry text and pictures to provide that more elusive quality: knowledge. To achieve this, they rely on the authority of locally based writers and photographers.

This book turns the spotlight on one of the most exhilarating cities in the world. Travellers have been drawn to Rome for centuries. Today they flock here in their millions not only to see the ancient city, the Vatican and to eat in traditional trattorias, but also to experience the newer side of the city – modern architecture, boutique hotels, and designer bars and restaurants. From the classical to the contemporary, *Insight Guide: Rome* covers the best of everything the city has to offer.

Contacting the Editors

We would appreciate it if readers would alert us to errors or outdated information by writing to:

Insight Guides, P.O. Box 7910, London SE1 1WE, England.
insight@apaguide.co.uk

The Contributors To This Book

This new edition of *Insight Guide: Rome* was commissioned by **Carine Tracanelli**, a senior commissioning editor, and edited by **Catherine Dreghorn**, assistant editor, at Insight Guides' London office, implementing a vibrant design by **Klaus Geisler**.

Solveig Steinhardt, who has spent the last seven years discovering the Eternal City's hidden treasures, was tasked with trekking the city streets to fully update the chapters and hotel and restaurant listings. She regularly works as a Rome correspondent for a number of travel magazines and guidebooks. Her favourite spots are the Terme di Caracalla at night, especially during the summer opera festival, and the Auditorium music hall. Solveig also updated the shopping chapter, originally written by **Annie Shapero**, a long-time resident and regular contributor to the Rome edition of *Where* magazine.

Travel writer and journalist **Marc Zakian** contributed a number of the short features, including *Rome on Film*, while writer and broadcaster **Lisa Gerard-Sharp** penned the incisive account of modern Rome and what makes the Romans tick.

This edition builds on excellent foundations laid down by many past contributors, including **Rowlinson Carter**, who wrote the original history chapter, **Jon Eldan**, who penned the food and drink chapter, and **Giovanna Dunmall**, who contributed to many of the previous updates. Additional material was supplied by **Jason Best**.

The majority of new photographs were by **Susan Smart**, with other images by **Britta Jaschinski, Anna Mockford, Nick Bonnetti** and **Alessandra Santarelli. Tom Smyth** undertook the picture research, proofreading was by **Sue Pearson** and the index compiled by **Helen Peters**.

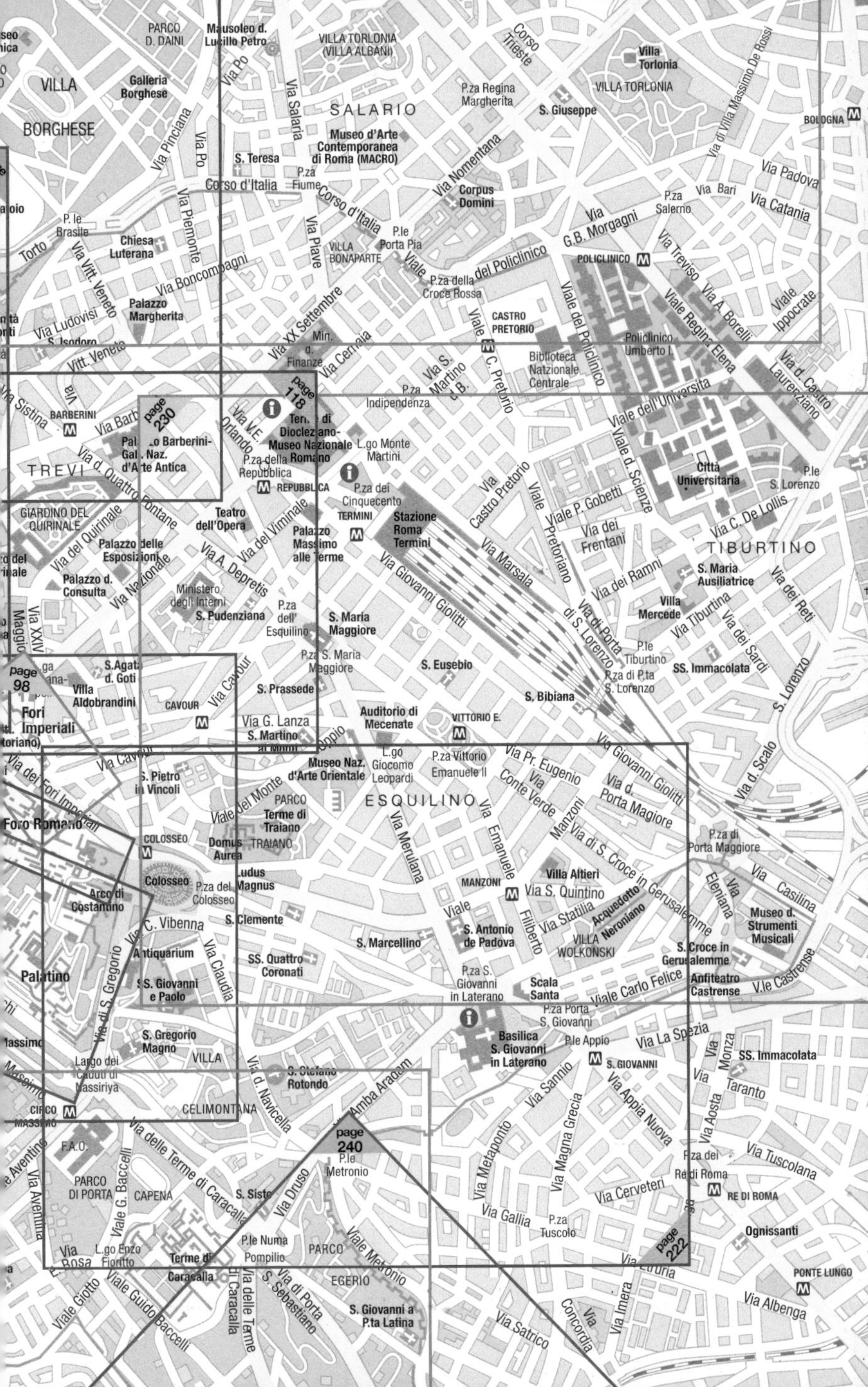

PARCO D. DAINI
Mausoleo d. Lucillo Petro
VILLA TORLONIA (VILLA ALBANI)
Corso Trieste
Villa Torlonia
VILLA TORLONIA
Via di Villa Massimo De Rossi
VILLA BORGHESE
Galleria Borghese
Via Po
Via Salaria
SALARIO
P.za Regina Margherita
S. Giuseppe
BOLOGNA
Via Pinciana
Museo d'Arte Contemporanea di Roma (MACRO)
S. Teresa
P.za Fiume
Via Nomentana
Corso d'Italia
Via Padova
Corpus Domini
P.za Salerno
Via Bari
Via Catania
P. le Brasile
Via Piemonte
Via Piave
P.le Porta Pia
VILLA BONAPARTE
Via G.B. Morgagni
Chiesa Luterana
Via Vitt. Veneto
Via Boncompagni
Viale del Policlinico
POLICLINICO
Via Treviso
P.za della Croce Rossa
Via A. Borelli
Viale Regina Elena
Viale Ippocrate
Palazzo Margherita
Via XX Settembre
CASTRO PRETORIO
Via Ludovisi
S. Isodoro
Min. d. Finanze
Via Cernaia
Viale C. Pretorio
Biblioteca Nazionale Centrale
Viale del Policlinico
Policlinico Umberto I.
Via d. Castro Laurenziano
Via Sistina
BARBERINI
Via Barberini
page 230
Via V.E. Orlando
page 118
Terme di Diocleziano-Museo Nazionale Romano
P.za Indipendenza
Via S. Martino d. B.
Viale dell'Università
Palazzo Barberini-Gal. Naz. d'Arte Antica
L.go Monte Martini
TREVI
Via d. Quattro Fontane
P.za della Repubblica
REPUBBLICA
P.za dei Cinquecento
Via Castro Pretorio
Viale Pretoriano
Viale d. Scienze
Città Universitaria
P.le S. Lorenzo
GIARDINO DEL QUIRINALE
Teatro dell'Opera
Via del Viminale
TERMINI
Stazione Roma Termini
Viale P. Gobetti
Via dei Frentani
Via C. De Lollis
TIBURTINO
Via del Quirinale
Palazzo delle Esposizioni
Palazzo Massimo alle Terme
Via Marsala
Via A. Depretis
Via Nazionale
Via Giovanni Giolitti
Via dei Ramni
S. Maria Ausiliatrice
Via dei Reti
Palazzo d. Consulta
Ministero degli Interni
S. Pudenziana
P.za dell' Esquilino
S. Maria Maggiore
Via di Porta di S. Lorenzo
Villa Mercede
Via Tiburtina
Via dei Sardi
P.le Tiburtino
P.za S. Maria Maggiore
S. Eusebio
P.za di P.ta S. Lorenzo
SS. Immacolata
S. Lorenzo
page 98
S.Agata d. Goti
Villa Aldobrandini
Fori Imperiali
CAVOUR
Via Cavour
S. Prassede
S. Bibiana
Via G. Lanza
S. Martino ai Monti
Auditorio di Mecenate
VITTORIO E.
Via dei Fori Imperiali
S. Pietro in Vincoli
Museo Naz. d'Arte Orientale
L.go Giocomo Leopardi
P.za Vittorio Emanuele II
Via Pr. Eugenio
Via Conte Verde
Via d. Porta Magiore
Via Giovanni Giolitti
Via d. Scalo
Foro Romano
Viale del Monte Oppio
PARCO Terme di Traiano
ESQUILINO
Via Merulana
Via Emanuele Filiberto
Via Manzoni
Via di S. Croce in Gerusalemme
P.za di Porta Maggiore
COLOSSEO
Domus Aurea
TRAIANO
Villa Altieri
Via Eleniana
Via Casilina
Colosseo
P.za del Colosseo
Ludus Magnus
MANZONI
Via S. Quintino
Arco di Costantino
Viale Manzoni
Via Statilia
Acquedotto Neroniano
Museo d. Strumenti Musicali
Via C. Vibenna
S. Clemente
S. Antonio de Padova
VILLA WOLKONSKI
S. Marcellino
S. Croce in Gerusalemme
Antiquarium
Via Claudia
SS. Quattro Coronati
Palatino
S. Giovanni e Paolo
P.za S. Giovanni in Laterano
Scala Santa
Viale Carlo Felice
Anfiteatro Castrense
V.le Castrense
Via di S. Gregorio
P.za Porta S. Giovanni
Basilica S. Giovanni in Laterano
P.le Appio
Via La Spezia
S. Gregorio Magno
Largo dei Caduti di Nassiriya
VILLA CELIMONTANA
S. Stefano Rotondo
S. GIOVANNI
Via Monza
SS. Immacolata
Via Taranto
CIRCO MASSIMO
Via d. Navicella
Via Amba Aradam
Via Sannio
Via Appia Nuova
Via Aosta
Via Aventina
F.A.O.
Via delle Terme di Caracalla
page 240
P.le Metronio
Via Metaponto
Via Magna Grecia
P.za dei Re di Roma
RE DI ROMA
Via Tuscolana
PARCO DI PORTA CAPENA
Viale G. Baccelli
S. Sisto
Via Druso
Via Cerveteri
Via Gallia
P.za Tuscolo
page 222
Ognissanti
L.go Enzo Fioritto
Terme di Caracalla
P.le Numa Pompilio
PARCO EGERIO
Viale Metronio
Via Etruria
PONTE LUNGO
Viale Giotto
Viale Guido Baccelli
Viale di Caracalla
Via delle Terme
Via di Porta S. Sebastiano
S. Giovanni a P.ta Latina
Via Satrico
Via Concordia
Via Imera
Via Albenga

The Guide at a Glance

The book is carefully structured both to convey an understanding of the city and its culture and to guide readers through its attractions and activities:

◆ The Best Of section at the front of the book helps you to prioritise. The first spread contains all the Top Sights, while Editor's Choice details unique experiences, the best buys or other recommendations.

◆ To understand Rome, you need to know something of its past. The city's history and culture are described in authoritative essays written by specialists in their fields who have lived in and documented Rome for many years.

◆ The Places section details all the attractions worth seeing. The main places of interest are coordinated by number with the maps.

◆ A list of recommended restaurants, bars and cafés is printed at the end of each chapter.

◆ Photographs throughout the book are chosen not only to illustrate geography and buildings, but also to convey the moods of the city and the life of its people.

◆ The Travel Tips section includes all the practical information you will need, divided into five key sections: transport, accommodation, activities (including nightlife, events, tours and sports), shopping, and an A–Z of practical tips. Information may be located quickly by using the index on the back cover flap of the book.

◆ Two detailed street atlases are included at the back of the book, complete with a full index. On the second one, you will find all the restaurants and hotels plotted for your convenience.

Places & Sights

Colour-coding at the top of every page makes it easy to find each area in the book. These are coordinated by specific area on the orientation map on pages 82–3.

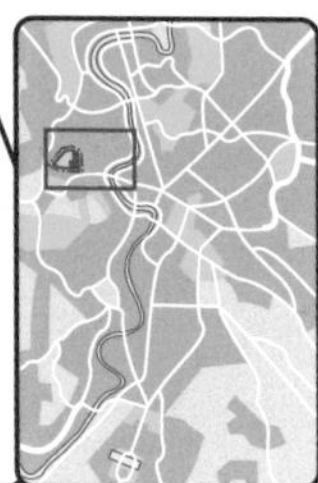

A locator map pinpoints the specific area covered in each chapter. The page reference at the top indicates where to find a detailed map of the area highlighted in red.

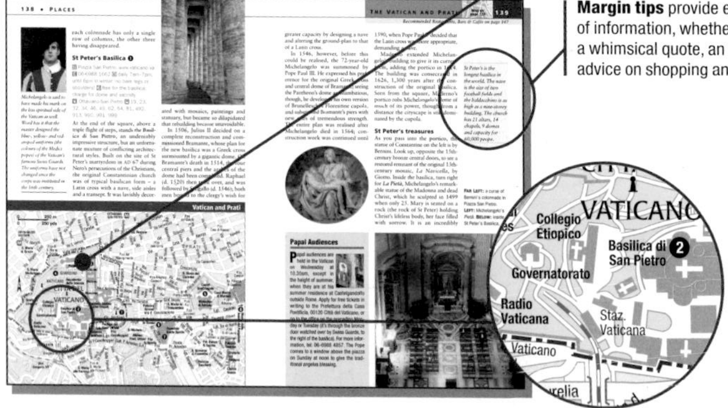

Margin tips provide extra little snippets of information, whether it's a practical tip, a whimsical quote, an historical fact or advice on shopping and eating.

A four-colour map provides a bird's-eye view of the area covered in the chapter, with the main attractions coordinated by number with the main text.

PHOTO FEATURES

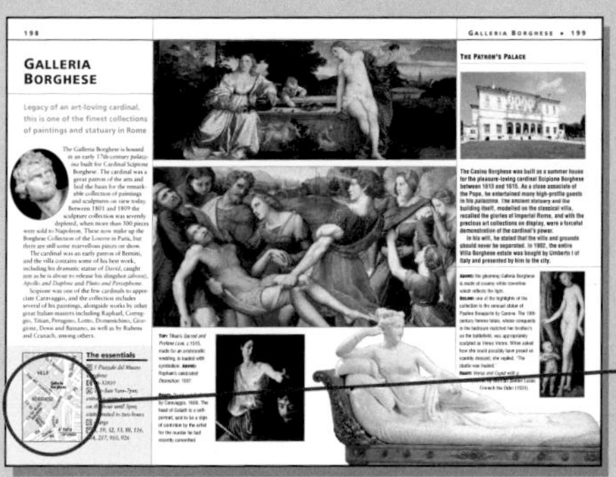

Picture stories offer visual coverage of major sights or unusual attractions. The map shows where it is, while vital statistics convey practical information: address, contact details, website, opening times, and if there's a charge.

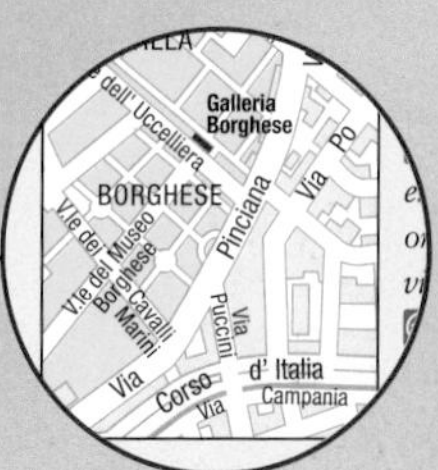

RESTAURANT LISTINGS

Restaurant listings feature the best establishments within each area, giving the address, phone number, opening times and price category followed by a useful review. The grid reference refers to the atlas at the back of the book.

In a pedestrianised alleyway, this rustic restaurant offers decent if a little unadventurous food. A nice touch is that you can choose which home-made pasta to go with which home-made sauce.

TRAVEL TIPS

GETTING AROUND

From the Airport

From Fiumicino, there are frequent train services to the city – every 15–30 minutes to Trastevere Station and every 30 minutes to Stazione Termini. Trains to Stazione Termini (the Leonardo Express) run from 6.37am to 11.37pm; the journey takes 35 minutes and the ticket

Advice-packed Travel Tips provide all the practical knowledge you'll need before and during your trip: how to get there, getting around, where to stay and what to do. The A–Z section is a handy summary of practical information, arranged alphabetically.

Contents

Best of Rome

Introduction

History

Features

Insights

Places

Restaurants & Bars

Travel Tips

Maps

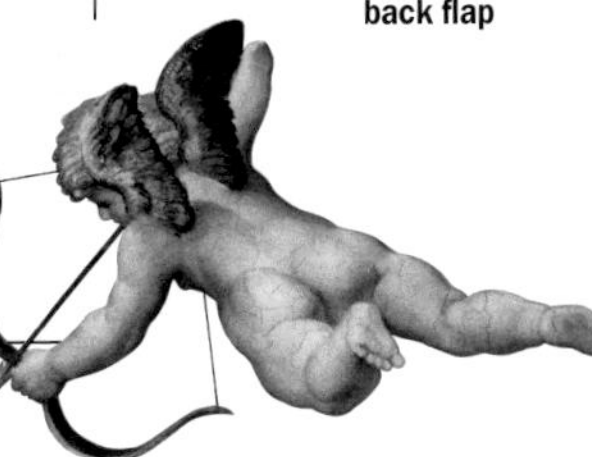

THE BEST OF ROME: TOP SIGHTS

Here, at a glance, are the city's must-sees, from the iconic monuments of Ancient Rome to the vibrant squares of Campo de' Fiori and Trastevere, and the tranquil gardens of the Villa Borghese

△ The majestic ruins of the **Forum**, the civic centre of Ancient Rome, are best seen on a Sunday when the busy thoroughfare that cuts through the site is closed to traffic. *See page 100.*

◁ The **Vatican Museums** merit a lifetime's study, but if you only have a few hours, be sure to include the Sistine Chapel in your tour of this vast repository of art. Michelangelo's breathtaking ceiling is a triumph of fresco painting. *See page 141.*

◁ The **Colosseum** is a shadow of its marble-clad imperial days, but it's impressive nonetheless and, as the symbol of Rome, remains one of the city's key sights. *See page 111.*

△ For a real insight into life in Ancient Rome, follow a tour of the Forum with a visit to the **Capitoline Museums**, an imposing collection of ancient art and Roman statuary. Among its most famous exhibits is the original bronze statue of a she-wolf suckling Romulus and Remus. *See page 89.*

◁ All human life converges on the **Spanish Steps** at the heart of Rome's main shopping district. *See page 129.*

▷ The old working-class district **Trastevere**, across the Tiber, is now a trendy quarter full of boutiques, restaurants and wine bars. *See page 201.*

▽ The best-preserved of all Ancient Rome's buildings is Emperor Hadrian's perfectly proportioned **Pantheon**. *See page 153.*

▷ When a voluptuous Anita Ekberg frolicked in the **Trevi Fountain** in Fellini's *La Dolce Vita*, she turned it into a Roman icon. Throw a coin in the water and enjoy an ice cream on the steps. *See page 117.*

◁ Della Porta's masterpiece, the *Fountain of Neptune*, stands at the northern end of elegant **Piazza Navona**, a totally enclosed square full of buskers, street performers, street artists and tourists. *See page 158.*

▽ By day the **Campo de' Fiori** is awash with the colour and activity of the daily market. It's also a great place to eat out at night. *See page 170.*

▽Leafy **Villa Borghese** is perfect for picnicking and home to two world-class museums. *See page 188.*

The Best of Rome: Editor's Choice

Unique attractions, festivals and events, top shops, pizzas and piazzas, church art, family outings... here are our recommendations, plus some money-saving tips

Best Views

- **The Gianicolo hill** Worlds away from the tightly packed streets of Trastevere and the chaos of the city below. *See page 206.*
- **Piazza Venezia** Fine views from the Vittoriano monument have the added advantage of excluding the hulking monument itself. *See page 90.*
- **Caffè Capitolino** Romantic views of terracotta rooftops and countless cupolas from the Capitoline Museum's pretty café. *See page 91.*
- **The Tabularium** Take in the Forum and the Palatine from a terrace in the ancient archive of Roman Law. *See page 89.*
- **Pincio Gardens** Views from the Villa Borghese Gardens stretch from Monte Mario to the Gianicolo and the piazza below. *See page 189.*
- **Castel Sant'Angelo** Views of the Tiber. *See page 143.*

Best Churches for Art

- **San Luigi dei Francesi** The dramatic paintings by Caravaggio in the Contarelli Chapel were the artist's first great religious works. *See page 158.*
- **Santa Maria in Trastevere** A pretty medieval church with spectacular mosaics on the facade and in the apse. *See page 202.*
- **Basilica di San Pietro** Michelangelo's tender and moving *Pietà* in St Peter's was completed when the artist was only 25 and remains one of his most famous works. *See page 138.*
- **San Pietro in Vincoli** This church houses another Michelangelo masterpiece, the newly restored statue of *Moses*. *See page 231.*
- **Santa Maria della Vittoria** So sensual is Bernini's famous sculpture of the *Ecstasy of St Teresa* that many suggest the rapture on her face is more than an expression of piety. *See page 187.*
- **Santa Prassede** The 9th-century church is filled with magnificent Byzantine mosaics. *See page 230.*
- **Santa Maria del Popolo** is a treasure house of art, with paintings by Raphael and Pinturicchio, plus two impassioned Caravaggios. *See page 125.*

Best Getaways

- **Ostia Antica** Well-preserved ruins of an old Roman port town. *See page 251.*
- **Tivoli** See the sumptuous Villa d'Este and its fountain-filled garden, and the remains of Hadrian's magnificent villa. *See page 257.*
- **Etruscan tombs** Cerveteri is the most atmospheric of the many Etruscan necropolises outside Rome. *See page 276.*
- **Oasi di Ninfa** An enchanting English-style garden with medieval ruins. *See page 263.*
- **Beaches** Head for Ostia or Fregene, or to Lazio's southern coastal stretches. *See page 254.*

Rome for Families

- **Villa Borghese Gardens** Laid out over rolling hills, this is the perfect city park for picnicking and relaxing. Attractions include museums, a zoo, a kids' playhouse, a boating lake and bikes for hire. *See page 188.*
- **Castel Sant'Angelo** Drawbridges, trapdoors, cannons, ditches and dungeons … everything but dragons in this ancient castle. *See page 143.*
- **Children's Museum** Explora is a delightful "playtown" where kids can touch, draw and play to their heart's content. *See page 306.*
- **Puppet shows** Free Punch and Judy shows on the Gianicolo hill. *See page 206.*
- **Coins in the fountain** A coin tossed in the Trevi Fountain is said to guarantee your return to Rome. *See page 117.*
- **A leisurely ride** on the No. 116 electric bus, which weaves its way from Via Veneto to the Vatican. Lovely for sightseeing and a welcome relief for sore feet. *See page 285.*
- **Villa Torlonia park** Let your older kids (11-15) interact with technology or simulate the set of a TV programme at Techno town, then relax in the fairytale setting of the Casina delle Civette (*see pages 194–5*).

OPPOSITE TOP LEFT: views from the Vittoriano monument. **OPPOSITE TOP RIGHT:** Michelangelo's *Pietà*. **OPPOSITE BELOW:** Santa Maria in Trastevere mosaic. **ABOVE:** Hadrian's Villa. **LEFT:** cycling in Villa Borghese. **RIGHT:** Piazza Navona.

Best Piazzas

- **Piazza Navona** Baroque grandeur, spectacular fountains and lively atmosphere. *See page 158.*
- **Piazza Farnese** A welcome relief from the chaos of neighbouring Campo de' Fiori. *See page 177.*
- **Piazza Mattei** A small piazza with a playful fountain and trendy café. *See page 173.*
- **Piazza Santa Maria in Trastevere** This neighbourly square buzzes with activity round the clock but never seems crowded. *See page 202.*
- **Piazza San Pietro** Vast, colonnaded square designed by Bernini to accommodate those on the papal pilgrimage. *See page 137.*
- **Piazza del Campidoglio** For the beautifully elegant staircase designed by Michelangelo. *See page 89.*
- **Piazza di Spagna** A spectacular urban space, perfect for people-watching. *See page 129.*

Best Buys

- **Ice cream** Head for Il Gelato di San Crispino for colouring- and preservative-free ice cream. *See page 66.*
- **Valentino** Ready-to-wear from Rome's beloved designer. *See page 132.*
- **Handbags** from Fendi and Furla are the ultimate in classic chic. The less discerning can pick up a cheap designer knock-off from any of the street vendors that congregate around tourist hotspots. *See pages 299–300.*
- **Shoes** from Fratelli Rossetti, a classic Italian footwear maker. *See page 300.*
- **Food** Two legendary delis for Roman specialities are Volpetti in Testaccio and charmingly old-fashioned Innocenzi in Trastevere. *See page 302.*
- **Jewellery** In New York there's Tiffany, in Paris there's Cartier, and in Rome there's Bulgari, where extravagant jewellery reigns supreme. Serious money. *See page 301.*

Above: a contented cat colony member. **Below Left:** arcane potions made by monks. **Below:** the spectacular Colosseum.

Only in Rome

- **Cat colonies** There are thousands of cats in Rome, many of them living wild among the ancient ruins. *See page 172.*
- **Priestly couture** Papal party gear, nuns' underwear, incense burners and more can be found in shops for religious garments and accessories on Via dei Cestari and Via di Santa Chiara. *See page 153.*
- **Cappuccino** Rome is full of atmospheric cafés serving excellent coffee. Piazza Rotonda and Piazza Farnese are prime spots, but the neighbourhood cafés frequented by locals are more fairly priced.
- **Catacombs** Three of the largest underground burial sites are to be found in the vicinity of the Appian Way. *See page 245.*
- **Made by monks** The potions and lotions, teas and preserves on sale at Ai Monasteri are all made by monks. *See page 301.*

Best Festivals and Events

- **RomaEuropa** An experimental arts festival held every autumn.
- **Estate Romana** "Roman Summer" is the collective name for all the events held outdoors in parks, villas, monuments and ancient sites, from June to September.
- **Easter week** torchlit processions and a huge open-air Mass in St Peter's Square. Plus chocolate and pastries galore.
- **Rome Film Fest** Rome's official film festival. Held at the Auditorium in October.
- **Il Natale di Roma** On 21 April Rome celebrates its founding with fireworks, music and other events.

For more about Rome's festivals see pages 306–9.

Best Small Hotels

- **Casa Howard, Via Capo Le Case** Tucked away in a secluded *palazzo*, the rooms are decorated with real flair. *See page 290.*
- **Aleph** Intriguing boutique hotel. Bedrooms inspired by 1930s design with hi-tech details, huge beds and a great spa. *See page 289.*
- **Locarno** Appealing Art Deco touches (the ornate cage lift alone is memorable). Oodles of charm and class. *See page 291.*
- **Due Torri** A delightful, historic hotel in a former cardinal's palace down a cobbled street. *See page 293.*
- **Teatro di Pompeo** Perched just off picturesque Campo de' Fiori, a homely mood prevails in the tasteful bedrooms. *See page 295.*

Best Pizzas

- **Dar Poeta** A special yeast-free dough is this Trastevere pizzeria's trademark. A local favourite. *See page 209.*
- **Formula Uno** The best and most down-to-earth pizzeria in the San Lorenzo university quarter, which is known as pizza central. *See page 237.*
- **Da Baffetto** A legendary pizza venue with fast-moving queues outside all night long. Brash but efficient service adds to the quintessential Roman experience. *See page 166.*
- **Napul'è** More than 40 types of authentic Neapolitan pizza. *See page 147.*
- **O' Pazzariello** A Neapolitan pizzeria with lots of ambience in a fairly small space. *See page 166.*
- **PizzaRé** Serves a huge range of crusty Neapolitan-style pizzas that are reliable and appetising. *See page 135.*
- **Zi' Fenizia** A kosher take-away in the Jewish Ghetto which has a permanent queue. *See page 183.*

ABOVE: inviting rooms at the Casa Howard. **RIGHT:** pizzas may have originated in Naples, but there are many excellent ones to be found all over Rome.

Money-Saving Tips

Free museums
EU citizens under 18 and over 65 years old get free entry to all state and city museums.

Free churches
All the basilicas and churches in Rome are free, as is the Pantheon.

Settimana della Cultura
Cultural Week is held all over Italy in late April or May, when entrance is free to all state-run museums and historical sites (log onto www.beniculturali.it for more details). *See page 307.*

Bus tours
Buses in Rome are cheap and efficient. An army of small, electric buses (116, 117 and 119) wind their way through the most scenic parts of Rome where cars and "real" buses cannot venture. *See page 285.*

Cheap eats
Anywhere marked *tavola calda*, where you can choose from well-stocked buffets, or *pizza al taglio*, where you can buy slices of pizza to enjoy on the steps of a nearby fountain or square.

Free Vatican
Entrance to the Vatican Museums is free on the last Sunday of the month, but be prepared for long queues. *See page 141.*

"Roman Summer" events
Anything that is part of the Estate Romana programme is usually fairly cheap (€8–€15). *See page 309.*

BVLGA

Immagina
da
ogni

SCALINATA R·IV
DELLA TRINITÀ
DEI MONTI

ROME AND THE ROMANS

Dubbed the Eternal City by poets and artists, Rome is one of the world's most exhilarating and romantic travel destinations. It is a city that inspires the mind, appeals to the senses and captures the heart

The 21st century has brought a waft of fresh air to the world's most ancient city. The millennial revamp for Holy Year 2000, which gave the city's ancient sites a much-needed facelift, sparked a number of changes in the dormant artistic and architectural scenes, and the revolution is on-going. Revamped galleries, new contemporary art museums, a cinema festival and the creation of a superb music complex turned Rome into a modern city that stays true to its glorious past while facing the future with confidence. While not a new *Dolce Vita*, there is a cinematic gloss to the emerging city, with eclectic festivals, a funky club scene, sleek cafés, boutique hotels and a more cosmopolitan air.

Not that Rome will ever wear its history lightly. The Eternal City remains chaotic but compact, bewildering but walkable, beguiling but exhausting. Unfortunately, the public transport system, from the pointless metro to the overcrowded buses, is woefully inadequate, with buses shunned by most middle-class Romans and the metro going nowhere relevant for most visitors. Work on a new metro line, running northwest to southeast, will slice through the heart of the Imperial city, but this is not due for completion until 2018 at the earliest. Fear of damaging ancient sites and becoming mired in bureaucracy are why radical measures have never been contemplated before.

The Eternal City has shaken off its dusty toga and slipped into contemporary clothes. As the mayor says: "Rome dares to dream again".

For now, cynical Romans see a decent transport system as a gift to their grandchildren, much as straight roads were a gift to the Empire's grateful colonies. Until then, the demented locals will continue to fume in traffic jams, flit by on flimsy Vespas or rattle around in speed-crazed buses. For visitors, the good news is that, with stoicism, sturdy shoes and enough caffeine-fuelled café stops, Rome is still a heavenly walking city.

PRECEDING PAGES: Gucci, Vespas and Bulgari – quintessentially Italian; a Caffe Castroni espresso. **LEFT:** Piazza di Spagna. **ABOVE:** Piazza del Popolo.

Neighbourhoods

The locals jest that Rome is not for Romans: few Romans live in the historic centre any more. In the 1960s the tradesmen moved to the suburbs in search of comfortable apartments while the *centro storico* succumbed to gentrification; once-crumbling *palazzi* were snapped up by astute investors, from bankers to politicians. Yet individuals remain attached to their *rione* or neighbourhood: the original 14 date from the time of the Emperor Augustus, but have grown to 22, each with its own civic crest. Moreover, Romans also harbour attachments to mythologised quarters in the *centro storico*, such as the Ghetto, the former Jewish district, or Campo de' Fiori, once peopled by mere fruit-sellers and furniture-restorers but now full of funky bars and fashion victims.

Outsiders often see Rome as devoted to Imperial posturing, whether of the ostentatious Colosseum-Forum variety or Mussolini's self-aggrandising EUR district. Yet local neighbourhoods can be both cosmopolitan and homely, ranging from the formalised domesticity of Parioli, framed by embassies, to mellow Trastevere, louche yet intimate, dotted with arty bars and galleries. Looming above Trastevere is the leafy, *fin de siècle* Gianicolo district, home to retiring residents and expatriate newcomers.

Rome can be rough around the edges, but its lack of manicured perfection is part of its charm. The Esquilino area,

All Aboard

For the cheapest, most chaotic tour through the time machine that is Rome, hop on the 87 bus, which runs from east to west, scoring a cross-section of the city's history. The route runs from bustling Piazza Cavour to the rural Via Appia Antica archaeological park, replete with tombs, ruins, cats and ghosts. En route are swathes of the Imperial, Early Christian, Renaissance and Baroque city in all its glory, from the gladiatorial Colosseum to seductive Piazza Navona, the Tiber and the legendary Seven Hills of Rome. Flashing past your eyes is all Roman history, from monumentality to murder most foul.

To see Rome as Fellini saw it, ride the No. 3 tram, which Fellini claimed gave him inspiration.

around the Fascist-Modernist Termini Station, nicknamed "the dinosaur", is a case in point, as is Testaccio, the former meat-packing district that is, with Ostiense, the pulsating heart of clubland. Once dilapidated, these districts are being gentrified but retain their edginess, youthful spirit and multi-ethnic flavour. Rome is more cosmopolitan than at any time since the Empire, though hardly on the same scale.

Yet beyond its bustle and bravado, the Eternal City feels static, imprisoned by its past. Rome is *the* place for contemplating the passage of time and the vanity of human wishes. "Within a short time you forget everything; and everything forgets you," said Marcus Aurelius. The world-weary population has little inclination to relive the glory, decline and fall. Nonetheless, there is a residual melancholy and romantic nostalgia for the grandeur of Imperial Rome.

The temporal and the spiritual

Novelist Alberto Moravia used to say: "Rome is an administrative city dominated by two institutions: the State and the Church." While an oversimplification, Rome *is* the meeting place of temporal and spiritual powers and, as the capital, lives and breathes politics. As for piety, the Vatican has traditionally been treated as a temporal power, as the corporate arm of the papacy. "Faith is made here but believed elsewhere," is the local dictum.

Essentially, the Romans are more ritualistic than religious, even if the death of John Paul II saw an outpouring of emotion that surprised cynical Rome-watchers.

At work, Romans have an inbuilt resistance to Milanese efficiency, schedules and short lunch breaks. Life is too Latin for a Protestant work ethic. Indeed, there are few qualms about playing the tourist at home, from eating an ice cream on Piazza Navona to tossing a coin in the Trevi Fountain, visiting the Vatican museums on a Vespa, lolling around the Villa Borghese Gardens, or peeking into the Pantheon while on a café crawl.

> *As the writer Alberto Moravia said: "There are no Romans, only people from all parts of Italy who adopt Roman characteristics".*

The first Pantheon was built by Marcus Agrippa. Even though Hadrian's later version in AD 117 was an improvement, he gave credit to his predecessor. Agrippa, who built aqueducts, baths and colonies, was too industrious to be a typical Roman. As the local saying goes: "*ce piace mangia bene ce piace poco lavora*" – we prefer eating and drinking to working.

FAR LEFT: guards outside the Palazzo del Quirinale. **TOP LEFT:** shopping on the Campo de' Fiori. **MIDDLE LEFT:** in-line skating in the Villa Borghese. **ABOVE:** local in Campo de' Fiori. **ABOVE RIGHT:** Rome's most efficient form of transport.

Romans at play

Bar aficionados believe you can tell a lot about a Roman by his café of choice. Cardinals favour the upstanding Caffè San Pietro near the Vatican, while haunts such as Caffè Rosati on Piazza del Popolo are proud of being the place *not* to be seen – here, celebrity regulars unwind in a discreet Art Nouveau ambience.

Roman café-owners proudly announce that "this was Fellini's favourite place", "Mastroianni's haunt", or that "Bertolucci prefers our pastries". Bar Canova, near Piazza del Popolo, was Fellini's second home: he came straight from his Oscar success to a party in the bar. The back room, where the visionary director held meetings, is now a Fellini shrine.

Yet the best bars compel a sentimental attachment that goes well beyond celebrity-worship: the journalist wife of former mayor Francesco Rutelli even dedicated a book to her local bar-owner in Caffè del Teatro Marcello.

Nightlife is less tribal than café culture, inspired by "*vivere e lascia vivere*," a "live and let live" philosophy. Party-goers start late and finish late, with clubbers calling into a bar for a *cornetto* (sweet croissant) and cappuccino before heading home. San Lorenzo, a city within a city, is an erstwhile immigrant district that is now the heart of the main university quarter, around Via dei Volsci. By night, books are exchanged for bar crawls, with Happy Hour an excuse for wine-tasting, tapas bars, emerging bands and, bizarrely, even board games.

Clubland is centred on Testaccio and Via Ostiense, particularly since the Roma Tre university campus has revitalised the area. However, more mellow visitors may feel more at

ESTATE ROMANA

Estate Romana (Roman Summer) is the name of the umbrella festival promoting art shows and music, cinema, dance, museum, theatre and kids' events, which takes place from July to August every year. Created more than 30 years ago, it was first intended to amuse the unlucky few who weren't able to escape the Rome heat and go away for the month of August as per Italian tradition. But the times they are a-changin' and with the economy in a downturn, more people are unable to afford to close up shop and take a holiday. On the bright side, *Estate Romana* is getting more popular every year. The main venues are the city parks, hosting high-level concerts every night: there's a jazz festival in Villa Celimontana, world music in Villa Ada, opera in Terme di Caracalla, classical music and dance in Villa Adriana. On the Tiber Island, sidewalks are set up with an array of stands selling crafts, CDs, clothes, jewellery and food, and there's an open-air cinema. Other summer attractions include a swimming pool by the Colosseum, an outdoor gym in Flaminio, and a faux beach on the river below Castel Sant' Angelo. Get the programme at www.estateromana.comune.roma.it.

home with Trastevere's arty ambience, and an evening spent in cool bars, listening to the Blues, followed by an *affogato* ice cream, drenched in liqueur.

High culture

As for high culture, Rome has seen a swathe of renovations and reopenings. The most radical project is MAXXI, a recently inaugurated grand project by Anglo-Iraqi architect Zaha Hadid, which sees a former army barracks reborn as the Museum of 21st-Century Arts. More traditional is the major refurbishment of the Palazzo Barberini and Gallery of Ancient Art, set in a palace designed by Borromini and Bernini, the founder of the Italian Baroque style. The rest of this great collection resides in Palazzo Corsini over the river, but is due to be displayed under one roof in Palazzo Barberini – but only when the privileged Officers' Club decamps from its palatial residence there.

In leafy Villa Borghese, the city's best-loved gardens, the Orangery (Aranciera) has been transformed into a modern art museum dedicated to Carlo Bilotti, an Italo-American collector. Close to vibrant Campo de' Fiori, the new Museo Barracco showcases Egyptian, Etruscan and Roman sculpture and, unlike most didactic Roman museums, uses a multimedia approach.

The most controversial new site is the Ara Pacis Museum, a steel, glass and marble structure designed to house a 2,000-year-old Altar of Peace that, ironically, was used for sacrifices. Created by Richard Meier, this is the first new public monument erected in the historic centre since Mussolini's day, and it divides local opinion. Art critic Vittorio Sgarbi called it "an indecent cesspit", while others have praised it as an airy, accessible building that lets citizens see into the mindset of Emperor Augustus and Ancient Rome.

The Romans have a reputation for being artistic connoisseurs and cultural raiders rather than creative artists. As blasé sophisticates, they have seen it all before and bought the T-shirt. Yet despite their love of bread and circuses, contemporary citizens have cultivated a dynamic arts scene, with one of the most vibrant music venues in Italy. Much credit is

FAR LEFT: waiter at the News Café. **LEFT:** party-goers start late and finish late. **ABOVE:** Easter concert performance at the Auditorium.

due to the Parco della Musica, Renzo Piano's theatrical space, where beetle-like pods create perfect acoustics in settings suitable for symphonies or soul, Rachmaninov or Lou Reed. Casa del Jazz, in the gardens of Villa Osio, a property confiscated from a Mafia boss, has grown into the city's major dedicated jazz venue, and, while the new Cinema Festival may not rival Venice's, it seeks to involve the Roman public rather than outsiders.

In trendy Testaccio, the Mattatoio, a former slaughterhouse, houses MACRO Future, a hip art museum. In the San Lorenzo area, near Termini Station, galleries in unconventional settings combine literary cafés with installations, photographic displays and performance art. Dotted around the city are concept stores and bookshops that double as bars and multimedia venues. Rome also playfully mixes art and entertainment: in eclectic club Brancaleone, crowds dance the night away before installations and video art screenings, while the Literature Festival in May is housed amid the marvellous ruins of Maxentius' Basilica.

Fashion parades

Rome is that rare thing – a city on the international shopping circuit that somehow manages to keep small shops in business. Svelte Romans saunter down Via del Corso and Via Condotti to windowshop for chic designer names. As for

EASTER IN ROME

Easter is the most heartfelt Roman festival, when history and tradition merge with common piety and cheerful consumerism. At Easter, the Eternal City is never more at ease with its Roman and Christian heritage, from St Peter's "Roman" relics to the Scala Santa, the marble staircase that Christ supposedly ascended to meet Pontius Pilate. In San Giovanni in Laterano, where the staircase arrived from Palestine, the faithful dutifully climb to the top on their knees. On Good Friday, the Pope retraces Christ's Via Crucis on a moving candlelit procession, ending in a huge open-air Mass on St Peter's Square on Easter Sunday. On becoming Pope, Benedict XVI opened up the Porta Santa Rosa entrance to the Vatican, as a gesture of openness, but the queues of pilgrims remain just as long. The Easter procession winds from the Colosseum to Monte Palatino, re-enacting the 14 Stations of the Cross, from Christ's death sentence to his entombment, with the Pope uttering a prayer at each station. Thousands of pilgrims gather with torches to follow this solemn procession, which coincides with classical music concerts in many city churches. Not that Roman festivals eschew gaiety and self-indulgence. The city's pastry shops display Easter eggs stuffed with tiny silver picture frames or costume jewellery. Wealthier Romans even instruct their favourite chocolatiers to encase treasured gifts in the eggs, ranging from engagement rings to car keys or symbolic crosses. Despite their sophistication, Romans love the chocolate-wrapped trappings of piety, and tangible symbols of truth, a reminder that even Christian Rome was founded on relics.

Roman brands, the leading lights are Valentino, renowned for his red-carpet style, Brioni, dresser to James Bond, and Fendi, displaying bespoke bags and politically incorrect furs in the gorgeous Palazzo Fendi at the foot of the Spanish Steps. More individualistic shopping awaits in the art galleries and workshops of Trastevere and the Borghetto Flaminio antiques market. Rome is full of *botteghe*, and many artisans' workshops will copy a marble bust on demand. Come nightfall and *aperitivo* time, the fashionistas emerge, to parade around lively Campo de' Fiori and the beguiling Piazza Navona area.

Summer in the city

The summer heat drives most Romans out of the city in search of sea or mountain air. Those who remain are wooed by summer festivals and hedonistic nightlife, especially during the *Estate Romana* festival. Summer is a riot of outdoor events staged in villas, parks and squares, from open-air cinema on Tiber Island to concerts and parties in the park. Equally lovely are the Terme di Caracalla, the high-vaulted Roman baths, used to showcase opera.

In the lush Villa Borghese Gardens, the Globe Theatre Roma is a replica of London's Elizabethan theatre of the same name, and stages Shakespearean drama and experimental theatre from June to September.

Set in stone

Despite all the surface glitz, there is no escaping the architecture, which assails one's senses around every corner. The Romans were arguably the greatest builders of antiquity, combining monumentality and utility with Greek grace and a sense of creation for eternity. The Pantheon remains an inspiration to contemporary architects, while down-to-earth football fans are equally struck by the Stadio Olimpico, Mussolini's Olympic Stadium, which hosts the deadly rivals, Roma and Lazio.

For an architectural overview, the Crypta Balbi displays recent archaeological finds and traces the city's development from the pre-Imperial era to Early Christian and medieval times. While some city museums are unduly didactic, the theatrical streets are a revelation.

Given its cinematic glamour, Rome can't help resembling a film set. Memories of gladiatorial contests are inescapable, superimposed on scenes of Fellini-esque excess or *Dolce Vita* charm, a *Roman Holiday* with Gregory Peck and Audrey Hepburn. Not that Hepburn will suddenly hitch up her Givenchy skirt and hop on a Vespa – the *Dolce Vita* doesn't linger on, despite the retro sexiness of the city. But a certain sultriness does linger, combining with the ancient stones to ensure this Eternal City continues to appeal to all who visit. ❑

FAR LEFT: graffitied doorway in Campo de' Fiori. **ABOVE LEFT:** leather craftsman at work in his San Lorenzo studio. **ABOVE:** Italy celebrate winning the FIFA World Cup in 2006. **ABOVE RIGHT:** Via dei Condotti swarms with shoppers and tourists.

THE MAKING OF ROME

Emperors and popes, dictators and rebels, philosophers and barbarians, saints and sinners, from immense wealth to pillage and ruin – Romans really have seen it all

Romulus and Remus, the twins famously suckled by a she-wolf, are not the only candidates for the title of founders of Rome. One account offered by Pliny the Elder was of a noblewoman who was surprised by a male organ rising from the ashes of a hearth. The resulting child became King Servius Tullius, builder of the first wall around Rome.

The Livy version

Implausible pregnancy is a feature of many of the legendary accounts, and this is no accident. Archaeology has unearthed evidence of scattered settlements in the Roman hills in 1200 BC, but these early Latins were culturally overshadowed by Etruscans and Greeks. Roman historians preferred a neat break with the past. Miraculous conception was just the ticket.

Rome is the only great city that has a birthday – 21 April, Il Natale di Roma, *the precise day when, according to Livy, Romulus founded the city back in 753 BC.*

A large part of Livy's vast *History of Rome*, written in the 1st century BC, is devoted to weighing up theories on its origins, including that of the poet Virgil, who relished the idea of the Greek world as Rome's spiritual cradle. Aeneas, the hero of Virgil's *Aeneid*, is a survivor of the sacking of Troy who drifted to North Africa and was sent by the gods to found Rome. Livy added more divine intervention: King Numitor of Alba Longa, the city founded by Aeneas's son Ascanius, was usurped, Livy explains, by his brother Amulius, and Numitor's daughter Rhea Silvia hid in a cave. She was visited there by the war god Mars, who became the father of her twins Romulus and Remus. Doubting this unlikely story, Amulius had her thrown into the Tiber, while the twins were put in a basket and cast adrift to meet their fate. The basket was washed up below the Palatine Hill, and the babies' cries attracted a she-wolf, who suckled the boys until they were rescued by a

LEFT: detail showing battle scenes from the Column of Marcus Aurelius. **ABOVE:** the Etruscan art masterpiece, *The Apollo of Veio.*

shepherd. Mars later appeared to the twins and pointed them towards their glorious destiny. They founded Rome, wrote Livy, in 753 BC.

Relations between them then soured. Remus proposed a site on the Aventine, and the name Rema; Romulus demanded the Palatine and the name Roma. Remus ridiculed Romulus' new walls, jumping over them. Furious, Romulus killed his brother, and the walls were ritually annointed with his blood.

Again as Livy tells it, Rome's population grew fast, but with many more men than women. Romulus decided to lay on games so magnificent all the surrounding tribes were bound to attend. What they did not know was that their women would not be going home. This has been immortalised as the "rape of the Sabine women".

Republican virtues

Seven kings were said to have ruled Rome after Romulus. Most – despite the legends – were Etruscans, indicating that Rome was still subordinate to the older civilisation. The city's institutions took shape: the patrician class provided priests and judges, while plebeians took care of agriculture, cattle-breeding and trade.

Tensions were frequent between Etruscans and Romans. They came to a head over another notorious rape, of Lucretia, the virtuous wife of a Roman, Collatinus, by the degenerate son of Rome's Etruscan King Tar-

ROMAN FAMILIES – THEORY AND PRACTICE

In Roman law men had absolute power over women – in theory. The head of a family or *pater familias* enjoyed total authority over all the women in it, and on marriage a woman simply passed from his authority to that of her husband. If she fell short of "virtue in all things" he could instantly divorce her, or punish her. Reality, though, often intervened. Wars sent high-born men away for years on end, leaving their wives in charge of their property, and created many wealthy widows. The rich woman with a string of lovers and a far-off husband was a stock figure for Roman gossips. Laws were relaxed to allow upper-class women to manage estates, or even engage in trade.

At the start of the Empire Augustus tried to re-establish old disciplines with fierce punishments for misbehaviour and restrictions on women, but without much success: one of the first victims was his own daughter Julia, who was exiled for adultery.

quinius Superbus. As Roman historians tell it, the populace rose up against the licentiousness of the Etruscan court, and drove Rome's last Etruscan king into exile. In 509 BC Lucius Junius Brutus, leader of the revolt, was elected one of the two Consuls who ruled Rome, as it became a republic. An Etruscan attempt to retake the city was seen off at the bridge across the Tiber by the hero Horatius.

The Roman Republic was tightly organised, above all for war – to which every Roman citizen had to contribute – but had no democracy. Only patricians could vote and sit in the Senate, to which the Consuls were responsible. In 494 BC the post of Tribune was created to protect plebeian interests, and from 450 BC the Twelve Tables of laws were displayed in the Forum, but the thousands of slaves had no rights at all.

Continental domination

Rome made little effort to develop an economic base: it simply lived on the proceeds of conquest. The Republic prospered against the backdrop of an invasion by the Gauls in 390 BC, when cackling geese sounded the alarm; the wars with Carthage, when Hannibal led his elephants across the Alps and almost brought Rome's progress to a dead stop, and the steady growth of its Empire, as the Romans expanded into Spain and to the banks of the Danube. With the final defeat of Carthage in 146 BC, Rome dominated the entire Mediterranean.

A mighty military machine was needed to control the conquered provinces, and successful generals became the most powerful figures in the state, with violent rivalries between them. In 91 BC two generals, Marius and Sulla, put down a revolt in several Italian cities, but then fought each other, and the unscrupulous Sulla took advantage of the situation to seize power and install Rome's first brief military dictatorship. The Roman Republic was dying.

> *The Roman Republic stood out among its neighbours for its military organisation and belligerent belief in its right to conquer allcomers.*

ABOVE LEFT: the rape of the Sabine women, as seen by David in the 1790s. **ABOVE:** the Roman Senate in session. **ABOVE RIGHT:** Pan and a Maenad depicted on a ceramic bowl.

Enter Caesar

The squabbles of the Roman élite continued after Sulla's death, but were interrupted by a vast slave revolt in 73 BC, led by the gladiator Spartacus. It was finally crushed by Crassus, which helped him become for a time the Empire's foremost general. From 59 BC he shared power in the First Triumvirate with Pompey and Julius Caesar, a brilliant commander who was about to conquer Gaul and lead his legions across the English Channel.

While in Gaul, he made sure a generous share of his booty went back to the capital to buy political support, and the friendship between him and Pompey turned into bitter enmity. Caesar was forbidden to return to Italy, but in 49 BC he defied the Senate by crossing the River Rubicon with his army, with the aim of seizing power. Defeated by Caesar's legions in Greece, Pompey fled to Egypt, where he was killed by his former Egyptian friends. Caesar followed him, and lingered in Egypt, besotted by its young queen Cleopatra, with whom he had a son. When he returned to Rome, she accompanied him.

Caesar now had unchallenged power, and endeared himself to the people with a spectacular building programme. Rome still had Republicans determined to resist dictatorship, however, and a band of senators led by Brutus cut Caesar down, on the Ides of March, 44 BC.

Gods and Empire

Caesar's murder did not lead to a restoration of the Republic but a new civil war, in which the conspirators were easily defeated by an alliance of Caesar's nephew and adopted son Octavian and Caesar's leading general, Mark Antony. These two, though, were also rivals, and became open enemies when Antony developed his passion for Cleopatra, which provided romantic interest for the next 13 years. After the two famous lovers committed suicide, Octavian, who took the name Augustus or "revered one", emerged as victor and – although the Senate remained in place, with little power – the first Roman emperor.

Cleopatra's expropriated treasure funded Augustus' transformation of Rome from "a city of brick into a city of marble". The Augustan Age was Rome's cultural apex, producing Virgil, Ovid and Livy. To end the political bickering of earlier years, Augustus gave Rome a much stronger civil service, which kept the Empire and its capital going throughout all the bizarre misbehaviour of his successors.

To reinforce his power (and ego) Augustus encouraged the worship of Julius Caesar and the rest of his family as gods, and this was taken to heart by his descendants, who literally believed they could do anything. Emperors such as Tiberius, Caligula and Nero acted like monsters at the pinnacle of society,

NERO'S DREAM HOME

Nero's extravagance was extraordinary even for one of the Caesars. After Rome's great fire in AD 64 – which many said he started – he seized 80 hectares (200 acres) of land by the Forum to build his Domus Aurea or "Golden House", with facades clad in gold, ivory and mother-of-pearl tiles, and fountains sprinkling perfumes. "At last", he said when it was finished, amazingly quickly, "I can live like a human being." So hated was Nero, though, that demolition began immediately after his death in AD 68, and his artificial lake-bed was used as the site of the Colosseum, to entertain the masses.

FAR LEFT: the grape harvest, in a Roman mosaic.
LEFT: noble Romans: Caesar (left) and Brutus.
ABOVE TOP: portrayal of a Roman orgy with dancer.
ABOVE: the poet Virgil, from an early manuscript.
RIGHT: philosopher-emperor Marcus Aurelius.

rivalling each other in their decadence, gleefully related by the later writer Suetonius. Alongside Roman excess there was a strange devotion to formality; the Greek Plutarch wrote long treatises on morality and etiquette, including which subjects to discuss at dinner.

The satirist Juvenal said that Roman emperors ruled with "bread and circuses" – doling out free grain to the poor, and dazzling the masses with lavish spectacles and bloody gladiatorial combats.

Honour was restored to the throne after the death of Nero in AD 68 by a succession of effective emperors, notably Trajan, Hadrian and the philosopher-emperor Marcus Aurelius, who between them led Rome to the height of its power in the second century AD. With over 1 million inhabitants, it was a city without equal anywhere in the world, attracting people from every part of its Empire and the known world.

Constantine and Christianity

Over the centuries, defending its vast possessions against a host of potential invaders imposed immense strains on the Empire. In 286, Emperor Diocletian decided ruling the Empire had become too big a job for one man, and divided it into two halves, Eastern and Western. After his death this led to more fighting between rival emperors, which ended, briefly, in 312 when Constantine the Great emerged as sole emperor. He, however, reaffirmed the division between East and West, and moved his main capital to the shores of the Black Sea, to the city he gave his name, Constantinople. Rome, once the *caput mundi* or "head of the world", was left just a shadow of its former self.

Constantine's other world-changing decision was to grant tolerance to Christianity, which only recently had been fiercely persecuted. In 324, he effectively made it the state religion of the Empire. In Rome itself the new faith and old pagan traditions coexisted for decades, but Constantine's decisions established Christianity

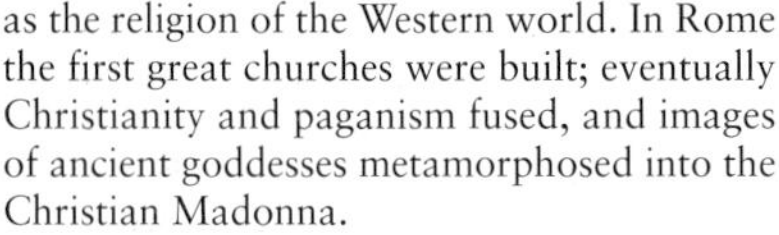

as the religion of the Western world. In Rome the first great churches were built; eventually Christianity and paganism fused, and images of ancient goddesses metamorphosed into the Christian Madonna.

Hard times

Rome was still the seat of the so-called Western emperors, who clung on, relying on armies of barbarian mercenaries. In 410, Emperor Honorius failed to pay the Visigoth leader Alaric, who sacked Rome, an event seen as the real end of the Roman Empire in the West.

Political collapse left a leadership vacuum increasingly filled by the new religion, and especially the bishop of Rome, the Pope – in contrast to the East, where Christian patriarchs were subordinate to the Byzantine emperors. In 452, Pope Leo I played a major part in buying off the hordes of Attila, the "Scourge of God", but he was unable to stop another sack of Rome, by the Vandals in 455. The city's essential aqueducts were no longer maintained, and Rome was partly abandoned.

Germanic tribes dominated Italy, and in 476 the Ostrogoth king Theodoric finally deposed Romulus Augustulus, theoretically the last

Western Roman emperor. In the next century, the Byzantine emperor Justinian sought to restore the old Empire and succeeded in regaining control of most of Italy, but even then his governors ruled from Ravenna, not Rome, and they were unable to resist another Germanic invasion, by the Lombards. The popes left Ravenna and returned to Rome, installing themselves in the Castel Sant'Angelo.

A major part in building up the role of the papacy was played by Gregory the Great, pope from 590–604. Seized by the beauty of Anglo-

> *Around AD 100 Rome's population was we over 1 million; by AD 600 it had no more than 20,000 people, living among the ancient ruins and using them as a quarry.*

Saxon youths in Rome's slave market, it is said, he was inspired to send missionaries to convert their country to Christianity. Missionary expeditions were also used across the Continent to assert papal authority over all the Christian communities of Western Europe, which until then had largely gone their own way.

Nostalgic Empire

The papacy's search for a Christian ruler to protect the Church focused on an alliance with the Frankish kings, sealed on Christmas Eve 800 when Pope Leo III crowned Charlemagne as Holy Roman Emperor in Rome. By this act Leo sought to make it clear that popes preceded emperors, but this was only the prelude to centuries of struggle for supremacy between the two. The "Holy Roman Empire" evoked the stability of the past, but it was never clear what the powers or role of this Empire were.

Rome was attacked by Muslim Saracens, in 846, and Romans fought Romans in political factions. Pope Gregory VII, elected in 1073, established many characteristic institutions of the Catholic Church, including the College of Cardinals and compulsory celibacy for priests. He also attempted to claw back authority over the Holy Roman Empire at the expense of Emperor Henry IV. He looked for new allies in the Normans, but this led to disaster *(see below)*.

Popes frequently excommunicated rulers who displeased them, but this only encouraged disrespect for the papacy. In 1309 France imposed its own candidate as pope and even moved the papacy to Avignon, from where seven successive popes reigned in the papacy's "Babylonian captivity".

Return to splendour

The papacy returned to Rome in 1377, but this was just the prelude to the Great Schism, when there were two or even three popes at the same time. The papacy was only unified with the election in 1417 of Martin V, of the aristocratic Roman Colonna clan.

Rome was in a ruinous state, but the restored papacy enjoyed a new authority that enabled it to demand funds from across Europe, so immense wealth began to flow into the city. Pope Nicholas V (1447–55) is credited with bringing the Renaissance to Rome, founding the Vatican Library and first proposing the complete rebuilding of St Peter's, which was on the verge of collapse. Posterity is indebted to the

Renaissance popes for their lavish patronage of the arts, but it was viewed with suspicion at the time, as Northern Europeans suspected they were just Italian princes extending their power. Fears were reinforced by Machiavelli's *The Prince* of 1513, a study in political intrigue based on the life of Cesare Borgia, illegitimate son and soldier-henchman of the Spanish Pope Alexander VI (1492–1503). Stories circulated around Europe of the worldliness, love of luxury and sexual pecadilloes of the popes, and one,

UNSUITABLE ALLIES

In his struggle with Emperor Henry IV, Pope Gregory VII lacked an army, so he tried to get Robert Guiscard *(pictured)*, the ferocious Norman warrior-ruler of southern Italy, to support him. However, when Guiscard reached Rome in 1084 he found that its people had already surrendered to Henry, and instead of protecting the Pope the Norman army (which included many Saracen mercenaries, indifferent to squabbles among Christians) set about sacking Rome, surpassing anything done by Goths or Vandals. Pope Gregory was blamed. Hated by Romans, he lived out his life in exile.

FAR LEFT: Ancient Rome's last great monument, the Arch of Constantine. **LEFT:** the founding of Constantinople, as depicted in a tapestry. **ABOVE:** Alaric and his Visigoths sack Rome. **ABOVE RIGHT:** Mass of Pope Gregory the Great, from an 11th-century manuscript.

Julius II (1503–13) – as well as being one of the greatest patrons of art and architecture – sought to end the papacy's dependency on untrustworthy monarchs by building up a large army of his own. Called "the warrior-pope", he launched a war against Venice, and played a full-blooded part in all the intrigues of Italian and foreign rulers for dominance in Italy.

Enormous wealth had also made Italy, and Rome, great prizes over which the European powers, especially France and Spain, fought for 60 years. In the 1520s Pope Clement VII mistakenly favoured the French against the mighty Emperor Charles V – then ruler of Spain and Austria – and in 1527 the emperor's army, which included many German Lutherans, took revenge in the infamous Sack of Rome. The Swiss Guard were killed to a man, "old nuns beaten with sticks, and young nuns raped and taken prisoner". This was the end of the papacy's pretentions to be an independent power. Clement VII, fortunate to be alive in his Castel Sant'Angelo refuge, was the first of a series of popes who threw in their lot with Charles V and his Spanish successors. Artists who had fled Rome gradually drifted back, but with a changed spirit. Michelangelo's *Last Judgement* in the Sistine Chapel (1536) is said to reflect the sombre mood of the time.

God's Banker

The richest man in Renaissance Rome was Agostino Chigi. He made a fortune trading in salt and alum (used in textile-dyeing), then made himself still richer by extending loans to several popes, to the point of being named Julius II's official treasurer. Dubbed *il magnifico*, he was a legendary bon vivant and art connoisseur; his mistress Imperia was famed as Rome's most beautiful courtesan. In 1508 he had a dazzling villa built by the Tiber, with paintings by (among others) Giulio Romano, Perugino and Raphael, including *The Triumph of Galatea*. So wealthy was he it was said that after banquets he had silver plates thrown into the Tiber rather than use them again (though it was also said he had his servants lay secret nets to catch them). His heirs were less successful, and in 1580 the villa was sold to the Farnese clan, to become the Villa Farnesina.

Counter-Reformation

The shockwaves of the Reformation were soon felt in Rome. In 1545 Pope Paul III convened the Council of Trent to define the "Counter-Reformation", the Catholic

Church's response to the crisis. A newly severe religious discipline was to be maintained, heretical ideas were to be stamped out, and militant new religious orders such as the Jesuits were encouraged to combat Protestantism. Art was required to have a far more emphatic religious message, seen in the growth of the Baroque.

In Rome, some saw an improvement in the social and religious climate. "Several popes in succession have been men of irreproachable lives," wrote Paolo Tiepolo, almost with surprise, in 1576, "hence all others are become better, or have at least assumed the appearance of being so... the whole city has become much more Christian-like in life and manners."

LEFT: Coronation of Pope Pius II, by Vecchietta. **ABOVE TOP:** father and son: Pope Alexander VI and Cesare Borgia. **ABOVE:** detail from Michelangelo's *Last Judgement*. **RIGHT:** warrior-pope and art patron, Julius II.

Nevertheless, while the extravagances of Renaissance Rome may have faded, the papacy remained hugely wealthy, and the popes were now able to dedicate more time and resources to Rome itself. This was the background to the extraordinary creativity that produced Baroque Rome, which perhaps marked the city visually even more than the High Renaissance. No longer a political power, Rome could still be a giant symbol of the glory of the Church. This could be kept up so long as the flow of wealth into Rome continued, but from around 1650 the papacy faced tighter times.

> *The Medici Pope Leo X loved extravagant banquets. "God has given us the papacy," he said to his brother, "let us enjoy it."*

Napoleon upsets things

In 1796 Napoleon issued a proclamation: "Peoples of Italy, the French army comes to

break your chains... we have no quarrel save with the tyrants who enslave you." After defeating the papal army, he demanded money and art treasures from the Vatican, and sovereignty over the Papal States. Pope Pius VI was bundled across the French border to Valence, but his successor, Pius VII, agreed to recognise Napoleon and crown him emperor in return for being allowed to return to Rome. Napoleon installed his mother in a palace in Piazza Venezia, and married his scandalous sister Pauline to the Roman Prince Camillo Borghese, who reciprocated by selling him the Borghese art collection, for 13 million francs.

The Original Tourists

After 1700 Rome and the papacy were no longer major players in European power politics. Instead, the city settled down into being the Continent's first great tourist attraction, as a "Grand Tour" of Italy and its ancient relics became an essential part of a Northern European gentleman's education. Writers such as Gibbon, Smollett, Goethe and Keats all wandered the ruins of Ancient Rome, pondering on its lost civilisation. Romans responded enthusiastically, and streets like Via Condotti were full of servants, guides and "artists' models" looking for tourist business.

Risorgimento

After Napoleon's fall papal rule was restored at the Congress of Vienna in 1814–15, together with Austrian dominance over Italy. This was the background to the Risorgimento, the rise of modern Italian nationalism, and the liberal and nationalist conflagration that swept Europe in 1848. Pope Pius IX was perceived as a liberal reformer, but was also terrified of revolution.

As unrest grew in Rome, he fled to Naples in November 1848, and a Roman Republic was proclaimed, led by a "triumvirate" including the idealist Giuseppe Mazzini. France's new ruler Napoleon III, however, needed Catholic support, and saw the restoration of the pope as a way to win it. Garibaldi (a key revolutionary figure) and his 4,000 red-shirted volunteers were no defence against French troops, but after resisting for months Garibaldi escaped with the remains of his band across Italy, to gain immortality.

Pius IX was protected by French troops for 20 years, while the Italian states threw off their princes and united, not behind Mazzini's Republic but a kingdom of Italy under Victor Emmanuel II of Piedmont. The Pope meanwhile convened the First Vatican Council. It had just asserted the doctrine of Papal Infallibility when in 1870, after Napoleon III's downfall led to French withdrawal, an explosion rocked the old Aurelian Wall and the Italian army poured through the breach. The Pope barricaded himself in the Vatican, and Rome began to adjust to life after 11 centuries of papal rule.

The capital of united Italy

When Rome was proclaimed capital of united Italy in 1871, a third of its population, then about 200,000, were beggars. For decades the clerical elite had paid no attention to mundane matters like drainage, at which the ancients had excelled, and every flood on the Tiber cascaded through the Old City. The new state unleashed an unprecedented round of new building, as old *palazzi* were converted into ministries, wide new streets were laid out and giant edifices were put up to house governement offices. The spectre of the Paris Commune in 1871 persuaded the city fathers the new Rome would be better off without a resident working class, so the poor were forced into shanty towns on the city's edge.

World War I was, for Italy, virtually a private fight against the Austro-Hungarian forces in the north, and Rome itself was not directly affected. Repercussions came later in the person of Benito Mussolini, the former editor of a socialist paper, who came out of the war "burning with patriotism and bursting with ambition, a *condottiere* of fortune… shrinking from no violence or brutality".

Garibaldi and Italian patriots called for "Rome o morte" *– Rome or death – but the papacy bitterly resisted the city's incorporation into the new Italian nation.*

FAR LEFT: the Tiber in the 18th century. **LEFT:** caricature *The Dancing Congress* shows the Sovereigns of Austria, Russia and Prussia at the Congress of Vienna. **ABOVE:** the Italian army ends papal rule, 1870. **ABOVE RIGHT:** patriarch of Italian nationalism, Garibaldi.

Mussolini and Fascism

Mussolini named his black-shirted party after the *fasces,* the symbol of authority in Ancient Rome. In 1922 he marched on Rome, ostensibly to save Italy from Communism. With King Victor Emmanuel III nominally still on his throne, Mussolini pushed through sweeping changes in Italian society. He dreamed of creating a new Roman Empire, with Rome as its showpiece. Roads were bulldozed through the old centre to modernise the city and its traffic.

FOOD FOR WARRIORS

In 1930 the Futurist artist and Fascist Filippo Marinetti launched a campaign against pasta, which, he said, made Italians fat, lazy and apathetic. It had not been part of the diet of the ancient Romans, it was said, when they had conquered Europe. Mussolini himself often said he wanted to make Italians tougher and more dynamic, less addicted to pleasure and more to combat and heroism, and for a time the campaign was taken up by the regime – which also wanted to lower Italy's dependence on imported wheat. Most Italians, though, ignored it, and remained as devoted to pasta as ever.

Pope Pius XI, a semi-recluse in the Vatican, warmed to the dictator as he restored the crucifix to schools and worked towards a treaty between the Vatican and the Italian state, formalised in the concordat of 1929.

In pursuit of his imperial dreams, Mussolini invaded Ethiopia and Albania. He took Italy into World War II in June 1940, when he felt sure Germany would win. But Fascist power proved to be made of straw, and one military disaster followed another. By July 1943 the Allies were preparing to invade Sicily. With the support of the king, senior generals had *Il Duce* arrested and Marshal Badoglio made head of government. Hitler, however, guessing the new government would make peace with the Allies, sent German troops into Italy and paratroops to rescue Mussolini, who became puppet ruler of a Fascist republic in the north.

> *"All merely picturesque things are to be swept away", proclaimed Mussolini in his plans for Rome, "and must make room for the dignity, hygiene and beauty of the capital".*

The next two years of war devastated Italy, but Rome – after some Allied bombing in 1943 – was declared an "Open City", which would not be directly fought over by either side, a period captured in Rossellini's remarkable film *Rome, Open City*. Acts of resistance were met with severe reprisals. Rome had no strategic value, but was a great symbolic prize. Rome was liberated on 4 June 1944, yet it was not until 28 April 1945 that Mussolini was captured, shot and hung from a lamp-post in Milan.

Slicing up the post-war cake

Conditions in Rome after the war were vividly portrayed in films of the era such as Vittorio de Sica's *Bicycle Thieves*. A common backdrop was the high-rise blocks that proliferated under Salvatore Rebecchini, mayor 1947–56. Property developers bribed bureaucrats, and empty spaces filled with illegal buildings.

The 1957 Treaty of Rome spelt out a vision of a European Common Market, but Italian political life was blighted by strikes and instability. The Communists were the largest single party, but all other parties agreed they must be kept from power by any means; no other party was big enough to form a government, so the result was a run of short-lived coalitions. Nevertheless, Italy managed an economic miracle, and instead of being associated with poverty, Rome began to attract new waves of tourists with the image of *La Dolce Vita*, enshrined in another film, by Fellini, from 1960.

In 1978, the Polish cardinal Karol Wojtyla became the first non-Italian pope in 450 years, as John Paul II. He brought a new international prestige to the Vatican, but it was also damaged by irregularities in its finances, and in 1985 the government ended Catholicism's status as the state religion of Italy.

Modern times

Ever since 1945 the Christian Democrats had been the constant in every government coalition, but over the next decade their dominance disintegrated as the judicial system cracked down on organised crime. This campaign spread to the worlds of business and politics in 1992, under the name *mani pulite* (clean hands), and the system of corruption and kickbacks that had ruled post-war Italy began to crumble.

It seemed like an opportunity for a completely new beginning, but the hole left by the Christian Democrats on the right was filled by media mogul Silvio Berlusconi and his Forza Italia party. Bringing a new brash populist style to Italian politics, Berlusconi has been often accused of being more interested in solving his numerous judiciary cases than the country's structural problems. The centre-right leader briefly led the country for the first time in 1994. In 1996 an unstable centre-left coalition came into power under Romano Prodi, but in 2001 Berlusconi won the election and became prime minister for the second time. His five-year tenure, Italy's longest-lived government since 1945, was followed in 2006 by the return to power of Prodi on an even more unstable basis.

Meanwhile, Berlusconi turned Forza Italia into the wider People of the Freedom (PoF) party and was elected again at the early election of March 2008. In the same year, Rome's mayoral election was won by Gianni Alemanno, a member of the former post-Fascist party Alleanza Nazionale, that also joined the PoF party. Unlike his predecessor, former centre-leftist mayor Walter Veltroni, Alemanno does not consider the proliferation of cultural events as one of the Eternal City's priorities. One of his first actions was the cancellation of the much-appreciated Notte Bianca (White Night), an all-night-long festival of free museums and concerts. In 2005, another era of Rome ended with the death of Pope Jean Paul II, succeeded by German cardinal Joseph Ratzinger as Benedict XVI. ❑

FAR LEFT: Mussolini holds forth.
LEFT: Italians read of his fall from power, 1943.
ABOVE: Pope Benedict XVI, shortly after his election.
ABOVE RIGHT: Rome's mayor, Gianni Alemanno.

MAMMA MIA SILVIO!

Three-times prime minister Silvio Berlusconi will undoubtedly leave a trace in Italy's history. Not only is the Cavaliere the rich and powerful owner of AC Milan football club and of three TV channels, who's been accused of abuse of power and suppressing free speech, he is also a man in his seventies who will not hide his surgical retouches. A refined international politician who chaired three G8 summits, he thinks that most problems can be solved with a friendly pat on the shoulder. He has the ability to understand his electors' feelings but isn't ashamed to indulge in jokes about foreign countries or women.

DECISIVE DATES

The Roman Republic: 753–27 BC

753 BC
Traditional date when Rome is said to have been founded by Romulus, on 21 April.

***c*.600 BC**
First parts of Forum built.

509 BC
Rome becomes a republic.

390 BC
Gauls sack Rome, but are then driven off.

264–146 BC
Punic Wars against Carthage: after its destruction in 146 BC Rome is the dominant power in the entire Mediterranean.

100 BC
Birth of Julius Caesar.

58–48 BC
Caesar conquers Gaul, invades Britain, then leads his army back into Italy, challenging the Senate. He defeats Pompey and is made dictator of Rome.

44 BC
Caesar assassinated.

31 BC
Octavian (Augustus) defeats Mark Antony and Cleopatra at the battle of Actium, in Greece.

The Roman Empire: 27 BC–AD 476

27 BC
Augustus declared Princeps or sole ruler, and founds the Empire. Peace is established and the arts flourish, especially in Rome.

AD 14
Death of Augustus, to be succeeded by Tiberius.

AD 64
Great fire in Rome: Nero builds his Domus Aurea or Golden House. First major persecution of Christians.

69–79
Emperor Vespasian builds the Flavian Amphitheatre (Colosseum). In AD 81 the Arch of Titus is erected to commemorate the destruction of Jerusalem by Vespasian and his son and successor Titus.

98–117
The Roman Empire achieves its greatest extent under Emperor Trajan, after his conquests in Dacia (Romania), Persia and Arabia, extending from northern England to the Persian Gulf. The arts flourish across the Empire.

117–38
Hadrian builds walls to secure the Empire's borders against barbarian invasions.

161–80
Reign of Marcus Aurelius. His column, with reliefs showing his victories over Danubian tribes, stands in Rome's Piazza Colonna.

193–211
Septimius Severus leads campaigns against the Parthians, commemorated by a grand arch in the Forum.

284–305
Emperor Diocletian divides Empire into Western and Eastern halves. Intense persecution of Christians.

312
Constantine defeats his rival Maxentius at the Milvian Bridge, near Rome.

313
Edict of Milan establishes toleration of Christianity; in 324 it is officially recognised.

330
Constantinople made the new capital of the Empire.

395
Division of the Roman Empire made permanent.

410
Rome sacked by Visigoths.

476
Romulus Augustulus, last Western emperor, deposed by Ostrogoth leader Theodoric, who declares himself king of Italy.

Surviving: 476–1377

536–68
Rome and most of Italy recaptured by Eastern Empire, with a stronghold at Ravenna, but the Byzantine armies are overwhelmed by another invasion, by the Lombards.

590–604
Pope Gregory the Great protects Rome by making peace with the Lombards, and sends missionaries throughout Europe.

750s
Pepin, king of the Franks, aids Pope Stephen III, returns lands taken by the Lombards, and lays the foundations of temporal sovereignty of the papacy.

800
Charlemagne is crowned Holy Roman Emperor by Pope Leo III in St Peter's.

962
Saxon King Otto I becomes Holy Roman Emperor.

1084
Rome is sacked twice, by Emperor Henry IV and by the Normans.

1309
Clement V moves the seat of the papacy to Avignon.

Papal Rome: 1377–1801

1377
Papacy returns to Rome under Gregory XI, but rival popes still contest the claims of his successors.

1417
Single papacy re-established in Rome, under Martin V.

1450s–1520s
Rome enjoys great prosperity during the High Renaissance. The popes attract great artists, among them Bellini, Botticelli, Bramante, Donatello, Michelangelo and Raphael.

1527
Charles V's army sacks Rome.

1545–63
Council of Trent initiates the Counter-Reformation.

1568
Jesuit order begins building the Church of the Gesù.

1585–90
Pope Sixtus V orders major public works in Rome, including the restoration of ancient aqueducts and fountains.

1626
Consecration of St Peter's.

1796–9
The French Revolutionary armies under Napoleon take Rome and make it a Republic. Pope Pius VI dies in exile in France in 1799.

1801
Pope Pius VII agrees a concordat with Napoleon in order to be allowed to return to Rome.

1811
Napoleon makes his baby son the king of Rome.

Rome in Italy: 1814–1945

1814–15
Papal States are restored to Pius VII by the Congress of Vienna.

1848–50
Pope Pius IX gives Papal States a constitution but refuses to support Italian unification and flees Rome. Radicals declare Roman Republic; Rome is besieged by French troops, who restore papal rule and protect Rome until 1870.

1870
French troops withdraw: Italian troops take over Rome, which is declared capital of the kingdom of Italy. The popes refuse to recognise the state and withdraw to the Vatican.

1871–1910
New Italian government undertakes massive building works in Rome, including the Tiber embankments.

1922
Mussolini marches on Rome and seizes power. More new building, with broad avenues and monuments, and suburbs around the city.

1929
Lateran Treaty: Church recognises the Italian state, which acknowledges the Vatican as an independent state with the Pope at its head.

1940
Italy enters World War II.

1943
Mussolini arrested; Allies land in southern Italy; Germans occupy the north.

1944
The Allies liberate Rome, on 4 June.

1945
Mussolini is killed by partisans.

Modern times

1946
After a referendum, Italy becomes a republic.

1957
The European Economic Community (now the European Union) is established by the Treaty of Rome; Italy is one of six founder members.

1960
La Dolce Vita is released, and Rome hosts the Olympics.

1962–5
Second Vatican Council.

1978
Cardinal Karol Wojtyla becomes the first Polish Pope, as John Paul II.

1981
Ali Agca tries to assassinate Pope John Paul II in St Peter's Square.

1993
Corruption scandals rock Italy, and national unity government formed. Francesco Rutelli becomes Rome's first directly elected mayor.

1994
Media magnate Silvio Berlusconi briefly becomes prime minister.

1995
Giulio Andreotti, seven times Italian prime minister, goes on trial for Mafia association.

1996
First left-wing government in Italian post-war history.

1998
Massimo D'Alema is first former Communist to head an Italian government.

2000
Millions flock to Rome for Holy Year celebrations, after a frenzy of restoration work. Centre-left government coalition falls.

2001
Berlusconi becomes prime minister for the second time. Walter Veltroni of the centre-left wins Rome's mayoral elections.

2005
Pope John Paul II dies: Cardinal Joseph Ratzinger elected Pope Benedict XVI.

2006
Berlusconi loses power by the narrowest of margins to a centre-left coalition led by Romano Prodi.

2008
Berlusconi becomes prime minister for the third time and the Romans elect their first right-wing mayor, Gianni Alemanno.

Rome on Film

Italian cinema was born in Rome in 1905. The country's first feature, *La Presa di Roma* – a dramatic tale of the city's incorporation into Italy in 1870 – marked the beginning of the Eternal City's enduring love affair with celluloid. It remains the heart of Italian cinema.

The silent era was dominated by historical spectaculars, epitomised by Giovanni Pastrone's kidnap drama set in the Punic Wars, *Cabiria* (1914). The success of these toga tales had industrialists and aristocrats queuing to finance Rome's burgeoning film industry.

The birth of Cinecittà

Mussolini saw film as the perfect propaganda vehicle for Fascism, and in a typical attempt to trump the Americans he built his own Hollywood-on-the-Tiber at Cinecittà, the largest film-making complex in Europe. Directors with the right ideological credentials were bankrolled by the regime, but created little of much merit. Nevertheless, some of Italy's greatest directors were meanwhile learning their trade at the studios, as second-unit directors or writers.

Neo-realism

The fall of Fascism marked the emergence of one of the world's great film movements: neo-realism. Stimulated by the desperate state of Italy at the end of the war and tired of escapist spectacle, the *neorealismo* auteurs set out to record the life of ordinary people.

At their forefront was Roberto Rossellini, who began shooting his masterwork, *Rome, Open City* (1945), on the devastated streets around Via Prenestina even before the German troops had left. It revolves around an extraordinary performance from Roman actress Anna Magnani, as a defiant matriarch.

The signature film of neo-realism was Vittorio de Sica's *Bicycle Thieves* (1948). The story of a man and his son in the Rome slums was a huge international success. De Sica bankrolled the film himself, and used non-professional actors. Other directors influenced by neo-realism included Federico Fellini and, in the 1960s, Pier Paolo Pasolini, whose subject matter was a Roman underworld of small-time thieves and desperate love. "We discovered our own country," said Fellini, "and its reality was so extraordinary we couldn't resist photographing it."

Fellini's devotion to Cinecittà made him the uncrowned king of the studios. He placed his adopted city under a microscope: *Roma* (1972) presented a fantastic vision of Rome, while *La Dolce Vita* (1960) satirised the idle rich who hung around the then glamorous Via Veneto, and left us the enduring image of Anita Ekberg cooling off in the Trevi Fountain.

Epics and comics

It's ironic that Mussolini's film city finally found fame with the Americans he was trying to outdo. In the 1950s good light, the pleasures of working in Italy and the renowned skills (but low costs) of its technicians brought Hollywood to Rome – turning Cinecittà into a household name for millions around the world.

For over a decade Cinecittà was synonymous with the epic – titles like *Quo Vadis* (1951), *Ben-Hur* (1959), Taylor and Burton's *Cleopatra* (1963) – but also made the film that launched a thousand tourist trips, *Roman Holiday* (1953). In its glory

years the studios produced over 1,000 films, employing hundreds of actors, extras, technicians and directors.

International productions brought added glamour to Cinecittà, but its bread and butter was Italian commercial moviemaking. Italians have always loved their comedy stars. Each city has its hometown clown: Naples is forever linked with Totò and Massimo Troisi, while Florence has Roberto Benigni. When Rome's chief jester, Alberto Sordi, died in 2003, over 80,000 people crammed the streets for his funeral; in a 50-year career he had appeared in over 100 films, including Fellini's 1953 classic *I Vitelloni*.

By the 1980s, though, Italian domestic film production was falling, as Hollywood movies filled Italian cinemas.

LEFT: Anita Ekberg exudes glamour and sex appeal in *La Dolce Vita*. **ABOVE LEFT:** neo-realist classic, *Bicycle Thieves*. **ABOVE:** poster for Cinecittà Burton and Taylor epic *Cleopatra*. **RIGHT:** taking a break on the set for big-budget HBO/BBC series, *Rome*.

Cinecittà's comeback

Television production replaced cinema as Cinecittà's everyday business. Home-grown comedies still play well in Italy, but in recent years there have only been fleeting glimpses of Rome in films shown outside the country. An exception is *La Finestra di Fronte* (The Window Opposite, 2003), in which Turkish-born director Ferzan Ozpetek used his adopted city, setting the film in the Ghetto.

Rome's most acclaimed film-maker is Nanni Moretti, Italy's Woody Allen. The city is often centre stage in his films, notably *Caro Diario* (1994), where he scooters around the concrete suburbs in search of the essence of Rome. Moretti, known for his distinctively languid, ironic style,

returned to film-making in 2006 after a long gap with *Il Caimano* (The Caiman), an acid satire on the Italy of Silvio Berlusconi.

After years in the wilderness Cinecittà is back. Now that so many film sets are computer-generated, this is the best place in the world to find the skills and craftsmanship that can create real sets.

In 2002, Martin Scorsese reconstructed entire blocks of 19th-century New York here for *Gangs of New York*. This heralded a slew of international productions including Mel Gibson's *The Passion of the Christ* (2004) and – recalling the scale of the old epics – the lavish HBO/BBC series *Rome*. Local film-makers can only hope this may pave the way for a new wave of international success for Italian cinema. ❑

DIVO ANTONINO ET

ART AND ARCHITECTURE: THE CREATION OF A CITYSCAPE

Three great eras – the ancient city, the Renaissance and the Baroque – have largely defined Rome's visual identity, blending in an astonishingly harmonious mix, studded with masterpieces

Walking through Rome's Centro Storico, one is frequently amazed by the sheer size and grandeur of the buildings crammed into narrow, winding streets. At other times one might be struck by an exquisite fountain or facade that, although obviously the work of a major artist and worthy of being the pride of any other city, is ignored by the traffic and pedestrians rushing past.

Rome has the kind of beauty that provokes passionate responses. It has also been a centre of power throughout its 2,700-year history, home to ancient emperors, then popes, and even Mussolini. Every era has left its mark.

A visible past

Romans' indifference to their extraordinary surroundings is nothing new. Rightly or wrongly, they have been blamed for mistreating their architectural heritage since ancient times.

Every corner seems to have something worth stopping to look at: a shady courtyard with a bubbling fountain, a Baroque facade above a street market, an obelisk blocking traffic in a way no modern planner would allow.

Emperor Maxentius (AD 306–12) accused contemporaries of tearing down "magnificent old buildings" to get material for new houses. Pope Pius II (1458–64) shuddered at people burning marble monuments to obtain lime.

LEFT: the Temple of Antoninus and Faustina was converted to San Lorenzo in Miranda in the 1100s.
RIGHT: St Peter's dome from Castel Sant'Angelo.

Goethe, visiting in the 1780s, complained that "what the barbarians left standing, modern architects have destroyed", and a century later the German historian Gregorovius thundered against the Piedmontese remodelling of the papal city. In the 20th century Alberto Moravia classified four-fifths of Rome "a disaster area of civic architecture". Yet these critics all stayed on in Rome, unable to desert it.

Locals' disregard has a natural explanation in overfamiliarity. Rome is a city standing on the shoulders of its predecessors, where layers of history run into each other. Materials have

been taken from older buildings to make new ones, and buildings adapted to suit changing needs. Medieval churches rise from the remains of ancient houses; a Renaissance palace balances on top of the Theatre of Marcellus, next to 20th-century apartments. Even if buildings disappear, their shapes remain. A key feature of Italian city life – the piazza – is a direct descendant of the ancient Forum.

THE FIRST FORUM

"Forum" is one of the most pervasive words the Romans have given to European languages. The marshy area below the Capitoline Hill was drained by Rome's Etruscan rulers as early as 600 BC, and served as a common space for every purpose – meeting up, buying and selling, settling disputes – and the site of the temple where the Vestal Virgins guarded the Sacred Flame, which ensured Rome's survival. Its grandeur grew with that of the city: around 180 BC the humblest market traders were driven out, and permanent law courts and trading halls were built. Later rulers added new Fora as monuments to themselves, but the original Forum remained the heart of the ancient city.

First steps

Rome's first permanent civic buildings were erected in the Forum. Most of the area now called the Centro Storico was little-populated for centuries, and much of it kept empty as the Campus Martius, the training ground where Roman men kept themselves ever-ready for war. Wealthy families built villas on top of Rome's hills, especially the Palatine, Viminal and Esquiline, while the dip between them – only just west of the Forum – was the Subura, the great slum of ancient Rome.

Republican Rome, though, grew in a fairly haphazard fashion, with few of the monumental symmetries now associated with Roman cities, and little of the splendour its imperial role seemed to demand. Accordingly Julius Caesar was the first to set out on a programme to improve the city. Soon Rome was flaunting its wealth; under Caesar, 640 gladiators wore silver armour at the city's games.

Caesar's nephew the emperor Augustus (27 BC–AD 14) liked to boast that he had found Rome made of brick and left it of marble. The urbanisation of the Campus Martius began, and was divided into *rioni* – the zones of central Rome that still exist today. Large parts of the Imperial Fora also date from these years.

The capital of the world

With over 1 million people – a size not reached by any other city for nearly 2,000 years – Ancient Rome was closely packed, noisy and crowded. While the wealthy lived in elegant houses – relics of many of which have survived – the Roman masses lived in insanitary *insulae* or apartment blocks of mud-bricks and timber, and fires, house collapses and epidemics were common. The *insulae* grew so rapidly and rose so high that after the fire of AD 64 destroyed the city centre, a decree of Nero limited their height to 20 metres (60ft).

In the wake of the fire, disagreement raged between those who wanted Rome's old alleys retained and Nero, who wanted broad avenues on which to display monuments to himself. As has gone down in legend, it was also rumoured that Nero had started the fire himself, to clear space for his vast palace, the Domus Aurea or Golden House. More practically, though, Nero forbade the use of wooden ceilings and insisted on the provision of water buckets in houses.

Little of Nero's constructions remains because they were destroyed by his successors Vespasian (69–79) and his sons Titus and Domitian. To win popularity and dissociate themselves from Nero they erected more democratic centres of enjoyment, among them the Colosseum, on land originally covered by Nero's private lake. Domitian's legacy was the stadium over which Piazza Navona was built.

One of Rome's greatest architects was Apollodorus of Damascus, master builder of Emperor Trajan (98–117), responsible for Trajan's Forum and the semicircular market behind it – a revolutionary idea, regarded as one of the wonders of ancient Rome, and still astonishingly well-preserved. Trajan also built a massive bath complex, on another part of the land that was once part of the Domus Aurea.

Rome's emperors built on until their last

ANCIENT ARCHETYPES

Around 55 BC Caesar's rival Pompey sponsored Rome's first permanent theatre, the Theatre of Pompey. Intended to offer sophisticated Greek-style theatre rather than the bloody spectacles ancient Romans usually enjoyed, it was so large the Senate often met there. The shape of the round building can still be seen behind Campo de' Fiori; Via di Grotta Pinta follows its curve. A few years later, Caesar built his own Basilica Giulia in the Forum. A combination of law court and trading centre, it consisted of a piazza surrounded by a double row of buildings, with shops on one side and mezzanine floors with embossed rounded arches, a style often copied in Renaissance architecture.

FAR LEFT: the triple arch of Septimius Severus and the Column of Phocas. **ABOVE LEFT:** the Colosseum. **ABOVE:** Trajan's Markets. **RIGHT:** drawing showing what the Theatre of Pompey would have looked like.

days – one of the last great monuments is the Arch of Constantine, completed only a few years before he left for Constantinople – but then centuries of construction came to a halt, and within decades much of the city was a ghost town. Few civic buildings survive from the centuries between the fall of the Empire and the Renaissance, but this was the time when Rome's major churches were founded, often incorporating parts of pagan temples. Defensive towers were also built, like the Torre delle Milizie (1309), above Trajan's Market.

The ruins of ancient Rome served later builders as a giant quarry for centuries, until many dwindled away to nothing.

The great rebirth

A huge proportion of Rome's architectural gems date from the years between 1454 and 1670, when Rome was again one of Europe's great power centres, and at the heart of Renaissance and Baroque art and architecture.

The Renaissance – Rebirth – stemmed from a rediscovery of the ancient art and culture that had been abandoned after the Roman Empire fell in the 5th century. It began in Italy in the late 14th century and, over 150 years, swept across Europe, leading to fundamental changes in culture, intellectual life and the way people lived and saw their place in the world.

Christopher Columbus and Vasco da Gama discovered new countries and trade routes, and philosophers such as Erasmus reapplied the humanist philosophies of the ancients. While not yet questioning the supremacy of God, this attitude of enquiry encouraged a questioning of the dogma of the Catholic Church, which led ultimately to the birth of Protestantism.

In Italy, however, it was in art and architecture that the new movement was most visible – in the development of perspective, the more naturalistic presentation of subject matter and especially the human body, and the use of classical proportions and styles in building.

The Renaissance first developed in northern Italy, particularly Florence. Nevertheless, most great artists of the era came to Rome at some point, to study the classical lines of ancient relics, or carry out commissions for the popes.

Rome's own renaissance

In the mid-15th century, two factors aided the re-emergence of Rome as a cultural centre. First, the papacy of Nicholas V (1447–55) began a line of powerful popes with time, money and the desire to improve Rome's appearance. Secondly, the Italian League of 1455 ushered in a period of relative peace across Italy, leaving the popes free to occupy themselves with broader ambitions.

Many changes made in the ensuing 70 years still define the look of Rome today. Nicholas V believed Rome had to be made majestic again to be a worthy centre of the Christian world. Highly learned, he was a patron of artists, craftsmen and scholars: advised by the architect Alberti, he was also the first to propose that Constantine's Basilica of St Peter – which was threatening to fall down in any case – should be demolished and replaced with a giant new focus for the Church. This suggestion would not be fully taken up until 1506, by Pope Julius II (1503–13), and work would go on for 120 years, but over the decades the new St Peter's incorporated contributions from nearly all the greatest masters of Renaissance painting, sculpture and architecture.

These same masters left their mark elsewhere in Rome: Bramante, Julius II's first choice as architect of the basilica, had earlier built the lovely Tempietto beside the church of San Pietro in Montorio on the Gianicolo, revolutionary in its use of classical form and considered the first true Renaissance building in Rome. Raphael, a later director of works at St Peter's, painted frescoes that can be seen in the Vatican and Villa Farnesina, and Michelangelo, who aged over 70 designed St Peter's dome in the 1540s, had earlier painted the Sistine Chapel, sculpted the *Pietà* and, in 1536, designed the Campidoglio for Pope Paul III.

Artists continued to flock to Rome until the 1527 Sack, to work for the popes or the great families who vied for the papal throne – the Barberini, Borghese, Farnese, Pamphilj and others.

FAR LEFT: the spectacular apse mosaics of Santa Maria in Trastevere. **ABOVE CENTRE:** fresco by Annibale Carracci in the Palazzo Farnese. **LEFT:** Michelangelo's staircase leading to the Campidoglio. **ABOVE RIGHT:** Bramante's Tempietto.

PAPAL STREET PLANS

The Renaissance popes changed the face of Rome in many other ways as well as in their individual buildings and great monuments. Sixtus IV (1471–84), patron of the Sistine Chapel, commissioned the Ponte Sisto or Sistine Bridge, the first new Tiber bridge in over 1,000 years. Leo X (1513–21) had Via di Ripetta created to link the Medici family palace and Porto di Ripetta, while another Medici pope, Clement VII (1523–34), commissioned Via del Babuino, thereby completing the *Tridente* or "Trident" of (today very fashionable) streets that, with Via del Corso, flow south from Piazza del Popolo.

Dating from this time are churches such as Santa Maria del Popolo and Santa Maria della Pace, the *palazzi* on Via Giulia and of course great works of art, now mostly in the Vatican or the *palazzi* Barberini and Doria Pamphilj.

The popes left an indelible stamp on the layout of Rome after the Sack, too *(see page 35)*. The greatest papal "planner" was Pope Sixtus V (1585–90). His network of streets built to link the city gates and improve access for pilgrims is still mostly intact: Via Felice (now Via Sistina, and other names) led straight to Santa Maria Maggiore and Santa Croce in Gerusalemme from Piazza del Popolo, one of four nodal points where obelisks were erected, with Santa Maria Maggiore, San Giovanni in Laterano and St Peter's.

The Demon Caravaggio

Caravaggio (1571–1610) was the greatest artist working in Rome at the end of the 16th century, but his fame lasted only a decade. Despite Counter-Reformation injunctions to show the realities of suffering, his dramatic lifelike figures and earthy details, his saints with dirty fingernails, did not meet with the approval of many art patrons used to the reverence of a Raphael or a Michelangelo, while many in the Church found such naturalism blasphemous.

Even more of a problem was his character: violent and argumentative, he had to flee Rome after killing a man in a brawl in 1606. Trouble followed him to Naples, Sicily and Malta, and it has never been clear how he died.

City of the Baroque

In the latter part of the 16th century, creativity was curbed by papal decree, in response to the threat of Protestantism. The Council of Trent laid down guidelines for Church commissions: all art was to have an unmissable religious message. Realism was allowed, but there was to be no prettification, and emphasis had to be put on the suffering of martyrs to remind people of the infernal torments awaiting them if they offended the Church. Niccolò Pomarancio's gruesome frescoes of martyred saints in Santo Stefano Rotondo and Santi Nereo e Achilleo date from this time.

While the Renaissance was imported from Florence, Baroque style had its home in Rome. It may seem strange that the sombre images of the late 16th century should lead to the ornate Roman Baroque of the 17th, but both were provoked by the fear of Protestantism. Both sought to promote Catholicism, but while one used shock tactics, the other sought to dazzle.

Size and visual impact were the main themes explored in Baroque architecture: the aim of religious art and building was to exalt the greatness of the Church and create a foretaste of heaven, and to this end every kind of visual effect could be deployed. By the 1620s, extravagantly decorated churches with *trompe l'œil* ceiling paintings and gold-encrusted altars

were thought more likely to keep people in the Catholic fold than portrayals of suffering. The basic form of these buildings might still owe much to classical models, but now everything was highly decorated with statuary and reliefs.

It was no accident Rome's first major Baroque churches were built for the new religious orders of the Counter-Reformation: the great Jesuit churches such as Il Gesù (1568–75) and Sant'Ignazio de Loyola (1626–50), and the initially less ornate Chiesa Nuova (1575–99) of the Oratorians, founded by San Filippo Neri, loved in Rome for giving charity to the poor.

> *The object of Baroque painting and building was to give the onlooker a vivid image of both the horrors of hell and – more frequently – the joys of heaven.*

FAR LEFT: grand stairway in the Palazzo Barberini. **TOP LEFT:** fountain opposite the Pantheon (1575). **LEFT:** *Bacchus* by Caravaggio. **ABOVE TOP:** Chiesa Nuova. **ABOVE:** frescoed ceiling of Il Gesù. **RIGHT:** the Fountain of the Four Rivers, Piazza Navona.

This was the age of Bernini and Borromini, whose facades grace streets and piazzas, and whose fountains and sculptures decorate Piazza Barberini and Piazza Navona, Ponte Sant'Angelo, Villa Borghese and the Vatican.

As well as exalting the Church, the Baroque could add grandeur to more earthly powers, and was eagerly taken up by great monarchs such as the Spanish Habsburgs and Louis XIV of France. Rome's great families were just as keen to demonstrate their wealth, by building massive city palaces and villas amid gardens. The Villa Borghese dates from this time, as do parts of Palazzo Doria Pamphilj, Villa Doria Pamphilj and the Palazzi di Montecitorio and Barberini. Once again artists flocked to Rome to study and find patrons among its great families. Velázquez, Rubens and Poussin all worked here, and left major works in Rome.

After about 1660, however, funding dried up, and the papacy and Roman aristocracy had to moderate their designs. No era since the Baroque has marked the city so deeply. The monuments of Bernini, Borromini and their contemporaries remain, stunning pieces of work that create a cityscape that is as Roman as the Colosseum and the Forum. ❑

Bernini and the Baroque

The Roman Baroque style, perfected by Bernini, was the model for European Baroque

Gianlorenzo Bernini (1598–1680) was at the forefront of Roman Baroque, pioneering sublime and spectacular effects. Although more restrained than elsewhere in Europe, Roman Baroque is theatrical, bold, at times bombastic. Bernini's Rome is an open-air gallery of fountains and façades. Palaces and churches boast sweeping curves, majestic façades and theatrical vistas flanked by flights of steps. As a virtuoso architect and sculptor, Bernini worked in broad brushstrokes, with illusionistic verve. At ease with interiors and exteriors, he was a showman renowned for his theatricality and technical brilliance.

Bernini's style found favour with a succession of popes. Even St Peter's is, in part, a Bernini creation, graced by enfolding colonnades. Other masterpieces include the witty design for an elephant to bear the obelisk of Santa Maria sopra Minerva and the graceful angels on Ponte Sant'Angelo. As for palaces, Palazzo Barberini (1629–33) heralded the Baroque style and was completed by Bernini, assisted by Borromini, who became his arch-rival *(see opposite)*.

Above: having worked for decades on the interior of the basilica, Bernini was commissioned to redesign St Peter's Square (1656–67). The colonnaded arms of the keyhole-shaped piazza reach out to Catholics in a symbolic embrace from the Mother Church, according to Bernini.

Left: Bernini's Sant'Andrea al Quirinale (1658–70) is a subtle tour de force inspired by Michelangelo's architectural feats.

LEFT: Rome's loveliest Baroque square, Piazza Navona, is home to three fountains and other works by rival architects Bernini and Borromini. In the foreground is Bernini's Fontana del Moro. His sumptuous fountains vie for attention with Borromini's church of Sant'Agnese, with its striking interplay of towers, domes and façade. **ABOVE:** Bernini's obelisk-carrying elephant outside Santa Maria sopra Minerva church. **LEFT:** *Apollo and Daphne*, which is displayed with other Bernini masterpieces in the Galleria Borghese. This is Bernini's most famous sculpture. The magnificent, youthful work shows the nymph fleeing from the sun god. **BELOW:** in the church of Santa Maria della Vittoria is what many consider to be Bernini's sculptural masterpiece, *The Ecstasy of St Teresa*.

FRANCESCO BORROMINI

Borromini (1599–1667) made use of revolutionary, gravity-defying architectural forms. While Borromini lacked the confidence and all-round virtuosity of Bernini, his churches abound in visual trickery. His work is characterised by a sculptural quality, the alternation of convex and concave forms, and a conspicuous fondness for geometric designs as well as for subtle plays of light and shade.

San Carlo alle Quattro Fontane *(see page 120)* was Borromini's first solo commission. Based on an oval design, the ingenious church is notable for its illusionistic dome. The sinuous, seemingly swaying, walls inspired countless Baroque artists.

In his time Borromini's genius was not fully recognised, partly because of his temperament (he was a depressive who eventually committed suicide) and his rivalry with Bernini, but he is now considered one of the great masters of Baroque.

THE SHAPE OF MODERN ROME

In a city that is regularly compared to a giant museum, the intrusion of modern streets, suburbs and rail lines has just as often been condemned as vandalism. Rome's survival, though, has always depended on its ability to integrate past and future

So pervasive is the past in Rome – in the visual impact of Ancient Rome, the Renaissance and the Baroque – that it's easy to think this represents the whole city. And yet Rome has grown vastly since 1700, and has never ceased to grow, build and adapt.

By the time of the death of Bernini in 1680 the extraordinary impetus behind the creation of Baroque Rome had visibly fallen away. The Church continued to commission buildings and improvements in the 18th century, but on a far smaller scale. Stylistically, rococo flourishes were added to the Baroque, but most of the city's architects lived on the legacy of the past.

Nevertheless, two of Rome's most famous, and most popular, sights date from this time. The Spanish Steps, built to link the French church of Trinità dei Monti with Piazza di Spagna, were completed in 1726, while Nicola Salvi's Trevi Fountain, designed for Pope Clement XII, was finished in 1762.

The new Italian state set about the most rapid burst of new building seen in Rome since the days of the Empire.

Modernity arrives

The changes brought by the 19th century were as much utilitarian as aesthetic. In 1856 Rome acquired its first railway line, to Frascati, and in 1862 the first part of Stazione Termini was built. These few novelties in sleepy papal Rome, however, were as nothing compared to the transformation that came after the city's incorporation into a united Italy in 1870.

LEFT: Richard Meier's new museum pavilion housing the ancient Ara Pacis altar. **RIGHT:** Rome is very well connected by rail to Italy and the rest of Europe.

The new state's rulers were modernisers, but found in their new capital a decaying, archaic city impassable to modern communications. Some needs could be met by recycling: Bernini's Palazzo di Montecitorio became Italy's Chamber of Deputies. Other changes were far more drastic. All-new, wide, un-Roman-looking avenues, such as Via Cavour, Via Nazionale and Corso Vittorio Emanuele II, were cut through to "open up"

Mussolini's Legacy

When we think of Roman architecture, we think mainly of Ancient Rome and the Renaissance, but Mussolini's Fascist regime of the 1920s and 1930s has left a powerful imprint on the city as well.

Whole areas of Rome are dominated by massive, conspicuous buildings with facades of white rectangular columns against a plain white or reddish-brown background, adorned with statues of naked athletes and grim-faced women holding ears of corn or bunches of grapes. This style even continued – shorn of its more obvious ideological symbols – after World War II, when Mussolini's regime had collapsed.

In contrast to Hitler, whose taste in art and architecture was always backward-looking, Mussolini liked to show he was in touch with 20th-century trends, and his regime recruited some of Italy's most innovative modern architects for its schemes, notably Marcello Piacentini and Angiolo Mazzoni. The style they came up with was a mix of austere Modernist functionalism and an evocation of Ancient Rome, with an added touch of the monumentalism that was a Fascist essential.

Some of the most striking examples are Piacentini's Città Universitaria, and the rebuilt Stazione Termini, begun by Mazzoni in 1937 but only completed (with major changes) in 1950. Another is the building south of the Circus Maximus, now used by the United Nations Food and Agriculture Organization, originally intended as the administrative hub of the African Empire of which Mussolini dreamed.

Some of Mussolini's projects involved not building but large-scale demolition. He wanted Italians to be more conscious of their Roman heritage, and so commissioned excavations of the Roman Fora. However, his interest was not academic, for he simultaneously destroyed a part of the Fora by driving Via dei Fori Imperiali through the middle of them, as a route to hold parades with the ancient ruins as an unbeatable backdrop. The construction of Via della Conciliazione into the Vatican, a symbol of reconciliation between the Holy See and the Italian state, involved demolishing the Spina, one of Rome's most celebrated historic streets.

However, the most prominent examples of Fascist architecture can be seen at the Foro Italico *(see page 195)*, and the area in south Rome known as EUR (pronounced *ay-oor*). The *Esposizione Universale di Roma* was to have been held in 1942, as a giant exhibition to mark 20 years of Fascist rule. The war prevented it from taking place, but building continued after 1945, and the EUR district is today a strange monument to Fascist taste *(see page 216)*. ❑

LEFT: the Palazzo della Civiltà del Lavoro, EUR.
ABOVE: the Via dei Fori Imperiali.

the old centre and connect it to an expanded Termini Station. The new Italy wanted to add its own touches of grandeur to Rome to compete with those of the ancients and the popes, and did so in a bombastic style epitomised by the vast Vittorio Emanuele monument on Piazza Venezia.

Other developments included the creation of new residential areas such as that around Piazza Vittorio Emanuele (1886), and – one of the most positive – the building of the Lungotevere or Tiber embankment in the 1870s, which put a stop to Rome's disastrous floods.

20th-century transformations

These innovations were detested by lovers of Old Rome, but they effectively created Rome as a modern city, around its ancient core. They also enabled Rome to accommodate a flood of immigrants from rural Italy, which had been gaining momentum ever since Unification. In 1922 Rome had about 800,000 people; by the end of World War II it would have 1.8 million.

The idea of building self-contained estates on the edge of Rome, the Agro Romano, was first mooted in 1907. Expansion had started before 1922, with the Art Nouveau Coppedè Quarter for the wealthy in the north of the city, and the engaging Garbatella workers' quarter south of Testaccio. Then Mussolini ushered in his own dramatic changes, to build a city fit to be the seat of his intended empire *(see left)*.

He also decided Rome needed "living space and greatness", and began building the *borgate* (estates) of Prenestina, Pietralata and San Basilio. Depressing in form and materials, they soon became symbols of wretchedness.

Post-war, slums girdled Rome, while at the other end of the social scale the wealthy got planning permission to build on the Via Appia. Slum clearance began in 1976: older *borgate* were given lighting, power, mains water and bus routes, while others were replaced by supposedly exemplary new suburbs such as Tor Bella Monaca or Tor de' Cenci. However, these too developed the usual problems of poverty, poor services, unemployment and drugs.

Rome urgently needed to improve living standards and integrate its outer sprawl into the rest of the city by improving the inadequate transport system, but solutions to urban blight seemed lost in the tangle of local politics. Since 1993, though, the city authorities have taken on a new prestige, and initiated impressive city-wide improvements in services and a swathe of new building. ❑

ABOVE: gateway in the Art Nouveau enclave known as the Quartiere Coppedè. **RIGHT:** apartment block in Garbatella district, south of Testaccio.

> *Modern Rome's sprawling suburbs contain both urban disaster zones and charming, tree-lined experiments in city living.*

Modern Architecture

In a city weighed down by its monumental past, some of the best-known modern architects are daring to make their mark

Modern architecture was a rarely seen phenomenon in Rome until a few years ago, when the state-of-the-art Auditorium by Genoese architect Renzo Piano, which opened in 2002, spawned a wave of major architectural projects by big-name architects. In the same year, a huge designer hotel opened near the station, one of the first completely new buildings in the historic centre in recent years.

Further out of town, the uplifting Jubilee

Above: the striking white "sails" of Richard Meier's Jubilee Church. **Left:** Meier's more controversial Ara Pacis pavilion.

Church designed by superstar architect Richard Meier was a welcome addition to the unremarkable eastern suburb of Tor Tre Teste. Meier's design for the new pavilion housing the Ara Pacis, an ancient Roman altar, which opened in 2006, proved more controversial, but like it or loathe it, it's a major new landmark on the cityscape.

The biggest among Rome's many new arts centres *(see right)* is Anglo-Iraqi architect Zaha Hadid's new museum of contemporary art in the northern suburbs, inaugurated in 2010, while in the southern EUR suburb a futuristic expo centre, a suspended, amorphous structure, was completed in 2006.

Across the city, disused industrial buildings have been transformed. In the Marconi area, the vast Città del Gusto (City of Taste) complex in a remodelled granary is a beacon of culture and activity in an industrial wasteland, while Dutch architect Rem Koolhaas is converting an old food market on the southwest side of the city into a "City of Youth". As well as this wave of public building, there is a residential building boom. Rome's renaissance, it seems, is in full swing.

ABOVE: Zaha Hadid's contemporary art centre, MAXXI, contains a complex network of interior and exterior spaces, which house two museums for the state collections of modern art and architecture.

LEFT: the library of the es hotel. This huge designer hotel near the station (on Via Filippo Turati) was one of the first completely new buildings in the historic centre in recent years. Owned by Radisson Blu, the slick establishment is an essay in minimalism. It has its own museum of 2nd-century ruins unearthed during construction.

RIGHT: Renzo Piano's Auditorium has three shell-like (or, some say, whale-shaped), concert halls, built around an outdoor amphitheatre, and is set in parkland in the northern suburb of Flaminia.

NEW GALLERIES

The list of the city's innovative new spaces dedicated to the arts is impressive. Apart from Zaha Hadid's ambitious new museum *(see left)*, MACRO, Rome's contemporary art museum, is now spread over two sites, one a converted Peroni brewery, the other a converted slaughterhouse. An old power station is now home to the overspill of the Capitoline collection, while the stables of the hilltop Quirinale Palace have been converted into a clean, crisp space for high-profile exhibitions.

ABOVE: part of the Capitoline Museums' vast collection of ancient statuary can now be viewed in the fabulous Centrale Montemartini museum, an imaginatively converted electrical power plant in Ostiense.

ABOVE: in the up-and-coming Testaccio neighbourhood, an old abbatoir on the edge of the Tiber has been converted into a site for cultural activities. Two of its pavilions have been given over to MACRO to house temporary exhibitions of contemporary art.

LEFT: the revamped Termini Station, one of the few successful pieces of post-war architecture in Rome, with its long, modernist facade in travertine stone, and graceful double curved roof.

PANINI
SANDWICHES

FOOD AND DRINK

Whether it's a long Sunday lunch or a stop-off for an ice cream on an evening stroll, eating in Rome is a very social activity – and one with 2,000 years of tradition, customs and ingenuity behind it

Culinary traditions run deep in Rome, reaching back to the ancient peoples who first populated the region. For centuries Romans have held firm against the influence of new ingredients, dishes and cooking techniques that have come as a result of Rome's contact with the rest of the world, as well as from the fads and fancies of the upper classes, emperors and popes.

The exotically spiced sauces, fancy game dishes and "delicacies" like fried parrots' tongues dressed with honey that delighted Roman emperors have faded into history, but something does remain from the high cuisine of the past: the unreserved pleasure with which Romans go to table. This is probably not the city to hunt down the top restaurants – few consider *la cucina romana* the best of Italy's regional cuisines – but Rome may well be one of Italy's most pleasurable cities in which to eat. Most restaurants plan on one seating per evening, so you will not be rushed, or pressured to leave. When in Rome, make a point of having a long, lingering meal – and have it in the open air, if the weather is good.

Often, what might seem to be slow service is merely the Roman way of stretching a meal far into the night.

LEFT: fast food, Roman-style.
RIGHT: pizza is a Roman staple; there are more pizzerias in the city than restaurants.

La cucina romana

Quite a lot of the local cuisine involves offal, the so-called *quinto-quarto* (fifth quarter) of the animal. Long-time favourites include *rigatoni con pajata* (pasta with veal intestines) and *trippa alla romana* (tripe with tomato sauce, mint and pecorino), but you will find that most restaurants in the centre of town tend to avoid such specialities in favour of dishes from other parts of Italy that are more familiar to an international clientele, such as pasta with pesto sauce (from Genoa), risotto and polenta.

But you needn't eat innards to eat Roman. Every restaurant will have at least a few home-grown dishes, all sharing the frugality that

marks the region's food. One current trend is known as "creative cuisine", is spreading by the minute, and involves chefs experimenting with local and international ingredients to offer adventurous (and delicious) dishes with long names. Most of them will advertise their cuisine as "based on tradition with a touch of creativity". The menu of a typical Roman establishment, however, tells a less complicated story: *spaghetti alla carbonara* (with bacon, egg and pecorino cheese), *cacio e pepe* (with pecorino and black pepper), *all'amatriciana* (with bacon or *guanciale*, cured pork jowl, and tomato), and *bucatini alla gricia* – Rome's own tube-shaped style of pasta with *guanciale* – all share an undeniable simplicity. Pasta even makes its way into Roman soups: *pasta e ceci* (chickpea soup flavoured with rosemary) and *broccoli e arzilla* (clear soup of broccoli and skate). *Gnocchi alla romana* (potato

APERITIVO HOUR

The Milan-born tradition of an early-evening *aperitivo* accompanied by buffets of savoury munchies has exploded onto the scene in Rome. Gone are the days of humble olives and nuts; opulent spreads now top the counters of even the tiniest bars from around 6 to 8pm every evening. Tramezzini sandwiches bursting with tuna, mozzarella and tomatoes, mini pizzas, focaccia sandwiches and omelette chunks left over from lunch grilled to a crispy finish and sliced up in quarters are typical. Fancier places offer pasta and rice dishes, salads, *bruschetta* and all manner of tempting *fritti* (deep-fried foods).

Most bars advertise their *aperitivo* as "happy hour", and offer drink specials as well. The classic Roman aperitif is bubbly Prosecco; Campari and soda is another best-seller. Otherwise opt for a glass of red or white wine, or the cocktail of your choice.

The establishments listed here represent a slice of Rome's ever-vibrant *aperitivo* scene.

Doppio Zero *68 Via Ostiense, tel: 06-5730 1961.*

Fluid *46/47 Via del Governo Vecchio, tel: 06-683 2361.*

Freni e Frizioni *4/6 Via del Politeama, tel: 06-454 97499.*

Magnolia *4 Campo de' Fiori, tel: 06-683 09367.*

Obikà *26 Via dei Prefetti, tel: 06-683 2630.*

Oppio Caffé *72 Via delle Terme di Tito, tel: 06-474 5262.*

Palatium Enoteca Laziale *94 Via Frattina, tel: 06-692 02132.*

Red *30 Via Pietro de Coubertin, tel: 06-806 91630.*

dumplings in a meat sauce) are traditionally prepared on Thursday, while *baccalà* (salt cod) is served on Friday.

Nor is fish fussed over: clams tossed with spaghetti and olive oil become *spaghetti alle vongole*, and *pesce azzurro* (fish from the sea) is baked in the oven *(al forno)* or cooked on the grill (*ai ferri* or *alla griglia*). Two common meat dishes are *saltimbocca alla romana* (veal slices rolled with prosciutto and sage) and the arch-Roman *coda alla vaccinara* ("oxtail butcher's style", slow-braised in a garlic, pepper, tomato and celery sauce), but the meat to try is *abbacchio* (milk-fed lamb), which is usually roasted with herbs and garlic or served *alla scottadito* (as grilled chops).

Greens on the side

Save room for vegetables, which abound in Rome's markets all year long and are usually

Romans are the undisputed masters of the artichoke, which you can try prepared in several different traditional styles.

served simply prepared, often steamed or blanched and then briefly sautéed. November to April is the season for another Roman speciality, artichokes, which can be served many different ways. Among them are *carciofi alla giudia* ("Jewish-style" and so typical of the Ghetto – deep-fried) and *carciofi alla romana*

(stuffed with garlic and mint, and stewed).

A typical winter salad is *puntarelle*, made by shredding the stalks of locally grown chicory and serving them with a lemon-anchovy dressing. Summer brings roasted peppers, aubergines and courgettes (zucchini) served in a variety of ways, and large tomatoes stuffed with herbs and rice, while in spring you'll see asparagus and *fave con pecorino* (raw broad beans with pecorino cheese).

Many Italians like to have just one main dish and finish a meal with a piece of fruit, then a coffee. Accordingly, appetisers and desserts get little attention in most Rome restaurants. A few common starters are melon or figs with prosciutto and *fiori di zucca* (deep-fried zucchini flowers filled with mozzarella and anchovies). Popular desserts are *torta di ricotta* (ricotta tart), *panna cotta* (eggless, firm creamy custard with a fruit sauce) and *tiramisù* (coffee trifle).

Find your wine

The local wines that still dominate the wine selections of most Roman restaurants – those from Frascati are the best-known – are nowadays much better than they used to be, but

FAR LEFT: chef at RistorArte, one of a new generation of restaurants serving modern Roman cuisine. **TOP LEFT:** tagliatelle and parmesan; tomato and mozzarella salad. **ABOVE:** olives are a common *antipasto*. **RIGHT:** artichokes are a Roman favourite.

still pale in comparison with wines produced in other parts of Italy, which are now widely available in the capital. For a good wine, it's usually better to bypass the house wine and choose a non-local label.

Italians rarely drink without eating, but stopping by a bar for an early-evening aperitif with a snack has become one of fashionable Rome's biggest fads (*see box, page 64*). Wine bars *(enoteche)* are also very popular. They have much better wine selections than most restaurants, and offer a great alternative to a restaurant meal, with a relaxed, easy-going atmosphere. Choose from usually about a dozen wines available by the glass (or from more than a thousand different labels by the bottle), and a great selection of high-quality cheeses, salami and other cured meats and smoked fish, as well as soups and salads, quiches and gratins, and sometimes home-made desserts.

Roman pizza

The Neapolitans are credited with inventing pizza, but Romans eat their fair share. There are more *pizzerie* than restaurants in town, and Romans have their own version of this staple dish: whereas a big Neapolitan pizza is made with a thick, softish dough and has a raised rim, a *pizza romana* is plate-sized,

ICE CREAM HEAVEN: ROME'S STAR *GELATERIE*

Romans have enjoyed ice cream since ancient times: Nero ate ice transported all the way from Vesuvius, mixed with fruit topping. Modern Rome has no shortage of fine parlours, and locals like nothing better than an evening *passeggiata* accompanied by a fresh *gelato.*

Many Roman bars and cafés sell ice cream, but don't be fooled – for the real thing, you must be more selective. Most of Rome's genuine artisan ice-cream makers have a long pedigree, and some are legendary. Here is a selection of the city's favourites.

Gelateria del Teatro 22a Piazza San Simeone (Centro Storico). Hidden away, this newcomer is the pride and joy of Roman Stefano and his Peruvian wife. Their artisan ice cream uses fresh fruit bought daily from the market.

Il Gelato di San Crispino 42 Via della Panetteria (Fontana di Trevi), 56 Via Acaia (San Giovanni) and Fiumicino Airport. Closed Tues. The cognoscenti consider this the best. Tubs only (cones would interfere with the taste) and flavours according to season.

Giolitti 40 Via Uffici del Vicario (Piazza Montecitorio) and Casina dei Tre Laghi (EUR). Open daily. Grandma Bernardina established the Giolitti brand in 1890 by seating her eight *bambini* outside while they ate ice creams; when passers-by asked her how she raised such beautiful children, she told them it was her milk products that did the magic.

Palazzo del Freddo di Giovanni Fassi 65–7 Via Principe Eugenio (Esquilino). Open summer noon–midnight, winter noon–9pm, closed Mon. The jazzy interior belies a tradition that dates back to 1890. Flavours are augmented by specialities such as the fruit or chocolate *pezzo duro.*

Fata Morgana 36A Via Ostiense (Piramide). This gluten-free ice cream parlour scoops up delicious and unusual flavours like Kentucky tobacco-scented dark chocolate, camomile and lavender, and ricotta and coconut.

I Tre Scalini 28–32 Piazza Navona (Centro Storico). Closed Wed. The home of the *tartufo* ice cream sits on Piazza Navona beckoning passers-by to try its famed chocolate truffle.

and rolled very thin and flat. Both kinds must be baked in a wood-burning stove *(forno a legna)*. A night out at a pizzeria (few are open for lunch) is a quintessential Roman experience.

On the go

For Romans, *gelato* (ice cream) is not so much a dessert as an afternoon or after-dinner snack to accompany a leisurely stroll around town. Accordingly, *gelaterie* are never far away and stay open late. Other treats that can be picked up from street vendors all over town are roasted chestnuts in the autumn and winter, and refreshing *grattachecca* (shaved ice with syrup) and watermelon wedges in summer.

Romans often stop at the local bar a couple of times a day, first for a breakfast of espresso or cappuccino and a *cornetto* (the Italian version of the croissant), then another espresso and perhaps a snack, such as a *panino* or *tramezzino* (small sandwiches) later in the day.

Pizza a taglio (by the slice) is also easy to find. Thicker than pizzeria pizza and topped with dozens of imaginative combinations, *pizza al taglio* is always sold by weight; an *etto* (100 grams) is a small portion. Many of the same shops also sell *supplì* (fried balls of rice and mozzarella), a classic Roman snack.

> *Romans may love a leisurely meal, but stopping for slices of pizza, a few scoops of ice cream or a shot of fruit and crushed ice is also an essential part of any* passeggiata.

A good *alimentari*, or grocery shop, is worth visiting as this is where you'll find regional products from all over the country. The local cheese to try is *pecorino romano*, made from ewe's milk in big wheels, bathed in brine and aged for 18 months. A by-product is *ricotta di pecora*, brought in fresh from the farms and delicious on its own. A memorable sandwich can be made from *porchetta* (whole roasted pig, sliced to order), a speciality of the hill towns around Rome. ❑

ABOVE LEFT: Roscioli, a popular Roman deli and small restaurant near Campo de' Fiori. **ABOVE:** Romans like their sweets simple, fresh and preferably home-made. **ABOVE RIGHT:** an espresso, the way to start the day and end a meal.

BVLGARI
10

SHOPPING

When it comes to shopping, Rome does more than hold its own against its more famous northern rival, Milan. It has enough haute couture, chic boutiques, designer homeware and leatherware stores to satisfy the hungriest of style vultures

For years Rome has been vying with big brother Milan for status as a fashionista magnet. While history hawks and culture vultures perpetually head for the Eternal City, serious shopaholics are quick to name Milan as the hands-down fashion capital of Italy. Yet times are changing. Not only can Rome boast a thriving market for high-quality handcraftsmanship, in the face of sibling rivalry, Gucci, Prada, Armani and company have set up shop in the prestigious Piazza di Spagna area, and boutiques are springing up every which way.

Made in Rome

For the keen-eyed and eager shopper, there are unique purchases to be had, from that hand-cut leather jacket you've always dreamed of, to handwoven textiles and home-grown Roman designer wear. They may not be parading the catwalks yet, but these unique up-and-comers are worth seeking out. In a city that refuses to leave behind the values of solid craftsmanship, so intrinsic to the "Made in Italy" mark, a savvy shopper will delight in the objects on offer.

Now more than ever, Rome boasts a shopping scene for all tastes – from the seekers of chic to lovers of all things ornate and original.

LEFT: Via dei Condotti, designer-store central.
RIGHT: window shopping by the Spanish Steps.

Be aware that the big guns of Italy don't necessarily cost less on their own soil. Those with an eye on the major labels would be wise to peruse price tags at home before landing in the capital. The outlets outside Rome, although cheaper, are a bit of a trek, so think twice about stocking up on your Prada, Fendi and Ferragamo.

The good news is that younger Roman labels like AVC (fabulous shoes) and Arsenale (a truly art gallery-esque women's boutique) are springing up, paving the way for fresh Roman fashion.

For a rundown of the various neighbourhoods and where to buy what, *see pages 72–3*.

Vintage fashions

There's a well-rounded vintage scene, with most shops clustered along Via del Governo Vecchio, just off Piazza Navona, and Via del Boschetto in Monti. For an ultra Roman experience, spend the afternoon trying on 1970s leather jackets and boho dresses, before refuelling at one of Via del Governo Vecchio's copious wine bars. The penchant for yesteryear continues in nearby Via dei Coronari, a street dotted with tiny antique shops.

When to hit the shops

Opening hours in Rome are a law unto themselves. What visitors find most surprising is the tendency for many shops to close for at least two hours at lunchtime and all of Monday morning. However, in highly commercial and touristy areas such as the Tridente, Via del Corso, the Trevi Fountain and Via Nazionale, most shops, especially the chain stores, department stores and high-fashion boutiques, now operate a so-called *orario continuato* (continuous opening hours), sometimes called the not-quite-English *orario no-stop*, both of which mean they do not close at lunchtime, and may be open Monday morning.

Sunday opening is another recent novelty. Again, it's mainly the big names, chain stores and department stores in touristy areas that open on a Sunday. Another thing to remember is that in July and August, as the heat starts to become oppressive, local and independent shops may close on Saturday afternoon, and most close for at least two weeks for their annual holiday.

GETTING AROUND

Getting from one area to another in Rome is easy. If you are staying in the city centre and are armed with a decent map, you can walk almost everywhere, and will definitely find it a more pleasant experience than trying to jam yourself onto one of the packed buses that chug through the traffic-choked city's central thoroughfares. Keep an eye out for the small electric buses (116 is the favourite) that snake quietly through the city though, as they can provide welcome relief for tired feet. For the more outlying areas there is usually a handy bus or a metro stop not too far away, to make it easier to carry your purchases home.

Roman service

It won't be long before you experience a phenomenon well known to regular visitors to Rome – the unhelpful shop assistant. Although there are many exceptions, most notably the designer boutiques who are dependent on tourist trade, and the small independent stores, Roman retail staff are not known for polite customer service. Shop assistants may seem either too bored or too busy talking to pay you any attention. Don't take it personally; simply ask firmly for what you want and you'll find the assistants usually snap to attention.

Bargain-hunting

Discounts are not generally given in most types of stores, although you may be able to get one if you are making a large purchase, or you happen upon a small defect of manufacture. One exception is the many large *profumerie* (perfume and cosmetics stores) where most items are sold at a *prezzo scontato* (discount price). Another way of getting reliable bargains is the end-of-season sales *(saldi)*.

The two main sales periods start in early January, continuing into February (or as long as they've got anything left on the racks), and in mid-July, lasting until mid-September. At other times of the year, interesting deals can often be had at stores showing a *liquidazione* sign, which indicates a closing-down sale.

The Fashion District outlets of Valmontone, 40km (25 miles) outside Rome, are definitely worth visiting for excellent deals and discounts. Among the stores represented are Gianfranco Ferre, Pierre Cardin, Calvin Klein Jeans, La Perla, Rosenthal, Bassetti, Adidas, Lotto and loads more. Trains leave hourly from Termini Station. Castel Romano hosts over 100 stores and offers up to a 70 percent discount on merchandise. Buses for Pomezia Via Pontina depart regularly from Metro B station Laurentina. Ask the driver to indicate the stop.

Don't underestimate the goods on offer at the open-air markets around town. For secondhand gems, Porta Portese, Via Sannio and Borghetto Flaminio are prime *(see page 75)*.

FAR LEFT: Trastevere artisan at work. **LEFT, ABOVE AND BELOW:** well-made bags, shoes, belts and other leather goods are good buys. **ABOVE:** inspecting the merchandise. **RIGHT:** retro homewares.

Designer fakes

Another way to get your "designer" goods cheaply is to buy them from the street vendors who populate the city's most touristy thoroughfares and bridges. Of course, they are selling bags that only look like real Prada, Gucci, Fendi and Louis Vuitton numbers, often to an unsuspecting international clientele. Remember, though, that when you are given prices at a fraction of those of the original labels, the goods are definitely not the real thing, and that trade in counterfeit goods is actually illegal. It's not an unusual sight to see the sudden scattering of such vendors at the sight of a police car rolling by. ❑

Shopping Areas

Most shoppers make a beeline for Tridente, but there are many other less busy, often cheaper shopping districts to discover

The Centro Storico: Rome's shopping scene is often summed up by one glorious avenue: Via del Corso, the road stretching from Piazza del Popolo to Piazza Venezia. It is here that you'll find everything from the national and international retail stores, high- and lower-end labels, and all the books, music and trinkets you're after. Many turnoffs lead to Piazza di Spagna and, most famously, Via Condotti. This is where the real designer glitz resides – that and about 99 percent of the tourist masses. For a far more leisurely shopping experience, weave your way through the backstreets, starting from Piazza del Popolo. Be sure not to overlook the hip Via del Babuino. The entire triangle is referred to as Tridente.

The areas around Piazza Navona, the Pantheon and the Campo de' Fiori are teeming with boutiques, homeware shops and fabulous shoes and accessories, not to mention some delicious food shops and pampering perfumeries.

BELOW: in the more upscale area around Piazza Fiume and the beginning of Via Salaria, you'll find Rinascente department store, and some retailers of pretty clothing, shoes and accessories.

ABOVE: shop windows in Via del Corso.

RIGHT: the Vatican-Prati neighbourhood to the north is home to shopping mega-street Via Cola di Rienzo. A slightly shorter jaunt than Via del Corso, this popular strip is lined with youthful retail chains, some great boutiques, and COIN, Rome's best department store. You'll also find some of the finest selections of speciality food and drink anywhere in town.

LEFT: dip into the hilly side streets of Monti, where art galleries, bric-a-brac shops and funky boutiques are turning this area into the next trendy hotspot.

RIGHT: in and around Piazza Vittorio (Rome's modest Chinatown near the station), ethnic clothing and accessories abound. The major Via Nazionale *(pictured right)* is the place to go for bags and shoes. Numerous stockists carry the best of this year's collections ranging in style and price.

BELOW: across the Tiber from the historic centre, Trastevere is bursting with knick-knack shops, artisans' workshops and some great jewellery stores. It is also the site of Porta Portese, the massive Sunday market selling just about anything *(see page 204)*.

DESIGNER HIT LIST

There's no reason to ignore your inner fashion muse, but in the midst of a designer shop-a-thon, fashionistas may wish to keep the following tips in mind:

For bags it's **Prada**, **Fendi**, **Furla** and **Gucci.**

For shoes, the best shops are **Prada**, **Ferragamo** and **Tod's**.

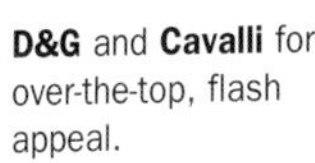

Trussardi and **Armani** for jeans.

D&G and **Cavalli** for over-the-top, flash appeal.

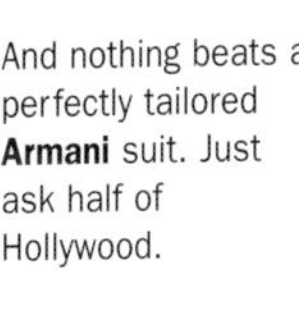

Valentino and **Laura Biagiotti** for evening allure.

And nothing beats a perfectly tailored **Armani** suit. Just ask half of Hollywood.

Markets in Rome

Neighbourhood markets are an essential part of the Roman way of life and are full of local colour

Rome has about 150 official *mercati rionali* (neighbourhood markets) which run from Monday to Saturday, where there's generally an abundance of the freshest fruit and vegetables, as well as stalls selling meat, fish, cheeses, hams and spices, and others loaded with kitchenware, household linens, clothing and toys. Although supermarkets are competing hard, there are a number of reasons why the tradition of buying from markets will be hard to extinguish. In the city centre a lack of space dictates that the supermarkets that do exist are still comparatively small, and have no convenient parking spaces. Buying from markets is still often more convenient, both economically and in terms of location.

Also extremely important are the personalised service and human contact. Many older people value this highly, and will spend time chatting to stallholders and other customers as they make their purchases. Markets, especially flea markets, also offer the opportunity to do some bargaining. Whether you go to buy or to browse, Rome's markets are worth visiting for their atmosphere alone.

Above: Rome's biggest flea market is Porta Portese, held on Via Portuense and adjacent streets between Piazza Porta Portese and Via Ettore Rolli.

Below: although supermarkets have sprung up all over Rome in recent years, most Romans still prefer to buy fresh produce from their local daily market.

ABOVE: the city's best-known food market is Campo de' Fiori. Here you will find everything from upmarket stalls selling exotic fruits and rare herbs at exorbitant prices to stalls where fresher-than-fresh produce on show is grown by the farmer who is serving you.

BELOW: another classic Roman market is held on Via Sannio, just behind the Basilica of San Giovanni in Laterano. This is the place to come for jeans, leather jackets, sports gear and shoes. There are also several stalls selling retro and second-hand clothes.

THE HIGHLIGHTS

The best of Rome's many street markets are listed below. Most of the produce markets are open from Monday to Saturday, 7am–2pm. **Campo de' Fiori** (Centro Storico) is Rome's most characteristic fruit and vegetable market. **Mercato dei Fiori**, Via Trionfale (Prati). A huge wholesale flower market that is open to the public on Tuesday morning only. Just south of here, **Mercato Trionfale**, on Via Andrea Doria (Prati), is an enormous fenced-in market that sells a large variety of produce. **Mercato di San Cosimato**, Piazza San Cosimato (Trastevere) is a small but popular fruit and vegetable market. **Nuovo Mercato Esquilino**, Via Ricasoli (Esquilino) is the most multicultural produce market, with exotic herbs and spices, yams, sweet potatoes and okra, and lots of other goods as well.

Smaller traditional markets can be found in San Lorenzo's **Largo degli Osci** (fewer tourists, low prices) and **Piazza dell'Unità**.

Specialist markets, and those selling goods other than fresh produce, include:

Mercato delle Stampe (Largo della Fontanelle Borghese, Centro Storico; Mon–Sat 8am–sunset), which sells prints and second-hand or antiquarian books.

Mercato di Via Sannio (Via Sannio, Piazza San Giovanni in Laterano, San Giovanni; Mon–Fri 8am–2pm, Sat 8am–5pm) sells new and second-hand clothes; the occasional vintage gem can be found here for a bargain price.

Porta Portese (Trastevere; Sun 7am–2pm). This is the best flea market in Rome. Skill is required to get a real bargain, but it's great fun. Hang onto your bags and look out for pickpockets.

The **Soffitta Sotto i Portici** market (Piazza Augusto Imperatore, under the porticoes; first and third Sun of every month, except Aug, 9am–sunset) is an antiques and collectors' market.

Borghetto Flaminio (Piazza della Marina, north of Piazza del Popolo; Sun 10am–7pm; closed Aug). All the stallholders here are private individuals, selling heirlooms and clothing, so there is a wide range in quality and price. There's a small admission charge.

Dior
Dior

BIKINI
BOCCHINI

ORIENTATION

The Places section details all the attractions worth seeing, arranged by area. The areas are shown on a colour-coordinated map on pages 82–3. Main sights are cross-referenced by number to individual maps

Rome is crammed with great sights. In no other city are the accumulated layers of history so evident. Every corner and crest seems to lead to a famous monument, church or square. However, for first-time visitors trying to grapple with the layout of its seven hills, the city can seem confusing. The best way to orientate oneself is to look upon Via del Corso as a spine, with the leafy Villa Borghese quarter at the top, the archaeological zone at the bottom, the Centro Storico to the west, Piazza di Spagna to the east, and the Vatican and Trastevere on the far bank of the River Tiber.

The first two chapters cover the main archaeological sites – namely the Capitol, Forum, Palatine and the Colosseum – reflecting the city's foundation and key episodes in its history. Trevi Fountain and the Spanish Steps are the focal point of the next two chapters, which cover these most iconic of Rome's landmarks and the maze of streets around them.

What is referred to as the Centro Storico, or historic centre, is the dense centre of Rome contained in the great bend of the River Tiber; this is covered in the chapters on Piazza Navona and the Pantheon, and Campo de' Fiori and the Ghetto.

The Vatican and Trastevere chapters take you across to the west bank of the Tiber for a tour of St Peter's and the Vatican Museums, and the fashionable Trastevere district and the Gianicolo (Janiculum Hill) for one of the finest views of the city.

The book also dips into the quarters verging on these key areas – the Villa Borghese quarter, the Aventine and Testaccio, Monti and Esquilino, the Appian Way and other neighbourhoods beyond the usual tourist routes. For those who want to escape the noise and heat of the city, there's a selection of day-trips into Rome's environs. Advice on getting around the city, shopping, nightlife, accommodation and other essential information is contained in the Travel Tips section of this guide. ❑

PRECEDING PAGES: Piazza di Spagna; Campo de' Fiori backstreet.
LEFT: reach for the sky – fragments of an enormous statue of Constantine.

Central Rome

Top Sights

Vatican Museums
page 141

Piazza Navona
page 158

Pantheon
page 153

Campo de' Fiori
page 170

Capitoline Museums
page 89

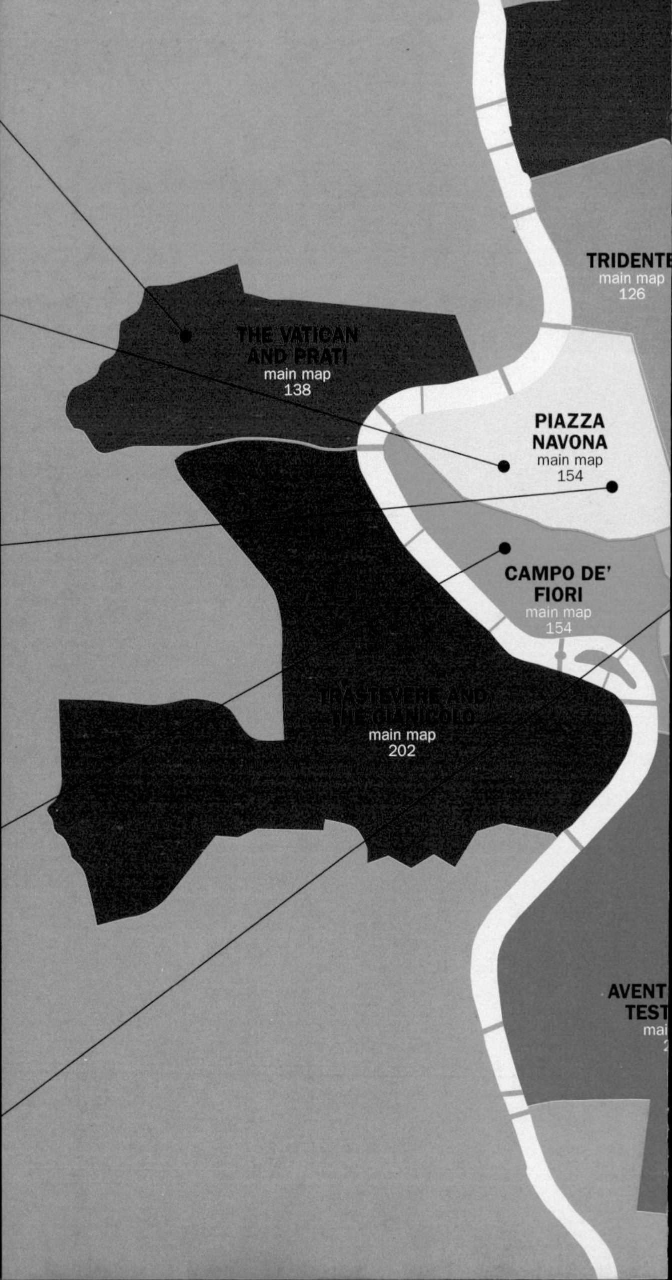

TRIDENTE
main map
126

THE VATICAN AND PRATI
main map
138

PIAZZA NAVONA
main map
154

CAMPO DE' FIORI
main map
154

TRASTEVERE AND THE GIANICOLO
main map
202

AVENT
TEST
mai

VIA VENETO AND
ORGHESE, and NORTH ROME
main maps 186 and 190

IRINALE
n map 118

MONTI AND
ESQUILINO
main map
230

E

ENT
ME
naps
) and 110

CELIO AND
SAN GIOVANNI
main map
222

APPIAN WAY
main map
240

Villa Borghese
page 188

Spanish Steps
page 129

Trevi Fountain
page 117

Forum
page 100

Colosseum
page 111

Rome

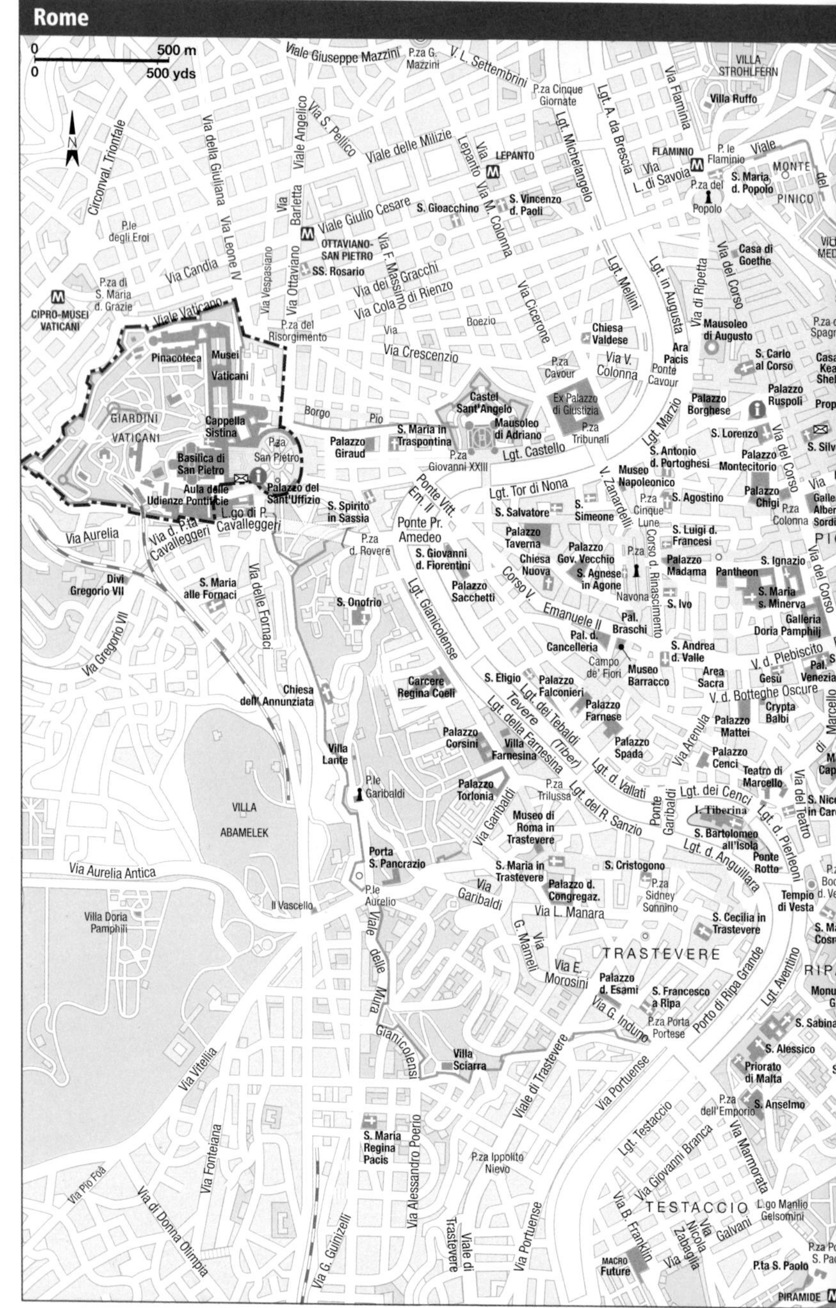

0 500 m
0 500 yds
Viale Giuseppe Mazzini
P.za G. Mazzini
V. L. Settembrini
P.za Cinque Giornate
VILLA STROHLFERN
Villa Ruffo
Via Flaminia
Lgt. A. da Brescia
Lgt. Michelangelo
Via della Giuliana
Circonval. Trionfale
Viale Angelico
Via S. Pellico
Viale delle Milizie
Via Lepanto
LEPANTO
FLAMINIO
P. le Flaminio
Viale
MONTE PINICO
S. Maria d. Popolo
P.za del Popolo
Via L. di Savoia
S. Vincenzo d. Paoli
S. Gioacchino
Via M. Colonna
Viale Giulio Cesare
Via Barletta
P.le degli Eroi
Via Leone IV
OTTAVIANO-SAN PIETRO
SS. Rosario
Via F. Massimo
Via dei Gracchi
Via Cola di Rienzo
Via Candia
Via Vespasiano
Via Ottaviano
P.za di S. Maria d. Grazie
CIPRO-MUSEI VATICANI
Viale Vaticano
P.za del Risorgimento
Boezio
Via Cicerone
Lgt. Mellini
Lgt. in Augusta
Via di Ripetta
Via del Corso
Casa di Goethe
Mausoleo di Augusto
Chiesa Valdese
Via
Via Crescenzio
P.za Cavour
Via V. Colonna
Ponte Cavour
Ara Pacis
S. Carlo al Corso
Pinacoteca
Musei Vaticani
GIARDINI VATICANI
Cappella Sistina
P.za San Pietro
Basilica di San Pietro
Aula delle Udienze Pontificie
Palazzo del Sant'Uffizio
Borgo Pio
Palazzo Giraud
S. Maria in Traspontina
Castel Sant'Angelo
Mausoleo di Adriano
P.za Giovanni XXIII
Ex Palazzo di Giustizia
P.za Tribunali
Lgt. Castello
Lgt. Marzio
Palazzo Borghese
Palazzo Ruspoli
S. Lorenzo
S. Antonio d. Portoghesi
Palazzo Montecitorio
Museo Napoleonico
Via del Corso
S. Silv
Lgt. Tor di Nona
V. Zanardelli
P.za Cinque Lune
S. Agostino
Palazzo Chigi
P.za Colonna
Ponte Vitt. Em. II
S. Spirito in Sassia
L.go di P. Cavalleggeri
Via d. P.ta Cavalleggeri
Via Aurelia
P.za d. Rovere
Ponte Pr. Amedeo
S. Salvatore
S. Simeone
Palazzo Taverna
S. Luigi d. Francesi
Corso d. Rinascimento
S. Giovanni d. Fiorentini
Palazzo Gov. Vecchio
Chiesa Nuova
S. Agnese in Agone
P.za Navona
Palazzo Madama
Pantheon
S. Ignazio
Divi Gregorio VII
S. Maria alle Fornaci
Via delle Fornaci
S. Onofrio
Palazzo Sacchetti
Lgt. Gianicolense
Corso V. Emanuele II
S. Ivo
S. Maria s. Minerva
Galleria Doria Pamphilj
Via del Corso
Via Gregorio VII
Pal. Braschi
Pal. d. Cancelleria
Campo de' Fiori
Museo Barracco
S. Andrea d. Valle
V. d. Plebiscito
Chiesa dell' Annunziata
Carcere Regina Coeli
S. Eligio
Palazzo Falconieri
Lgt. dei Tebaldi
Tevere (Tiber)
Lgt. della Farnesina
Palazzo Farnese
Area Sacra
Gesù
Pal. Venezia
V. d. Botteghe Oscure
Crypta Balbi
Palazzo Mattei
Palazzo Spada
Via Arenula
Palazzo Cenci
Teatro di Marcello
Palazzo Corsini
Villa Farnesina
Villa Lante
VILLA ABAMELEK
P.le Garibaldi
Palazzo Torlonia
Via Garibaldi
P.za Trilussa
Lgt. d. Vallati
Lgt. dei Cenci
Ponte Garibaldi
I. Tiberina
Lgt. del R. Sanzio
Museo di Roma in Trastevere
S. Bartolomeo all'Isola
Lgt. d. Pierleoni
Via del Teatro
Via Aurelia Antica
Porta S. Pancrazio
S. Maria in Trastevere
S. Cristogono
Lgt. d. Anguillara
Ponte Rotto
Palazzo d. Congregaz.
P.za Sidney Sonnino
Tempio di Vesta
Il Vascello
P.le Aurelio
Via Garibaldi
Via L. Manara
Villa Doria Pamphili
S. Cecilia in Trastevere
Viale delle Mura Gianicolensi
Via G. Mameli
Via E. Morosini
TRASTEVERE
Palazzo d. Esami
S. Francesco a Ripa
Via di Ripa Grande
Porto di Ripa Grande
Lgt. Aventino
Via G. Induno
P.za Porta Portese
S. Sabina
S. Alessio
Villa Sciarra
Viale di Trastevere
Via Portuense
Priorato di Malta
Via Vitellia
P.za dell'Emporio
S. Anselmo
Lgt. Testaccio
Via Giovanni Branca
Via Marmorata
S. Maria Regina Pacis
Via Alessandro Poerio
P.za Ippolito Nievo
Via Fonteiana
Via Pio Foà
Via di Donna Olimpia
Via G. Guinizelli
Viale di Trastevere
Via Portuense
Via B. Franklin
TESTACCIO
L.go Manlio Gelsomini
Via Nicola Zabaglia
Via Galvani
MACRO Future
P.ta S. Paolo
PIRAMIDE

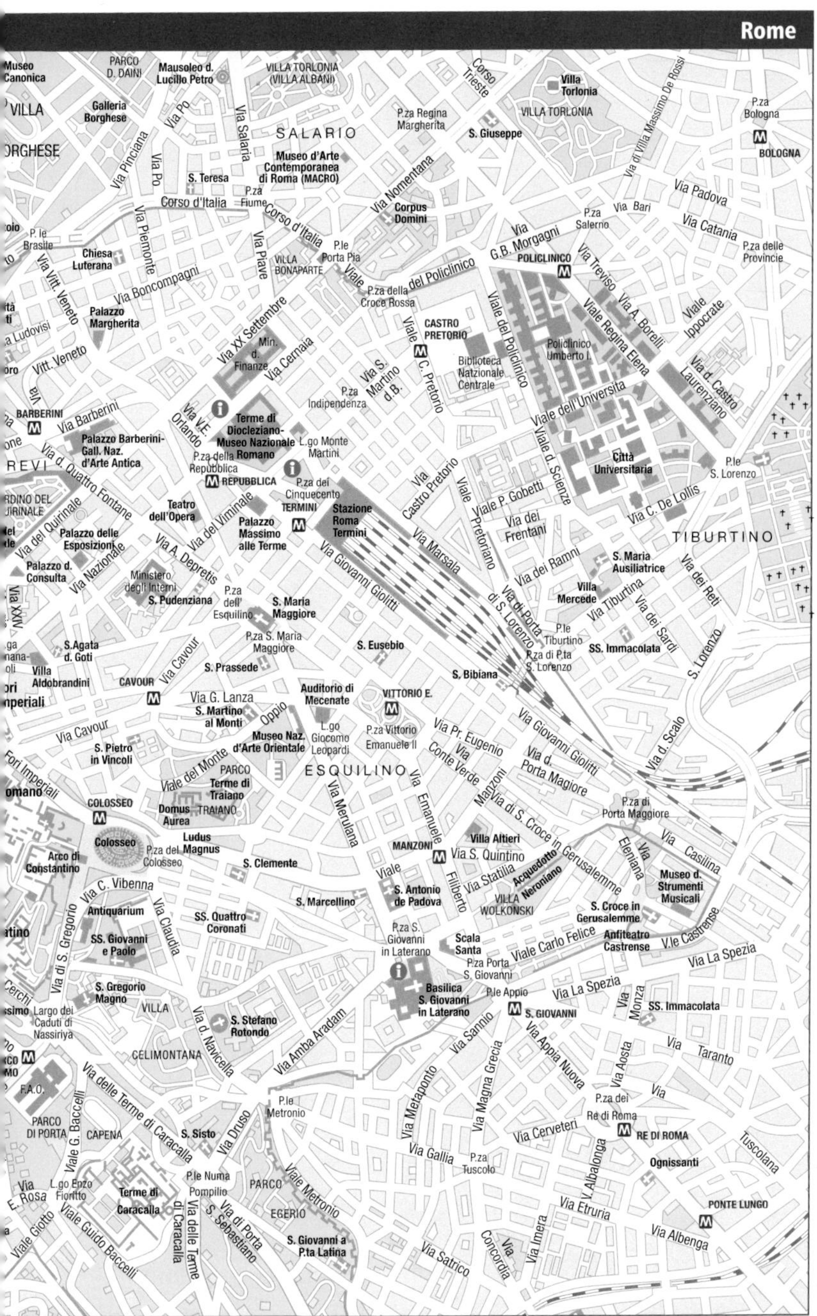
SALARIO
Villa Torlonia
VILLA TORLONIA
Mausoleo d. Lucillo Petro
Galleria Borghese
Museo d'Arte Contemporanea di Roma (MACRO)
S. Teresa
S. Giuseppe
Corpus Domini
POLICLINICO
BOLOGNA
CASTRO PRETORIO
Biblioteca Natzionale Centrale
Policlinico Umberto I.
Città Universitaria
Terme di Diocleziano-Museo Nazionale Romano
REPUBBLICA
TERMINI
Stazione Roma Termini
Palazzo Massimo alle Terme
Teatro dell'Opera
Palazzo delle Esposizioni
Palazzo Barberini-Gall. Naz. d'Arte Antica
BARBERINI
Palazzo Margherita
Chiesa Luterana
S. Maria Maggiore
S. Pudenziana
S. Prassede
S. Eusebio
S. Bibiana
CAVOUR
VITTORIO E.
S. Martino al Monti
S. Pietro in Vincoli
Museo Naz. d'Arte Orientale
Auditorio di Mecenate
ESQUILINO
TIBURTINO
S. Maria Ausiliatrice
Villa Mercede
SS. Immacolata
COLOSSEO
Colosseo
Arco di Constantino
Domus Aurea
Terme di Traiano
Ludus Magnus
S. Clemente
MANZONI
Villa Altieri
S. Antonio de Padova
S. Marcellino
SS. Quattro Coronati
Antiquarium
SS. Giovanni e Paolo
S. Croce in Gerusalemme
Museo d. Strumenti Musicali
Anfiteatro Castrense
Scala Santa
Basilica S. Giovanni in Laterano
S. GIOVANNI
SS. Immacolata
S. Gregorio Magno
S. Stefano Rotondo
CELIMONTANA
S. Sisto
Terme di Caracalla
S. Giovanni a P.ta Latina
RE DI ROMA
Ognissanti
PONTE LUNGO
Via Nomentana
Via Salaria
Corso d'Italia
Via XX Settembre
Via Cavour
Via Merulana
Via Appia Nuova
Via Tiburtina
Via Marsala
Via Giovanni Giolitti
Via La Spezia
Via Casilina
Via Tuscolana

Recommended Restaurants, Bars & Cafés on page 91

THE CAPITOLINE HILL

The Capitoline Hill was the political power centre of the ancient world, beautified by Michelangelo's designs during the Renaissance and now home to the world's oldest museums. Close by, the Vittoriano monument overlooks traffic-clogged Piazza Venezia, linking the ancient world with our own

The Capitoline Hill started life as a fortified stronghold and later became the city's religious and political centre. As a 12th-century guidebook, *Mirabilia Romae (The Marvels of Rome)* stated: "The Capitol was the head of the world, where consuls and senators abode to govern the earth." At only 50 metres (150ft), it may be the lowest of the city's seven hills, but Rome was founded at its feet. During the Renaissance, it was glorified with the Piazza Campidoglio, a harmonious square designed by Michelangelo, and second only to Piazza San Pietro in its architectural symmetry.

The twin crowns

In ancient times the hill looked quite different, with steep cliffs of porous tufa rock falling steeply on all sides of its twin crowns. On the southern crown, known as Campidoglio (the Capitol), stood the Tempio di Giove (Temple of Jupiter), which was the religious hub of the state. Originally the size of a football pitch, it was begun by the Etruscan kings and dedicated in 509 BC, the first year of the Republic. Behind its six-pillared, south-facing frontage a great anteroom led to the shrines of three great gods – Jupiter, Juno and Minerva. Every New Year's Day, the consuls were inaugurated in a formal ceremony on the Capitol.

The triumphal processions followed Via Sacra, the holy road, coming up the hill from the Forum. Remnants of the basalt paving of this street can be seen quite clearly from Via di Monte Tarpeo. Anyone guilty of treason was thrown from

Main attractions

SANTA MARIA IN ARACOELI
THE CAPITOLINE MUSEUMS
MAMERTINE PRISON
IL VITTORIANO MONUMENT
MUSEO DEL RISORGIMENTO
MUSEO DI PALAZZO VENEZIA

LEFT: Michelangelo's staircase leads to the Campidoglio, watched over by the twin gods, Castor (pictured) and Pollux.
RIGHT: Piazza Venezia viewed from the steps of the Vittoriano monument.

The spacious interior of Santa Maria in Aracoeli, and the stairway to its entrance (right).

BELOW: statue of Marcus Aurelius in the Campidoglio.

the Rupe Tarpea (Tarpeian Rock), the Capitol's southern precipice. The other crown of the hill housed the temple to Juno Moneta, the goddess who is supposed to have warned the Romans of an attack by Gauls in 390 BC by making her sacred geese honk. The mint also stood here, hence the word *moneta*, meaning money.

Santa Maria in Aracoeli ❶

✉ Scala dell'Arce Capitolina 12
🕒 daily 9am–12.30pm, 2.30–5.30pm (6.30pm in summer) € free
🚌 *see Musei Capitolini*

The site of the ancient Temple of Juno Moneta is now occupied by the church of Santa Maria in Aracoeli (St Mary of the Altar in the Sky). The church hides behind a 13th-century brick façade, but its origins go back much further, as its ancient columns testify. Records from AD 574 mention a church on this site. The present church was built by Franciscans in around 1250. The interior features an ornate coffered ceiling dating from 1572–5 and a striking Cosmatesque floor. This style of intricate, geometric polychrome patterns is named after Lorenzo Cosmati (1140–1210), its inventor. In the first chapel on the right are Renaissance frescoes by Pinturicchio depicting the life of St Bernard. The recent restoration of the

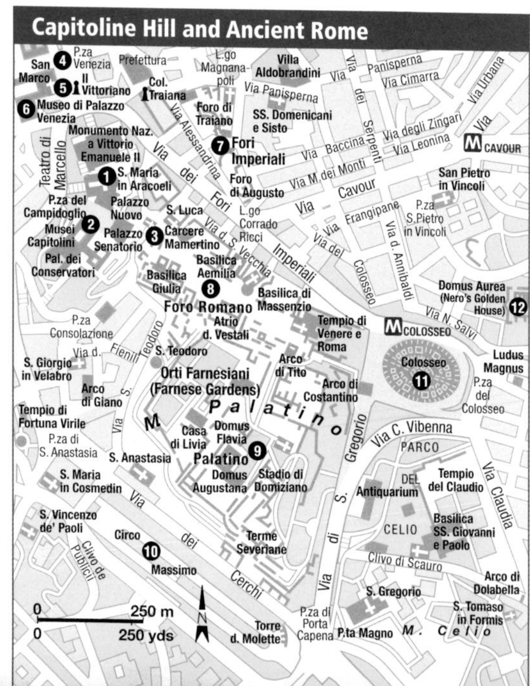

Recommended Restaurants, Bars & Cafés on page 91

Chapel of San Pasquale Baylon revealed beautiful 13th-century frescoes concealed behind 16th-century works. Steps lead down from the exit in the right transept to the level of the Piazza del Campidoglio.

PIAZZA DEL CAMPIDOGLIO

Between the hill's two peaks sits the **Piazza del Campidoglio** (Capitol Square). In ancient times it was the site of the Asylum, a sacred sanctuary that protected the persecuted, said to date back to the time of the founder of the city, Romulus. The magnificent square, its buildings and the broad staircase leading up to it were designed by Michelangelo for Pope Paul III, who wanted a majestic setting for the reception of the Holy Roman Emperor Charles V on his visit to Rome in 1536.

As it turned out, the square wasn't completed until the 17th century. Standing guard at the top of the **Cordonata**, as the staircase is known, are two imposing statues of Castor and Pollux. The piazza's centrepiece is a first-rate copy of an immense equestrian statue of Emperor Marcus Aurelius. The original is kept inside the Capitoline Museums.

Straight ahead is the **Palazzo Senatorio**. At the bottom of its double staircase is a fountain of Minerva flanked by two statues representing the Nile (left with the Sphinx) and the Tiber (right with the she-wolf).

The Musei Capitolini ❷

1 Piazza del Campidoglio
06-0608 Tue–Sun 9am–8pm
charge 30, 40, 44, 46, 60, 62, 63, 64, 70, 81, 84, 85, 87, 95, 117, 119, 160, 170, 175, 271, 492, 571, 628, 630, 715, 716, 780, 781, 810

The two grand *palazzi* on either side of the square – Palazzo Nuovo (New Palace) and Palazzo dei Conservatori (Conservators' Palace) – house the oldest public museums in the world. The **Musei Capitolini** are entered via the Palazzo dei Conservatori, on the right of Michelangelo's Cordonata. Together they contain a rich collection of ancient sculpture, and late Renaissance and Baroque art *(see pages 51–5)*.

The two palaces are connected via a passage lined with artefacts that runs underneath the square. From here you can visit the **Tabularium**, Rome's ancient archive (from 78 BC). It was built around the even older Temple of Veiovis, and rose four storeys high, with 10 arches opening onto the Forum, although all but three of them are now bricked up.

FOOD

Avoid the refreshment stands dotted around the major tourist sites unless you're absolutely desperate for a drink. They're overpriced and prey on thirsty tourists. If you don't want to be ripped off, it's worth stocking up on a supply of bottled mineral water from a grocery store, or take advantage of the water gushing out of the drinking fountains.

ABOVE LEFT: the she-wolf suckling Romulus and Remus. **BELOW:** fragments of a colossal statue of Constantine in the Palazzo dei Conservatori.

Some of the best views of the city can be seen from the cafés in the Palazzo dei Conservatori and the Vittoriano monument. Take the lift (€7) and spare your feet 196 steps.

ABOVE RIGHT: tomb of the Unknown Soldier. **ABOVE:** admiring the view from the Tabularium. **BELOW:** the Vittoriano monument.

Memorable views across the Roman Forum can be had from here.

Mamertine Prison ❸

✉ 1 Clivo Argentario (currently closed for restoration)

A road winds its way down from the left of the Palazzo Senatorio to the church of San Giuseppe dei Falegnami and the **Carcere Mamertino.** Defeated kings and generals, having been paraded through the streets in their victor's triumphal march, were imprisoned here before being executed. A small chapel next to a spring commemorates St Peter, who is said to have been incarcerated here, and to have baptised his guards with water from a spring he miraculously created. From the prison, the road leads down to Via dei Fori Imperiali *(see page 97)*.

PIAZZA VENEZIA ❹

If all roads lead to Rome, then all roads in Rome seem to lead to Piazza Venezia, the hub of the city's road network since 1881. Some 800,000 Romans squeeze their cars through

here every day, and it's not the best place to be during rush hour.

Il Vittoriano ❺

✉ Piazza Venezia ◷ daily summer 9am–5.30pm, winter 9.30am–4.30pm € free ▣ *see Musei Capitolini*

Compared to the grace and majesty of the Campidoglio, Il Vittoriano, which dominates the square, while undeniably impressive, is a bombastic structure. Romans refer to it irreverently as the typewriter, the wedding cake or even Rome's false teeth. In the 19th century, a whole swathe of medieval streets was razed to make way for this hulking white monument erected in honour of Victor Emmanuel II of Savoy, the first king of the newly unified Italy. However, entrance is free and visitors can climb the steps (or pay €7 for the elevator ride) for wonderful views of the city and welcome refreshments in the outdoor café behind it *(see below)*.

Below the equestrian statue of Victor Emmanuel II is the tomb of the Unknown Soldier flanked by perpetually burning flames and two armed guards. The monument also has a permanent museum complex. **The Museo del Risorgimento** recounts the history of the Risorgimento (literally "Resurrection"), a turbulent period of war and political wrangling that led to the reunification of Italy. However, few of the exhibits are labelled in English, and it's of limited appeal to those with only a passing interest in military history.

Around the back of the building is a space used for high-profile international exhibitions, while on the other side there's a brand-new museum focusing on Italian emigration.

Palazzo Venezia ❻

118 Via del Plebiscito 06-6999 4319 Tue–Sun 8.30am–7.30pm charge *see Musei Capitolini*

Although the Vittoriano is the most dominant, the Palazzo di Venezia is the most interesting building on this square. Built by Cardinal Barbo in 1455 and enlarged when he became Pope Paul II, it was later handed over to the Venetian ambassadors and then the Austrians, until Mussolini decided it would make a perfect office. He addressed the crowds from its balcony, the very balcony from which Pope Paul II watched the races along the Corso *(see page 127)*.

This palace now holds the **Museo di Palazzo Venezia**, with displays of medieval paintings, sculptures and artefacts, terracotta models (some by Bernini), bronze sculptures, and glass, silver and ivory objects. A permanent collection of Renaissance arts and crafts is joined by regular exhibitions dedicated to national and international artists and art movements.

Behind the palace is the church of **San Marco** (8.30am–12.30pm and 4–7pm; closed Mon am and Wed pm), with a lovely mosaic in its 9th-century apse. Outside the church stands the buxom **statue of Madama Lucrezia**, one of Rome's so-called "Talking Statues" *(see page 162)*. ❑

Piazza Venezia is one of central Rome's busiest hubs. It is also a major bus terminus.

BEST RESTAURANTS, BARS & CAFÉS

The restaurants and bars in this area are very touristy and not really recommended, but we detail a few places worth visiting, as much for the views and atmosphere as for food and drink.

Restaurants

Vecchia Roma

18 Piazza Campitelli 06-686 4604 L & D Thur–Tue. **€€€€** [p339, D1]

At Vecchia Roma you pay for the location, the service and some of the city's finest outdoor seating. The classic dishes are usually good, although occasionally only competent, and the wine is excellent. It's expensive for what you get, but memorable.

Bars and Cafés

Caffè Capitolino (top of Palazzo dei Conservatori, adjacent to Piazza Campidoglio) has one of the most panoramic views in Rome. Outdoor seating under sunshades, on the so-called "Terrazza Caffarelli", is expensive but delightful if it's not too hot. Inside, cafeteria-style service is cheaper. Open until 8pm in summer.

The **Ara Coelis Café** (behind the Vittoriano monument; also accessible from the Piazza del Campidoglio) is another great, if touristy, spot for a drink and affords fine views of the Forum and the Roman skyline.

Just off Piazza Venezia to the east is a former theatre that attracts a thirty-something Roman crowd looking for a quirky night out. **Il Centrale Ristotheatre** (6 Via Celsa) has a bar with a lounge area and restaurant with live music, theatre or cabaret. From 7.30pm–midnight on Sundays there's an all you can eat buffet, plus one drink, for a set price.

*Price includes dinner and a half-bottle of house wine. **€€€€** = more than €60, **€€€** = €40–60, **€€** = €25–40, **€** = under €25.*

Palazzo dei Conservatori

The larger of the two Capitoline Museums has a varied collection of artworks, from ancient statues to Baroque paintings

Divided between two palaces on either side of the Campidoglio, the Capitoline Museum collection is the oldest public collection of classical sculpture in the world – the first exhibits were made over to the people of Rome by Sixtus IV in 1471. A visit to the museums begins in the Palazzo dei Conservatori (to the right of the Michelangelo staircase, as you face the equestrian statue of Marcus Aurelius), where the ticket office and cloakrooms are.

One of the most iconic exhibits here is the much-copied she-wolf wet-nursing Romulus and Remus, symbol of Rome. The wolf is Etruscan, dating from the 5th century BC, but the twins were added in the 15th century by Florentine artist Pollaiuolo. You can also get a good close-up view of the original equestrian statue of Marcus Aurelius (the one on the square is a copy) exhibited in an airy, skylit room. Other highlights include a graceful 1st-century BC figure of a boy removing a thorn from his foot, an earlier Venus, a fine collection of Renaissance and Baroque art, and fragments of a huge statue of Constantine.

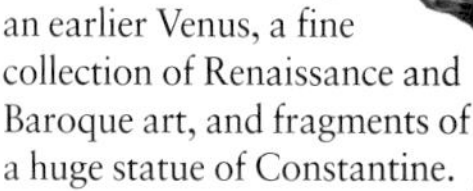

The essentials

Piazza del Campidoglio; www.museicapitolini.org

06-0608

Tue–Sun 9am–8pm

charge

30, 40, 44, 46, 60, 62, 63, 64, 70, 81, 84, 85, 87, 95, 117, 119, 160, 170, 175, 271, 492, 571, 628, 630, 715, 716, 780, 781, 810

Above: detail from the vast frescoes decorating the Hall of the Orazie and Curiazi where the Public Council of Conservators convened. Painted by Mannerist Cavaliere d'Arpino (1595–1640), they illustrate the origins of Rome as told by the Roman historian Livy.

ABOVE: *The Rape of the Sabine Women* by Pietro da Cortona. He was a contemporary of Bernini, and together they pioneered a true Baroque style, as illustrated by the movement, richness of colour and theatricality of this painting. **BELOW:** this vivid portrait of Hannibal riding an elephant is central to the 15th-century murals that decorate the Hannibal Room which records the Punic Wars fought between Rome and arch-rival Carthage.

ABOVE: in the courtyard of the Palazzo dei Conservatori are the surreal fragments of a colossal statue of Constantine, which once stood in his basilica in the Forum. The gigantic marble head is 2 metres (6ft) high. **RIGHT:** the celebrated bronze *Lo Spinario*, a delightful 1st-century BC statue of a boy plucking a thorn from his foot, inspired many Renaissance works. **BELOW:** sensual portrayal of St John the Baptist by Caravaggio.

ABOVE: the Palazzo dei Conservatori and Palazzo Nuovo are linked by an underground tunnel which leads to the Tabularium, the ancient Roman State Record Office, erected in 78 BC. It affords fine views of the Forum.

Palazzo Nuovo

The smaller of the museum duo holds some of the finest examples of ancient Roman statuary in the city

An underground passageway lined with artefacts connects the Palazzo dei Conservatori with the Palazzo Nuovo, via the Tabularium *(see page 89)*, which offers an excellent view of the Forum. This second museum in the Capitoline duo is filled with row upon row of portrait busts of Roman emperors, while the first floor contains some exquisite examples of Roman statuary. The most famous piece here is the *Dying Gaul*, a beautifully evocative statue of a fatally wounded warrior.

Other artworks worth singling out include the voluptuous *Capitoline Venus (pictured left)* and the red marble *Satyr Resting*, a copy of an original by Praxiteles. This is the statue which inspired Nathaniel Hawthorne's novel *The Marble Faun*. "It is impossible to gaze long at this stone image", wrote Hawthorn in the novel, "without conceiving a kindly sentiment towards it, as if its substance were warm to the touch, and imbued with actual life."

More earthly subjects on display include a drunken woman and children with various animals.

Keep a look out also for the Mosaic of the Doves from Hadrian's villa and the 2nd-century mosaic of theatre masks.

Below: in the courtyard of the Palazzo Nuovo is a fountain which incorporates a 1st-century BC statue of a river god. Known as "Marforio", this is one of Rome's famous "talking statues", to which placards containing satirical comments on the events of the day were attached during the Renaissance.

Left: Cupid and Psyche, a Roman copy of a Greek original portraying the god of love embracing the goddess of the soul.

Below Left: the *Capitoline Venus* is another Roman copy of a Hellenistic original, which Goethe considered the finest ancient statue in Rome. This sensual statue portrays the goddess of love and beauty rising from the water, modestly – but ineffectively – trying to cover her body. It's likely that such an accomplished sculpture decorated a prestigious imperial home.

Below: the Hall of the Emperors contains portrait busts of Roman emperors and their families, while the Hall of Philosophers includes busts of Socrates, Sophocles, Demosthenes, Euripides and Homer.

Right: the poignant statue of the *Dying Gaul*, thought to be the statue of a gladiator – "butchered to make a Roman holiday" in Byron's words – was discovered with another equally moving statue, the *Galata Suicide*, now housed in the Palazzo Altemps *(see page 160)*.

RIGHT: interspersed among the busts displayed on the ground-floor rooms are a variety of funerary reliefs, plinths and sarcophagi, the most famous of which is the 3rd-century sarcophagus depicting scenes from the life of Achilles.

ABOVE: the central exhibit in the Hall of the Doves is the exquisitely crafted mosaic of drinking doves found in Hadrian's Villa at Tivoli. In the same room is another highly expressive 2nd-century mosaic of two Greek theatre masks, probably from an imperial villa on the Aventine Hill.

ABOVE: the centrepiece of the design for the Piazza del Campidoglio was the magnificent statue of Marcus Aurelius (now a copy; the original is in the museum). Michelangelo found the statue so lifelike that he stood before the horse and commanded it to walk.

Recommended Restaurants, Bars & Cafés on page 113

ANCIENT ROME

This chapter shows you some of the places where Ancient Rome thrived, declined and eventually fell. Here lie the remains of the Fora, the Palatine, the Colosseum and Nero's Golden House

Main attractions

- THE IMPERIAL FORA
- THE FORO ROMANO
- PALATINE HILL
- CIRCUS MAXIMUS
- THE COLOSSEUM
- NERO'S GOLDEN HOUSE

By 7.30 in the morning, a traffic jam usually blocks the intersection of Via Labicana and Via dei Fori Imperiali which leads to the Colosseum and the Appian Way. This boulevard, commissioned by Mussolini for the greater glory of the Fascist Empire, slices through the heart of Rome's ancient sites. Here, Nero built an artificial lake to grace his palace. Then the Flavians – in a bid to return the tyrant's palace to the people – built the Colosseum. The construction of Via dei Fori Imperiali in 1932 was a relatively recent attempt to use Ancient Rome's monuments to underwrite modern political ambition.

Bulldozers flattened one of the city's oldest medieval quarters to make way for the route, destroying ancient walls, imperial palaces, temples and arches, some dating from the 3rd century BC. Architects ignored the archaeological massacre. When *Il Duce* ordered the removal of a pile of stones near the Colosseum, nobody pointed out that they marked the Meta Sudans, an ancient spring. Ludwig Curtius, then director of the German Archaeological Institute, said: "It would have been easy while building the street to excavate those parts of the Fora of Julius Caesar and of Trajan still lying underground, and to direct the road over them as a bridge, but the dictator, concerned only for his next demonstration of power, was in a hurry…"

Originally, Mussolini had hoped to excavate the Imperial Fora, which would have served as decoration alongside his new processional road, symbolically connecting his regime with the glory of Roman antiquity. If these plans had been followed, an

LEFT: the Arch of Septimius Severus.
RIGHT: 21st-century centurion and friend.

The simplest way to reach the Forum is to take metro line B or one of the buses indicated to Colosseo or Piazza Venezia. From Trastevere, the Aventine or Villa Borghese take tram No. 3. The entrance to Trajan's Markets is only a 10-minute walk away from the Colosseum.

RIGHT: Julius Caesar.
BELOW: Via dei Fori Imperiali.

archaeological park would have extended from the excavated Forum area to the ruins of the Baths of Caracalla and on to Via Appia Antica. But the project was never realised and the road became a major thoroughfare. It is unlikely that the ruins beneath it will ever come to light.

THE IMPERIAL FORA ❼

✉ Via dei Fori Imperiali ☎ 06-3996 7700 ⏲ Tue–Sun 8.30am–one hour before sunset ⓔ charge Ⓜ Colosseo 🚌 60, 63, 64, 70, 75, 84, 85, 87, 117, 170, 175, 186, 810, 850

The remains of the Fori Imperiali lie on either side and buried beneath the Via dei Fori Imperiali. As Rome grew in power, its population increased and the original Roman Forum was no longer big enough to serve the city's needs. The Imperial Fora were built by a succession of emperors from Caesar to Trajan.

The **Imperial Fora Visitor Centre** Ⓐ is located on the Via dei Fori Imperiali between Via Cavour and the Colosseum metro stop. Inside you can find background information on the site and toilets.

Caesar's Forum Ⓑ

On the south side of the Via are the remnants of Caesar's Forum (Foro di Cesare), the first Imperial Forum, built in 51 BC by Julius Caesar when the original became too small for Rome's increasing population. It was dedicated, still unfinished, in 46 BC and completed under Augustus (23 BC–AD 14). Following Hellenistic models, it was square and enclosed by pillars. On its western side stood the Temple of Venus Genetrix (look for three reconstructed columns), built as Caesar believed himself to be a descendant of the goddess.

Recommended Restaurants, Bars & Cafés on page 113

Forum of Augustus Ⓒ

The Foro di Augusto across the street was built to celebrate the emperor's victory and revenge over the army of Cassius and Brutus, who had led the conspiracy to assassinate Julius Caesar, his adoptive father. In the centre stood the temple of the war god Mars Ultor (Mars the Avenger), and in the great apses of the square stood statues of the mythical ancestors of Augustus' family.

Trajan's Forum and Trajan's Markets

The **Foro di Traiano** Ⓓ was a massive complex of temples, libraries and markets, surrounded by colonnades, that outdid the other Fora in size and splendour. It was designed in AD 106 by Apollodorus of Damascus, the best architect of his time. Building it meant removing a small hill between the Quirinal and the Capitol. To the northwest, it was bound by the vast Basilica Ulpia, which had five naves. In its western apse, the Atrium Libertatis, slaves were liberated.

Trajan also commissioned his architect to build the **Mercati di Traiano** Ⓔ (Trajan's Markets; entrance 94 Via IV Novembre; tel: 06-6978 0532; Tue–Sun 9am–7pm; admission charge), the ancient equivalent of a multi-storey shopping mall. Its remains stand behind the Forum on the slopes of the Quirinal, between two libraries on Via IV Novembre. They reveal a complex system of streets on various levels, with shops, administrative offices and spaces reserved for the distribution of grain to the public.

While there is also a lower entrance, the upper one on Via IV Novembre offers the best view of this marvellously preserved testament to Roman daily life. You'll first enter the Great Hall, which recently reopened after restoration. This was most likely the place for grain

Before working your way around the Forum and trying to make sense of the ruins, it's a good idea to get an overview of the site. The best vantage point for this is the Tabularium or the terrace behind the Capitol *(see pages 89–90)*. You can also refer to the detailed map of the Roman Forum on *pages 100–1*.

ABOVE LEFT: refreshment stands are a familiar sight. **BELOW:** Trajan's Markets.

Trajan's Column.

rations. From the adjoining terrace are good views down to the commercial spaces below, which would have held offices and shops. Nearby is Via Biberatica, which judging from its name (*bibere* means "to drink" in Latin) once housed bars for thirsty shoppers and businessmen.

The magnificent **Colonna Traiana** ❻ (Trajan's Column) was erected in AD 113 to celebrate Trajan's victory over the Dacians (inhabitants of today's Romania). The 40-metre (120ft) -high column is decorated with a spiral frieze of bas-reliefs depicting various phases of the Dacian campaigns (AD 101–2 and 105). Originally the reliefs were brightly painted and would have been visible from the balconies of the libraries. In AD 177, a golden urn containing the emperor's remains was buried under the column. The statue topping the column is of St Peter, commissioned by Pope Sixtus in 1587 to replace what was once a statue of Trajan.

THE FORO ROMANO ❽

Via dei Fori Imperiali 06-3996 7700 daily summer 8.30am–one hour before sunset charge, ticket also includes Palatine Hill, Palatine Museum and Colosseum Colosseo 60, 63, 70, 75, 81, 84, 85, 87, 160, 175, 186, 628, 810, 850

The best place to begin a tour of the Foro Romano is at the main entrance on Via dei Fori Imperiali, roughly level with Via Cavour. Originally a marshy valley between the Capitoline and Palatine hills, the area was drained by the Cloaca Maxima, the great sewer, and the site became a marketplace that developed into the religious, political and commercial centre of Republican Rome. By the time excavations began in the 18th century, most of the Forum was buried under rubble, and the place was known as Campo Vaccino (Cow Field), since it was used for grazing cattle.

Forum (Foro Romano)

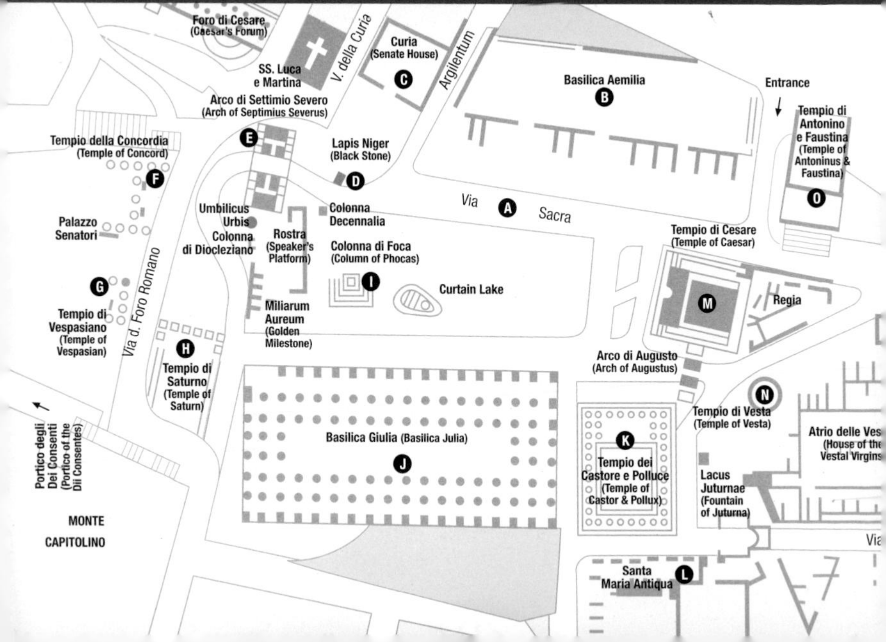

Foro di Cesare (Caesar's Forum)
SS. Luca e Martina
V. della Curia
Curia (Senate House) C
Argilentum
Basilica Aemilia B
Entrance
Tempio di Antonino e Faustina (Temple of Antoninus & Faustina) O
Arco di Settimio Severo (Arch of Septimius Severus) E
Tempio della Concordia (Temple of Concord) F
Lapis Niger (Black Stone) D
Via Sacra A
Palazzo Senatori
Umbilicus Urbis
Colonna di Diocleziano
Rostra (Speaker's Platform)
Colonna Decennalia
Colonna di Foca (Column of Phocas) I
Curtain Lake
Tempio di Cesare (Temple of Caesar)
Regia
M
G
Tempio di Vespasiano (Temple of Vespasian)
Via d. Foro Romano
H
Tempio di Saturno (Temple of Saturn)
Miliarum Aureum (Golden Milestone)
Arco di Augusto (Arch of Augustus)
N
Tempio di Vesta (Temple of Vesta)
Atrio delle Ves (House of the Vestal Virgins
Basilica Giulia (Basilica Julia) J
K
Tempio dei Castore e Polluce (Temple of Castor & Pollux)
Lacus Juturnae (Fountain of Juturna)
Portico degli Dei Consenti (Portico of the Dii Consentes)
MONTE CAPITOLINO
Via
Santa Maria Antiqua L

Recommended Restaurants, Bars & Cafés on page 113

Via Sacra Ⓐ

From the entrance a path leads down to the Via Sacra (the Sacred Way), the oldest street in Rome, which once ran through the Forum from the Arch of Titus up to the Capitoline. Triumphal processions of victorious generals in horse-drawn chariots parading their prisoners and spoils of war, and followed by their soldiers, would pass along the street to the Temple of Jupiter on the Capitol, where they would make sacrifices to Jupiter, the supreme god.

Walking westwards in the direction of the Capitoline, to the right lie the remains of the **Basilica Aemilia** Ⓑ, a massive assembly hall for politicians, businessmen and traders dating from

Even if you don't know any Latin, you'll be able to pick out familiar names carved into the stone in the Roman Forum.

LEFT: Carrera marble sculpture by modern artist Jiménez Deredia, on the Via Sacra.

Forum (Foro Romano)

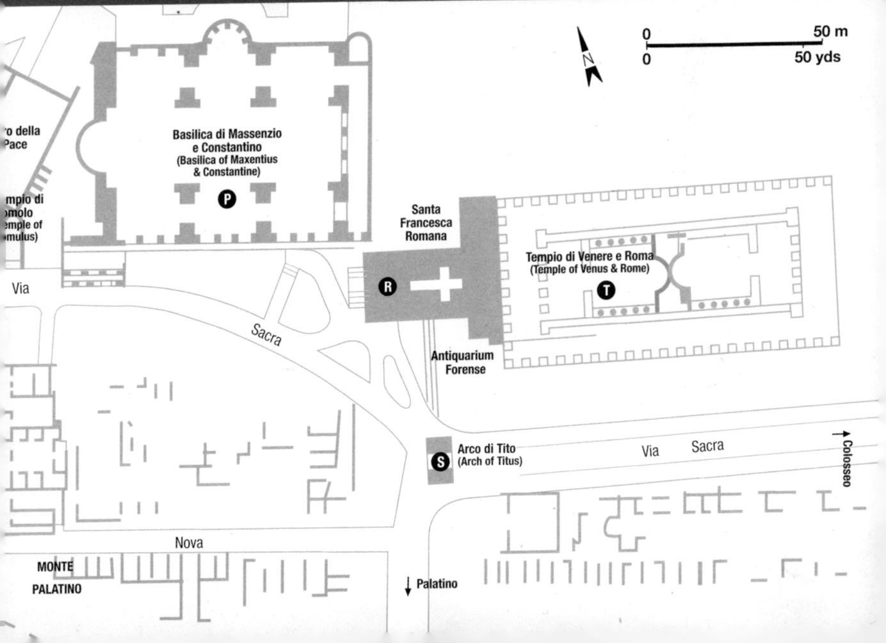

0 50 m
0 50 yds
N
Basilica di Massenzio e Constantino (Basilica of Maxentius & Constantine) Ⓟ
Santa Francesca Romana Ⓡ
Tempio di Venere e Roma (Temple of Venus & Rome) Ⓣ
Antiquarium Forense
Via Sacra
Arco di Tito (Arch of Titus) Ⓢ
Via Sacra
→ Colosseo
Nova
MONTE PALATINO
↓ Palatino

The Via dei Fori Imperiali is closed to traffic on some Sundays.

the 2nd century BC. It was rebuilt by Augustus after a fire, and then again after another fire in 410, when Alaric and his Goths invaded the city during the conquest of Rome. You can still see the stains left by coins burnt into the floor. Until 1500, most of the hall was still standing, but Bramante, Rome's chief architect during the High Renaissance, used some of it to build Palazzo Torlonia in the Borgo quarter. On the steps, you can see the remains of a temple to Venus, nicknamed *Cloacina* because the small circular building marks the spot where the **Cloaca Maxima** (the city's main sewer, built in the 1st century BC) empties into the valley of the Forum.

Beyond the Basilica Aemilia is the **Curia** Ⓒ, the ancient Senate House that was the centre of political life in Republican Rome. In the Middle Ages, the Curia was consecrated as a church, but the current building, a replica of Diocletian's, dates from 1937. The bronze doors are copies of the originals, which were transferred in the 17th century to the Basilica of San Giovanni in Laterano *(see page 221)*. In the cavernous inner hall (30 metres/90ft long, 20 metres/60ft wide, 20 metres/60ft high), the 300-strong Senate would gather to control the destiny of the Empire. In front of the Curia is the Comitium, where the Popular Assembly met.

Even older is the **Lapis Niger** Ⓓ (Black Stone), a pavement of black marble laid to mark a sacred spot; according to legend, the tomb of Romulus, Rome's mythical founder, lies here. The remains of a monument from the 6th century BC have been excavated from under the Lapis Niger, and, while they do not prove the existence of the grave, they are evidence that Romulus was already venerated in early Rome.

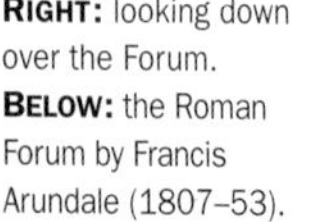

RIGHT: looking down over the Forum. **BELOW:** the Roman Forum by Francis Arundale (1807–53).

Recommended Restaurants, Bars & Cafés on page 113

Arch of Septimius Severus E

Behind looms the imposing Arco di Settimio Severo. The triple arch is 25 metres (75ft) wide, 10 metres (30ft) deep and 20 metres (60ft) high. It was built in AD 203 to celebrate the 10th anniversary of the emperor's ascent to the throne. The reliefs on the arch depict the victorious campaigns Septimius Severus and his two sons, Geta and Caracalla, fought against the Arabs and the Parthians (in present-day Iran). In earlier years, the arch was topped by a statue of the emperor in a four-horse chariot.

Later, Caracalla had his brother murdered in the arms of their mother and then placed him under *damnatio memoriae* (exile from memory) by ordering the deletion from monuments of all references to Geta and replacing them with laudatory titles to himself. You can still see the chisel marks on the inscriptions, which were originally inlaid with metal.

Beside the arch is the **Umbilicus Urbis**, a navel-shaped piece of stone that marked the centre of the city. Here, too, stood the **Miliarum Aureum**, a gilded bronze milestone that marked the start (or end) of all the Imperial roads connecting the main towns of the Empire to Rome. Beside it stood the **Rostra**, the speaker's platform moved here from the Comitium by Julius Caesar. It was once decorated with the prows or beaks *(rostra)* of ships captured at the battle of Actium in 31 BC. Trophies from Cleopatra's fleet are reputed to have been displayed here as well.

Behind, to the right, are the remains of the **Tempio della Concordia** F (Temple of Concord), a reconstruction by the Emperor

During the Middle Ages, part of the Arch of Septimius Severus, which was half buried in rubble, was used as a barber's shop.

ABOVE: 1st–2nd-century statue in the Curia, said to portray either Hadrian or Trajan. **BELOW:** Arch of Septimius Severus.

Roman *Domus*

On Clivio di Scauro, south of the Colosseum, and under the Basilica of Saints John and Paul on the Caelian Hill, 20 underground rooms dated between the 2nd and 4th centuries AD were recently reopened to the public after extensive restoration work. A series of residences and private baths built in the 2nd century AD were transformed into a single, luxurious house *(domus)* a century later by a wealthy owner and decorated with frescoes. The Roman *Domus* is now open to tourists (tel: 06-7045 4544; www.caseromane.it; Thur–Mon 10am–1pm and 3–6pm; admission charge). Entrance to the site is allowed every 30 minutes. Book in advance if you want a guided tour.

During the festival of Saturnalia, masters and their slaves briefly traded places; generous banquets were held and gifts exchanged. The festival originally lasted for one day only, but became so popular with the people that it later continued for a whole week. Scholars widely agree that Christmas was established around this time of year to coincide with the widespread pagan holiday.

Tiberius (AD 14–37) of the sanctuary erected to mark the peace accord between the patricians and plebians following the Class Wars of 367 BC.

Two temples

After their deaths, many emperors were automatically deified and had temples consecrated to them. All that remains of the **Temple of Vespasian** Ⓖ (AD 69–79), erected by his sons Titus and Domitian (both of whom later became emperors) are the three Corinthian columns that rise up behind the Rostra.

In the northwestern corner of the Forum stands the **Tempio di Saturno** Ⓗ (Temple of Saturn), which housed the Roman state treasury. All that remains of this, the most venerated temple of Republican Rome, consecrated in 498 BC, are eight Ionic columns on a podium. Saturn was god of agriculture and ruler of the mythical "Golden Age". Each year in December the festival of Saturnalia was celebrated *(see left)*.

RIGHT: Romans celebrating the Saturnalia. **BELOW:** remains of the Temple of Saturn, and the three Corinthian columns of the Temple of Vespasian.

Two columns

Heading eastwards now along the Via Sacra (with your back to the Capitol), to your left stands the Corinthian **Colonna di Foca** Ⓘ (the Column of Phocas), the most recent of the classical monuments in the Roman Forum. This column was erected in 608 by Smaragdus, the Byzantine exarch (governor) for Italy, in honour of the Eastern Emperor Phocas who donated the Pantheon to the Church. Next to it, a bronze inscription commemorates one of the sponsors of the paving of the Forum, L. Naevius Surdinus, in the 1st decade BC. A fig tree, an olive tree and a vine, which used to grow here, together with a statue of Marsyas, symbolised Roman justice.

Recommended Restaurants, Bars & Cafés on page 113

Between the Column of Phocas and the Rostra is the base of the **Colonna Decennalia**, raised in AD 303 to celebrate 10 years of rule by the two emperors Diocletian and Maxentius. The relief on the base shows the *Souventaurilia*, the ceremonial state sacrifice of a boar, a ram and a bull.

Basilica Giulia J

On the other side of the Via Sacra stood the **Basilica Giulia**. Started by Julius Caesar in 50 BC and completed by Augustus, it was originally the largest building in the Forum (101 metres/330ft long and 49 metres/160ft wide). All that remains of this two-storeyed, marble-faced structure are its pillared foundations. The basilica housed four courts of law, was the seat of the Roman office of weights and measures, and was a meeting place for bankers.

The Temple of Castor and Pollux K

Heading in the direction of the Colosseum, you'll come to the three surviving columns of the Tempio di Castore e Polluce, built in 448 BC to commemorate the decisive battle of Lake Regillus fought between Latins and Romans in 499 BC. The Romans believed victory was secured by the miraculous appearance of Castor and Pollux, Jupiter's twin sons, and built the temple in their honour. A block of marble from this temple was used by Michelangelo as the base for the equestrian statue of Marcus Aurelius he made for the Piazza del Campidoglio.

Behind the pillars is a small marble altar with reliefs of the heavenly twins, and the site of the **Lacus Juturnae** (Fountain of Juturna), the sacred well at which the Dioscuri (the collective name for Castor and Pollux) watered their horses after bringing news of the Roman victory.

On the other side of the temple, at the foot of the Palatine, is the oldest Christian structure in the Forum: the church of **Santa Maria Antiqua** L was built in AD 365 on the site of a temple to Augustus.

Temple of Caesar M

A path leads away from the church entrance back past the temple of

Dramatic remains of the Temple of Castor and Pollux.

BELOW LEFT: detail from the Arch of Septimius Severus. **BELOW:** the Emperor Vespasian by Peter Paul Rubens (1577–1640).

Vespasian

Emperor Vespasian was one of Imperial Rome's more successful rulers. His reign (AD 69–79) brought a welcome period of peace and prosperity to a city and an Empire in disarray following the death of Nero.

Vespasian put to shame the extravagances of Roman nobles by the simplicity of his own life. In order to restore state finances after the disastrous extravagances of Nero (AD 54–68), he renewed old taxes and instituted new ones; one such tax was levied on urine, which was collected from public urinals (it was a useful raw material for dyeing wool). When asked by one of his sons how he could make money with such a malodorous substance, he replied *"Pecunia non olet"* – money doesn't smell. These taxes helped finance the building of great public works, not least of which was the Colosseum.

Vestal Virgins had seats of honour in the circus and theatre and lived in luxury, but if they broke their vow of chastity, they were buried alive.

ABOVE RIGHT: Caesar's funeral pyre, 15 March 44 BC. **BELOW:** detail of the remains of the Regia walls.

Castor and Pollux to the Tempio di Cesare, which occupies the site where Caesar's corpse was cremated after his assassination on the Ides of March in 44 BC. So great was the grief of the people that they kept his funeral pyre burning for days. After the cremation, his ashes were washed with milk and wine, then buried. The temple was built on the site of the pyre by his adopted son, the emperor Augustus.

Behind the Temple of Caesar lie the remains of the walls of the **Regia**, the official residence of the Pontifex Maximus, the Chief Priest of Ancient Rome; the title is still held by the Pope today.

Temple of Vesta Ⓝ

Directly opposite, 20 Corinthian columns surround the remains of the circular Tempio di Vesta, goddess of the hearth and patron of the state. Here the Vestal Virgins kept the eternal flame of Rome burning and watched over the sacred image of Minerva (daughter of Jupiter and Juno), saved, according to legend, from blazing Troy by Aeneas. The

Vestals entered divine service as young girls and lived a chaste life for at least 30 years in the **House of the Vestal Virgins**, the rectangular structure next to the temple, a once luxurious building.

Monumental temple

Back near the main entrance of the Forum, a broad flight of steps leads up to the **Tempio di Antonino e Faustina** Ⓞ (Temple of Antoninus and Faustina), built in AD 141 by the emperor in memory of his wife and converted to a church in the 12th century. It is the only Forum building that gives a real indication of just how monumental Roman temples were.

Recommended Restaurants, Bars & Cafés on page 113

Basilica of Maxentius and Constantine P

The eastern half of the Forum is dominated by the Basilica di Massenzio e Constantino, a three-aisled basilica that was begun by Emperor Maxentius (303–12) and completed by his successor, Constantine (306–337). Only the northern nave remains. The central nave was crossed by cruciform vaults, each resting on eight side pillars, one of which has been outside the church of Santa Maria Maggiore since 1613.

Numerous Renaissance architects are said to have used its apse and arches as models, the most famous being Michelangelo, who studied its hexagonal coffered arches when designing the dome of St Peter's.

In the western apse, a **Colossus of Constantine** was discovered in 1487. Bits of the huge statue, including head, feet and hands, can be seen in the courtyard of Palazzo dei Conservatori *(see page 92)*.

Temple and church

Next to the basilica is the circular **Tempio di Romolo** Q (Temple of Romulus), dating from AD 309, which now forms the apse of the church of Santi Cosma e Damiano, converted in the 6th century. Beneath the temple are the remains of tiny rooms believed to have been part of a brothel.

With its colourful brickwork, the Romanesque belltower of the church of **Santa Francesca Romana** R will have caught your eye. The present building is 13th-century, though the facade was added in 1615. Francesca Romana is the

You can take a picnic into the Forum/ Palatine area. Officially, it's not allowed, but if you are discreet and tidy, there will be no problem.

LEFT: Temple of Antoninus and Faustina. **BELOW:** Basilica of Maxentius and Constantine.

Underneath the Farnese Gardens is a long tunnel built by Nero, possibly a secret route to other parts of the Palatine. The tunnel is also a welcome escape from the blazing heat of the Roman summer. Relax in the shade as long as you can without blocking tourist traffic.

patron saint of motorists, and on her festival day – 9 March – cars are parked as close as possible to the church to be blessed.

Arch of Titus ❸

Beyond the church, marking the end of the Via Sacra, stands the majestic Arco di Tito, the oldest triumphal arch in Rome, built by Domitian to celebrate the capture of Jerusalem in AD 70 by his brother Titus and father Vespasian. Reliefs inside the arch show Titus in his chariot with Nike, goddess of victory, and the spoils of war, including a menorah, the ritual Jewish seven-branched candelabra, being carried in triumphal procession.

RIGHT: Farnese Pavilions on the Palatine. **BELOW:** the Palatine Hill.

Temple of Venus and Rome ❼

Between the Arch of Titus and the Colosseum is the **Tempio di Venere e Roma,** originally built by Hadrian (AD 117–38) and rebuilt by Maxentius in 307 after a fire. At 110 by 53 metres (361 by 174ft), it was the largest temple in Rome and comprised two shrines placed opposite one another, surrounded by pillared halls in the Greek style. It is well documented that Hadrian was an ardent admirer of Greek culture.

PALATINE HILL ❾

✉ Palatine Hill ☎ 06-3996 7700 ⏲ daily 8.30am–one hour before sunset € charge, ticket includes entry to Palatine Museum, Colosseum and Roman Forum 🚇 Colosseo 🚌 60, 75, 81, 84, 85, 87, 117, 175, 271, 571, 673, 810, 850

From the Arch of Titus, the road goes up to the **Palatino,** where Rome's Imperial rulers lived in luxury. Legend holds that Romulus killed his twin brother Remus on the Palatine Hill before founding Rome here in

Recommended Restaurants, Bars & Cafés on page 113

753 BC. Whatever the truth of this, archaeological remains do confirm the existence of a sheep-herding population whose simple homes were excavated on top of the hill. At the height of Roman opulence, the area offered a beautiful panorama of the city away from the chaos below, and expansive villas packed the area. It wasn't until the 16th century that Cardinal Farnese recognised the value of the land and purchased most of it.

Farnese Gardens

Paths and steps lead up to the **Orti Farnesiani** Ⓐ (Farnese Gardens). These pleasure gardens were laid out in the 16th century for the cardinal, over the ruins of the Palace of Tiberius. They end at a viewing terrace with a fine panorama over the Forum. A subterranean vaulted passageway leads to the **Casa di Livia** Ⓑ (House of Livia; *see right*).

In the southwest corner of the hill, excavations have revealed the oldest traces of a settlement in the city (8th century BC). The story goes that the Iron Age hut known as the **Capanna di Romolo** Ⓒ (Hut of Romulus) was the dwelling of a shepherd who raised Romulus and Remus, after they were suckled by the wolf in a nearby cave.

Domus Flavia and Domus Augustana

South of the gardens lay the **Domus Flavia** Ⓓ, built by Emperor Domitian, who is said to have lined his throne room with mirrors in order to see approaching enemies from any angle. The room with a pattern traced on its floor was the courtyard; behind that was the dining room, and the room to the right was the *nymphaeum*, where diners retired for breaks during banquets.

Next to this palace was the **Domus Augustana** Ⓔ (House of Augustus), private residence of the emperor. The oval building next to it, the vast outline of which can be

In 1860 excavations of the Casa di Livia revealed gloriously frescoed walls and elaborate mosaics. Some of these can be seen at the Palazzo Massimo (see page 233) and at the Capitoline Museums (see page 89).

ABOVE LEFT: Faustulus entrusting Romulus and Remus to his wife, Acca Larentia, *c.*1643.

An umbrella pine provides atmosphere but scant shade for the ruins of the Palatine Hill.

clearly discerned, was a stadium built for the emperor's private games. To the south are the impressive ruins of the **Terme Severiane** (Baths of Septimius Severus).

Palatine Museum F

The tall grey building sandwiched between the Domus Flavia and the Domus Augustana is the Museo Palatino (tel: 06-3996 7700; www.pierreci.it; daily 8.30am–one hour before sunset; charge, ticket includes entry to Palatine Hill, the Colosseum and Roman Forum). Inside is a fine collection of artefacts found during the course of excavations on the site.

Circus Maximus 10

The remains of the Palatine palaces overlook the Circo Massimo, one of the oldest Roman arenas. Not much of this 6th-century BC stadium remains, but you can make out the track, which was used mainly for chariot races. There are traces of seating to the south (the tower is a medieval addition). In its heyday the arena held around 300,000 spectators, and not only hosted chariot races, but also staged sea battles,

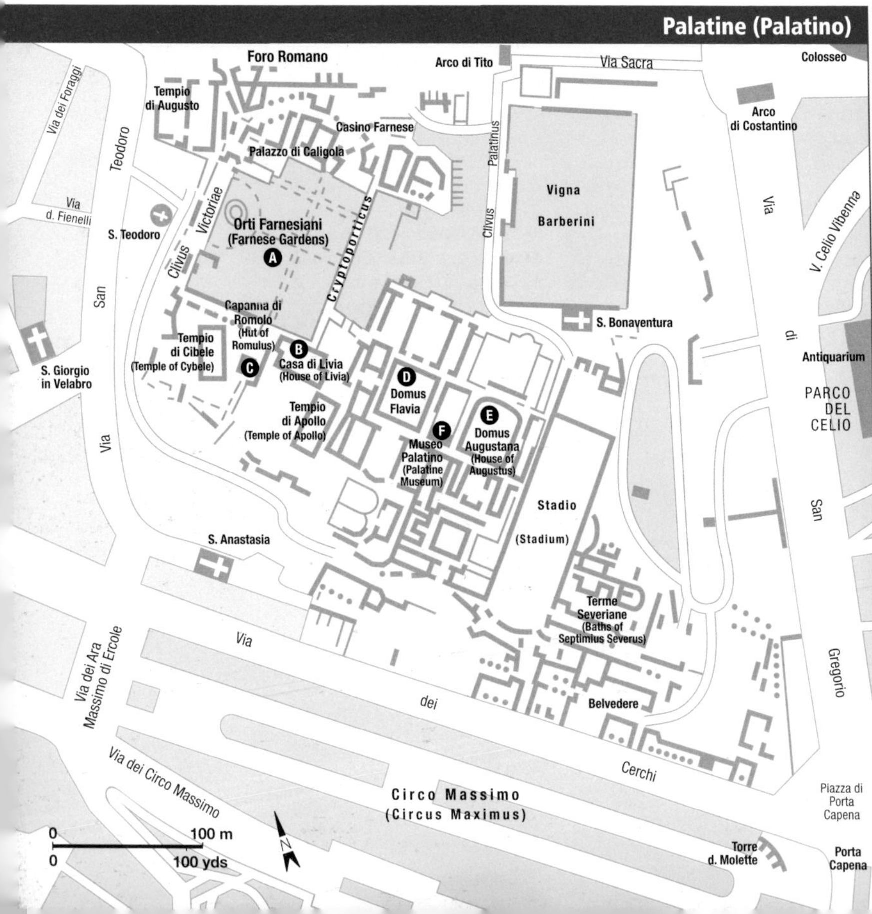

Palatine (Palatino)

Foro Romano
Arco di Tito
Via Sacra
Colosseo
Tempio di Augusto
Casino Farnese
Arco di Costantino
Via dei Foraggi
Teodoro
Palazzo di Caligola
Clivus Palatinus
Vigna Barberini
Via d. Fienelli
Clivus Victoriae
Cryptoporticus
Via di San Gregorio
V. Celio Vibenna
S. Teodoro
Orti Farnesiani (Farnese Gardens) A
Capanna di Romolo (Hut of Romulus)
S. Bonaventura
Tempio di Cibele (Temple of Cybele) C
B Casa di Livia (House of Livia)
Antiquarium
S. Giorgio in Velabro
D Domus Flavia
PARCO DEL CELIO
Tempio di Apollo (Temple of Apollo)
F Museo Palatino (Palatine Museum)
E Domus Augustana (House of Augustus)
Via San Teodoro
Stadio (Stadium)
S. Anastasia
Terme Severiane (Baths of Septimius Severus)
Via dei Cerchi
Via dei Ara Massimo di Ercole
Belvedere
Via dei Circo Massimo
Circo Massimo (Circus Maximus)
Piazza di Porta Capena
0 100 m
0 100 yds
N
Torre d. Molette
Porta Capena

Recommended Restaurants, Bars & Cafés on page 113

which required the pumping of gallons of water into the stadium space.

THE COLOSSEUM ⓫

Piazza del Colosseo 06-3996 7700 daily 8.30am–one hour before sunset charge, ticket includes entry to Palatine Hill, Palatine Museum and Forum Colosseo 3, 60, 75, 81, 85, 87, 117, 175, 186, 204, 673, 810, 850

At the far end of the Roman Forum lie the remains of the majestic **Colosseum**, the most enduring symbol of Ancient Rome. Its monumental grandeur and violent history have enthralled and appalled visitors for over 2,000 years. Work on its construction began in AD 72 under Vespasian, who decided to build it on the site of Nero's artificial lake, and was completed by his son Titus. The vast amphitheatre measured 190 metres (570ft) long and 150 metres (450ft) wide, had 80 entrances and could seat between 55,000 and 73,000 spectators. It opened in AD 80 with a three-month programme of games to satisfy a bloodthirsty audience. Christians fought lions, gladiators fought each other and wounded contestants lived or died according to the emperor's whim, expressed by the Imperial thumb, which pointed either up or down. Today, the walls of the various dungeons, cages and passageways, gruesome reminders of the centuries-long slaughter that took place here, can be seen through the caved-in floor of the arena.

The **Ludus Magnus**, the nearby training ground of the gladiators, was connected to the arena by a tunnel. The remains of seating for up to 3,000 people shows how much the public

Try and visit the Colosseum first thing in the morning, before the crowds build up.

LEFT: a reconstruction of the Colosseum. **BELOW:** the defining image of Rome.

The Arco di Constantino, another triumphal arch built for the glory of the emperors.

ABOVE RIGHT: history lesson on site.
BELOW: a wonder of the world – inside the Colosseum.

liked to watch gladiators learning the tricks of their trade.

Gladiatorial combat was banned by Honorius in AD 404, and over time the amphitheatre became a quarry supplying material for many of Rome's buildings, including Palazzo Venezia and St Peter's. In 1744, Benedict XIV consecrated the arena to the memory of Christian martyrs who died in it *(for more about the Colosseum, see pages 114–15)*.

Between the Colosseum and the Palatine Hill is the **Arco di Constantino** (Arch of Constantine), built to commemorate Constantine I's victory over Maxentius at the Ponte Milvio in AD 312 *(see page 196)*.

NERO'S GOLDEN HOUSE ⓬

✉ 1 Viale della Domus Aurea; www.pierreci.it ☎ 06-3996 7700 (currently closed for restoration) Colosseo 🚌 60, 75, 81, 85, 87, 117, 175, 186, 204, 673, 810, 850

A short walk uphill from the Colosseum is Nero's Golden House (Domus Aurea). Work began here in AD 64 immediately after a fire had devastated a large chunk of Rome.

Made up of a series of pavilions surrounded by pastures, woods, vineyards and a small artificial lake (on which the Colosseum now stands), it originally extended from the Palatine to the Caelian and Oppian hills. The enormous complex was filled with Greek statues and monumental fountains.

According to the Latin biographer Suetonius, its vestibule was large enough to contain a statue of Nero 40 metres (120ft) high, and the house was covered in gold and decorated with precious gems and mother-of-pearl. There were dining rooms with ivory ceilings from which rotating panels showered guests with flowers, and fitted pipes sprinkled them with perfume. The palace had its own aqueducts to supply water for the fountains, and the baths could be filled with sea or sulphurous water, according to Nero's whim.

The main building was decorated with shiploads of plundered Greek works of art. But Nero did not have long to enjoy it. He committed suicide in AD 68 after he was condemned to death by the Senate.

Almost immediately the house began to be stripped, demolished or built on by his successors. In the early 16th century, frescoes belonging to the house were discovered by artists, including Raphael and Michelangelo, but no-one linked these cave-like rooms to the emperor's outrageous abode until centuries later.

It is hard to get an idea of the opulence and size of the extraordinary 250-room mansion, built on an estate that covered a third of Ancient Rome; only the skylit Octagonal Hall gives any real idea of its former architectural grandeur. Some 30 rooms are usually open to the public, but recent structural problems forced the city to close the site for restoration; it is due to reopen in 2012. ❑

Enjoy a cocktail with a killer view of the illuminated Colosseum at the Hotel Gladiatori (www.hotelgladiatori.it; *see page 227*).

LEFT: fresco showing the birth of Adonis, from Nero's Golden House.

BEST RESTAURANTS, BARS AND CAFÉS

Restaurants

The overpriced tourist restaurants around the Colosseum should be avoided, but if you wander eastwards into the huddle of streets behind it you'll find some good neighbourhood eateries.

Forum Pizzeria

✉ 34–38 Via San Giovanni in Laterano ☎ 06-7759 1158 ⏲ L & D daily. **€** [p340, B2]
A large pizzeria serving delicious, thick-crusted pizzas from a wood-fired oven.

Ristorante Mario's

✉ 9 Piazza del Grillo ☎ 06-679 3725 ⏲ L & D Tue–Sun. **€–€€** [p339, E1]
Traditional Roman food (fish is their speciality) at affordable prices. Has a lovely pergola in the square outside.

San Teodoro

✉ 49–51 Via dei Fienili ☎ 06-678 0933 ⏲ L & D Mon–Sat. **€€€€** [p339, E2]
Located in a tranquil piazza, this elegant restaurant offers traditional food successfully updated and centred on seasonal availability. Staples are fish carpaccios and home-made pasta.

Bars and Cafés

The gay bar **Coming Out** (8 Via San Giovanni in Laterano, *pictured right*), across from the Colosseum, in an area known as "gay street" serves hot food until 2am. A lively scene ensures a faithful following, not just from the gay community.

At **Oppio Caffè** (72 Via delle Terme di Tito) hi-tech meets classical Rome: plexiglass and video screens contrast with ancient brickwork. Outside seating provides stunning views of the Colosseum. Open all day, with live music some nights.

Price includes dinner and a half-bottle of house wine.
***€€€€** = more than €60, **€€€** = €40–60, **€€** = €25–40, **€** = under €25.*

THE GRIM GLORY OF THE COLOSSEUM

"While the Colosseum stands, Rome shall stand; when the Colosseum falls, Rome shall fall; when Rome falls the world shall fall"

The Colosseum is the city's most stirring sight, "a noble wreck in the ruinous perfection" in Byron's words. It was begun by Vespasian, inaugurated by his son Titus in AD 80, and completed by Domitian (AD 81–96). It could seat over 50,000 bloodthirsty spectators who revelled in the spectacle of gladiators fighting to the death. "Bread and circuses" was the judgement of Juvenal, the 1st-century poet, on the way the city's rulers kept the populace happy. With the fall of the Empire, the Colosseum fell into disuse. During the Renaissance, the ruins were plundered of their valuable travertine to build churches and palaces all over Rome.

Quarrying was only halted by Pope Benedict XIV in the 18th century and the site dedicated to Christian martyrs.

ABOVE: Renaissance historians believed that ancient Roman arenas were sometimes flooded to stage mock naval battles, but there is scant evidence to suggest that such a display ever took place in the Colosseum.

BELOW LEFT: the Gate of Life was reserved for victorious gladiators, while vanquished gladiators were sent to the Gate of Death, as depicted in this relief found at the Colosseum.

BELOW: views from the higher tiers down to the arena show a maze of passageways normally hidden from view. The moveable wooden floor was covered in sand to soak up the blood. The subterranean section concealed the animal cages and sophisticated technical apparatus, from winches and mechanical lifts to ramps and trap doors.

The essentials

Piazza del Colosseo; www.pierreci.it *tel: 06-3996 7700* *daily 8.30am until one hour before sunset; ticket office shuts one hour before closing time* *charge* Colosseo *3, 60, 75, 81, 85, 87, 117, 175, 186, 204, 673, 810, 850*

ENTERTAINMENT FOR THE MASSES

The Roman appetite for bloodshed was legendary, with the barbaric *munera*, or blood sports, introduced as a corrupt version of the Greek games. Although supremely public, the Colosseum was a stratified affair. The podium, set on the lowest tier, was reserved exclusively for the Emperor, senators, magistrates and Vestal Virgins. Above them sat the bourgeoisie, with the lower orders restricted to the top tier, and the populace on wooden seats in the very top rows. Shortly before the games began, the Emperor and his followers would enter the amphitheatre, and spectators would show their reverence by clapping, cheering, and chanting their sovereign's honorifics.

A trumpet call started the games and spectacles began with cries of "Hail to the Emperor, those about to die salute thee". If a gladiator tried to retreat into the underground chamber, he was pushed forward with whips and red-hot irons. The gladiators mostly fought to the death. A wounded man could beg for mercy by lifting a finger of his left hand. If the crowd waved handkerchiefs, he was saved. Thumbs down meant death. After the gladiators came the wild beasts, which were made to fight one another or human beings – armed or unarmed. The animals, mostly imported from Africa, included lions, elephants, giraffes, hyenas, hippos, wild horses and zebras.

On the arena's opening day, 5,000 animals were slaughtered. In AD 248, the millennium of the founding of Rome was celebrated by gladiatorial contests. The last gladiatorial fight took place in AD 439, while animal fights ended the following century.

RIGHT: gladiators, named after the Roman sword, *gladius*, were mostly condemned criminals, prisoners of war or slaves. They were trained to fight then pitted against each other and against various exotic animals.

LEFT: men dressed in traditional Roman costumes stroll around the perimeter of the Colosseum – some indulge in light-hearted role-playing for the benefit of tourists, others will fleece you for a photo.

BELOW: school children learn the gory details of life in Ancient Rome with a history lesson in situ.

RIGHT: the Colosseum is Rome's top tourist sight, and when floodlit at night it creates a wonderful spectacle. It has been used as an arena for crowd-pulling concerts – Simon and Garfunkel played here on their 'Old Friends' tour.

CLEMENS XII PONT MAX
AQVAM VIRGINEM
COPIA ET SALVBRITATE COMMENDATAM
CVLTV MAGNIFICO ORNAVIT
ANNO DOMINI MDCCXXXV PONTIF VI
PERFECIT BENEDICTVS XIV PON MAX
POSITIS SIGNIS ET ANA
CLEMENTIS XIII PONT MAX
SOLVTVM A DOM MDCCLXII

FONTANA DI TREVI AND QUIRINALE

The Quirinal, Rome's highest hill, is synonymous with Italian politics. Its summit is crowned with the President's official residence and at its foot, hidden in the maze of narrow streets, is the Trevi Fountain, one of Rome's most iconic sights

Main attractions

TREVI FOUNTAIN
ACCADEMIA DI SAN LUCA
PALAZZO DEL QUIRINALE
SCUDERIE DEL QUIRINALE
SANT'ANDREA AL QUIRINALE
SAN CARLO ALLE QUATTRO FONTANE
BARBERINI PALACE
PIAZZA BARBERINI
PORTA PIA
SAN VITALE
PALAZZO DELLE ESPOSIZIONI
PALAZZO COLONNA

The Quirinal Hill, the highest of Rome's seven classical hills, is crowned by the Piazza del Quirinale and the imposing presidential palace. The square is somewhat austere, but the labyrinth of surrounding streets are well worth exploring.

Trevi Fountain ❶

A good place to begin a tour of the area is the Fontana di Trevi (Trevi Fountain), which rose to fame in Fellini's 1960 classic *La Dolce Vita* when blonde bombshell Anita Ekberg plunged provocatively into it for a midnight bathe. Nowadays, if you try to put a foot in the water, a whistle blast from the city police will stop you in your tracks. That, and a €170 fine.

However, no one will stop you from throwing a coin in the fountain (over your shoulder with your back to the fountain), an old custom said to ensure your return to the Eternal City. The steps around the fountain are always packed with tourists tossing coins, eating ice creams and taking endless photos.

The flamboyant rococo-style fountain was designed in 1762 by Nicola Salvi, "some sculptor of Bernini's school gone absolutely mad in marble" was Nathaniel Hawthorne's assessment. Its central figure is the sea god Neptune standing astride a giant shell drawn by winged horses led by Tritons. One horse is placid, the other agitated, symbolising calm and stormy seas. In the niches on either side are statues of Health (right) and Abundance (left). Above the latter, a marble relief shows Agrippa commissioning the aqueduct in 19 BC, which still supplies the fountain to this day.

LEFT: the Trevi Fountain. **RIGHT:** guards outside the Quirinale Palace, official residence of the President of the Republic.

With arguably the finest ice cream in town, the Gelateria San Crispino near the Trevi Fountain serves up original flavours made with all-natural ingredients. The signature flavour, Il Gelato di San Crispino, is a basic Italian *crema* made with wild Sardinian honey.

Accademia di San Luca ❷

✉ 77 Piazza dell'Accademia; www.accademiasanluca.it ☎ 06-679 8850 ⏲ Mon–Sat 10am–12.30pm € free Ⓜ Barberini 🚌 52, 53, 61, 62, 63, 71, 80, 81, 85, 95, 116, 117, 119, 160, 175, 492, 628, 630, 850

It's a five-minute walk from the fountain to the Galleria dell'Accademia di San Luca, Rome's school of art. The academy, named after St Luke, the patron saint of painters, was founded in 1577 to train artists in the Renaissance style. Bernini and Domenichino were former directors of this august institution.

The gallery, which has recently been extensively renovated, has a collection of portraits, drawings and landscapes of Rome spanning the centuries, including works by Titian, Guido Reni and Van Dyck.

There's also an impressive ramp, designed by Borromini, which spirals up to the top floors of the

palazzo. Free exhibitions are held by art students, and the academy organises a prestigious architecture prize.

THE QUIRINAL

Follow Via San Vincenzo uphill from the Fontana di Trevi, then turn left into Via Dataria and take the steps up to Piazza del Quirinale. In the centre of the square are colossal

Fontana di Trevi and Quirinale

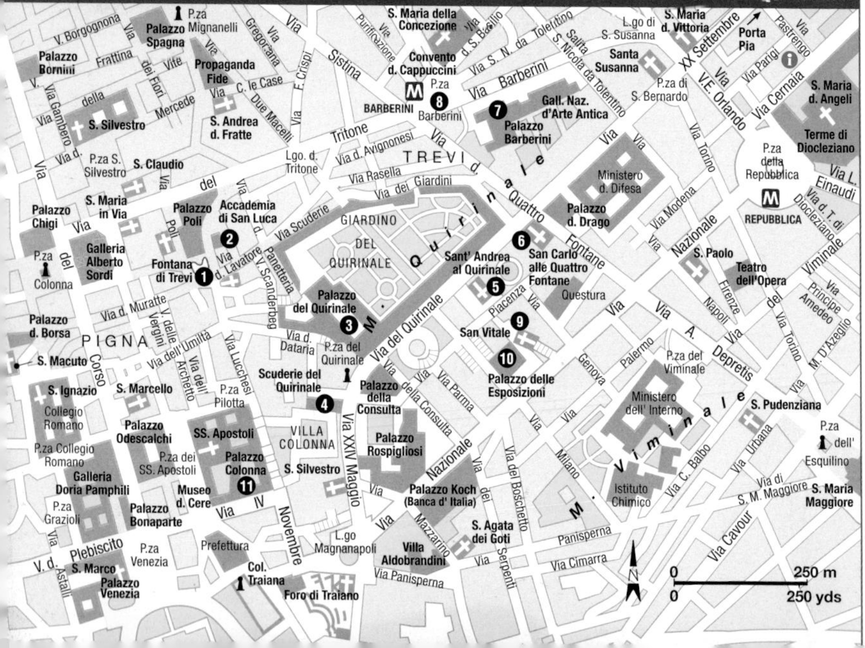

Map on page 118

Recommended Restaurants, Bars & Cafés on page 123

statues of the heavenly twins, Castor and Pollux, with their horses. They came from Constantine's baths and were arranged around the obelisk (taken from Augustus' mausoleum) in the 18th century.

Palazzo del Quirinale ❸

www.quirinale.it 06-46991 Sun 8.30am–noon (depending on state visits – check website) charge Barberini 40, 60, 64, 70, 117, 170, 640

The square is dominated by the **Palazzo del Quirinale**, which was the summer palace of the popes until 1870, when it became the palace of the kings of the newly unified Italy. Since 1947, it has been the official residence of the President of the Republic. The oldest part of the palace is open to the public most Sunday mornings.

Scuderie del Quirinale ❹

www.scuderiequirinale.it 06-3996 7500 daily 10am–8pm, Fri–Sat until 10.30pm charge Barberini 40, 60, 64, 70, 117, 170, 640

Part of the complex on the opposite side of Piazza del Quirinale, the former palace stables, or *scuderie*, is now a bright and spacious two-level museum space, which hosts important exhibitions all year round. The stairs leading from the top floor back to the lobby have a glass wall which offers fine views of the city.

Across the square from the Quirinale Palace sits the sugary-white **Palazzo della Consulta**, which houses Italy's supreme court. The structure was built atop the ruins of Constantine's baths.

FAR LEFT: obelisk in the Piazza del Quirinale. **LEFT:** flags fly over Palazzo del Quirinale. **BELOW:** the inauguration of Italy's new president, Giorgio Napolitano, in May 2006.

Not far from the Trevi Fountain, beneath the arthouse Trevi Cinema (which, incidentally, sometimes screens films in English), is the fascinating Area Archeologica del Vicus Caprinus (Thur–Sun 11am–5pm, Mon 4–7.30pm; admission charge). Here lie the remains of a 1st-century BC *caseggiato* – a communal Roman dwelling.

Baroque Masterpieces

Via del Quirinale runs along the southeast flank of the palace and, on the opposite side, passes two pretty parks (dotted with shaded benches if you need a rest), and two Baroque churches. **Sant'Andrea al Quirinale** ❺ (Wed–Sat and Mon 8am–noon and 3.30–7pm, Sun 9am–noon, 4–7pm) is the work of Bernini, whose genius is demonstrated in the elliptical plan, gilded dome and stucco work. Light from the clerestory windows illuminates the white-and-gold stucco work of the dome and the richly coloured inlaid marble of the walls and floor.

Further along is the tiny **San Carlo alle Quattro Fontane** ❻ (Mon–Fri and Sun 10am–1pm and 3–6pm, Sat 10am–1pm) by Bernini's arch-rival, Borromini (1599–1667). It may be small (it is often referred to as San Carlino), but with its concave and convex surfaces it illustrates Borromini's ingenuity at creating the illusion of space in an awkwardly shaped site. His love for illusion and *trompe l'œil* is evident throughout the structure, most notably in the cloister, which is rectangular but appears octagonal.

The church gets its name, Alle Quattro Fontane, from the four Baroque fountains at each corner of the busy crossroads, placed here in 1593, which represent the Tiber, the Nile, Diana and Juno. From here, the highest point of the Quirinal Hill, you can look down towards the Trinità dei Monti obelisk in one direction and the Santa Maria Maggiore obelisk in the other.

Barberini Palace ❼

✉ 18 Via Barberini, entrance on Via delle Quattro Fontane ☎ 06-32810 ⏱ Tue–Sun 8.30am–7.30pm

ABOVE RIGHT: park benches provide welcome shade. **BELOW:** Via delle Quattro Fontane.

Recommended Restaurants, Bars & Cafés on page 123

charge Barberini 52, 53, 61, 80, 95, 116, 119, 175, 492

From the Quirinal, Via delle Quattro Fontane leads to Palazzo Barberini, the family palace of Pope Urban VIII (1623–44), built by three of Rome's most prominent 17th-century architects, Bernini, Borromini and Maderno. It houses the newly renovated **Galleria Nazionale d'Arte Antica**, which displays works from the early Renaissance to the late Baroque, including *The Annunciation* by Lippi, canvases by Caravaggio, Raphael's celebrated *La Fornarina*, Pietro di Cosimo's *Maddalena*, a portrait of Henry VIII by Holbein and a fine ceiling fresco by da Cortona.

Bernini's fountains

In the **Piazza Barberini** 8 are two Bernini fountains. The **Fontana del Tritone** (1632–7) features four dolphins supporting a shell on which the water-spouting Triton sits. The **Fontana delle Api** (Bee Fountain, 1641), on the north side of the square, features the ubiquitous bee, symbol of the powerful Barberini

Mental torment and genius often go hand in hand, as was the case for Borromini. The church of San Carlino was his first solo job, completed when the artist was just 35 years old. Borromini had hoped to be buried in the crypt's splendid funerary chapter, but his suicide put paid to that, and he was dumped in an unmarked grave at San Giovanni dei Fiorentini.

ABOVE LEFT: *La Fornarina* by Raphael. **LEFT:** papal coat of arms on Sant'Andrea al Quirinale. **BELOW:** Fontana del Tritone on Piazza Barberini.

The Princess Isabella Apartment, the 15th-century wing of **Palazzo Colonna,** *has been preserved in all its original majesty. Decorated with ornate frescoes by Bernardino di Betto (known as Pinturicchio), there are many notable works of art here, including some magnificent small paintings on copper by Jan Brueghel the Elder.*

RIGHT: Porta Pia. **BELOW:** Palazzo Colonna's Room of the Apotheosis of Martin V takes its name from the subject of the ceiling painting by Benedetto Luti.

family. Running from the northwest of the piazza is Via Vittorio Veneto, the avenue rendered immortal in Fellini's film *La Dolce Vita* as the gathering place for the glitterati to see and be seen.

From here Via Barberini leads to Largo Santa Susanna and the church of **Santa Maria della Vittoria,** home to Bernini's *Ecstasy of St Teresa,* another masterpiece of Baroque sculpture *(see page 187).*

The end of Via XX Settembre is marked by **Porta Pia,** Michelangelo's last architectural work, and an excellent example of the transition from High Rennassiance to Baroque architecture. It is also the symbol of Italy's unification as on September 20 1870, the Italian army made a breach in the gate and defeated the Pope's soldiers, putting an end to the Church's secular power.

VIA NAZIONALE

Running parallel to Via del Quirinale is Via Nazionale (laid in 1870 when Rome gained its new status as capital), which links Piazza della

Repubblica with the Imperial Fora. Towards the southern end are **San Vitale** ❾ church, built in the 5th century and restored in the 15th century, and the **Palazzo delle Esposizioni** ❿ (194 Via Nazionale; www.palazzoesposizioni.it; tel: 06-3996 7500; Tue–Thur 9.30am–8pm, Fri–Sat 9.30am–10.30pm, Sun 10am–8pm; charge).

It is hard to miss this massive 19th-century edifice. The neoclassical structure was designed in 1883 by Pio Piacentini to house the Quadriennale d'Arte, a national art exhibition, and the first reactions were not very forthcoming: the Romans criticized the monumental entrance and the lack of windows on the facade (the rooms receive light from the glass ceilings). Originally containing fine art, the Palazzo now houses a vibrant cultural centre with an important programme of exhibitions and events, covering art, music, photography, film and theatre. There's also a café, restaurant and gift shop. Its large bookstore focuses on art, design and architecture books, and is open until late.

Across the road are the impressive **Palazzo Koch,** headquarters of the Banca d'Italia, and the **Villa Aldobrandini,** behind which is a small public park (whose entrance is on Via Mazzarino).

Palazzo Colonna ⓫

66 Piazza SS Apostoli, entrance on Via della Pilotta; www.galleriacolonna.it 06-678 4350 Sat 9am–1pm charge 40, 60, 64, 70, 117, 170

Via Nazionale curves around into Via IV Novembre (leading to Piazza Venezia), passing Trajan's Markets and the Palazzo Colonna. The *palazzo* housed over 23 generations of the Colonna family, and represents a fascinating, if often juxtaposing, architectural panorama spanning four centuries (1300–1700). Inside is a charming art gallery, with richly vaulted, frescoed ceilings, one of which portrays Marcantonio Colonna's victory at the battle of Lepanto (1571). Artists represented here include Lorenzo Monoco, Veronese, Jacopo and Domenico Tintoretto, Pietro da Cortona and Guercino. Be sure to look out for Bronzino's gloriously sensuous *Venus and Cupid*, and Annibale Carracci's *Bean-Eater*, the gallery's most prized work.

From the palace, Via della Pilotta leads back to the Trevi Fountain. ❑

Via della Pilotta, overhung by four elegant bridges, connects the Palazzo Colonna with the gardens of Villa Colonna.

LEFT: street stall.
BELOW: News Café.

BEST RESTAURANTS, BARS AND CAFÉS

Restaurants

Al Presidente
95 Via in Arcione 06-679 7342 L & D Tue–Sun. €€€ [p335, E3]
A family-run restaurant, with a lovely outdoor area. It offers high-quality food and a good wine list, which includes a few choice selections to be had by the glass. A real gem in this touristy area.

Le Tamerici
79 Vicolo Scavolino 06-6920 0700 L & D Mon–Sat. €€€ [p335, E3]
Innovative, seasonal cuisine from an all-female team, with a minimalist decor providing dramatic contrast to the Baroque extravagance outside. This level of refinement, quality and service does not come cheap.

Vineria Il Chianti
81–82 Via del Lavatore 06-678 7550 L & D Mon–Sat. €€ [p335, E3]
A buzzing, rustic locale with young staff and a Tuscan slant. Dishes likely to include hearty soups, quiche with courgette flowers and wild boar fillet. Pizzas in the evening and an appetising selection of cheeses served with honey or jam.

Bars and Cafés

Il Gelato di San Crispino (42 Via della Panetteria; closed Tue) serves ice cream like no other. In a wide variety of flavours, it is served in paper cups, as cones affect the taste according to its creators.

The **News Café** (72 Via della Stamperia) takes its name from the racks of newspapers available for customers to read. A good all-day option for salads, soups and pastas.

In an anonymous gallery off the street is attractive, olde-worlde **Dagnino** (75 Via V. E. Orlando), a vast Sicilian pastry shop (try their speciality, the ricotta-stuffed *cannoli*) and *tavola calda* serving all-day sweet and savoury specialities.

Price includes dinner and a half-bottle of house wine.
€€€€ = more than €60, €€€ = €40–60, €€ = €25–40, € = under €25.

Recommended Restaurants, Bars & Cafés on pages 134–5

PIAZZA DI SPAGNA AND TRIDENTE

The Spanish Steps provide a great spot for watching the world go by. Here, buskers play guitars, romantics pay homage to Keats and Shelley, backpackers sunbathe on the steps and shoppers crowd the windows of the elegant shops below. Off the Piazza di Spagna stretch the most fashionable shopping streets in Rome

Main attractions

PIAZZA DEL POPOLO
SANTA MARIA DEL POPOLO
THE CORSO
PIAZZA COLONNA
CASA DI GOETHE
SAN LORENZO IN LUCINA
SANTA MARIA IN VIA LATA
SPANISH STEPS
KEATS-SHELLEY HOUSE
VIA DEI CONDOTTI
ARA PACIS
MAUSOLEUM OF AUGUSTUS

The Tridente is a mecca for anyone interested in fashion, shopping or art; some tourists never stray from here. The area takes its name from the trio of streets built in the 16th century to relieve congestion in Rome's cramped medieval centre. Via del Corso, Via di Ripetta and Via del Babuino emanate like the prongs of a fork from the Piazza del Popolo, for centuries the main entrance to Rome for travellers coming from the north.

PIAZZA DEL POPOLO ❶

Piazza del Popolo is one of the most impressive squares in Rome. The paving was allegedly paid for by taxes levied on prostitutes, and the piazza was used for executions at one time. In the 19th century, the square was remodelled by Valadier, who created the oval form.

The most striking feature of this elegant square is the **obelisk**. Stolen from Egypt by Emperor Augustus, it once decorated the Circus Maximus, where it was used as a turning point during chariot races.

Standing at the ends of Via del Babuino and Via del Corso are two churches designed by Carlo Rainaldi in the 1660s. Though they appear identical, one is octagonal and the other is dodecagonal. Stand between them for a good view down the Via del Corso to Piazza Venezia and the facade of the Vittoriano monument.

Santa Maria del Popolo ❷

12 Piazza del Popolo, 06-361 0836, daily 8am–noon, 4–7pm, free, Flaminio, 88, 95, 117, 119, 490, 491, 495, 628, 926

LEFT: the twin towers of Trinità dei Monti atop the Spanish Steps.
RIGHT: relaxing in the Piazza del Popolo.

One of the four lion fountains by Valadier (1823) that grace the Piazza del Popolo. In the background are Rainaldi's twin Baroque churches.

RIGHT: Santa Maria del Popolo.
BELOW: Caravaggio's *Conversion of St Paul.*

Across the piazza, by Porta Flaminia, is the church of Santa Maria del Popolo, built in 1472 over a pre-existing 11th-century chapel. According to legend, Emperor Nero was buried on the site by his spiteful lover, and 1,000 years later Pope Paschal II had the chapel constructed to rid the site of evil spirits.

The church was rebuilt in the late 15th century, and is packed with Renaissance masterpieces. The biggest attractions are the two paintings by Caravaggio, *The Conversion of St Paul* and *The Crucifixion of St Peter*, but also worth seeking out are the beautifully detailed frescoes by Pinturicchio, and Guillaume de Marcillat's exquisite stained glass inside the Bramante-designed apse.

The small Chigi Chapel was designed by Raphael for influential banker Agostino Chigi, who commissioned numerous works of art and architecture, including the Villa Farnesina *(see page 205)*. Mosaics in the dome depict God creating the solar system and Chigi's astrological chart. The chapel was completed by Bernini, who added two of his characteristic statues, one of Daniel and one of Habakkuk.

THE CORSO

The most important of the trio of streets that fan out from the Piazza del Popolo is **Via del Corso**, a long thoroughfare that links the square with the Piazza Venezia, another of Rome's central squares and one of its most terrifying traffic roundabouts. The name "Corso" dates

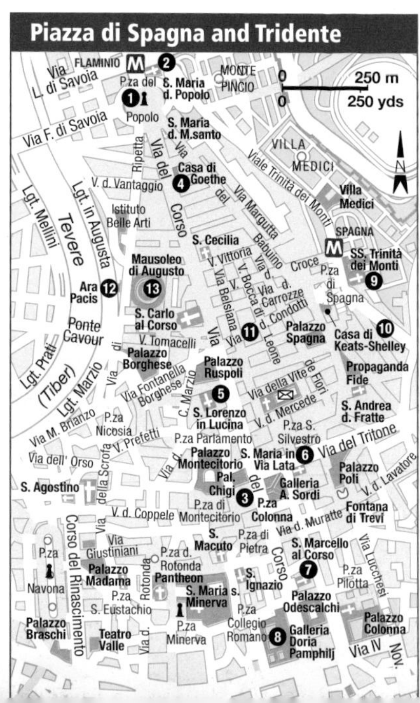

Recommended Restaurants, Bars & Cafés on pages 134–5

from the 15th century, when Pope Paul II introduced horse racing *(corse)* along its length. Pope Alexander VII straightened the road in the 16th century. The races were imitations of the ancient games (with all their atrocities), and it wasn't only horses that ran: there were races for prostitutes, for children, for Jews and for the crippled. The German poet Goethe, who lived at No. 18 *(see page 128)*, described the races in his *Italian Journey*. They were finally banned at the end of the 19th century.

Piazza Colonna ❸

These days, the only people racing along the Corso are politicians being whisked at high speed to **Palazzo Chigi**, the prime minister's official residence, and the neighbouring **Palazzo di Montecitorio**, the Chamber of Deputies, both on **Piazza Colonna.** This square marks the halfway point of the Via del Corso.

The southern half of the Corso between Piazza Colonna and Piazza Venezia is lined with stately palaces, most of which are banks, while the northern half, between Piazza Colonna and Piazza del Popolo, is a much more pedestrian-friendly shopping area. In the early evening and on Saturdays, Romans swarm into town to stroll up and down and window shop on this stretch of the Corso and the surrounding streets *(see shaded area on map opposite)*.

Two spas in the vicinity will boost your flagging spirits after too much sightseeing or shopping. Try the Caribbean rejuvenation treatment at the **Aveda Day Spa** (9 Rampa Mignanelli; tel: 06-6992 4257), or join the international jet set indulging themselves at the spa of the stylish **Hotel de Russie** (9 Via del Babuino; tel: 06-328 881).

LEFT: reliefs on the Column of Marcus Aurelius.
BELOW: Via del Corso.

Rome has been called the city of obelisks – it has at least 13. Most were brought back by triumphant armies and erected in public places to show the power of the Empire, but some – such as the one at the top of the Spanish Steps – are Roman imitations of Egyptian originals.

Dominating the Piazza Colonna is the street's only classical relic, the 30-metre (90ft) **Colonna di Marco Aurelio** (Column of Marcus Aurelius). It dates from AD 180, and the bas-relief around the shaft depicts the campaigns of Marcus Aurelius against the Germanic tribes and the Sarmatians. Stairs lead to the top, where the original statue of the emperor was replaced with one of the Apostle Paul in 1589.

Casa di Goethe ❹

✉ 18 Via del Corso; www.casadigoethe.it ☎ 06-3265 0412 ◷ daily 10am–6pm € charge 🚆 Flaminio 🚌 *see page 125*

ABOVE RIGHT: at the top of the Spanish Steps. **RIGHT:** Goethe. **BELOW:** the church of San Marcello.

Not far from the Piazza del Popolo is the apartment where German poet Goethe lived for two years in the late 18th century. He shared the house with painter Hans Tischbein, whose depictions of the poet are on display.

You can peruse the writer's journals and a room dedicated to all his works, either written in, or inspired by, the Eternal City. Among them are *Iphigenia*, *The Roman Elegies*, *Faust*, *The Roman Carnival* and *Italian Journey*.

Three churches

Further down the Via del Corso, in a small square to the west, is the 12th-century church of **San Lorenzo in Lucina** ❺ (16A Via in Lucina; tel: 06-687 1494; daily 8am–8pm).

It contains some busts by Bernini, and a grill, rumoured to be the very spot where the martyr St Lawrence was burnt to death for his refusal to hand over Church riches to the Roman city government. When questioned as to the whereabouts of the wealth, he is said to have presented the poor, crippled, and homeless, declaring that they were the true treasures of the Church.

On the other side of the Corso from Piazza Colonna is **Santa Maria in Via Lata** ❻, which has an impressive facade by da Cortona. In a side street next to the church is one of Rome's "talking" fountains, the *facchino* (or water-bearer). In the days before freedom of speech, the *facchino* and other "talking statues" were hung with satirical and

Recommended Restaurants, Bars & Cafés on pages 134–5

subversive messages and fulfilled much the same function as a newspaper *(see page 162)*.

Another noteworthy church is **San Marcello al Corso** ❼ (Mon–Sat 7.30am–noon and 4–7pm, Sun 9.30am–noon and 4–7pm), further along the Corso towards Piazza Venezia, which has a Van Dyck crucifix in the sacristy (you need to ask to see it).

The palace on the right at the end of the Corso houses the **Galleria Doria Pamphilj** ❽, details of which are included in the Piazza Navona chapter *(see page 156)*. There are several splendid buildings in the city called Doria Pamphilj (also spelt Pamphili), after one of the oldest aristocratic Roman families. One of their members, Giovanni Battista Pamphilj, became Pope Innocent X (1644–55). The current generation of the family still live in this *palazzo* and their private apartments are sometimes open for guided tours.

The Spanish Steps ❾

The sweeping Spanish Steps combine with the twin towers of the church of Trinità dei Monti on top and the harmonious square with its bizarrely shaped fountain below to form one of the most distinctive of Roman scenes. **Piazza di Spagna** is so called because there has been a Spanish Embassy to the Holy See here since the 17th century. The French, meanwhile, owned the land around the convent of **Trinità dei Monti** at the top of the steps, and so they claimed the right to pass through the square and named part of it French Square.

This petty rivalry between the French and Spanish reached a climax with the building of the Spanish Steps. The original design was intended to sing the praises of the

For a taste of old-fashioned English style in the heart of the capital, try Babington's Tea Rooms (23 Piazza di Spagna, tel: 06-678 6027). The creaky wood floors, serious black-skirted staff and all-round austere feel are like a trip back in time. However, the teapots for €11 a person will bring you right back to the present day, and to one of the world's most pricey piazzas.

LEFT: a Fiat 500, the ultimate city car, on the Via del Corso. **BELOW:** the Barcaccia in Piazza di Spagna.

Byron, who had claimed that Rome was the city of his soul, was disappointed to find it "pestilent with English". His fellow Romantic poet Shelley was equally disturbed by the Brits abroad: "The manners of the rich English are wholly insupportable, and they assume pretences which they would not venture upon in their own country."

French monarchy, and there was to have been a huge equestrian statue of Louis XIV. However, the Pope was against this idea, so when the architect de Sanctis finally started building the steps in the 18th century, the only reference made to France was the little fleur-de-lis on the pedestals.

The cascade of the Spanish Steps is perennially crowded with visitors. In spring, the crowds share the steps with pots of blossoming azaleas. The centrepiece of the square at the bottom of the steps is the fountain by Pietro Bernini, who was aided in its construction by his more famous son, Gianlorenzo. The so-called **Barcaccia** is a half-sunken boat fed by water from the ancient aqueduct *Aqua Virgo*.

The English ghetto

The Grand Tourists of the 18th century, most of whom were English aristocrats, stayed in this area on their visits to Rome (it came to be known as the English ghetto). In the 19th century many illustrious artists, writers and musicians followed in their footsteps: Keats, Tennyson, Stendhal, Balzac, Wagner and Liszt among them.

RIGHT: Caffè Greco. **BELOW LEFT:** *Shelley in the Baths of Caracalla*, by Joseph Severn. **BELOW RIGHT:** Keats-Shelley House.

Keats-Shelley House ⑩

✉ 26 Piazza di Spagna; www.keats-shelley-house.org ☎ 06-678 4235 ⏲ Mon–Fri 10am–1pm and 2–8pm, Sat 11am–2pm € charge Ⓜ Spagna 🚌 117, 119

In 1820, Keats spent the last few months of his life in a small room

Grand Tourists

The term "Grand Tour" first appeared in 1670 in Richard Lassels's *Voyage through Italy*, when the British priest and traveller declared that "young lords" must visit Italy and France to educate themselves in the culture of antiquity. In the following centuries Italy's great cities became the main stops on a secular pilgrimage of English aristocrats and aspiring gentlemen wishing to complete their education. For the Romans, this procession of "Sirs" and "Miladies" represented an opportunity to cash in. Houses were rented out in the fashionable districts of Rome on the Corso and Piazza di Spagna, and tea shops (such as Babington's), hotels and cafés sprung up. With the arrival of mass transport in the middle of the 1800s travel became cheaper and safer; many writers, including Byron and Shelley, felt that the Grand Tour was de rigueur. The dalliances and foibles of these British in Italy became the subject for literary satire in the novels of E.M. Forster and Henry James, many of which have been dramatised for cinema.

overlooking the Spanish Steps; he died of consumption there in 1821, aged just 25. In 1906, the house was bought by an Anglo-American association and turned into a museum and library dedicated to Keats and his fellow Romantics who had made Rome their home. The Keats-Shelley House has an intriguing collection of personal objects and documents relating to the lives of Shelley and Byron, but the main focus is on Keats – his prints, paintings, books and death mask are on display.

SHOPPING STREETS

The former artistic enclave is now the haunt of big spenders and wishful window shoppers who come to flex their credit cards in its elegant and expensive shops. The area between Piazza di Spagna and Via del Corso is for dedicated fashionistas. Elegant **Via dei Condotti** ⓫ is designer-label heaven.

This street, plus the parallel **Via Borgognona** and **Via Frattina**, which are linked by the equally sumptuous **Via Bocca di Leone**, are home to all the top fashion outlets. **Via del Babuino** is lined with interesting design and antique shops. Parallel to this is **Via Margutta**, a pretty, narrow street (once home to Federico Fellini), with artists' studios, galleries and workshops. Twice a year (May and September/October), the street holds a special art show dedicated to the works of local painters. Matching the expensive shops in this area are some of the best hotels in Rome.

Towards the end of Via dei Condotti is the world-famous tourist trap **Caffè Greco**, said to have been opened by a Greek merchant in 1760. The great and the good down the centuries have frequented this café, including Baudelaire, Wagner, Taine, Liszt, Stendhal, Goethe,

Rome's most opulent shopping street is Via dei Condotti, which starts at the Spanish Steps. The designer shops – Armani, Bulgari, Gucci and Prada among them – feature dazzling window displays and even more dazzling prices.

LEFT AND BELOW: shoppers mix with designer labels in Via dei Condotti.

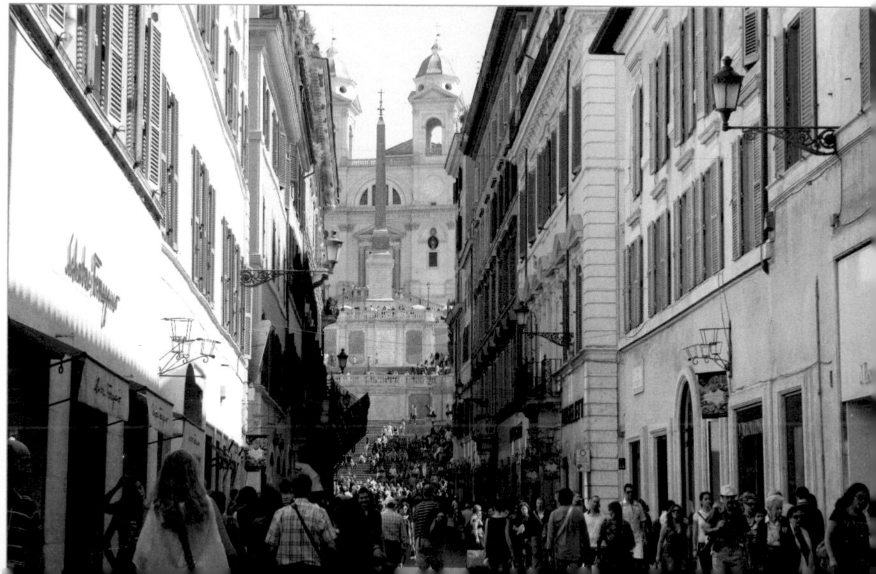

Roman Fashion

Many glamorous and highly sought-after couturiers are based in Rome, the hotspot being Via dei Condotti

While most of the Italian fashion business is centred on Milan, there are a handful of top designers who have made their base in Rome. The most famous of these is undoubtedly Valentino, who opened his Roman studio in 1959 and has enjoyed success ever since. His high-profile clients have included Sophia Loren, Audrey Hepburn and Jackie Kennedy, and his glamorous evening-wear is a constant winner at red carpet events.

Laura Biagiotti and Fendi are also big names in the world of international fashion who started in Rome. The former, who has been dubbed the "queen of cashmere", creates luxurious knitwear (coats included), silk separates and loose-fitting, feminine dresses. The designer is said to test-drive her designs personally for comfort. Her headquarters and home are located just outside Rome in the 15th-century castle of Marco Simone, a former medieval fortress. The four towers of the castle form the famous Biagiotti logo.

The second of the two, Fendi, is a company created by a married couple and their five daughters. They first set up their flagship shop on Via Borgognona on the site of a former cinema in the early 1950s. Over half a century on, the shop is one of the largest in the area and sells beautiful bags, shoes, luggage and ready-to-wear clothes.

Two other legendary names are worth checking out: Fontana and Capucci. The heyday of the Sorelle Fontana (Fontana Sisters) is associated with the glamorous *Dolce Vita* of the 1950s and 1960s, when droves of aristocratic women and just about all the successful foreign actresses in Rome visited their atelier. You can see their classic, elegant clothes at Via della Fontanella di Borghese. Roberto Capucci also emerged during the 1950s and is best-known for the sculptural quality of his garments that look as good off as on the body. His work has been shown in important design museums in Italy, Vienna, Munich and Paris, and he has a boutique/atelier on Via Gregoriana.

More recently, the young Gai Mattiolo has been making his mark both at home and abroad. He has his own-name boutique in the ultra-swanky Via Borgognona, and many more in cities throughout the world. Adriana V. Campanile is the new favourite for shoe fanatics. Her designs are modern and stylish, and easily pass for pricier Piazza di Spagna luxuries.

Of course, just about all the other well-known Italian designers, among them Versace, Armani and Trussardi, have shops in Rome as well, mostly around Via dei Condotti. However, visitors who cannot afford top designer names should not be put off; there are plenty of boutiques selling clothes with far less frightening price tags. Remember, too, that Italy produces stunning shoes, bags and leather accessories, and a wide selection can be found in the city's shops. ❑

LEFT: a trademark Laura Biagiotti white suit.

Recommended Restaurants, Bars & Cafés on pages 134–5

Byron, Keats and Shelley.

The third road in the trident of streets, **Via di Ripetta** (*ripa* means river bank: a reminder that there was once a harbour here, back when ships still plied the Tiber) connects Piazza del Popolo to the Vatican, via the Mausoleum of Augustus and the Ara Pacis, two ancient monuments dating from the time of Augustus.

Ara Pacis Museum ⓬

Lungotevere in Augusta, www.arapacis.it 06-0608 Tue–Sun 9am–7pm charge Flaminio 81, 117, 119, 224, 628, 913, 926

The **Ara Pacis**, a finely carved sacrificial altar built in 13 BC to commemorate the era of peace *(pax romana)* that followed Augustus' victories in Gaul and Spain, was painstakingly pieced together by archaeologists from original and reconstructed fragments, and erected in its current location by Mussolini in 1938. The altar is enclosed by a white marble screen decorated with reliefs illustrating mythological and allegorical scenes.

After years of neglect and botched

restorations, the altar is now the principal exhibit in a new museum complex, designed amid great controversy by US architect Richard Meier. Inaugurated in 2006, his striking glass-and-travertine design is the only work of modern architecture in the historic centre of Rome, and as such has provoked strong reactions *(see right)*.

Mausoleum of Augustus ⓭

Behind the museum is the **Mausoleo di Augusto**, built between 28 and 23 BC, long before it was intended for use. The first person buried here was Augustus' nephew Marcellus, then Augustus himself in AD 14. It's hard to believe now that this overgrown ruin was one of the most magnificent sights in Rome, covered as it was with marble pillars and statues. ❑

Critics of Richard Meier's Ara Pacis Museum have likened it variously to a petrol station, a pizzeria and a giant coffin. Vittorio Sgarbi, a celebrity art critic and former Deputy Culture Minister, publicly set fire to a model of the building, and recently declared it "an indecent cesspit by a useless architect".

ABOVE: Mausoleo di Augusto.
BELOW: the Ara Pacis.

BEST RESTAURANTS, BARS AND CAFÉS

Restaurants

Price includes dinner and a half-bottle of house wine:
€ = under €25
€€ = €25–40
€€€ = €40–60
€€€€ = more than €60

Al 34

34 Via Mario dei Fiori 06-679 5091 L & D Tue–Sun. **€€** [p335, E3]
The service is fast, the prices honest, the atmosphere lively and the food classical Italian. Sample the *tonnarelli al granciporro* (pasta with crab), the fresh fish *misto* (a mix of different fish), the home-made Neapolitan *caprese* cake, *semifreddo al torronocino* (nougat ice cream dessert) or the pear and chocolate tart.

La Baguette

24–25 Via Tomacelli 06-6880 7727 B, Br, L & D daily. **€–€€** [p335, D3]
The first Italian branch of a popular Belgian chain. Ideal for breakfast (exquisite croissants) or later, when large salads, quiches and open sandwiches made with fresh stone-ground bread can be washed down with organic wines, teas and fruit juices around large wooden tables. A terrace a couple of doors down is a major bonus in summer.

Dal Bolognese

1–2 Piazza del Popolo 06-361 1426 L & D Tue–Sun. **€€€–€€€€** [p335, D2]
On the theatrical Piazza del Popolo, this smart restaurant with paintings on the wall, uniformed waiters and couches on which to sip your *aperitivo* serves good-quality staples from the Emilia Romagna region to a loyal clientele of politicians, film producers and assorted artists and celebrities. Closed three weeks Aug.

Da Gino

4 Vicolo Rosini 06-687 3434 L & D Mon–Sat. **€€** [p335, D3]
Vaulted ceilings and frescoes adorn this trattoria, where affordable Roman specialities are served following the traditional weekly calendar, which means fish on Tuesday and Friday. For dessert, home-made *crostate* (tarts) and a legendary *tiramisù*. No credit cards. Closed Aug.

'Gusto

9 Piazza Augusto Imperatore 06-322 6273 L & D daily, Br Sat and Sun. Restaurant **€€–€€€**, pizzeria **€–€€** [p335, D2]
'Gusto is an empire: a pizzeria downstairs, an upmarket restaurant upstairs, a wine bar on the other side, an *osteria* next to that. There's even a well-stocked cookery store attached. The service is fast and friendly, and the general standard is high. An added feature is the outdoor seating most of the year under impressively austere 1930s porticoes that line the square. Booking advisable. Open late.

Hostaria dell'Orso

25c Via dei Soldati 06-6830 1192 D only Mon–Sat. **€€€€** [p335, D3]
Milanese superstar chef Gualtiero Marchesi is at the helm of the exclusive Hostaria dell'Orso in a *palazzo* that has been an inn since medieval times. Now a posh but hip restaurant-cum-piano bar-cum-disco, it has an expensive take on Italian haute cuisine which can be ordered à la carte or from four different set-price menus *(menù degustazione)*.

Il Margutta RistorArte

118 Via Margutta 06-3265 0577 L & D daily, Br Sun. **€€–€€€** [p335, E2]
This is one of Rome's oldest vegetarian restaurants and offers refined contemporary Italian cuisine. Walls are filled with modern art, echoing its location in the artsy Via Margutta. At lunch there is a set-price buffet, and there's a good brunch on Sunday.

Matricianella

3–4 Via del Leone 06-683 2100 L & D Mon–Sat. **€€** [p335, D3]
Traditional Roman food in a cheerful setting. To start, try their crispy *fritto vegetale* (fried vegetables) and then, if you are a carnivore, the fettuccine with chicken liver and minced beef is a good bet. Closed three weeks Aug.

Nino

11 Via Borgognona 06-679 5676 L & D Mon–Sat. **€€–€€€** [p335, E3]
A cordial setting where genuine Tuscan food has been consumed for over 70 years. Sample the leek soufflé, wild boar with polenta, and pappardelle with hare sauce. The wine list is well thought out and has a good selection of half-bottles. At the upper end of the price scale, and well worth it. Closed Aug.

L'Osteria

16 Via della Frezza 06-3211 1482 L & D daily. **€€** [p335, D2]
Informal but chic, and further proof that anything the 'Gusto team *(see left)* does turns to gold. Furniture and

ABOVE: Il Margutta RistorArte.

details have some 1930s touches, and the menu is a skilful combination of the traditional and the contemporary, with 400 cheeses, cured meats, deep-fried delicacies, omelettes, soups and good main courses. All served with hearty home-made bread and excellent wines by the glass or bottle from a selection of 1,700 labels.

Otello alla Concordia

✉ 81 Via della Croce ☎ 06-679 1178 ⏲ L & D Mon–Sat. € [p335, E2]

Authentically Roman food (*rigatoni all'amatriciana*, lamb and *tiramisù*) and fresh fish served in a room overlooking a pretty little courtyard, used in summer. Book ahead.

PizzaRé

✉ 14 Via di Ripetta ☎ 06-3211468 ⏲ L & D daily. € [p335, D2]

For a simple pizza after a heavy day's spending in the Spanish Steps' clothing mecca, try PizzaRé, maker of the thick and crusty Neapolitan variety. Set-price menus including pasta and grilled meats at lunchtime. Pizzas at reduced price on Monday evenings.

Porto Maltese

✉ 7 Salita di San Sebastianello ☎ 06-678 0546 ⏲ L & D Tue–Sun. €€–€€€ [p335, E2]

Trendy bar and restaurant with a friendly atmosphere. Waiters can be seen heading to and from a large open aquarium at the front, full of wriggling eel, crabs and lobsters. Alternatively, choose from a more sedate fish counter at the back.

Taverna Ripetta

✉ 158 Via di Ripetta ☎ 06-6880 2979 ⏲ L & D Mon–Sat, D only Sun. €€ [p335, D2]

Romantic and atmospheric, this restaurant is perfect for lunch as well as dinner. The menu incorporates pasta, meat and fish. Try the gnocchi with basil and cherry tomatoes, and the outstanding *semifreddo* for dessert.

Bars and Cafés

One of the most appealing wine bars in the area is the **Enoteca Antica di Via della Croce** (76b Via della Croce). It's cosy in winter in its cellar-like interior, and delightful in summer if you can nab one of the few outdoor tables. You can just sit and drink wine, or you can eat here too.

Two other buzzing venues are the wine bar in the excellent **'Gusto** complex (9 Piazza Augusto Imperatore, *see previous page*), and an ultra-modern rival pizzeria-restaurant-café-bar called **Recafè** (36 Piazza Augusto Imperatore).

Buccone (19 Via di Ripetta) existed long before wine bars became fashionable, and it is a joy just to take in the sheer authenticity of this high-ceilinged, old-fashioned emporium crammed with bottles of wine and regional specialities.

Old-fashioned, artsy hang-out **Café Notegen** (159 Via del Babuino) still has plenty of charm, although it is looking a little worse for wear these days. The all-day opening and affable manner are endearing.

There are a number of other historic cafés in this area. Long-time rivals **Canova** (16 Piazza del Popolo) and **Rosati** (5 Piazza del Popolo) face each other across the grand expanse of Piazza del Popolo. Both are good, but Rosati wins hands down for ambience. Furthermore, its cakes are mouth-watering, and the cocktails are a cut above the usual.

English tearoom **Babington** (23 Piazza di Spagna) was founded in 1835 and is still run by the same family. Order English and continental breakfasts, a traditional brunch, cocktails and excellent tea. All cakes, breads and muffins are baked fresh daily. Elegant, and decidedly expensive.

The beautiful **Antico Caffè Greco** (86 Via dei Condotti) with its marble tables and red-velvet chairs is frequented mostly by tourists, but the bar out the front makes delicious coffee. Drink it standing at the bar, as it's much cheaper than when you are sitting at a table.

For the ultimate view of Rome, climb up the Spanish Steps and turn left to **Ciampini al Café du Jardin** (Viale Trinità dei Monti), open only in summer, where you can have light meals and cocktails as the sun sets on the Eternal City.

Recommended Restaurants, Bars & Cafés on page 147

THE VATICAN AND PRATI

The Vatican City is a shrine to the power and extravagance of the Catholic Church through the ages, and to its extraordinary artistic taste

Main attractions

ST PETER'S SQUARE
ST PETER'S BASILICA
THE VATICAN MUSEUMS
THE SISTINE CHAPEL
CASTEL SANT'ANGELO
THE BORGO
PRATI
MUSEUM OF THE SOULS OF PURGATORY

The fabulous wealth and extravagance of the Catholic Church through the ages is celebrated without restraint in the Vatican State. The immense basilica of St Peter's, with its dome by Michelangelo and an interior sumptuously bedecked with Bernini's glistening creations, is impressive enough. Then there are the Vatican Museums, mile upon mile of rooms and corridors containing historic treasures, and, of course, the Sistine Chapel.

Covering a total area of little more than 40 hectares (100 acres), Vatican City is by far the world's smallest independent sovereign entity with its population of 800, only 30 of whom are women. The Lateran Treaty of 1929, concluded between Pope Pius XI and Mussolini, established its territorial limits. The Vatican has its own stamps, currency, media, railway and police force – the Swiss Guards. The city is roughly trapezoidal in shape, bounded by medieval walls on all sides, except on the corner where the opening of St Peter's Square marks the border with Rome.

ST PETER'S SQUARE

Piazza San Pietro ❶ was laid out by Bernini in 1656–67 for Pope Alexander VII. Its double-colonnaded wings symbolise the outstretched arms of Mother Church, embracing and protecting the congregation. The piazza itself is keyhole-shaped, echoing St Peter's role as holder of the keys to heaven. In the centre are fountains by Maderno and della Fontana, and an Egyptian obelisk, brought to Rome by Emperor Caligula in AD 37. Between the obelisk and each fountain is a round marble slab, from where the spectator obtains a typically Baroque illusion: that

LEFT: St Peter's Square. **RIGHT:** view of the keyhole-shaped square from the dome.

Michelangelo is said to have made his mark on the less spiritual side of the Vatican as well. Word has it that the master designed the blue-, yellow- and red-striped uniforms (the colours of the Medici popes) of the Vatican's famous Swiss Guards. The uniforms have not changed since the corps was instituted in the 16th century.

each colonnade has only a single row of columns, the other three having disappeared.

St Peter's Basilica ❷

✉ Piazza San Pietro; www.vaticano.va ☎ 06-6988 1662 ⏲ daily 7am–7pm, until 6pm in winter (no bare legs or shoulders) € free for the basilica; charge for dome and sacristy Ⓜ Ottaviano-San Pietro 🚌 19, 23, 32, 34, 46, 49, 62, 64, 81, 492, 913, 990, 991, 999

At the end of the square, above a triple flight of steps, stands the **Basilica di San Pietro**, an undeniably impressive structure, but an unfortunate mixture of conflicting architectural styles. Built on the site of St Peter's martyrdom in AD 67 during Nero's persecutions of the Christians, the original Constantinian church was of typical basilican form – a Latin cross with a nave, side aisles and a transept. It was lavishly decor-

ated with mosaics, paintings and statuary, but became so dilapidated that rebuilding became unavoidable.

In 1506, Julius II decided on a complete reconstruction and commissioned Bramante, whose plan for the new basilica was a Greek cross surmounted by a gigantic dome. On Bramante's death in 1514, the four central piers and the arches of the dome had been completed. Raphael (d. 1520) then took over, and was followed by Sangallo (d. 1546); both men bowed to the clergy's wish for

Vatican and Prati

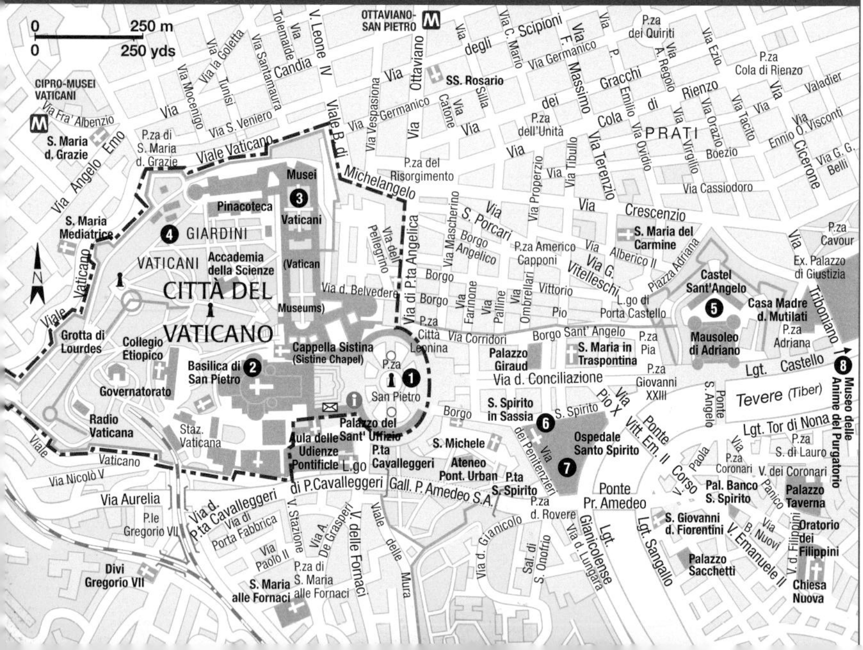

greater capacity by designing a nave and altering the ground-plan to that of a Latin cross.

In 1546, however, before this could be realised, the 72-year-old Michelangelo was summoned by Pope Paul III. He expressed his preference for the original Greek cross and central dome of Bramante; seeing the Pantheon's dome as unambitious, though, he developed his own version of Brunelleschi's Florentine cupola, and substituted Bramante's piers with new ones of tremendous strength. The entire plan was realised after Michelangelo died in 1564; construction work was continued until 1590, when Pope Paul V decided that the Latin cross was more appropriate, demanding a nave.

Maderno extended Michelangelo's building to give it its current form, adding the portico in 1614. The building was consecrated in 1626, 1,300 years after the construction of the original basilica. Seen from the square, Maderno's portico robs Michelangelo's dome of much of its power, though from a distance the cityscape is still dominated by the cupola.

St Peter's treasures

As you pass into the **portico**, the statue of Constantine on the left is by Bernini. Look up, opposite the 15th-century bronze central doors, to see a restored remnant of the original 13th-century mosaic, *La Navicella*, by Giotto. Inside the basilica, turn right for ***La Pietà***, Michelangelo's remarkable statue of the Madonna and dead Christ, which he sculpted in 1499 when only 25. Mary is seated on a rock (the rock of St Peter) holding Christ's lifeless body, her face filled with sorrow. It is an incredibly

St Peter's is the longest basilica in the world. The nave is the size of two football fields and the baldacchino is as high as a nine-storey building. The church has 21 altars, 14 chapels, 9 domes and capacity for 60,000 peope.

FAR LEFT: a curve of Bernini's colonnade in Piazza San Pietro. **LEFT:** Michelangelo's *Pietà*. **BELOW:** inside St Peter's Basilica.

Papal Audiences

Papal audiences are held in the Vatican on Wednesday at 10.30am, except in the height of summer, when they are at his summer residence at Castelgandolfo outside Rome. Apply for free tickets in writing to the Prefettura della Casa Pontificia, 00120 Città del Vaticano, or go to the office on the preceding Monday or Tuesday (it's through the bronze door watched over by Swiss Guards, to the right of the basilica). For more information, tel: 06-6988 4857. The Pope comes to a window above the piazza on Sunday at noon to give the traditional angelus blessing.

TIP

Tours of the Vatican Gardens must be booked in advance through the Vatican tourist office (tel: 06-6988 4676; every day except Wed and Sun). To visit St Peter's Necropolis, beneath the basilica, contact the Vatican's Ufficio Scavi (tel: 06-6988 5318; weekdays 9am–5pm; no children under 15).

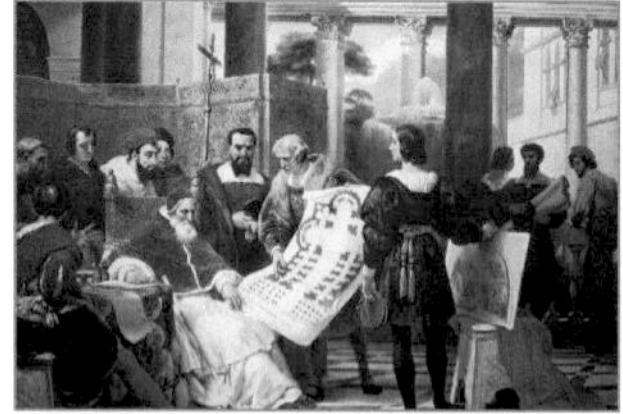

moving work and the only one Michelangelo ever signed.

Halfway down the nave the 13th-century statue of St Peter by Arnolfo di Cambio is so widely venerated that its foot, kissed by devout pilgrims for over seven centuries, is almost worn away.

In the centre of the basilica, directly under the dome is Bernini's **baldacchino** (1633), commissioned by the Barberini Pope Urban VIII. This huge bronze canopy (the largest free-standing bronze structure in the world) rises 26 metres (66ft) over the holiest part of the church, the legendary tomb of St Peter. The twisted columns are replicas of the ones that Christ apparently leant against in the Temple of Solomon. It was cast from metal stripped from the Pantheon's dome, leading locals to quip, "What the Barbarians didn't do, the Barberini did." Bernini added the vine leaves and the bees, symbols of the Barberini coat of arms.

To the right of the baldacchino, stairs lead down to the **grottoes** (daily 7am–7pm, until 6pm in winter; free) containing the tombs of several popes, including that of the recently deceased Pope John Paul II.

On the apse wall, framed by the baldacchino, is another Bernini creation, the **Cattedra di San Pietro** (1665), a gilded bronze throne said to have been the episcopal chair of St Peter. It is supported by statues of the four fathers of the Church, and above it angels and putti surround a halo of gilt stucco with a key to heaven and the dove of the Holy Spirit.

Don't miss the ghoulish **tomb of Alexander VII**, another of Bernini's patrons, to the left of the transept. Just above the door is Bernini's last work, representing a skeletal allegory of death clutching an hourglass, reminding us that death comes to us all. The draped skeleton is surrounded by four

ABOVE: Pope Julius II ordering Bramante, Michelangelo and Raphael to construct the Vatican and St Peter's, by Vernet. **BELOW:** the magnificent dome of St Peter's Basilica.

statues representing Justice, Truth, Prudence and Chastity.

The dome

The entrance to the **dome** (daily 9am–6pm; closed during ceremonies; admission charge) is on the right of the portico. The long climb to the top (there are 320 steps from where the lift stops) is rewarded by extensive views across the city.

The **Vatican Gardens** can be seen from the dome, but if you want a closer look you will have to book in advance *(see tip opposite)*.

THE VATICAN MUSEUMS ❸

100 Viale Vaticano; www.vatican.va 06-6988 4947/4676 daily 9am–6pm (last admission 4pm); closed Catholic holidays; no bare legs or shoulders charge; last Sunday in the month is free Ottaviano-San Pietro, Cipro-Musei Vaticani 19, 23, 32, 34, 49, 62, 64, 81, 492, 913, 990, 991, 999

The Vatican Museums are a good 15-minute walk from St Peter's Square; just follow the walls north until you reach the entrance. Expect a long queue, especially at weekends and on the last Sunday of the month, when the place gets mobbed as admission is free. To help visitors out, the museum authorities have devised four routes lasting from 1½ to 5 hours. All, including the shortest, take in the Sistine Chapel.

There are 10 collections in all, plus the papal apartments, but the undisputed highlights are the Sistine Chapel and the Raphael Rooms. Because different visitors have different tastes and because of the vast amount of exhibits contained in the museums, no single route is described here, only the main highlights. You'll find plenty of detailed information at the entrance.

Vatican post box. The Vatican has its own stamps, currency, radio station, newspaper and police force.

LEFT: detail from *The Creation of Adam,* on the Sistine ceiling.
BELOW: Giuseppe Momo's magnificent helicoidal staircase (1932).

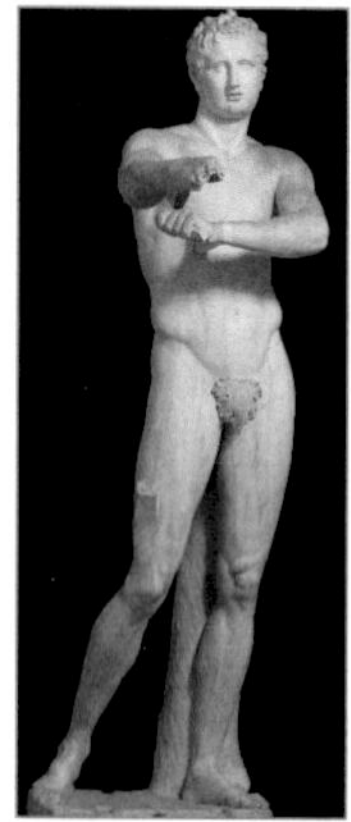

Statue of Apoxyomenos, the Greek representation of an athlete. This is a 1st-century AD Roman copy of a Greek original.

Sistine Chapel

No visit to the Vatican is complete without a look inside the Sistine Chapel. The walls, depicting scenes from the lives of Christ and Moses, were painted by some of the greatest masters of the Renaissance: Botticelli, Perugino, Ghirlandaio and Signorelli. It is Michelangelo's sublime frescoes, however, which have made the chapel universally famous *(see pages 150–1)*.

The Raphael Rooms

The Stanze di Raffaello are four rooms decorated by Raphael in the 16th century at the request of Pope Nicholas V. The first room, the **Sala di Constantino**, was the last to be painted and, since Raphael was on his deathbed, is mainly the work of his pupils. The frescoes depict scenes from the life of Constantine.

The **Stanza di Eliodoro** was decorated in the years 1512–14. The subject matter alludes to events in Pope Julius II's life. *Expulsion of Heliodorus*, with angels chasing a thief out of the temple, refers to Julius's success in expelling the enemy from Italy.

The next room, **Stanza della Segnatura**, was where the Pope's council met to sign official decrees. The frescoes (1509–11) mix pagan and Christian themes. In the *School of Athens* fresco, representing the triumph of philosophical truth, Raphael portrays ancient characters with the features of contemporary heroes. The bearded figure of Plato in the centre is da Vinci; Bramante appears as Euclid in the foreground, and the thoughtful figure of Heraclites on the steps is Michelangelo. The *Parnassus* fresco, representing poetic beauty, features Homer, Virgil, Ovid, Dante and Boccaccio.

The last room, the **Stanza dell' Incendio di Borgo**, takes its name from the fresco depicting a terrible fire in the Borgo in 847, miraculously extinguished by Leo IV making the sign of the cross. This room was painted after the first half of Michelangelo's Sistine ceiling was uncovered, and direct influences can be seen in the monumentality of the figures.

For information on the other Vatican collections, see *Treasures of the Vatican, pages 148–9*.

BELOW: *Dispute* from the Stanza della Segnatura, one of the Raphael Rooms.

Papal Insignia

Wherever you see a coat of arms with the crossed keys of St Peter topped with the triple crown, you know the building, sculpture or painting on which it appears was a papal commission. Each papal dynasty had its own insignia. Red balls signify the Medici popes, for example, while bees represent the Barberini, the greatest patrons of the Baroque. The Barberini bees can be spotted all over Rome, from Triton's Fountain to the baldacchino in St Peter's *(below)*. Other interesting papal symbols to look out for are dragons, doves, fleurs-de-lis, cypress and olive trees, stars and hills.

Vatican Gardens ❹

✉ Viale Vaticano; www.vatican.va
☎ 06-6988 4676 ⏲ guided tours every day except Wed and Sun
€ charge €30; ticket also grants entry to the Vatican Museums
Ⓜ Ottaviano-San Pietro, Cipro-Musei Vaticani 🚌 19, 23, 32, 34, 49, 62, 64, 81, 492, 913, 990, 991, 999

A place of meditation for the popes since 1279, the gardens were commissioned by Nicholas III who wanted an orchard, a lawn and a vegetable garden. The most important improvements were carried out in the 16th and 17th centuries by artists, including Bramente and Pirro Logorio. Renaissance culture, philosophy and art had an influence on the gardens' landscape, demonstrated by small temples and grottoes dedicated to the Virgin, and the impressive fountains. The ship-shaped Fountain of the Galley shoots water from its cannons, and the Eagle Fountain celebrates the arrival of water from the Acqua Paola aqueduct at the Vatican. There's also a French Garden, rare tree species and a notable example of Italian-style gardening, with hedges, trees and bushes trimmed to perfection to convey a sense of symmetry.

Castel Sant'Angelo ❺

✉ 50 Lungotevere Castello; www.castelsantangelo.com ☎ 06-681 9111 ⏲ Tue–Sun 9am–7.30pm

If you're travelling with children, the Castel Sant'Angelo, with its ramparts, trapdoors, prison chambers, drawbridges and cannonballs galore, will keep them amused.

ABOVE LEFT: view of St Peter's from Castel Sant'Angelo. **LEFT:** Bernini's angels on Ponte Sant'Angelo. **BELOW:** the Vatican Gardens.

The eye-rolling, ecstatic expressions of Bernini's ten angels on the Ponte Sant'Angelo have earned them the nickname "the breezy maniacs".

charge Lepanto 23, 34, 49, 62, 64, 80, 87, 492, 926, 990

Castel Sant'Angelo is approached from across the Tiber by means of the delightful **Ponte Sant'Angelo**, a pedestrian bridge adorned with statues of saints Peter and Paul and 10 angels sculpted by Bernini and his students in the 1660s *(see page 54)*. The three central arches were part of the bridge Hadrian built in AD 136 to link his mausoleum – now the Castel Sant'Angelo – to the centre of the city. Most of the present bridge dates from the 17th century, but it was altered in the late 19th century to accommodate the new Tiber embankment.

Construction of the castle began in AD 123, and 16 years later it became Hadrian's mausoleum. It has since been a fortress, a prison and the popes' hiding place in times of trouble, thanks to the *passetto*, the corridor that connects the Vatican Palace with the castle. The castle houses artefacts from all periods of Roman history, and many of the rooms, such as the Sala Paolina painted by del Vaga in 1544, are beautifully frescoed.

BELOW: Castel Sant'Angelo from the pedestrian Sant'Angelo bridge.

The papal chambers and other rooms are accessible via the spiral ramp inside, which is still in an excellent state of preservation. At the top of the ramp are the terraces and café, both with superb views of the Dome of St Peter's and the rest of Rome. (It was from this parapet that Puccini's heroine, Tosca, plunged to her death.) The gigantic bronze statue of the Archangel Michael that crowns the citadel was placed here in 1753.

The Borgo and Via della Conciliazione

If you've energy left after visiting St Peter's and the Vatican Museums, wander the warren of pedestrian streets just east of the Vatican. The first pilgrims to St Peter's were housed in hostels here, and the area is still a colony of international pilgrims today, making it the place to go for anyone wishing to buy religious items.

The relaxed charm of this atmospheric neighbourhood will soothe your tired feet as you meander along its medieval lanes and admire its ancient, ivy-clad *palazzi*. The quarter was formerly known as the Città Leonina after Leo IV, who built the fortified walls and connected the Vatican to Castel Sant'Angelo by an overhead passageway. Unfortunately a large part of the Borgo and its olde-worlde atmosphere were destroyed when Mussolini decided that St Peter's needed a more grandiose approach and tore the area in two with the Via della Conciliazione, which ruins the effect of Bernini's piazza, but allows for a full view of St Peter's.

An interesting sight on Via delle Conciliazione is the church of **Santa Maria Traspontina** (daily 7am–noon, 4–7pm), which stands on the site of an ancient Roman pyramid, said to have been Romulus' Tomb.

Map on page 138

Recommended Restaurants, Bars & Cafés on page 147

The church was built in 1527 and houses the columns to which Saints Peter and Paul are thought to have been chained before their martyrdom. Further down, the style of **Palazzo Torlonia** (30 Via delle Conciliazione, closed to public), closely resembles that of Palazzo della Cancelleria (the papal chancellery) and its facade is an example of Roman Renaissance. The Palazzo was built for a cardinal in 1496, but has had many owners, including the nobleman Giovanni Torlonia, after whom it was named, some members of the Medici family and Queen Christina of Sweden.

South of the boulevard is **Borgo Santo Spirito**. The church of **Santo Spirito in Sassia** ❻, built for the Saxons in 689, was rebuilt in the 16th century. Next door, the **Ospedale Santo Spirito** ❼ was set up by Pope Innocent III in the 13th century as an orphanage for unwanted babies. Within the hospital is the small **Museo Storico Nazionale dell'Arte Sanitaria** (3 Lungotevere in Sassia; tel: 06-678 7864; 10am–noon Mon, Wed, Fri), with an array of medical paraphernalia, and two frescoed wards.

PRATI

North of the Vatican lies the elegant residential area of Prati. Until the late 19th century, Prati was characterised by vast vineyards and gardens, hence the name, which means "meadows". The quarter was built in its present shape in response to an urgent need to expand the city after it was proclaimed capital of the newly unified nation in 1870.

Its strategic position just outside the Vatican walls makes this district convenient for sightseeing and shopping. Prati may lack the medieval charm of the Centro Storico, but if you want to get a deeper understanding of the real fabric and rhythm of everyday Roman life, then venturing into this neighbourhood is a great way to start.

Prati is easily reached on metro line A (get off at Lepanto, Ottaviano-San Pietro or Cipro-Musei Vaticani), or one of the many bus routes that terminate at Piazza del Risorgimento.

Most of the shops are concentrated around Via Cola di Rienzo and Via Ottaviano, around Piazza Mazzini, which is laid out in a large

SHOP

Another feature of Prati is its markets. The wholesale flower market at 45 Via Trionfale has blooms and plants at give-away prices. Essentially a trade market, it is open to the public on Tuesday mornings. Nearby Mercato Trionfale is one of the city's largest, and runs along Via Andrea Doria. Here you'll find fresh produce, as well as clothing and homewares. There's also a superb covered food market at Piazza dell'Unità.

BELOW: fresh produce at Mercato Trionfale.

star-shaped plan, and Piazza Cavour, immediately recognisable by its towering palms. Facing Piazza Cavour, with its rear towards the west bank of the Tiber, is the colossal **Palazzo di Giustizia** (Palace of Justice), dubbed *il palazzaccio* (the big, ugly building). Its riverfront facade is crowned with a bronze chariot and fronted by statues of the great men of Italian law.

The Museum of the Souls of Purgatory is housed within the Sacro Cuore del Suffragio (Sacred Heart of Suffrage). and was founded by Jouet, a missionary from Marseille.

Museum of the Souls of Purgatory ❽

✉ 12 Lungotevere Prati ☎ 06-6880 6517 🕒 daily 7.30–11am and 4.30–7.30pm € free 🚇 Lepanto 🚌 30, 70, 81, 87, 130, 186, 244, 492, 913, 926

A small neo-Gothic church on the Tiber's banks houses what is perhaps the strangest museum in Rome: the Museo delle Anime del Purgatorio, which some say holds proof of the existence of an afterlife. Following a fire that destroyed part of the church in the late 1800s, Father Jouet recognised the face of a suffering man in one of the smoke stains on the wall and, interpreting it as a sign from the otherworld, he decided to collect items to testify to the existence of Purgatory. Handprints on Bibles, faces marked on missals and stained nightgowns are among the few items on display in the small showcase, while many others have been removed by the church authorities because of doubts regarding their authenticity. ❑

RIGHT: the Sacro Cuore del Suffragio. **BELOW LEFT AND RIGHT:** the pleasant riverbank in the residential area of Prati.

BEST RESTAURANTS, BARS AND CAFÉS

Restaurants

Price includes dinner and a half-bottle of house wine:
€ = under €25
€€ = €25–40
€€€ = €40–60
€€€€ = more than €60

Dante Taberna de' Gracchi

✉ 266 Via dei Gracchi ☎ 06-321 3126 ⏲ D only, Mon–Sat. **€€–€€€** [p334, B2]
A relaxing pastel-coloured interior and classic cuisine based mostly on fresh fish, and a different soup every day. Choose a fine wine from an endless list.

Il Matriciano

✉ 55 Via dei Gracchi ☎ 06-321 3040 ⏲ L & D Thur–Tue. **€–€€** [p334, B2]
Just around the corner from St Peter's, this restaurant has served genuine local food for over 90 years. Its signature dish is an excellent *spaghetti all' amatriciana* (spaghetti with tomato, onion and cured pork sauce).

Napul'è

✉ 89–91 Viale Giulio Cesare ☎ 06-323 1005 ⏲ L & D daily. **€** [p334, B2]
Neapolitans approve of the pizza at this southern restaurant. Choose from 40 different styles, all boasting the typical thick crust (as opposed to the thin Roman pizza). Also serves pasta and meat dishes from the Campania region and offers live music some nights.

Osteria dell'Angelo

✉ 24 Via G. Bettolo ☎ 06-372 9470 ⏲ L Tue–Fri, D Mon–Sat. **€–€€** [p334, B2]
This neighbourhood trattoria with a fixed-price evening menu, including house wine, is always packed to the gills. Try the *fritti* to begin with, then a flavourful version of the Roman standard *tonnarelli cacio e pepe* (pasta with pecorino and pepper). Booking advisable. No credit cards.

La Pergola dei Cavalieri Hilton

✉ 101 Via A. Cadlolo, Monte Mario ☎ 06-3509 2211 ⏲ D only Tue–Sat. **€€€€** [off map p334, A1]
German superstar chef Heinz Beck has made this a place worth making a detour for. Enviable views, attentive staff and ultra-refined food *(pictured right)*. Elegant dress code.

Settembrini

✉ 25 Via Settembrini ☎ 06-323 2617 ⏲ L & D Mon–Sat. Closed in August. **€€€€** [p335, C1]
Serving both sushi and seafood pasta, Settembrini explores various cuisines and manages to combine them skilfully. The cheese and cold meat platters are the result of long ingredient research and the wine list is spectacular, with many sparkling wines.

Siciliainbocca

✉ 26 Via Faà di Bruno ☎ 06-3735 8400 ⏲ L & D Mon–Sat. **€€** [p334, B1]
Come here for a cheerful ambience and good Sicilian food seasoned with the island's flavours: lemons, olives, capers and plenty of sunshine. Their classic ricotta-filled *cassata* is excellent.

Taverna Angelica

✉ 6 Piazza Capponi ☎ 06-687 4514 ⏲ L & D Sun, D only Mon–Sat. **€€** [p334, B3]
Massimo Pinardi's restaurant has only been around a few years, but it quickly earned a reputation for high-quality food. Try smoked goose breast with celery, apple and walnuts, pasta with fennel and anchovy, or grilled swordfish with pesto.

Zen

✉ 243 Via degli Scipioni ☎ 06-321 3420 ⏲ L & D Tue–Fri & Sun, D only Sat. **€€–€€€** [p334, C2]
High-standard, fresh Japanese food is Zen's strong point. Pick your dishes as they roll past you on the city's first sushi and sashimi conveyor belt, or order the tempura and other heftier dishes à la carte. The restaurant closes for two weeks in August.

Bars and Cafés

Pellacchia (103 Via Cola di Rienzo) makes its own ice cream on the premises and is deservedly famous. On an otherwise residential street **Antonini** (19–29 Via G.Sabotino) makes the kind of cakes you bring to dinner parties when you want to impress – perfect for an aperitif. **Bar Bar** (17 Via Ovidio, www.barbar.it) is the first so-called lounge bar in the city; its long bar counter and sleek furniture give it a New York vibe.

Treasures of the Vatican

Sensory overload, known as "Stendhal's Syndrome", is a natural response to the Vatican's endless artistic riches

The Vatican Museums house one of the biggest and most important art collections in the world. They merit a lifetime's study, but for those who have only a few hours, there are some sights that simply should not be missed.

The Sistine Chapel *(see pages 150–1)* with Michelangelo's marvellous ceiling, and the four Raphael Rooms *(see page 142)* are the star attractions. The Museo Pio-Clementino contains some of the greatest sculptures of antiquity *(see opposite)*. The Pinacoteca picture gallery houses an extensive collection of paintings from Byzantine times to the present, with works by Giotto, Bellini, Titian, da Vinci, Raphael, Caravaggio and many others.

The Vatican Library contains a priceless collection of illuminated manuscripts and early printed books. The Chapel of St Nicholas has some exquisite frescoes by Fra Angelico, and frescoes by Pinturicchio can be seen in the Borgia Apartment.

More recent artwork is not neglected either, and the Modern Religious Art Collection, adjoining the apartment, displays works by Paul Klee *(far left picture)*, Francis Bacon, Max Ernst and Henri Matisse, among others. The Etruscan Museum, meanwhile, contains many artefacts found in tombs of the mysterious pre-Roman civilisation *(see pages 273–4 for more on the Etruscans)*. The Gregoriano Profano Museum houses finds from the Baths of Caracalla, on the old Via Appia.

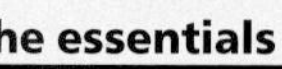

The essentials

✉ *100 Viale Vaticano; www.vatican.va*
☎ *06-6988 4947/4676*
🕘 *9am–6pm, ticket office open until 4pm* € *charge*
🚇 *Ottaviano-San Pietro, Cipro-Musei Vaticani*
🚌 *19, 23, 32, 34, 49, 62, 64, 81, 492, 913, 990, 991, 999*

CLASSICAL MASTERPIECES

The Museo Pio-Clementino houses some of the greatest sculptures of Greek and Roman antiquity. In the Octagonal Courtyard of the Belvedere are three masterpieces of classical art: the *Atleta Apoxyomenos*, a 1st-century AD copy of a 4th-century BC bronze, depicts an athlete washing himself after the exertions of a hard-run race. The beautiful *Apollo del Belvedere* , which depicts the Greek sun god, is another copy of a Greek original, which once stood in the Agora in Athens. The action-packed *Laocoön* (*pictured above*), a 1st-century BC copy of a 3rd-century BC bronze sculpture, was found near Nero's Golden House by the Colosseum. The marble statue depicts a Trojan priest of Apollo and his two sons struggling with two writhing sea serpents.

The remainder of the sculpture gallery is divided up into sections. The Hall of the Greek Cross (Sala a Croce Greca) houses porphyry sarcophagi of Emperor Constantine's mother and daughter. The Circular Hall (Sala Rotonda) has a huge gilded bronze statue of Hercules and a colossal head of Jupiter of Otricoli, a Roman copy of the Greek original. In the Hall of the Muses (Sala delle Muse) there are statues of Apollo and the Muses; in the centre, the *Belvedere Torso* (1st century BC) is a Greek work that was admired greatly by Raphael and Michelangelo.

The Animal Room (Sala degli Animali) is worth visiting for its remarkable animal statues by Antonio Franzoni (1734–1818), inspired by Roman originals. The Gallery of Statues (Galleria delle Statue) has more Roman copies of Greek originals. For the Mask Room (Gabinetto delle Maschere), intricate 2nd-century AD mosaics of theatrical masks have been brought from Hadrian's Villa at Tivoli, just outside Rome.

ABOVE (MAIN PICTURE): Borgia Pope Alexander VI (1492–1503) occupied six apartments in the Vatican Palaces and had them decorated by Pinturicchio and his pupils. The frescoes portraying scenes from the lives of the saints, with Lucrezia Borgia in the guise of St Catherine, is the undisputed highlight.
ABOVE: detail from Raphael's *School of Athens* (1510–11) showing Plato and Aristotle with students including Michelangelo (with his famous boots on), who considered Raphael an arch-rival. In the Raphael Rooms.
LEFT: Galleria delle Carte Geographiche (Gallery of Maps): this superb barrel-vaulted gallery is frescoed with maps of Italy. Most were designed by a 16th-century monk.
RIGHT: Known as the *Mars of Todi*, this 5th-century BC bronze is one of the highlights of the Etruscan art collection.

SISTINE CHAPEL

The dynamism of the figures and mastery of colour and light still astonish visitors, as they did Michelangelo's contemporaries

The Sistine Chapel was built by Sixtus IV in 1473–81 as the official private chapel of the popes. It was also used for the conclaves by which a new Pope is elected, a function the chapel preserves today. Michelangelo was engaged to paint the ceiling by Pope Julius II in 1508. He worked single-handedly, lying on his back, for four years (1508–12). When the work was finally unveiled, it set the seal on his reputation as the greatest living artist.

The ceiling depicts scenes from Genesis, starting with God dividing light from dark and ending with the drunkenness of Noah. The sides show the ancestors of Christ and, on marble thrones, the prophets and the classical sybils who prophesised Christ's coming. Above these are the *ignudi*, nude figures holding up festoons with papal symbols and medallions. In the four corners are scenes of salvation, including the dramatic hanging of Haman, and Judith swiping off Holofernes's head.

Critics cannot agree if the ceiling is a neo-Platonic statement or a theological programme devised with the help of religious experts, including, perhaps, Julius II.

ABOVE: *The Fall of Man.* One of the nine ceiling panels depicting stories of the Creation, the Fall and Noah. The panels (painted in reverse order) are as follows: 1) Separation of Light and Darkness 2) Creation of Sun, Moon and Planets 3) Separation of Land and Sea 4) Creation of Adam 5) Creation of Eve 6) the Fall, and Expulsion from Paradise 7) the Sacrifice of Noah 8) the Flood 9) the Drunkenness of Noah.

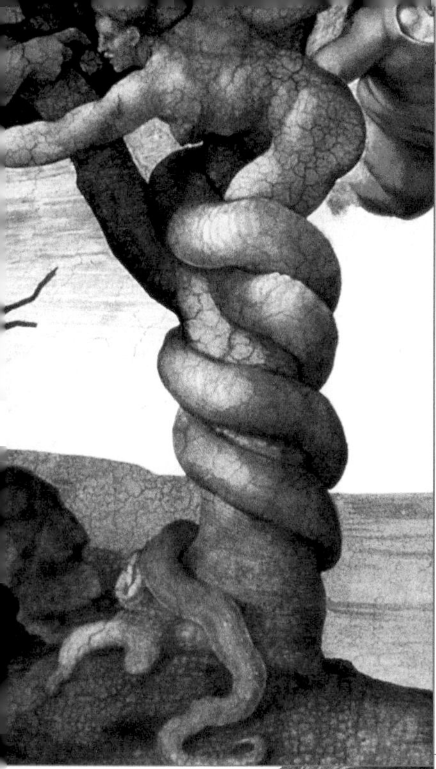

THE LAST JUDGEMENT

Some critics say the overall theme of the Sistine Chapel is salvation, reaching its climax in the Last Judgement fresco on the end wall (painted by Michelangelo between 1535 and 1541). It depicts a harrowing image of the souls of the dead rising up to face the wrath of God. The good are promoted to heaven, while the damned are cast down into hell. The figure of St Bartholomew is depicted to the right of the beardless Christ, carrying his flayed skin in his left hand. The tragic face depicted on it is Michelangelo's self-portrait; his pained expression reflected the spiritual crisis he was going through and his contemporaries' lack of comprehension.

The fresco aroused violent controversy. The nudity of the figures was criticised as indecent, but Michelangelo's patron, Paul III, was overwhelmed by the work, truly appreciating its greatness. Some of his successors were not so enlightened. In 1564, Pope Paul IV, in a fit of prudery, ordered drapery to be painted over some of the nude figures.

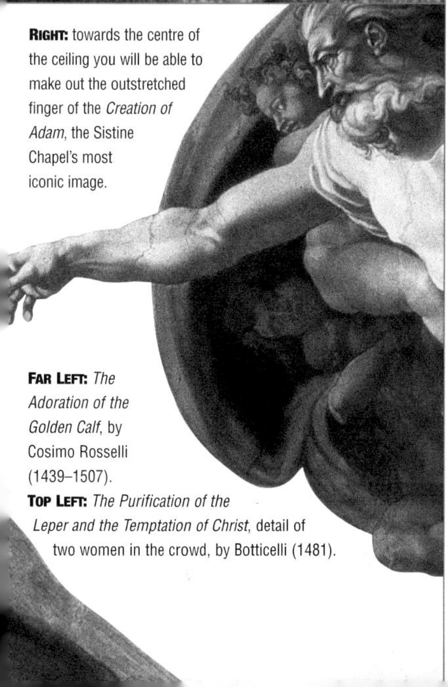

BELOW: the other paintings in the Sistine Chapel have been understandably overshadowed by Michelangelo's work. But the earlier frescoes on the lower walls illustrating scenes from the lives of Moses and Christ are worthy of more than a passing glance. They include works by Pinturicchio, Botticelli, Luca Signorelli and Perugino, who painted the fresco *Giving of the Keys to Saint Peter* (1481) pictured below.

RIGHT: towards the centre of the ceiling you will be able to make out the outstretched finger of the *Creation of Adam*, the Sistine Chapel's most iconic image.

FAR LEFT: *The Adoration of the Golden Calf*, by Cosimo Rosselli (1439–1507).

TOP LEFT: *The Purification of the Leper and the Temptation of Christ*, detail of two women in the crowd, by Botticelli (1481).

PIAZZA NAVONA AND THE PANTHEON

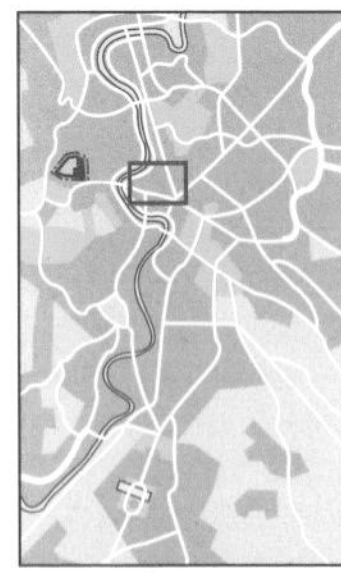

The Pantheon has stood in the heart of Rome for almost 2,000 years, while Piazza Navona is built on the foundations of a Roman stadium. Today this compact section of the Centro Storico is filled with Baroque buildings and churches, along with picturesque alfresco cafés

Main attractions

THE PANTHEON
SANTA MARIA SOPRA MINERVA
GALLERIA DORIA PAMPHILJ
GOVERNMENT BUILDINGS
SAN LUIGI DEI FRANCESI
PIAZZA NAVONA
PALAZZO ALTEMPS
SANT'IVO
PIAZZA DI PASQUINO
MUSEO DI ROMA
PONTE SANT'ANGELO
VIA DEI CORONARI

The area loosely referred to as the Centro Storico (the Historic Centre) is contained between the great bend of the Tiber to the west and Via del Corso to the east. In ancient times, the area centred on the Campus Martius (Field of Mars), an army training ground dedicated to the Roman god of war which lay outside the *Pomerium*, the sacred boundary of the city. It was here, in front of the nearby Temple of Apollo (three pillars of which can still be seen next to the Teatro di Marcello), that generals returning from their military campaigns reported to the Senate.

As building space around the central Fora became scarce, the city gradually spread beyond the ancient walls and out towards the Tiber. By Imperial times the old Campus Martius had all but disappeared, and the area was filled with theatres, baths, porticoes and arenas, and dotted with verdant public parks. All that is left to remind us of the existence of the Field of Mars is an elegant little square and street called Piazza and Via di Campo Marzio.

Rome's population shrank in the Middle Ages due to devastating plagues and the relocation of the Empire's capital to Constantinople. Those who remained moved towards the Tiber. The river was good for defence purposes, for water, which there was no access to further inland because so many of the ancient aqueducts had been destroyed, and because it provided a transport route safe from highway bandits. The river current also turned floating mills, which were tied up between the banks.

The ruins in the area also provided building materials for new houses, churches and papal

LEFT: the Pantheon, Piazza della Rotonda.

complexes. Some were used as forts or – as with the Pantheon – as churches. Almost all the major medieval, Renaissance and Baroque buildings in the Centro Storico are either expressions of an increasingly powerful Church, or reflect the intense competition for power and prestige among Rome's rich and aristocratic families.

But the Historic Centre has more to offer than churches and palaces. Its tangle of streets and alleys has been the home of the craft guilds since medieval times when these quarters were full of *botteghe* (workshops). The types of trade may have changed, but trade is still the lifeblood of the district. There are antique shops and fairs in and around Via dei Coronari and Via dell'Orso, while Piazza della Fontanella Borghese is the site of a print market.

AROUND PIAZZA DELLA ROTONDA

The Piazza della Rotonda is one of the busiest squares in the city. It's worth trying to beat the crowds by getting here as early as you can.

The Pantheon ❶

Piazza della Rotonda 06-6830 0230 Mon–Sat 8.30am–7.30pm, Sun 9am–6pm free 30, 40, 46, 62, 63, 64, 70, 81, 87, 116, 186, 204, 492, 628, 810

One of the most memorable and impressive of Rome's many architectural marvels is the Pantheon (Basilica di Santa Maria ad Martyres), the best-preserved ancient building in Rome. Originally built as a temple to all the gods, its subsequent conversion into a

One of the most interesting streets is Via dei Cestari (connecting the Pantheon and Largo Argentina). It is lined with shops selling religious raiments and equipment for the Catholic priesthood. Many facades incorporate old guild signs or pieces of ancient marble.

LEFT AND BELOW: street theatre artist and musicians.

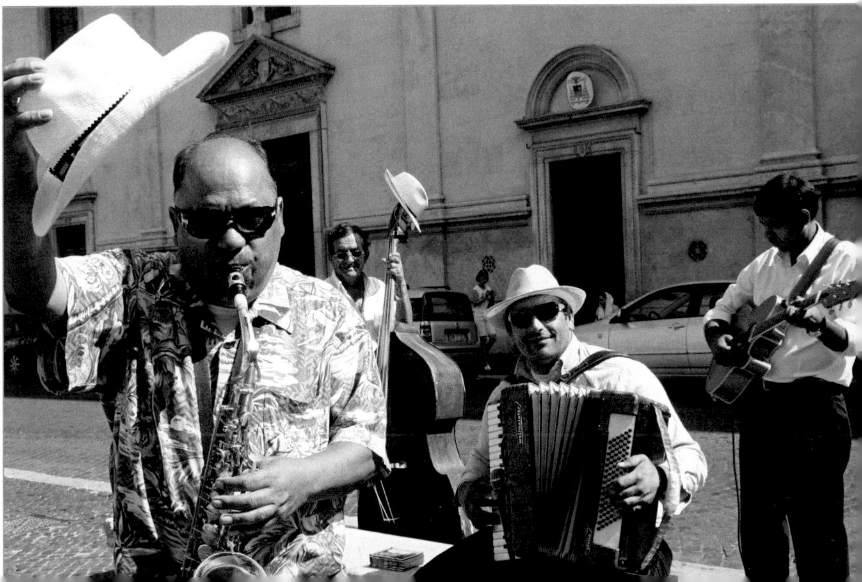

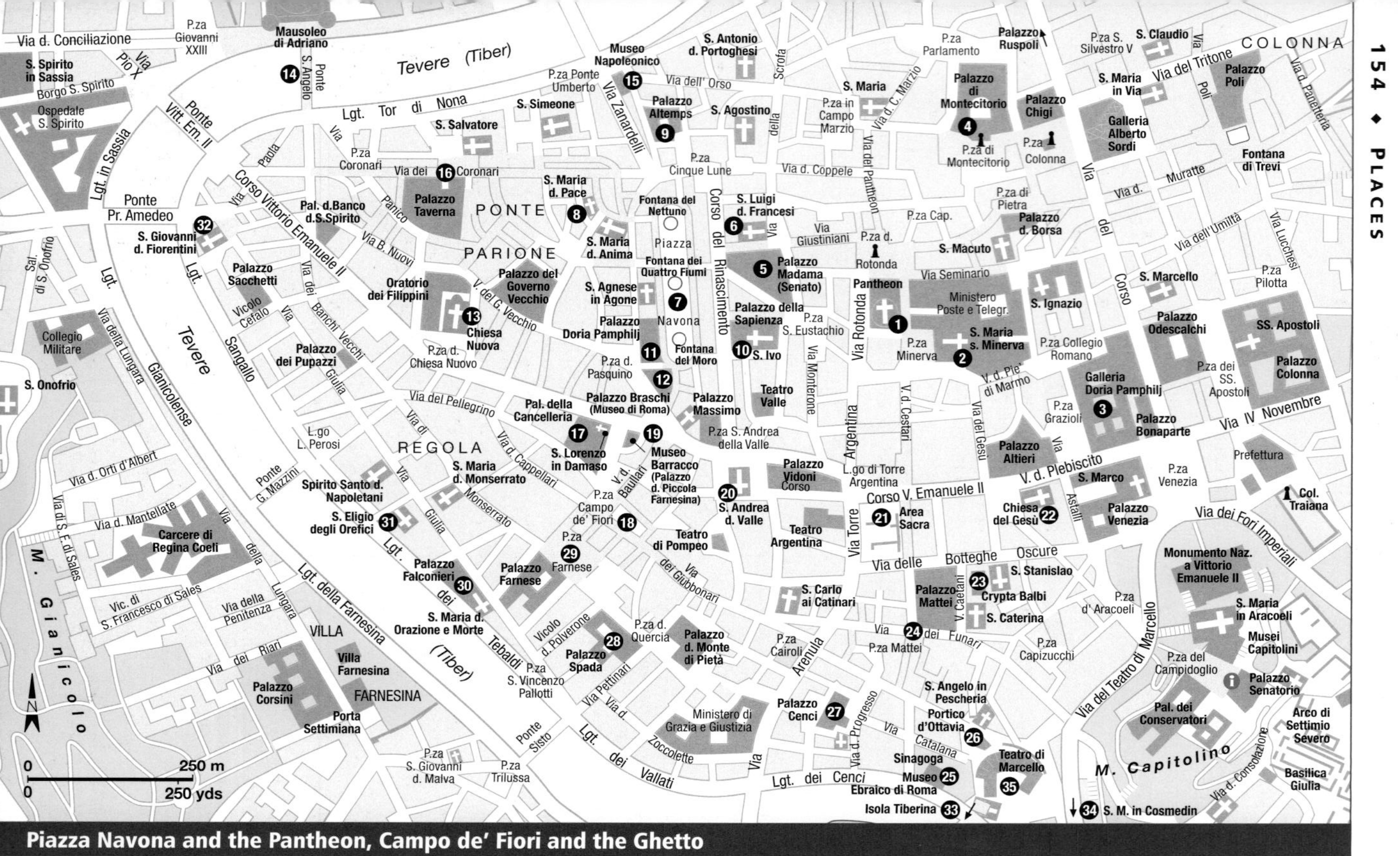

Piazza Navona and the Pantheon, Campo de' Fiori and the Ghetto

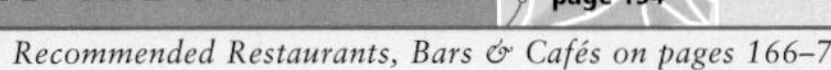

Recommended Restaurants, Bars & Cafés on pages 166–7

church in 609 saved it from being torn down. Only 15 metres (45ft) above sea level, the Pantheon is now the lowest point in Rome. The ditch around it shows just how much the rubble has raised Rome over the centuries: in ancient times one looked up to the Pantheon, not down.

As the inscription over the portico informs us, the statesman Marcus Agrippa, son-in-law of Augustus, built the original Pantheon in 27 BC in honour of the victory over Antony and Cleopatra at Actium. Agrippa's building, however, was severely damaged by fire in AD 80 and was completely rebuilt by Hadrian (AD 117–38), who has been credited as the building's architect, not just its patron.

The portico is stately and imposing: 16 massive Corinthian columns support a roof with a triangular pediment (the notches cut into the portico columns are said to have supported stalls for a fish and poultry market in the Middle Ages). The walls are 6 metres (20ft) thick and the huge bronze doors 8 metres (24ft) high. But the most striking aspect of the building is, of course, the dome *(see box below)*.

The Pantheon contains the tombs of kings and painters, Raphael (1483–1520) being one of them. The marble floor is an 1873 restoration.

Santa Maria sopra Minerva

Southeast of the Pantheon, **Santa Maria sopra Minerva** ❷ (Mon–Sat 7.10am–7pm, Sun 8am–noon and 2–7pm) is the only truly Gothic church in Rome. Built in the 8th century on the site of a temple of Minerva, its present form dates from around 1280 when it was rebuilt by Dominicans. Its most striking feature is the beautiful, Giotto-blue vaulted ceiling.

The church houses the tombs of

Living, great Nature feared he might outvie
Her works; and dying, fears herself may die.

The inscription on Raphael's tomb in the Pantheon as translated by Alexander Pope.

ABOVE: Bernini's marble elephant on Piazza Minerva supports a 6th-century obelisk.
BELOW LEFT: detail of the Pantheon facade.

The Pantheon Dome

A perfect hemisphere, and a symbol of beauty and harmony, the Pantheon dome had a profound impact on the architects of the Renaissance, influencing Brunelleschi's cathedral in Florence and Michelangelo's design for the dome of St Peter's. The height of the dome is the same as its diameter: 43.3 metres (142ft). The hole (oculus) in its centre is still the only source of light. On sunny days, a beam of light pours through the oculus and moves around the Pantheon's interior, illuminating the frescoes and tombs. Originally, the dome was covered in bronze, but the Byzantine emperor Constans II stripped the outer layer off and took it to Constantinople in 667. Almost 1,000 years later, in 1620, the Barberini Pope Urban VIII had the inner layer melted down to make cannons for Castel Sant'Angelo and Bernini's baldacchino in St Peter's. This act of papal vandalism inspired the quip that "What the Barbarians didn't do, the Barberini did".

Vaulting in Santa Maria sopra Minerva, the only true Gothic church in Rome.

several popes and cardinals, and the relics of St Catherine of Siena (the patron saint of Italy who died in the Dominican convent here in 1380). The last chapel on the right is decorated with a fresco of *The Assumption* by Filippino Lippi. In the bottom section the portraits of two young boys represent two Medici princes, future popes Leo X and Clement VII. To the left of the altar stands a Michelangelo sculpture of Christ the Redeemer, whose nudity shocked the Church at the time. It was carved as a nude figure in Florence, then sent to Rome, where it was ineptly finished by pupils.

Outside in Piazza Minerva, the jovial little **elephant statue** with an ancient Egyptian obelisk on its back was designed by Bernini in 1667.

On nearby Via del Pie' di Marmo (Street of the Marble Foot), set on a pedestal in a shadowy corner is the massive and very worn foot of an ancient Roman statue.

Beyond stands the church of **Sant' Ignazio** (daily 7.30am–12.20pm and 3–7.20pm), built between 1627 and 1685 to honour St Ignatius, founder of the Jesuit order. The interior is the usual Baroque combination of gold embellishments, marble and statuary, but the highlight is Andrea Pozzi's fantastic *trompe l'œil* views of heaven.

Just south of here (off Via del Corso) is Piazza del Collegio Romano and the entrance to the Galleria Doria Pamphilj.

Galleria Doria Pamphilj ❸

✉ Via del Corso 305; www.doriapamphilj.it ☎ 06-679 7323 ⏲ daily 10am–5pm Ⓔ charge (free audio guide) 🚌 62, 63, 81, 85, 95, 117, 119, 175

RIGHT: liturgical vestment shop on Via dei Cestari, "Religious Row". **BELOW:** priestly parade.

Recommended Restaurants, Bars & Cafés on pages 166–7

The Galleria Doria Pamphilj contains one of the best art collections in Rome, with over 400 paintings from the 15th to 18th centuries. The 17th-century palace was the residence of the once-powerful Doria Pamphilj dynasty (it is still the property of the Pamphilj family, who live in the opposite wing). Every inch of wall space in the ornate State Apartments is taken up with paintings, in keeping with the interior fashions of the time. The finest room here is the 18th-century Gallery of Mirrors – a Versailles in miniature. The light pouring in from the windows on both sides is reflected in the mirrors and gold frames to dazzling effect. The gallery is lined with sculptures, and ceiling frescoes depict the Labours of Hercules.

The collection was begun by Pamphilj Pope Innocent X, who was crowned in 1644, and expanded by subsequent generations. It includes the portrait of Innocent X by Velázquez (painted in 1649), with a penetrating gaze and a certain ruthlessness in his expression. Nearby is a bust of the Pope by Bernini, Titian's *Salomé* (one theory suggests that John the Baptist's head is a self portrait of Titian and Salomé that of a lover who rejected him), a double portrait by Raphael, and two masterpieces by a young Caravaggio – *Rest on the Flight to Egypt*, much lighter than the rest of his oeuvre, and the *Magdalene*.

Government buildings

Rome is still the centre of Italian government, and there are two important government offices in heavily guarded old *palazzi* in this area. Behind Piazza Colonna, **Palazzo di Montecitorio** ❹ is where the Chamber of Deputies has met since 1871. Before that, it was the Papal Tribunal of Justice. Bernini drew up plans for the building in 1650, and Carlo Fontana saw the design and building through to completion in 1697. Virtually all that remains of the 17th-century design is the convex curve of the facade – designed to make the building look even bigger than it is – and the rusticated columns.

The Egyptian obelisk in front of the *palazzo* dates from the 6th century BC. It was used by Emperor Augustus for an enormous sundial he laid out in 10 BC. The sundial was discovered in the crypt of the nearby church of San Lorenzo in Lucina.

Another ancient relic that was adapted to modern usage lies in the nearby Piazza di Pietra, east of Piazza della Rotonda. The **Palazzo della Borsa** takes its name from its one-time role as Rome's stock

TIP

The Palazzo Doria Pamphilj frequently hosts classical concerts, and keeps the gallery rooms open for concert-goers to visit during the performance interval. For up-to-date programme information visit www.doriapamphilj.it or www.lastravaganza musica.it.

BELOW: Titian's *Salomé* in the Galleria Doria Pamphilj.

The 6th-century BC *Egyptian obelisk stands in front of the Palazzo di Montecitorio, home to the lower house of government.*

BELOW: Bernini's Fountain of the Four Rivers.

exchange. Prior to that, the building, with its 11 ancient columns, was a customs house, and originally, in the 2nd century AD, it was the Temple of Hadrian, which is how it is mostly referred to now.

The Senate has occupied the elegant **Palazzo Madama** ❺ between Piazza della Rotonda and Piazza Navona since 1870. It was built for the Medici family in the early 16th century, and several of its members lived here before becoming Pope.

The palace gets its name from the Habsburg Madama Margherita (1522–86), the illegitimate daughter of Emperor Charles V and the wife of Alessandro de' Medici.

Caravaggio chapel

Opposite is the Baroque church of **San Luigi dei Francesi** ❻ (10am–12.30 pm and 4–7pm, closed Thur pm), the French national church in Rome, built in 1589. It contains works by Giacomo della Porta and Domenico Fontana, but it is the three Caravaggio masterpieces in the Capella Contarelli, showing scenes from the life of St Matthew (*The Calling of St Matthew*, *The Martyrdom of St Matthew* and *St Matthew and the Angel* – painted between 1599 and 1602) that make a visit very worthwhile. These wonderful and moving paintings demonstrate Caravaggio's astounding mastery of light and dramatic realism. Have a euro handy to light the chapel up.

AROUND PIAZZA NAVONA

Piazza Navona ❼ is one of the most animated squares in Rome, invariably full of Romans and foreign visitors wandering among stalls set up by hopeful artists, relaxing with a coffee in one of the many bars, or stopping for a chat by its gushing fountains.

Piazza Navona was built over the remains of the emperor Domitian's ancient athletics stadium: the stand forms part of the foundations of the flanking houses, and you can see one of the original entrances just behind the north end of the square.

The stadium originally measured 50 by 275 metres (150 by 825ft), with the seats rising to 35 metres (105ft). It was used for athletic contests and

horse races, and was probably still in use when the Goths invaded in the 5th century. However, the plundering of its fabric began under Constantius II (third son of Constantine the Great), who carried off works of art and decorative features in 356 to adorn his new residence in Constantinople, after the seat of the Empire had been moved there.

Three fountains

The piazza owes its Baroque appearance to the Pamphilj Pope, Innocent X (1644–55), who enlarged his family palace and commissioned the square's magnificent centrepiece, Bernini's **Fontana dei Quattro Fiumi** (Fountain of the Four Rivers). The rivers in question – the Danube, the Ganges, the Nile and the Plate – are represented by four huge allegorical figures who in turn represent the four continents Europe, Asia, Africa and America. The Nile is blindfolded because the source of the river was then still a mystery. Rising above the statues is an obelisk taken from the Circus of Maxentius. The obelisk is topped by the figure of a dove with an olive branch to show that this once pagan monument has been converted into a Christian one.

To the south of the square is the **Fontana del Moro** (Fountain of the Moor). Its central figure (which

Street artists and caricaturists make a good living from the regular flow of tourist traffic on Piazza Navona.

LEFT: *St Matthew and the Angel* by Caravaggio.
BELOW: Piazza Navona.

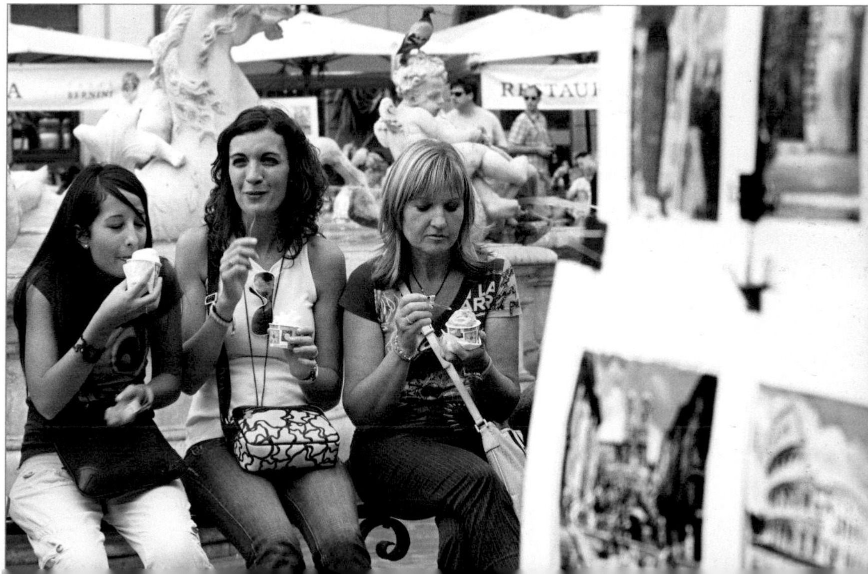

From December until early January, Piazza Navona hosts a colourful Christmas fair at which all sorts of decorations, toys, sweets and Baroque-style Nativity scenes are sold. It lasts until the Epiphany (6 January), when friendly old ladies on broomsticks (*befane*) hand candy to well-behaved children.

looks more like a Triton than a Moor) was designed by Bernini.

The **Fontana del Nettuno** (Fountain of Neptune) at the northern end was originally just a large basin. The sculptures were added in the 19th century to create symmetry.

Churches and palaces

Pope Innocent also commissioned the Borromini facade of **Sant' Agnese in Agone**. Here, it is said, the saint was pilloried and stood naked in the stocks until her hair miraculously grew to protect her modesty. Inside the church there are underground chambers where you can see the ruins of the stadium of Domitian, a Roman mosaic floor and medieval frescoes on the wall.

To the left of the church is **Palazzo Doria Pamphilj** (not to be confused with the Galleria Doria Pamphilj), designed by Rainaldi in the mid-17th century. It now houses the Brazilian Embassy.

Just off the square is the church of **Santa Maria della Pace** ❽ (Mon, Wed, Fri 9am–noon), rebuilt in 1482 and then restored in 1656, when the convex, Baroque facade was added. The church contains Raphael's frescoes of *The Four Sybils*.

The nearby **Santa Maria dell' Anima** (daily 9am–12.45pm and 3–7pm) is the German-speaking church of Rome and was founded in 1500, although the present building was heavily restored in the 19th century. Apart from a Romano altarpiece, most of the works of art inside are by pupils and followers of Caravaggio, Michelangelo and Raphael.

Palazzo Altemps ❾

✉ 44 Piazza di Sant'Apollinare (nr Piazza Navona) ☎ 06-3996 7700

RIGHT: Fountain of the Moor. **BELOW RIGHT:** one of the four allegorical figures in Bernini's Fountain of the Four Rivers. **BELOW:** Fountain of Neptune.

Tue–Sun 9am–7.45pm charge (combination ticket valid for three days includes Palazzo Massimo alle Terme, the Baths of Diocletian and Crypta Balbi) 30, 40, 46, 62, 64, 70, 81, 87, 116, 492, 571, 628, 916

Just north of Piazza Navona, Palazzo Altemps is one of the four sites of the Museo Nazionale Romano which holds the state collection of ancient treasures; the rest of the collection is split between Palazzo Massimo alle Terme, the Terme di Diocleziano, and the Crypta Balbi *(see page 173)*.

Full of tranquil rooms set around a central courtyard, this airy museum contains many treasures of classical statuary and art, most of which come from the priceless collection amassed by Cardinal Ludovisi. The prize exhibit is the Ludovisi Throne, a decorative Greek sculpture, thought to date from the 5th century BC, which Mussolini sold to Hitler in 1938, and which is now believed to be one of a pair. Upstairs, the vaulting of the loggia is intricately painted with a vine-covered pergola full of winged putti, flowers, fruits and exotic birds, inspired by the flora and fauna imported by the explorers of the New World. It is lined with busts of the 12 Caesars.

Other masterpieces here include an incredibly well-preserved carved sarcophagus from the 3rd century and the moving *Galata Suicide*, said to have been commissioned by Julius Caesar, purchased by the cardinal at the same time as the *Dying Gaul*, now in the Capitoline Museum *(see page 94)*.

The *palazzo* also contains many frescoes and bas-reliefs, a private chapel and parts of the ancient Roman houses on which its foundations can be seen.

Remedies for the sweet of tooth and fractious children. Gumdrops in this tempting display are poetically named "tears of love".

LEFT: the Ludovisi Throne. **BELOW:** courtyard of the Palazzo Altemps.

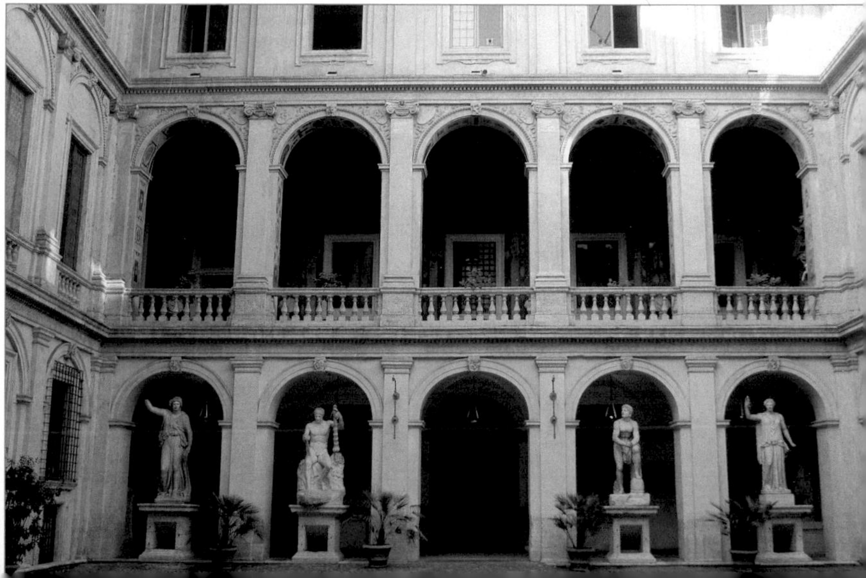

Talking Statues

Rome's "talking statues" were the mouthpieces of discontent in the city during the Renaissance

Rome's "talking statues" are a tradition born in the 1500s, when the citizens were governed directly by the Papacy. To avoid punishment they would secretly hang their caustic criticism, stinging epigrams and short satiric verses on a statue. This political dissidence often took place at night, the Romani enjoying a good laugh in the morning before the insults were removed by the authorities. The statues were sometimes draped with poems or jokes, but most often the postings were broadsides against the Vatican. The statues soon earned nicknames, the best-known being the Pasquino (Piazza di Pasquino, *see page 163*). This torso of a male figure, possibly from the 3rd century BC, is in such poor condition that it is hard to know who, or what, it represents. The roots of his nickname are recounted in a Roman legend saying he was "discovered" near a barber's shop or inn run by a Signor Pasquino.

The best-known "pasquinate" barb is a pun against Pope Urban VIII. This Pope from the Barberini family commanded Bernini to strip the ancient Roman bronze parts of the Pantheon to make the great baldacchino canopy for St Peter's altar. "*Quod non*

fecerunt barbari, fecerunt Barberini" ("What the barbarians didn't do, the Barberini did") quipped Pasquino. This statuesque satire became so fervent that Pope Adrianus VI (1522–23) wanted Pasquino cast into the Tiber. The risk of ridicule for punishing a lump of stone saved the statue from the river bed – but severe laws were issued to stop the practice, and Pasquino was put under surveillance.

Marforio is known as Pasquino's friend. He and Pasquino were a bantering double act: one posing questions about politics and popes, the other retorting ironically. Marforio's statue – a reclining river god – is now in the Capitoline Museum; he was silenced when he was removed from the Roman Forum and placed in the museum by the Vatican for "safe keeping".

The Facchino (Porter) is a small fountain on Via Lata (just off the Via del Corso). Dressed in a typical porter's costume, nobody knows who made the statue – though it was once, wrongly, attributed to Michelangelo.

Madama Lucrezia sits on the corner of Piazza San Marco (next to Piazza Venezia). This marble is probably associated with the goddess Isis. Her nickname derives from a 15th-century Lucrezia who fell in love with the married king of Naples. Lucrezia came to Rome to ask the Pope to let the king divorce, but permission was denied. When the king died, Lucrezia moved to Rome – living near the Piazza San Marco.

The statue of the Babuino (Baboon) gives the Via del Babuino its name. This diminutive statue of Silenus (the ancient Greek woodland satyr) reclines on a fountain outside the church of St Athanasius. His wicked grin and his grubby brown torso make him one of the best-known of the talking statues – which became known collectively as *il Congresso degli Arguti* (the Shrewd Congress).

Until very recently the Babuino was still opining, with modern Romans venting their spleen in graffito and messages on the wall behind him. In a strange echo of past political censorship, the "messages" on the wall were recently cleaned up, as were all the statues, which are now back to their original shade of white. ❑

ABOVE: Marforio, Pasquino's friend. **LEFT:** the marble torso on Piazza Pasquino is still festooned with comments on the events of the day.

East of Piazza Navona, on the parallel Corso del Rinascimento, is the **Palazzo della Sapienza,** which housed the headquarters of Rome's oldest university, La Sapienza, until it moved to the Stazione Termini area in 1935. It is now home of the State Archives. In the square is Borromini's **Sant'Ivo** ❿ (Sun 9am–noon only), a Roman Baroque church with a striking, white, spiralling bell-tower and unusual facade. On the main altar is a 1661 canvas by da Cortona showing St Ivo and other saints surrounded by angels.

LEFT: Sant'Ivo.
BELOW: inside Palazzo della Sapienza.

Piazza di Pasquino

Off the southern end of Piazza Navona is **Piazza di Pasquino** ⓫. The mutilated marble torso leaning against the wall is thought to date from the 3rd century BC. It was found in Piazza Navona and brought here in the 15th century when it became one of Rome's "talking statues".

The statue leans against a wall of the **Palazzo Braschi**, one of the last papal palaces built in Rome, in the 18th century. The *palazzo* is home to the newly renovated Museo di Roma.

Museo di Roma ⓬

10 Piazza San Pantaleo;
www.museodiroma.comune.roma.it
06-0608 Tue–Sun 9am–7pm
charge as for Palazzo Altemps

The Palazzo Braschi was built by Cosimo Morelli in the closing years of the 18th century as a papal residence for Pius VI (the chapel and staircase are by Valadier). It houses a

Avoid the overpriced cafés on Piazza Navona. For a glass of wine and plate of cheese, cold cuts, pâté or any combination of snacks and salads, the Cul de Sac wine bar on Piazza Pasquino is a good place to know about.

Palazzo Braschi, the former papal residence, now houses part of the Museo di Roma.

BELOW: *The Puppet Theatre*, by Achille Pinelli (1809–41), in the Museo di Roma.

sizeable collection of art and artefacts which document the daily life of Roman nobility from medieval times to the beginning of the 20th century.

Part of the collection is housed in the Museo di Roma in Trastevere, and the rest is shown in rotation. Most interesting among the paintings, which are of more historic than artistic value, is the series illustrating Roman festivities and processions.

Palazzo Massimo alle Colonne, next door to the Braschi, was designed in 1536 by Baldassare Peruzzi for the Massimo family, who occupy it to this day. The building is screened by a fine curved portico of Doric columns visible from the Via del Paradiso. Behind the palace, in Piazza de' Massimi, is an ancient column that may have come from the remains of Domitian's stadium.

Around Corso Vittorio Emanuele II

Towards the Tiber end of the Corso Vittorio Emanuele II stands the 16th-century **Chiesa Nuova** ⓭, built for San Filippo Neri, founder of a great spiritual order. St Philip had wished the interior to be plain, but in the centuries after his death his disciples commissioned da Cortona to paint the magnificent frescoes that decorate the vault, apse and dome. Among the church's other treasures are three altarpieces by Rubens.

Next to the church is the **Oratorio dei Filippini**, built by Borromini between 1637 and 1662 as a place of worship for St Philip Neri's fraternity. St Philip was a strong believer in the spiritual benefit of music and instituted the musical gatherings that later became known as oratorios. The building now houses the Capitoline Historical Archives. Its facade was inspired by "the human body

Recommended Restaurants, Bars & Cafés on pages 166–7

with open arms so as to embrace everyone who enters".

In **Piazza della Chiesa Nuova** is a 17th-century fountain that came from the Campo de' Fiori. On the rim of its basin is the inscription: *Ama Dio e non fallire – Fa del bene e lascia dire* (Love God and don't fail – Do good and make sure people talk about it).

The nearby **Palazzo del Governo Vecchio** was the residence of the governor of Rome from 1624 until the mid-18th century.

The embankment

A little further west along Corso Vittorio Emanuele II is the **Palazzo del Banco di Santo Spirito**. Its facade (1520s) is by Antonio da Sangallo the Younger. From here, Via Banco di Santo Spirito leads to the lovely **Ponte Sant'Angelo** ⓮ *(see page 144)*.

At the southern end of the next bridge upriver, Ponte Umberto I, is the **Museo Napoleonico** ⓯ (tel: 06-0608; Tue–Sun 9am–7pm; admission charge). Among the Bonaparte family memorabilia is a cast of the right breast of Napoleon's sister, Pauline, made by Canova in 1805, when he

started work on the reclining nude in the Galleria Borghese *(see page 192)*.

The nearby **Via dell'Orso** used to be lined with inns and was a favourite haunt of courtesans. Today, the area is better-known for its antique shops, interspersed with classy boutiques selling modern designer furniture. The **Via dei Coronari** ⓰ is packed with some of the best antiques and fine-arts shops in Rome. ❑

For nearly a century, La Mostra dell'Antiquariato, a twice-yearly antiques market, has been held on Via dei Coronari. Every May and October dealers literally roll out the red carpet along the street and stay open for late-night shopping, while torches and candles light the way.

ABOVE LEFT AND BELOW: the traffic-free Ponte Sant'Angelo is Rome's loveliest bridge.

BEST RESTAURANTS, BARS AND CAFÉS

Restaurants

Price includes dinner and a half-bottle of house wine:
€ = under €25
€€ = €25–40
€€€ = €40–60
€€€€ = more than €60

Da Baffetto

✉ 114 Via del Governo Vecchio ☎ 06-686 1617 ⌚ D only, daily. € [p335, C4]
One of the city's legendary pizzerias. Not the best pizza in town, but almost, its typically thin base always on the right side of crusty. Service is brisk and the turnaround is fast, but if you go early or late, it is more relaxed. Be prepared to queue as no bookings are taken. No frills, no tablecloths, no credit cards. Closed two weeks Aug.

La Cantina di Ninco Nanco

✉ 36 Via Pozzo delle Cornacchie ☎ 06-6813 5558 ⌚ L & D daily. €€ [p335, D4]
A friendly restaurant specializing in the authentic flavours of the southern region of Basilicata. The sunny countryside is reflected in the simple meat and pasta recipes. Friendly waiters and well-stocked wine cellar.

Casa Bleve

✉ 48–49 Via del Teatro Valle ☎ 06-686 5970 ⌚ L & D Tue–Sat. €–€€ [p335, D4]
Set against the stunning backdrop of the restored Palazzo Medici Lante della Rovere. An enormous semicircular counter is laden with all kinds of cold meats, salads and cheeses. Beyond, there's seating in a large, atmospherically-lit room. With an exceptional wine list, this is a high-level *enoteca* worth seeking out. Closed three weeks Aug.

Clemente alla Maddalena

✉ 4/5 Piazza della Maddalena ☎ 06-683 3633 ⌚ L & D daily. €€€ [p335, D4]
The owner prides himself on the freshness of the ingredients, and the menu changes according to the season, with fresh fish, selected meat cuts, and porcini mushrooms in autumn. The setting is charming and elegant, and there's a pleasant terrace for the summer.

Il Convivio Troiani

✉ 28 Vicolo dei Soldati ☎ 06-686 9432 ⌚ D only Mon–Sat, L by request for groups of 8 and over. €€€€ [p335, D3]
Run by three brothers, Il Convivio is one of the city's foremost gastronomic temples. Equal emphasis is placed on vegetable, fish and meat options, but they are always combined with something unexpected. Three elegant rooms and well-trained staff make for a truly rounded gourmet experience.

Cul de Sac

✉ 73 Piazza di Pasquino ☎ 06-6880 1094 ⌚ L & D daily. €–€€ [p335, D4]
One of the best-stocked wine bars in Rome. Space may be tight, but the atmosphere, prices and array of cheeses, cold meats, Middle Eastern-influenced snacks, hearty soups and salads all hit the right spot. It gets packed, so be prepared to queue as bookings aren't taken. Open late.

Il Fico

✉ 49 Via di Monte Giordano ☎ 06-687 5568 ⌚ L & D daily, in winter D only Mon. €€ [p335, C4]
This friendly eatery is very reasonably priced for its location, a stone's throw from Piazza Navona. All dishes are made with fresh seasonal ingredients. Try the pasta with mussels, pecorino cheese and cherry tomatoes.

Fortunato al Pantheon

✉ 55 Via del Pantheon ☎ 06-679 2788 ⌚ L & D Mon–Sat. €€–€€€ [p335, D4]
A place for those who don't want to take risks but want to eat well and be served quickly and efficiently. People keep coming back for the simple classical dishes, such as spinach and ricotta ravioli cooked with butter and sage, grilled squid or veal served with rocket.

Maccheroni

✉ 44 Piazza delle Coppelle ☎ 06-6830 7895. ⌚ L & D daily. €€ [p335, D3]
A lively trattoria with several rooms and some outdoor tables. It attracts a youngish clientele drawn by fair prices and typical, competent cuisine.

O' Pazzariello

✉ 19 Via Banco di Santo Spirito ☎ 06-6819 2641 ⌚ D only Tue–Wed, L & D Thur–Sun. € [p334, C4]
With an exhibitionist pizza-cook and *simpatico* waiters, this is a sure bet for a fun and affordable evening. The pizzas are thick-crusted and range from small to gigantic.

Osteria dell'Ingegno

✉ 45 Piazza di Pietra ☎ 06-678 0662 ⌚ L & D Mon–Sat. €€ [p335, E4]
Much frequented by politicians due to its

ABOVE RIGHT: Osteria dell'Ingegno.

location near parliament, this modern *osteria* specialises in light, inventive dishes. The sweets are home-made and the wines well chosen.

L'Osteria di Memmo

✉ 22 Via dei Soldati ☎ 06-6813 5277 ◷ L & D Mon–Sat. **€€–€€€** [p335, D3]

In an old *palazzo*, three elegant rooms have been made over in modern minimalist style. The menu is creative, though first courses are a bit hit and miss. However, the main courses, desserts and wines compensate for any shortcomings.

Riccioli Café

✉ 13 Via delle Coppelle ☎ 06-6821 0313 ◷ B, Br, L & D Mon–Sat (10–2am). **€–€€** [p335, D3]

Riccioli Café was the first oyster bar in the city and serves sushi and sashimi, all beautifully displayed on wooden counters. It's one of the buzziest bars in the area at *aperitivo* hour.

La Rosetta

✉ 8 Via della Rosetta ☎ 06-686 1002 ◷ L & D Mon–Sat, D only Sun. **€€€€** [p335, D4]

One of the best seafood restaurants in Rome, where the produce is guaranteed to have been caught that morning and prepared by an experienced chef. Unless you go for the "working lunch" or a set-price *degustazione* (tasting) menu, your bill is likely to tip the **€**100-a-head mark for a full meal.

Terra di Siena

✉ 77–78 Piazza Pasquino ☎ 06-6830 7704 ◷ L & D daily. **€€** [p335, D4]

Carnivores flock to this family-run restaurant, with dishes including succulent beef tagliata and the famed Fiorentina steak. The menu is 100% Tuscan, and portions are generous. The wine list includes a wide variety of Chianti labels.

Da Tonino

✉ 18 Via del Governo Vecchio ☎ 33 5587 0779 ◷ L & D Mon–Sat. **€** [p335, C4]

As the weekend queues testify, this is one of Rome's best-loved eateries. Excellent local food, served in generous portions. Thursday is fresh gnocchi and tripe night; Friday is fish and *pasta e ceci* (pasta and chickpeas) night. No credit cards.

Vecchia Locanda

✉ 2 Vicolo Sinibaldi ☎ 06-6880 2831 ◷ D only Mon–Sat. **€€** [p335, D4]

In a pedestrianised alleyway, this rustic restaurant offers decent if a little unadventurous food. A nice touch is that you can choose which home-made pasta to go with which home-made sauce.

Bars and Cafés

For a genteel snack lunch or tea with home-made cake, head to the delightful **Caffè Novecento** (12 Via del Governo Vecchio) not far from Piazza Navona.

The recipe for success at celebrated **Caffè Sant'Eustachio** (82 Piazza Sant'Eustachio) seems to lie in the water, coming from a 2000-year-old aqueduct, and in the wood-roasted Sant'Eustachio coffee blend.

The **Tazza D'Oro** (84 Via degli Orfani) serves some of the tastiest coffee in town. Standing room only.

For ice cream, **Giolitti** (40 Via Uffici del Vicario) has been scooping dozens of flavours since 1900, and has an olde-worlde dining room inside. **Cremeria Monteforte** (22 Via della Rotonda) makes some of the best-quality ice cream in Rome. The flavours are relatively few, but choosing is still difficult as they are all equally tantalising. Mini-cones are available to try a flavour out.

La Caffettiera (65 Piazza di Pietra) is a smart café where you can enjoy Neapolitan goodies.

Le Coppelle (52 Piazza delle Coppelle) has a central location and a great line in cocktails. Outdoor seating in summer, and a cosmopolitan vibe.

Recommended Restaurants, Bars & Cafés on pages 181–3

CAMPO DE' FIORI AND THE GHETTO

People have lived and worked in this picturesque part of Rome since the Middle Ages. The tangle of cobbled streets and alleys lead to the vibrant Campo de' Fiori market square and beyond into Europe's longest-surviving Jewish community

The southern part of Rome's Centro Storico is a triangle of tightly packed streets between the Corso Vittorio Emanuele II, Via Arenula and the river, with the lively little market square of Campo de' Fiori at its hub. In ancient times this area was part of the Field of Mars (Campus Martius), a main training ground for the Roman army *(see page 152)*, until Julius Caesar's reign when the moneyed citizens of Imperial Rome moved in and built great complexes and theatres. By the Middle Ages, the area was a warren of small, dark, narrow streets, with the eastern side occupied by the Ghetto, lively now but a poignant reminder of the Jewish community's suffering.

In 1880, the rulers of a newly unified Italy set about putting their mark on the city and built the Corso Vittorio over the ancient tract of Via Trionfale and the winding, medieval Via Papale, destroying beautifully proportioned Renaissance squares and buildings in the process.

The resulting avenue had none of the grandeur that was intended, and today it's a traffic-choked thoroughfare that disrupts the beauty and harmony of the medieval streets around it.

LEFT: Nuns at Campo de' Fiori produce market. **RIGHT:** Jewish quarter.

AROUND CORSO VITTORIO EMANUELE II

Set off down the Corso from the Ponte Vittorio Emanuele, then turn right into **Via dei Banchi Vecchi.** At No. 22 is the fanciful facade of **Palazzo dei Pupazzi**, built in 1504 and decorated with elaborate stucco designs by Mazzoni. This street leads to **Via del Pellegrino**, which winds past artisans' workshops, bookshops and antique dealers to **Palazzo della Cancelleria** ⓱, a splendid Renaissance palace built between 1485 and

Main attractions

- CAMPO DE' FIORI MARKET
- MUSEO BARRACCO
- AREA SACRA
- IL GESÙ
- CRYPTA BALBI
- PIAZZA MATTEI
- JEWISH GHETTO
- THE SYNAGOGUE AND MUSEUM
- PORTICO D'OTTAVIA
- PALAZZO CENCI
- PALAZZO SPADA
- PIAZZA FARNESE
- TIBER ISLAND
- SANTA MARIA IN COSMEDIN
- THEATRE OF MARCELLUS

With its reputation for being a carnal, pagan place, the Campo de' Fiori was a natural spot to hold executions. Of all the unfortunate victims, Giordano Bruno was the most important figure to be burnt at the stake here, in 1600. A priest and philosopher, he was found guilty of freethinking, claiming that the earth was not the centre of the universe but revolved round the sun, a belief which cost him his life.

1527. The architect is unknown but the beautiful courtyard is attributed to Bramante, who also modified the adjoining 4th-century basilica of **San Lorenzo in Damaso**. Bramante had a reputation for destroying medieval monuments (the ancient St Peter's basilica is a prime example), which earned him the nickname *Maestro Ruinante* (Master Ruiner).

The palace was built for Cardinal Raffaele Riario, who is said to have financed it from the proceeds of one night's gambling, before being confiscated by the Pope and used as the Apostolic Chancery. The Sala Riaria and the Salone dei Cento Giorni (the only two rooms of the palace that can be seen), along with the Salviati chapel, can be visited by appointment only (tel: 06-6989 3405, Mon–Sat).

ABOVE RIGHT AND BELOW: fresh produce, flowers and novelty t-shirts can all be bought at Campo de' Fiori.

Campo de' Fiori ⓲

South of the Cancelleria is the lively **Campo de' Fiori** (Field of Flowers), so named because it used to be a meadow that sloped down towards the Tiber. It has been the site of a produce market for centuries and was one of the liveliest areas of medieval and Renaissance Rome, when cardinals and pilgrims would rub shoulders with fishmongers, vegetable-sellers and prostitutes.

The Campo de' Fiori is the most secular of Roman squares, for although it is as old as Rome itself, it has never been dedicated to any

cult and to this day is free of churches. Its present aspect dates from the end of the 15th century, when the whole area was reshaped. It was surrounded by inns for pilgrims and travellers (there are still plenty of hotels in the area if you don't mind the noise). During the Renaissance, some of these hotels were the homes of successful courtesans, Vannozza Catanei, mistress of the Borgia Pope Alexander VI, among them. On the corner of the square and Via del Pellegrino you can see her shield, which she had decorated with her own coat of arms and those of her husband and lover.

Today, the Campo flourishes, thanks to a perfectly balanced infrastructure. It has everything from a butcher's and a baker's shop to clothes boutiques, a cinema and a bustling morning food market. At night, the Campo plays host to hundreds of Romans and visitors who frequent the bars and restaurants or simply hang out under the statue of Bruno, sipping beers until late into the night. Then the Campo has only a few hours to breathe before the market traders arrive to set up their stalls at the crack of dawn.

The streets around Campo de' Fiori still retain the names of trades originally practised in them. Via dei Baullari, the luggage-makers, leads to Piazza Farnese; Via dei Giubbonari, named after the sellers and makers of *gipponi* or bodices, is still lined with clothes shops, which are among some of the cheapest in town.

Museo Barracco ⓳

166 Corso Vittorio Emanuele; www.museobarracco.it 06-6880 6848 Tue–Sun 9am–7pm charge 30, 40, 46, 62, 64, 70, 81, 87, 116, 492, 628

Via dei Cappellari was where the hat-makers congregated, but is now full of furniture restorers, gilders and carpenters practising their trade on the street.

LEFT: Campo de' Fiori market trader. **BELOW:** visit Roscioli Alimentari for gourmet food.

Antique sculptures on display at the refurbished Museo Barracco.

Turning back up Via dei Baullari to Corso Vittorio, you reach **Palazzo Piccola Farnesina** in Piazza San Pantaleo. Built for a French prelate, Thomas Leroy, in 1523 and decorated with fleurs-de-lis, this elegant Renaissance palace is now home to the Museo Barracco, a prestigious collection of antique sculpture. Artworks include Assyrian bas-reliefs, Attic vases, rare examples of Cypriot art and exceptional Phoenician, Etruscan and Roman pieces. It's easy to see why Giovanni Barracco, who spent his life collecting these masterpieces, called ancient sculpture "the mother of all the arts".

Further along Corso Vittorio, the magnificent church of **Sant' Andrea della Valle** ⓴ (daily 7.30am–12.30pm and 4.30–7.30pm) has the second-largest dome in Rome after St Peter's. Its design is largely by Maderno, with frescoes by Lanfranco and Domenichino. The church is the setting for Act I of Puccini's much-loved opera, *Tosca.*

The church stands over some of the remains of the **Teatro di Pompeo**, a huge complex that spread from Campo de' Fiori to the temples at Largo Argentina. It was built in 55 BC as part of a plan to introduce some culture to Rome, but the Romans preferred the blood-and-guts entertainment of gladiators, fake battles and animal fights. You can ask one of the priests to take you downstairs for a look.

Next to the theatre was the **Curia Pompeia** where Julius Caesar was stabbed to death on the Ides of March (15 March), 44 BC. Remains of the theatre have been discovered in the cellars of the surrounding houses, and are visible at the Da Pancrazio and Da Costanzo restaurants, and in the breakfast room of Hotel Teatro di Pompeo, for those in the mood to eat or sleep amid famous ruins.

BELOW: one of Rome's many stray cats. **BELOW RIGHT:** Area Sacra.

Largo di Torre Argentina

Next stop on Corso Vittorio is Largo di Torre Argentina, one of the busiest crossroads in the city and a major bus interchange. Its architecture – *palazzi,* banks and insurance companies – isn't very exciting. Only **Teatro Argentina**, a state-funded theatre and

The Cat Women of Rome

The city's stray cat population numbers in the hundreds of thousands. Originally said to have boarded Rome-bound ships from Egypt, the felines made themselves at home among the ancient monuments. Since the excavation of the **Area Sacra** in 1929, stray cats have been taking refuge in the protected area below street level, sunning themselves amid the ruins at Largo di Torre Argentina. As their numbers grew, volunteer cat caretakers, referred to as *gattare* (cat women) fed and cared for the cats until an official sanctuary was established in 1993. The organisation receives donations and support from all over the world, and has even established a cat adoption agency. Visit the centre for more information and a look at some of Rome's oldest residents. Largo di Torre Argentina; www.romancats.de; tel: 06-454 2540; open daily noon– 6pm.

official home of the Teatro di Roma, radiates any atmosphere.

The real attractions lie in the middle of the square, several metres underground. During attempts to improve the road system in the 1920s, archaeologists excavated four temples (street levels in ancient times were some 10 metres/30ft below today's level). The **Area Sacra** ㉑ dates from Republican times, around the 3rd and 4th centuries BC. It is not known to which gods the temples were consecrated, so they are known simply as temples A, B, C and D. Some of the remains, inhabited by Rome's many stray cats *(see opposite)*, can be seen from above.

East of the square is the church of the **Gesù** ㉒ (7am– 12.30pm and 4–7.45pm), more properly called Santissimo Nome di Gesù. Built between 1568 and 1584 with funds provided by the powerful Cardinal Alessandro Farnese, it was Rome's first Jesuit church. The flamboyance of its design and decoration look forward to the Baroque churches of the next century. The founder of the Jesuit order, St Ignatius Loyola, is buried in the opulent Cappella di Sant'Ignazio di Loyola, built by Andrea del Pozzo in 1696. Above the chapel's altar is a statue of the saint, framed by gilded lapis lazuli columns.

Crypta Balbi ㉓

31 Via delle Botteghe Oscure
06-678 0167 Tue–Sun 9am–7.45pm charge 46, 62, 70, 87, 186, 492, 571, 810, 916

Not far from the Gesù church is the Crypta Balbi, one of the four homes of the Museo Nazionale Romano collection *(see page 161)*. This huge courtyard, originally annexed to a theatre built for Augustus at the end of the 1st century AD, was excavated in 1981 and forms the basis for the fascinating Crypta Balbi Museum, inaugurated in 2000.

It combines state-of-the-art technology with the preservation and interpretation of archaeological finds on the site itself, tracing the development of Roman society from antiquity to modern times. The ruins beneath the structure can be visited once an hour (on the hour) for short periods, and reveal the expansive lobby of the theatre, built by Cornelius Balbus, a friend of Augustus.

Piazza Mattei ㉔

Just south of here is the cosy little **Piazza Mattei**, with a funky bar, a

Ceiling detail in the Gesù church.

LEFT: Fontana delle Tartarughe.
BELOW: Crypta Balbi.

FOOD

The Ghetto is a great place to find that unique hybrid, Roman-Jewish food, and other non-Italian delicacies. If it's bagels, muffins and chocolate-chip cookies you're after, head for La DolceRoma bakery, an Austrian-owned spot at 20b Via del Portico d'Ottavia.

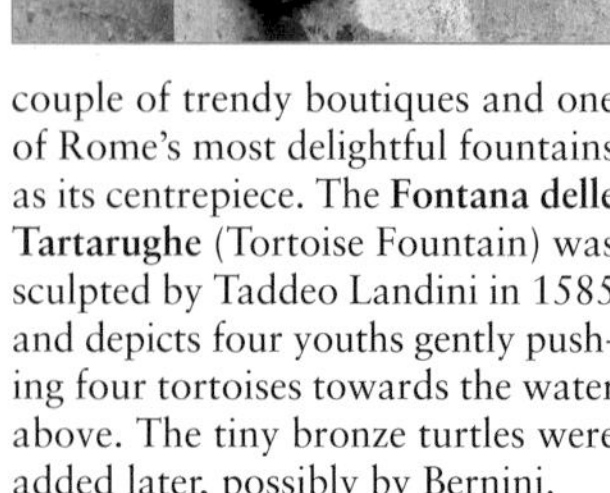

ABOVE: water pump in the Ghetto.
BELOW LEFT AND RIGHT: snapshots of the Jewish Ghetto.

couple of trendy boutiques and one of Rome's most delightful fountains as its centrepiece. The **Fontana delle Tartarughe** (Tortoise Fountain) was sculpted by Taddeo Landini in 1585 and depicts four youths gently pushing four tortoises towards the water above. The tiny bronze turtles were added later, possibly by Bernini.

JEWISH GHETTO

The Ghetto lies in the area between Largo Argentina, the river, Via Arenula and Teatro di Marcello. The first wave of Jewish settlers came in the 2nd century BC, and thrived peacefully here until Titus' victory over Jerusalem in AD 70, after which their status changed from free men to slaves (the Colosseum workforce was largely made up of Jewish slaves).

In the centuries that followed, their fortunes and status fluctuated. In the Middle Ages the Jewish population enjoyed relative freedom, and were generally appreciated for their financial and medical skills. But then in 1555, Pope Paul IV's zero-tolerance policy culminated in a papal bull ordering the confinement of the Jewish population into an enclosed area around the Portico d'Ottavia, which became known from then on as the Ghetto. The area was surrounded by high walls with doors that were locked from the outside at night.

The walls of the Ghetto were destroyed in the revolutionary year of 1848. When Rome fell to King Emmanuel II's troops in 1870, ending papal dominion over the city, the Jews were finally given the same rights as other Italian citizens. But persecution resumed with the outbreak of World War II, when the

Fascist regime deported 1,024 Jews to Nazi concentration camps.

Today, the area retains its Jewish heritage, and the streets are dotted with kosher shops and restaurants.

The Synagogue ㉕

✉ Tempio Maggiore, Lungotevere Cenci; museum: www.museoebraico.roma.it ☎ 06-6840 0661
⏲ Mon–Thur 9am–6pm, Fri and Sun 9am–12.30pm € charge 🚌 30, 40, 46, 62, 63, 64, 70, 81, 87, 186, 204, 271, 492, 571, 628, 630, 780

The Synagogue, consecrated in 1904, was built to a great height to send a message to the Vatican across the Tiber. On 13 April 1986, Pope John Paul II and Rabbi Elio Toaff held a historic meeting here marking the first time that a bishop of Rome had prayed in a Jewish house of worship. Pope Benedict XVI repeated the event on 17 January 2010.

Attached to the Synagogue (make sure you carry some form of ID, as security is strict) is the **Museum of Jewish Culture.** Reopened in 2006 after careful renovations, the museum recounts the story of Rome's Jewish population through art, relics and a documentary film. Six new exhibition spaces contain treasures from the community, including Renaissance-era embroidery, stunning ritual items and original marble blocks from some of the *Cinque Scole*, Rome's five ancient synagogues.

Portico d'Ottavia ㉖

The church of **Sant'Angelo in Pescheria** (Wed and Sat 3–8.30pm), where Jews were once forced to attend penitential services, was built on the ruins of the Portico d'Ottavia, originally the entrance to a colonnaded walkway erected in 147 BC by Augustus to display statues captured from Greece. It was dedicated to his sister, Octavia, the abandoned wife of Mark Antony. In the Middle Ages, the ruin was used as a covered fish market – above the arch of the portico, there is a Latin inscription demanding that all the fish exceeding the length marked have to be decapitated and their heads given to Conservatori (this was the preferred part for making fish soup).

Via del Portico d'Ottavia still has several medieval houses. At the end (No. 1) is **Casa di Lorenzo Manili** (not open to the public). Lorenzo Manili had this house built in 1468 and adorned it with a classical plaque. The Latin inscription dating the building employs the ancient Roman calendar that used the founding of Rome as its starting point. According to this, the year 1468 was 2221. Original Roman reliefs are embedded in the facades, as well as a fragment of an ancient sarcophagus.

TOWARDS PIAZZA FARNESE

A short distance west of here is the **Palazzo Cenci** ㉗, the family palace of the infamous Beatrice Cenci, who attracted sympathy for killing her brutal father, but was nevertheless condemned to death for witchcraft

The shop on the corner of Via del Portico d'Ottavia is a famous Jewish bakery specialising in a ricotta and black cherry torte. Ask for a slice of torta di ricotta e visciole. The tiny Forno del Ghetto is technically open Mon–Thur 8am–8pm, but the goodies are often gone by noon.

BELOW: in front of Portico d'Ottavia.

The best way to get a glimpse of the magnificent frescoed ceilings of Palazzo Farnese is to walk by just after sundown, while people are still inside, and lights are on. If you're en route to dinner in the area it's worth a look.

and murder, and beheaded on Ponte Sant'Angelo in 1599. Only parts of the original medieval building remain. The present facade and details are Baroque. Note the architectural quirk of an indented balcony on the front facing Via Arenula.

Crossing back over Via Arenula, Via degli Specchi leads to **Palazzo Monte di Pietà**, which was set up as a pawnshop in the 16th century and is still used as an auction house, open to the public every morning. From here, turn left and then right into Via Capo di Ferro.

Palazzo Spada ㉘

✉ 13 Piazza Capo di Ferro; www.galleriaborghese.it ☎ 06-683 2409 🕒 Tue–Sun 8.30am–7.30pm € charge 🚌 23, 30, 40, 46, 62, 63, 64, 70, 81, 116, 280, 492, 571, 628, 630, 780, 916

The large building on your left, with the facade covered in stucco reliefs by Mazzoni, is Palazzo Spada. The Spada family bought the palace in 1632 and Borromini restored it, adding the ingenious corridor to the courtyard. Borromini raised the floor and shortened the columns to create a false sense of perspective, making the corridor appear much longer than it actually is. At the end, a statue was placed against a painted garden backdrop. The statue is less than 1 metre (3ft) tall but from afar it seems to be life-size.

The *palazzo* is also home to the **Galleria Spada**, which has a fine collection of paintings, including work by masters Rubens, Domenichino, Guercino, Tintoretto, Reni and Artemisia, amongst others.

ABOVE RIGHT: head to Palazzo Spada to visit the Galleria's masterpieces. **BELOW:** Piazza Farnese.

Recommended Restaurants, Bars & Cafés on pages 181–3

Piazza Farnese 29

The end of the street opens into Piazza Farnese, linked by a short street back to Campo de' Fiori. Its twin fountains incorporate two huge basins from the Baths of Caracalla *(see page 227)*. You'll want to linger in this picturesque square, and there's an inviting (if overpriced) bar where you can stop for refreshment.

The **Palazzo Farnese**, a masterpiece of High Renaissance architecture, was commissioned by Cardinal Alessandro Farnese in 1517. The palace cost so much that for a while even the Farnese finances were strained. The original designs were by da Sangallo, but Michelangelo took over the work. When he died, Vignola and della Porta finished it off. Annibale Carracci frescoed the main salon. In 1874 Palazzo Farnese became the French Embassy, and it is now open to the public (one hour visits at 3, 4 and 5pm Mon and Thur. Book ahead, tel: 06-6889 2828).

Via Giulia

Near the palace is Via Giulia, named after Pope Julius II who commissioned it as a monument to the Apostolic Church. When Bramante began work on it in 1508, the intention was to make it Rome's most important thoroughfare, connecting the Vatican with Ponte Sisto and the Ripa Grande harbour, and thus the centre of papal Rome. The centrepiece of the street was to be the Palazzo dei Tribunali, but the building failed to get beyond the foundations stage.

The street became a prestigious address, and many high profile people lived in its sumptuous palaces, including Antonio da Sangallo, Raphael and Benvenuto Cellini. The parties in Via Giulia were among the best in Rome, and on one occasion wine gushed from the Mascherone Fountain for three full days.

All this is hard to believe now, as the street is quiet and lined with expensive antique shops and art galleries. The elegant arch crossing the street was designed by Michelangelo and was intended to connect Palazzo Farnese with the Villa Farnesina across the Tiber, but the bridge was never built.

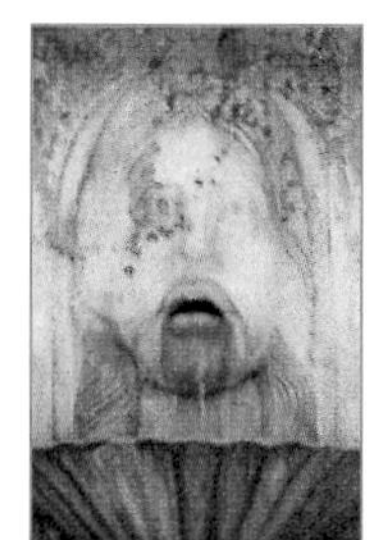

Mascherone Fountain, Via Giulia.

BELOW LEFT: Michelangelo's arch, part of an uncompleted bridge on Via Giulia. **BELOW:** one of the two fountains in Piazza Farnese.

If you're not too squeamish, pay a visit to the Criminology Museum (29 Via del Gonfalone; tel: 06-6889 9442; open Wed–Sun 9am–1pm and 2.30–6.30pm). It displays articles relating to some of Italy's most sensational crimes, the clues and evidence used to incriminate the culprits, and the gruesome instruments used to extract confessions and punish the guilty.

RIGHT: resident Tiber Island dog. **BELOW:** boat on the Tiber. **BELOW RIGHT:** a stroll on the river bank.

Next to the arch stands the church of **Santa Maria dell'Orazione e Morte** (Mass on Sun 6pm), which was redesigned by Ferdinand Fuga (1733). Fuga was a member of the Compagnia della Buona Morte, an association whose purpose was to give a decent burial to the poor. Grotesque and macabre arabesques of human bones – children's skulls, collarbones, ribs – decorate the walls of the crypt. The walls and the ceiling are covered with reliefs and mosaics.

Adjacent to the church is **Palazzo Falconieri** ㉚, which was modernised by Borromini for the Falcone family and is framed by two falcons' heads on female torsos. It is now the Hungarian Academy, and occasionally opens for exhibitions and concerts.

Off Via Giulia, in Via Sant'Eligio, is the beautiful little 16th-century church of **Sant'Eligio degli Orefici** ㉛ (Mon–Fri 9.30am–1pm), designed by Raphael, with a dome by Peruzzi.

Further along the street, past the derelict church of **San Filippo**, is the fortified building of the **Carceri Nuove** (New Prison), built in 1655 to replace the gruesome prisons of Tor di Nona and the nearby torture chambers of the Savella family, who until then were the papal gaolers.

Continuing past the Palazzo dei Tribunali, you come to several important Renaissance *palazzi*, including da Sangallo the Younger's palace at No. 66 and one of Raphael's houses at No. 85. The street ends with the church of **San Giovanni dei Fiorentini** ㉜ (daily 7.30am–1pm and 4–7pm; art collection closed in July and August), built in various stages by Sansovino, da Sangallo the Younger, della Porta and Maderno. The facade was added in the 18th century. Inside, there is a delightful sculpture of St John by the

Boat Trips on the Tiber

Rome launched a tourist riverboat service on the Tiber in 2003. A fleet of steamboats, led by the flagship *Rea Silvia* (christened after the mother of Romulus and Remus) started sailing between the Duca D'Aosta Bridge and Ponte Marconi in Trastevere. Until December 2008, services included river cruises to Ostia Antica and hop-on, hop-off trips, but torrential rains caused the river to swell to record levels, damaging some of the boats and forcing the companies to downsize.

Today, the services available include pleasure trips with on-board commentary (€15), night-time cruises with dinner on board (€50), and aperitivo cruises (€35). Pleasure trips run daily every 30 minutes, from 10am–6pm, while dinner cruises only operate Thur–Sat. Boarding points are Ponte Sant'Angelo and Isola Tiberina. For information and bookings, tel: 06-9774 5498; www.battellidiroma.it.

Recommended Restaurants, Bars & Cafés on pages 181–3

Sicilian Mino del Reame over the sacristy door, and an impressive apse altar by Borromini with a marble group, the *Baptism of Christ*, by Antonio Raggi. Both Borromini and Maderno are buried in the church.

TIBER ISLAND ㉝

The Isola Tiberina is a pretty island in the middle of the Tiber. It has long been associated with healing. Legend has it that in 293 BC the Romans asked the Greeks, and their god Aesculapius in particular, for help overcoming a plague. They were sent a shipful of snakes, whose venom was used to cure ailments. The plague was defeated and a temple to Aesculapius duly erected. The church of **San Bartolomeo** was built on the ruins of this temple in the 10th century. The island is also the site of the Fatebenefratelli (the "do-good-brothers") hospital founded in 1548.

The two bridges linking Isola Tiberina to the shore are among the oldest structures still in use in Rome. The **Ponte Fabricio** (leading to the north bank) was built in 62 BC by the civil engineer Lucius Fabricius, and there's an inscription to prove it. The **Ponte Cestio** was built in 42 BC by Lucius Cestius and restored in AD 370. The central arch is all that remains from that date; the rest is a late 19th-century reconstruction. This bridge leads into the heart of Trastevere.

Off the eastern end of the island are the remains of Rome's first stone bridge (142 BC), known as the **Ponte Rotto** (Broken Bridge). Most of what remains is from a 1575 reconstruction by Gregory XIII, the rest of which was washed away in 1598. The modern bridge behind it, **Ponte Palatino**, is sometimes called the English Bridge, because it is one of the very few stretches of road in Rome where cars are driven on the left.

Monument to St Bartholomew, whose relics are housed in the church of San Bartolomeo on Tiber Island.

ABOVE LEFT: ruins of Ponte Rotto.
BELOW: Tiber Island, a picturesque route to Trastevere.

Legend has it that if you tell a lie while your hand is in the Bocca della Verità, or Mouth of Truth, it will be bitten off. In a famous scene in William Wyler's 1953 classic film Roman Holiday, *Gregory Peck fooled Audrey Hepburn into believing – for a minute – he'd lost his hand to the statue.*

BELOW: Piazza Santa Maria in Cosmedin.

Santa Maria in Cosmedin ㉞

18 Piazza Bocca della Verità
06-678 1419 daily 9.30am–4.30pm (5.30pm in summer) free
23, 44, 63, 81, 95, 160, 170, 628, 715, 716, 781

Back on the mainland, east of the bridge, is the **Piazza della Bocca della Verità**, once the site of the Forum Boarium, the cattle market of Ancient Rome. The square is named after the Bocca della Verità *(see left)*, which is in the portico of the church of Santa Maria in Cosmedin. First built in the 6th century, with additions made throughout the centuries, the church is a lovely mixture of early Christian, medieval and Romanesque design. The floors were replaced with stunning Cosmati pavements, and a belltower was erected in the 12th century. You'll find a Roman bathtub on the altar, used for baptisms, and an 8th-century mosaic in the sacristy. The name Cosmedin is Greek (it means "splendid decoration"), and Rome's oldest Greek Christian community has been worshipping here since the 700s.

Temples of Hercules and Portunus

In the piazza are two well-preserved Republican-era temples. The round one was recently restored and determined by archaeologists to be the oldest marble structure in the city, built in the 1st century BC to Hercules. The nearby square temple is dedicated to Portunus, the god of harbours, which makes good sense considering the vicinity of the Tiber.

Theatre of Marcellus ㉟

What looks like a smaller version of the Colosseum attached to a Renaissance *palazzo* is in fact the remains of the Teatro di Marcello. The once-glorious performance space was completed under the reign of Emperor Augustus, who named it after his nephew Marcellus. In its heyday, the 20,000-seat theatre flaunted three tiers, each supported with a different style of column, from the basic Doric to the extravagant Corinthian, and the top level, which has collapsed, was adorned with decorative theatre masks. Call 06-0608 for a guided tour. ❑

BEST RESTAURANTS, BARS AND CAFÉS

Restaurants

Price includes dinner and a half-bottle of house wine:
€ = under €25
€€ = €25–40
€€€ = €40–60
€€€€ = more than €60

Antica Trattoria Polese

40 Piazza Sforza Cesarini 06-686 9543 L & D Wed–Mon. €€ [p335, C4]

Less packed than its rowdier neighbour Da Luigi, Polese has the better outdoor seating in a small piazza off Corso Vittorio, and a more refined Roman menu based on what is available at the market that morning. In the evening, pizza is also on the menu.

Ba'Ghetto

57 Via del Portico d'Ottavia 06-6889 2868 L & D Mon–Thur, L only Fri, D only Sat. €€ [p339, D1]

The Jewish, Libyan and Roman specialties are all strictly kosher. Try the fried *carciofi alla giudia* artichokes and ask the staff to decipher the complicated Arabic dish names on the menu.

Il Bacaro

27 Via degli Spagnoli 06-939 0558 L & D Mon–Fri, D only Sat. €€ [p335, D3]

Located in a small, quiet street behind the Pantheon, the Bacaro oozes charm, and is perfect for a romantic soirée. Its cobbled stone and trellised outdoor area, and tiny internal room are much sought after, so booking is essential.

La Bottega del Vino di Anacleto Bleve

9a Via Santa Maria del Pianto 06-686 5970 L & D Tue–Sat. € [p339, D1]

A quintessentially Roman *enoteca* (wine bar) whose buffet is loaded with dozens of delicacies such as smoked swordfish, salmon rolls, *sformati* (flans) and cod carpaccio. Locals come here for the good food, well-chosen wine list and the *simpatia* of its husband-and-wife owners, Tina and Anacleto. *Aperitivo* hour starts at 6.30pm and the *enoteca* closes at 8pm.

Ditirambo

74 Piazza della Cancelleria 06-687 1626 L & D Tue–Sun, D only Mon. €€ [p339, C1]

The atmosphere is busy but convivial. The varied menu includes numerous and unusually creative vegetarian options, such as ricotta flan with raw artichokes and a pomegranate vinaigrette, and wholemeal pasta with red onions and pecorino cheese. There are many good cuts of meat and plentiful fish dishes. The desserts are home-made, fresh and heavenly; the wine list is extensive and the waiters happy to tell you all about it. Closed three weeks in Aug.

Ar Galletto

102 Piazza Farnese 06-686 1714 L & D Mon–Sat. €–€€ [p339, C1]

A simple trattoria with Roman classics such as *spaghetti alla carbonara*, *abbacchio* (lamb) and *involtini* (meat rolls). The view of Michelangelo's Palazzo Farnese and Bernini's two fountains is unforgettable.

Da Giggetto al Portico d'Ottavia

22 Via del Portico D'Ottavia 06-686 1105 L & D Tue–Sun. €€ [p339, D1]

It may be very popular with tourists, but don't let that put you off. The standards are reliably high as they take their Roman-Jewish cooking very seriously here, and the service is equally efficient and pleasantly old-fashioned. Try one of five menus, all of which usually include *carciofi alla giudia* (deep-fried whole artichokes), stuffed courgette flowers or salted cod fillets.

Price includes dinner and a half-bottle of house wine:
€ = under €25
€€ = €25–40
€€€ = €40–60
€€€€ = more than €60

Il Gonfalone

✉ 7 Via del Gonfalone ☎ 06-6880 1269 ⊙ L & D daily. **€€** [p334, C4]

This restaurant with lovely outdoor seating is an understated gourmet experience. Vegetarians, fish-lovers and meat-eaters are equally well served. The cuisine style is a nouvelle take on Mediterranean. There's a bar and lounge area downstairs where people drink and dance until the small hours.

Hosteria del Pesce

✉ 32 Via di Monserrato ☎ 06-686 5617 ⊙ D only Mon–Sat. **€€€–€€€€** [p338, C1]

The scrubbed wood and streamlined interior set the tone for this quality restaurant which happily lives up to its pretensions. Hosteria del Pesce serves only the freshest fish, either raw or cooked, and the white-only wine list is judiciously composed.

Da Luigi

✉ 23–24 Piazza Sforza Cesarini ☎ 06-686 5946 ⊙ L & D Tue–Sun. **€€** [p335, C4]

Traditional (and therefore heavy) Roman fare at this always-packed venue on a small square off Corso Vittorio Emanuele. There's a pleasant breeze and a convivial atmosphere amongst the outdoor seating on the square. Frequented by tourists and locals alike.

Il Pagliaccio

✉ 129a Via dei Banchi Vecchi ☎ 06-6880 9595 ⊙ L & D Wed–Sat, D only Mon and Tue. **€€€** [p335, C4]

This smart restaurant has a limited but creative menu with an emphasis on beautiful presentation and quality ingredients. It's expensive but, as its regular customers agree, well worth it.

Der Pallaro

✉ 15 Largo del Pallaro ☎ 06-6880 1488 ⊙ L & D Tue–Sun. **€** [p339, C1]

This quintessentially Roman trattoria is owned by the jovial Fazi couple and is a reliable favourite for those with big appetites and smaller budgets. There is no menu, but for about €20 (house wine and water included) you are served several courses that will leave you more than satisfied. Unsophisticated but tasty; the artichokes are excellent and the desserts home-made. No fish. Open past midnight. No credit cards.

Dal Pompiere

✉ 38 Via S. Maria dei Calderari ☎ 06-686 8377 ⊙ L & D Mon–Sat. **€€–€€€** [p339, D1]

Waistcoated waiters dance attendance on customers in the wood-panelled and frescoed rooms of this fine restaurant occupying the first floor of the Palazzo Cenci. The food is Roman-Jewish and consistently good – which means the tables are consistently full.

Renato e Luisa

✉ 25 Via dei Barbieri ☎ 06-686 9660 ⊙ D only Tue–Sun. **€–€€** [p339, D1]

A reliable and affordable trattoria in a rustic, simple setting, serving classic dishes accompanied by good house wines. You could start with fettuccine with pachino tomatoes and buffalo ricotta, followed by turkey cooked with rosemary and honey, rounded off with a perfect crème brûlée.

Roscioli

✉ 21 Via dei Giubbonari ☎ 06-687 5287 ⊙ L & D Mon–Sat. **€€** [p339, C1]

This family-run deli-cum-

LEFT: Da Giggetto al Portico d'Ottavia.
ABOVE RIGHT: Roscioli.

restaurant receives rave reviews for its authentic produce and inventive food combinations, such as their signature dish, *tonnarelli* with grouper fish, pistachios and fennel seeds. Cheerful, pleasant atmosphere.

Sora Margherita

✉ 30 Piazza delle Cinque Scole ☎ 06-687 4216 ⏲ L Mon–Sat, D Mon, Wed, Fri and Sat. **€** [p339, D1]
A small, basic trattoria in the heart of the former Jewish Ghetto, serving simple and hearty fare (much of it vegetarian) accompanied by bread from renowned Trastevere bakery La Renella. The sweets are homemade, and the highly palatable local wine is from Velletri outside Rome. No credit cards.

Taverna degli Amici

✉ 37 Piazza Margana ☎ 06-6992 0637 ⏲ L & D Tue–Sat, D only Sun. **€€–€€€** [p339, D1]
A refined alfresco restaurant in an ivy-draped square in the Ghetto district. It serves subtly different versions of Roman classics as well as plenty of interesting vegetarian dishes.

Trattoria Moderna

✉ 16–17 Vicolo dei Chiodaroli ☎ 06-6880 3423 ⏲ L & D daily. **€€** [p339, D1]
A lively restaurant with appealing decor. The owners are experienced Roman restaurateurs, and the menu is classical Mediterranean with some modern touches.

Zio Ciro

✉ 1 Via della Pace ☎ 06-686 4802 ⏲ L & D daily. **€** [p335, D4]
Succulent, Neapolitan-style, thick-crusted pizzas (the Roman ones have thinner bases) and a range of pasta dishes and salads. Excellent value by Roman standards. Outdoor seating.

Bars and Cafés

Zi' Fenizia (31 Via dell' Umilta) has been declared the best take-away pizzeria in the city by Gambero Rosso, Italy's answer to the Michelin guides. It's all kosher, and their signature pizza topping is a tasty combination of anchovy and endives.

Il Goccetto (14 Via dei Banchi Vecchi) has been serving good wines and even better cheeses for over two decades in this medieval bishop's palace with frescoed ceilings. Some 800 different labels are available for sale, of which about 40 can be tasted by the glass.

Award-winning ice cream maker **Alberto Pica** (12 Via della Seggiola) has been making *gelato* all his life and is rather better at it than most. People travel from all over Rome to enjoy his superlative ice creams.

La Vineria (15 Campo de' Fiori) is the perfect spot to sit back and people-watch. Order a glass of wine or a beer, or, if it's cold, ask for a heart-warming vin brulé.

A kitsch but quintessentially Roman place, **Jonathan's Angels** (16 Via della Fossa) is bright, full of colour and filled with quirky memorabilia, including dozens of portraits of the owner with his children. It also boasts the most memorable loos in town, complete with their own fountain.

Sciam (56 Via del Pellegrino) is a laid-back Middle Eastern tea room with a tempting selection of sweet and savoury dishes. You may even be tempted to take a puff of the aromatic hookah pipes. Open until 2am.

The tables at **Kosher Bistrot** (66/69 Via Santa Maria del Pianto) spill onto the pedestrianised streets of the Jewish ghetto for a pleasant snack, lunch, or drink in the sun.

Bohemian-styled interiors and occasional live concerts are the main elements of chic bar **Bartaruga** (8 Piazza Mattei), a favourite among local celebrities and models.

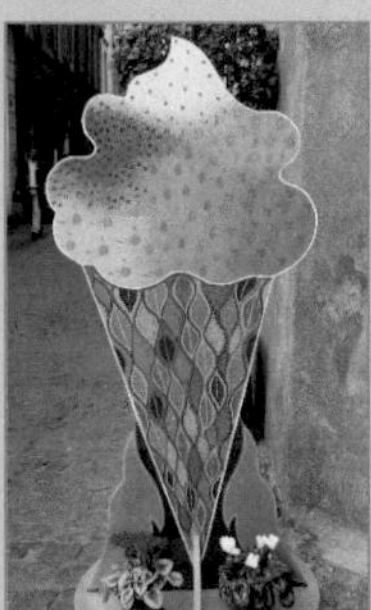

HARRY'S BAR
ROMA
HB
HB
HB

Recommended Restaurants, Bars & Cafés on page 197

VIA VENETO AND VILLA BORGHESE

The country estates of wealthy Romans were carved up after Unification and transformed into elegant boulevards lined with imposing *palazzi*. Only the Villa Borghese was saved and turned into a vast public park containing some of the city's finest museums

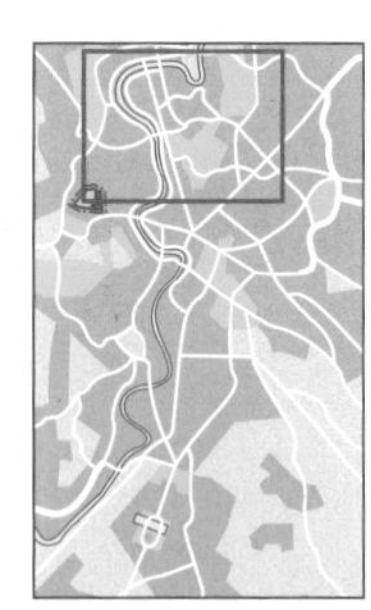

This chapter takes you from Via Veneto, which leads north from the city centre, up to the Villa Borghese Gardens, Rome's finest park, with a gallery of remarkable paintings and sculptures.

VIA VENETO

The southern end of **Via Veneto** begins in **Piazza Barberini** ❶, a busy square with a cinema and fast-food joints. In its centre sits, rather forlornly, Bernini's **Fontana del Tritone** (Triton Fountain), *pictured on page 121*. Via Veneto itself, lined with plane trees and pavement cafés, was once the symbol of Roman fashion and style. However, the glorious days of *La Dolce Vita*, immortalised on screen by Fellini, are long gone. Anita Ekberg now lives in retirement in the Castelli Romani, and the intellectuals have drifted to Piazza del Popolo and the area around Piazza Navona. The long, twisting avenue is now filled for the most part with luxury hotels, embassies and offices, as well as numerous anonymous restaurants with glass-enclosed outdoor seating, hungry for the tourist dollar. Only a few historic cafés – Harry's Bar at No. 150, Café de Paris at No. 90 and the Art Deco Doney's at No. 145 – still bear witness to the street's heyday as the place to be seen in Rome.

SANTA MARIA DELLA CONCEZIONE ❷

27 Via Vittorio Veneto; www.cappucciniviaveneto.it 06-487 1185 daily, church: 7am–noon, 3–7pm, crypt: 9am–noon, 3–6pm donation expected Barberini 52, 53, 61, 62, 63, 80, 95, 116, 119, 175, 492, 630

Main attractions
- PIAZZA BARBERINI
- SANTA MARIA DELLA CONCEZIONE
- SANTA MARIA DELLA VITTORIA
- VILLA BORGHESE GARDENS
- GALLERIA BORGHESE
- CATACOMBE DI PRISCILLA
- QUARTIERE COPPEDÈ
- MACRO
- VILLA TORLONIA
- FORO ITALICO
- THE AUDITORIUM
- MAXXI

LEFT: Harry's Bar on Via Veneto.
RIGHT: Via Veneto ends at the Porta Pinciana, part of the old Roman Aurelian walls.

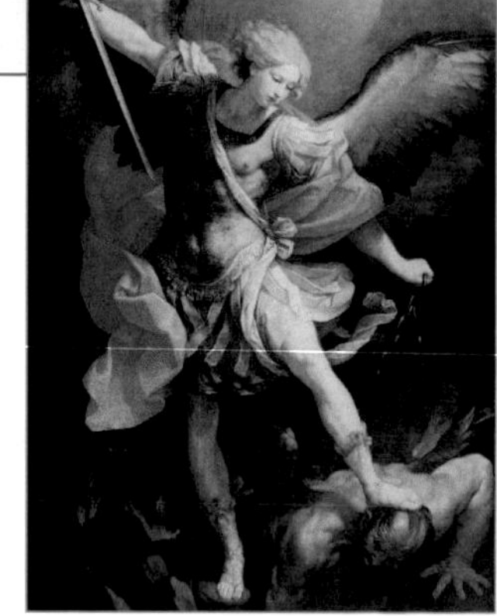

That most popular of Italian drinks, cappuccino, is named after the garb worn by Capuchin monks. The colour of the milky coffee is reminiscent of their brown robes and the pointed hoods of the peaks of milky foam. The word cappuccino literally means "little hood" or "monk's cowl".

ABOVE RIGHT: *The Archangel Michael Slaying the Devil* by Guido Reni. **BELOW:** outside Café de Paris on Via Veneto.

At the southern end of the Via Veneto, this Baroque church also goes by the name of I Cappuccini (The Capuchins). The Capuchin friars broke away from the Franciscans in 1525, but still emulate the humble lifestyle of their patron saint, dressing in a simple brown robe with a cord belt, and sandals without socks. This church has been the home of the Capuchin order in Rome since 1631.

It has two noteworthy paintings: *The Archangel Michael Slaying the Devil* by Guido Reni and *St Paul's Sight Being Restored*, by Pietro da Cortona. But the main draw is in the crypt, which contains the bones and skulls of 4,000 Capuchin friars, ornately displayed *(see box on right)*.

Gardens of Sallust

The **Horti Sallustiani** (Gardens of Sallust) lie between Via Veneto and the Villa Borghese Gardens. Gaius Sallustius, a historian and profiteer who made enormous fortunes out of the campaigns of 40–30 BC, embellished his home with magnificent gardens. Soon hailed as one of the wonders of the world, they were quickly appropriated by the Empire. Vespasian and Titus preferred this part of Rome to the Palatine.

Fountains, pools and mosaic floors once drew awed visitors. Now the gardens lie 15 metres (45ft) below street level, buried by the rubble from collapsed houses and the building activity of the 19th century.

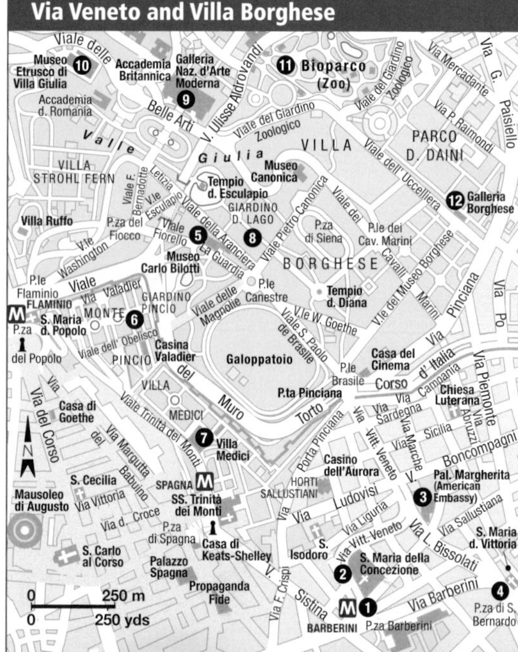

Recommended Restaurants, Bars & Cafés on page 197

Archaeological finds from the gardens include the obelisk at the top of the Spanish Steps and those on show as part of the collection of the Museo Nazionale Romano *(see page 233)*.

In the Middle Ages, the family of Ludovisi-Boncompagni injected new life into the by then unkempt gardens by planting 30 hectares (74 acres) of vineyards. They lasted until the property boom of the 1880s, which spelt their demolition. The Società Generale Immobiliare, backed mainly by German and French capital, made an irresistible offer to the Ludovisi princes, and the villa was split up. All that remains is the 16th-century **Casino dell'Aurora** in the gardens of the Swiss Cultural Institute.

Palazzo Margherita ❸

The other part of the gardens spared by developers is **Palazzo Margherita**, which was completed in 1890 and now houses the American Embassy. One of the Ludovisi princes had this gigantic building constructed as a substitute for his lost garden, but his money ran out and he had to sell it to the Savoy royal family, who moved the queen mother in. It bears her name to this day.

SANTA MARIA DELLA VITTORIA ❹

✉ 17 Via XX Settembre 🕒 daily 9am–noon, 3.30–6.30pm € free 🚇 Repubblica 🚌 16, 38, 60, 61, 62, 84, 86, 90, 92, 217, 360, 910

To the south of the *palazzo*, on the corner of Piazza San Bernardo and Via XX Settembre, stands the church of **Santa Maria della Vittoria**, begun by Carlo Maderno in 1605. It contains Bernini's famous Baroque Cornaro side-chapel, which uses natural lighting effects to highlight the *Ecstasy of St Teresa*, a sculpture of Teresa of Avila, one of the great saints of the Counter-Reformation, portrayed with open mouth and half-closed eyes at the climax of her vision of Christ. She described how an angel pierced her heart with a flaming golden arrow. It has prompted many writers and critics over the centuries to suggest that the love she is experiencing may not be entirely divine.

In its Dolce Vita *heyday, the five-star Excelsior on Via Veneto played host to some of the most glamorous stars of the day. Many a tempestuous scene between hot-headed lovers Frank Sinatra and Ava Gardner was played out within its walls.*

BELOW LEFT: Bernini's *Ecstasy of St Teresa.*

Bone Idols

Beneath the church of Santa Maria della Concezione is an extraordinary crypt which contains the bones of 4,000 monks. Many churches have charnel houses, but this arrangement of skeletal remains into intricate designs is unique. The crypt is full of unusual tableaux: brown-cowled skeletons bow to visitors under arches of hip bones and pelvises; an infant skeleton attached to the ceiling brandishes a scythe, surrounded by rosettes made from vertebrae; a large clock comprises finger and foot bones. And in case this is not enough to remind you of mortality, a sign ominously informs us that: "What you are now, we once were. What we are now, you shall someday be".

The origins of this death cult are unclear. The church says that when French Capuchin friars came to Rome they found a shortage of burial space and created this monument. There is also the legend of "a half-mad monk with time on his hands and a certain passion for tidiness." Whatever the motives, this is Rome's most artistic cemetery.

ABOVE: the Pincio Gardens. **BELOW:** retreat to the park if the heat gets too intense.

VILLA BORGHESE

At the northern end of Via Veneto, outside the Porta Pinciana, is the **Villa Borghese**, which was founded at the beginning of the 17th century by Cardinal Scipione Borghese Caffarelli, a nephew of Pope Paul V. The family later extended their property by buying some nearby land, so that 100 years ago the park encompassed 75 hectares (190 acres), which the Borghese frequently opened to the public. Property developers cast a greedy eye on the villa in the late 19th century, and their plans provoked the first battle to save the Romans' traditional society promenade.

Eventually, in 1901, the state bought the villa and, two years later, gave it to the people. The Villa Borghese, along with the Pincio Gardens and the Villa Giulia, is now home to a handful of museums, a cinematic cultural centre and the city zoo.

The **Villa Borghese Gardens** are laid out over rolling hills with winding paths, little lakes, statues and pretty flower beds. On Sunday, the people of Rome take over the park. Every corner is full of picnicking families, strolling lovers, cyclists and joggers, and squealing children at play.

There are several entrances to the park, but the main one is at the top of Via Veneto, at Porta Pinciana.

Carlo Bilotti Museum ❺

✉ Viale Fiorello La Guardia, Villa Borghese; www.museocarlobilotti.it ☎ 06-0608 ⏲ Tue–Sun 9am–7pm € charge Ⓜ Flaminio 🚌 95, 116, 490, 495

A wide *viale* leads downhill from the Porta Pinciana, passing the **Galoppatoio** (horse track) on the left and a statue of Goethe on the right. A

Recommended Restaurants, Bars & Cafés on page 197

little further ahead, the old orangery (Aranceria) has been restored and transformed into a museum containing a collection of works by Carlo Bilotti, an Italo-American collector who favoured modern art. The core of the collection is made up of 22 paintings and sculptures by Giorgio de Chirico. There is also a portrait of the larger-than-life arts patron Larry Rivers, and one of Bilotti's wife and daughter, the *Portrait of Tina and Lisa Bilotti* (1981) by Andy Warhol. Other key works include *Summer* by Gino Severini and the large bronze *Cardinal* by Giacomo Manzù. The complex regularly houses important modern and contemporary art exhibitions.

Pincio Gardens ❻

From Piazzale Canestre walk down Viale delle Magnolie and head over the bridge, crossing busy Viale del Muro Torto below, into the **Pincio Gardens** at the southwest corner of the park. These formal gardens were designed by Valadier in the 19th century. Look out for the fanciful water clock and the **Casina Valadier**, once an elegant café visited by the intellectuals of the Roman *belle époque*. Nowadays, it is an expensive restaurant with a fabulous view from its terrace (www.casinavaladier.it; tel: 06-6992 2090; daily 12.30–3pm, 8–11pm).

Outside the restaurant is a stand full of bicycles and pedal-carts for hire – not a bad idea, especially if you plan on visiting the museums across the park. The romantic terrace of the Pincio overlooks Piazza del Popolo and offers a splendid vantage point to view the city. It's a particularly delightful spot for an evening stroll.

Just inside the park, on the other side of the Porta Pinciana, stands the new Casa del Cinema (www.casadelcinema.it). The lovely converted villa boasts several screening rooms (showing the occasional film in English), a book and DVD shop, and a cinema library containing scripts and movie stills. The CineCaffè (daily 9am–7pm), which serves drinks and light meals in an airy atmosphere, is an appealing place to add to your Villa Borghese itinerary.

LEFT: Sunday activity.
BELOW: view of Piazza del Popolo from the Pincio Gardens.

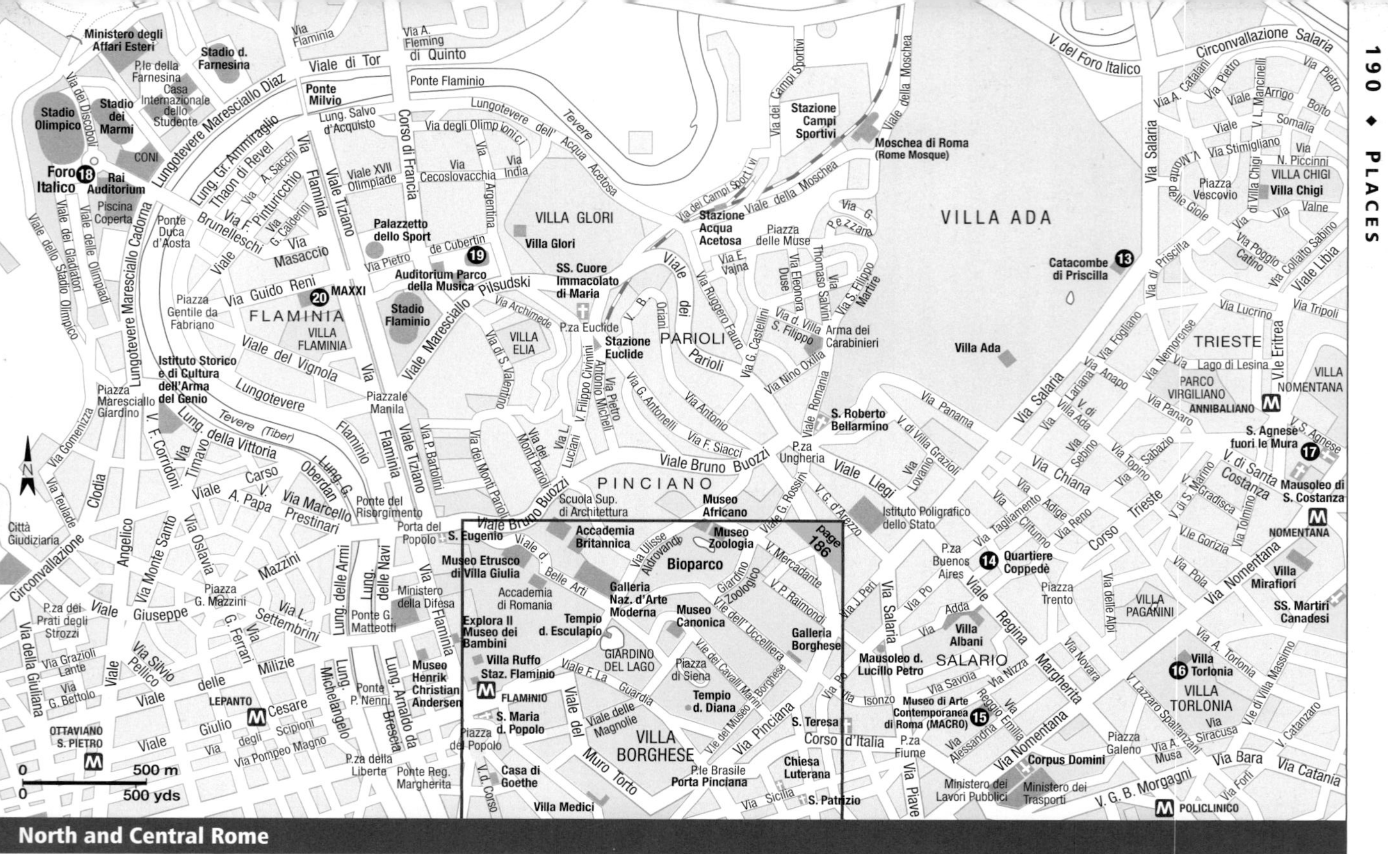
North and Central Rome
VILLA ADA
Villa Ada
Catacombe di Priscilla
Moschea di Roma (Rome Mosque)
Stazione Campi Sportivi
Stazione Acqua Acetosa
VILLA GLORI
Villa Glori
SS. Cuore Immacolato di Maria
Stazione Euclide
PARIOLI
PINCIANO
VILLA ELIA
Auditorium Parco della Musica
Palazzetto dello Sport
Stadio Flaminio
MAXXI
FLAMINIA
VILLA FLAMINIA
Istituto Storico e di Cultura dell'Arma del Genio
Stadio Olimpico
Foro Italico
Stadio dei Marmi
Rai Auditorium
CONI
Piscina Coperta
Ministero degli Affari Esteri
Stadio d. Farnesina
Casa Internazionale dello Studente
Ponte Milvio
Ponte Flaminio
Ponte Duca d'Aosta
Ponte G. Matteotti
Ponte P. Nenni
Ponte del Risorgimento
Ponte Reg. Margherita
Tevere (Tiber)
Museo Etrusco di Villa Giulia
Explora Il Museo dei Bambini
Villa Ruffo
Staz. Flaminio
FLAMINIO
S. Maria d. Popolo
Casa di Goethe
Villa Medici
VILLA BORGHESE
Porta Pinciana
Tempio d. Diana
Museo Canonica
Galleria Borghese
Bioparco
Museo Zoologia
Museo Africano
Galleria Naz. d'Arte Moderna
Accademia Britannica
Accademia di Romania
Tempio d. Esculapio
GIARDINO DEL LAGO
Scuola Sup. di Architettura
S. Eugenio
page 186
Museo Henrik Christian Andersen
Ministero della Difesa
S. Teresa
Chiesa Luterana
S. Patrizio
Mausoleo d. Lucillo Petro
Museo di Arte Contemporanea di Roma (MACRO)
SALARIO
Villa Albani
Quartiere Coppedè
Istituto Poligrafico dello Stato
S. Roberto Bellarmino
VILLA PAGANINI
VILLA TORLONIA
Villa Torlonia
Corpus Domini
Ministero dei Trasporti
Ministero dei Lavori Pubblici
POLICLINICO
Villa Mirafiori
SS. Martiri Canadesi
NOMENTANA
S. Agnese fuori le Mura
Mausoleo di S. Costanza
TRIESTE
PARCO VIRGILIANO
ANNIBALIANO
VILLA NOMENTANA
VILLA CHIGI
Villa Chigi
LEPANTO
OTTAVIANO S. PIETRO
Città Giudiziaria
Viale Tiziano
Via Flaminia
Corso di Francia
Via Salaria
Viale Regina Margherita
Via Nomentana
Viale dei Parioli
Viale Bruno Buozzi
Via Piave
Corso d'Italia
Via Po
Viale Liegi
Lungotevere Maresciallo Cadorna
Lungotevere Maresciallo Diaz
Via della Giuliana
Circonvallazione Clodia
Circonvallazione Salaria
V. del Foro Italico
Viale delle Olimpiadi
Viale dei Gladiatori
Viale dello Stadio Olimpico
Viale Mazzini
Via Oslavia
Via Monte Santo
Viale Angelico
Lung. della Vittoria
Lung. Michelangelo
Lung. delle Armi
Lung. delle Navi
Lung. Arnaldo da Brescia
Viale del Muro Torto
Via Pinciana
500 m
500 yds

Recommended Restaurants, Bars & Cafés on page 197

Villa Medici ❼

Further down the Pincio hillside is the majestic **Villa Medici**. Rebuilt in the 16th century for the Crescenzi family, it was then passed to the Medicis, before being confiscated by Napoleon in 1803 and made the home of the French Academy. It is open for occasional exhibitions and concerts. There are also guided tours of the gardens on Saturday, Sunday and Wednesday mornings (advance booking, tel: 06-67611).

Giardino del Lago ❽

Backtrack and cross the bridge to where a wide *viale* leads up to **Piazza di Siena** on the right. This oval track is the site of the International Horse Show in May – an important social and sporting event.

To the left is the pretty **Giardino del Lago**, with a tiny lake in the middle of which stands a reproduction of a Greek temple of Aesculapius. Rowing-boats can be hired for a brief paddle. Nearby, you will find the **Fountain of Fauns**, created in 1929 by Giovanni Nicolini.

Galleria Nazionale d'Arte Moderna ❾

131 Viale delle Belle Arti; www.gnam.arti.beniculturali.it 06-3229 8221 Tue–Sun 8am–7.30pm charge 3, 19, 231, 926

Two sloping ramps lead to Viale delle Belle Arti and the neoclassical facade of the Galleria Nazionale d'Arte Moderna (GNAM). It has a permanent collection of 19th- and 20th-century pieces (dating until the 1960s) by Italian and foreign artists including de Chirico, Van Gogh, Modigliani, Degas, Cézanne, Courbet, Kandinsky, Mondrian, Klimt, Henry Moore and others. The gallery also frequently hosts travelling exhibitions of international importance. There is a café and a reasonably priced restaurant.

Nearby **Museo Henrik Christian Andersen** (20 Via Pasquale Stanislao Mancini, Piazzale Flaminio; www.museoandersen.beniculturali.it; tel: 06-321 9089; Tue–Fri 9am–7pm) is a branch of the GNAM, and offers a look at the Norwegian-American artist, whose bold, bronze statues of men in all their glory were not always so well received.

Next door, in the Piazza Winston Churchill, is the **Accademia Britannica**, designed by Lutyens and home to visiting scholars.

Museo Etrusco di Villa Giulia ❿

9 Piazzale di Villa Giulia 06-322 6571 Tue–Sun 8.30am–7.30pm

Entrance to the National Gallery of Modern Art, housing a collection of 19th- and 20th-century art, including a group of paintings by the Macchiaioli, Italy's answer to France's Impressionists.

ABOVE LEFT: Fonte Gaia in the Villa Borghese gardens.
BELOW: Villa Medici.

TIP

Add some romance to your jaunt in the park. Pick up a gourmet picnic-to-go from nearby Piazza di Spagna-area restaurant GiNa. Luxury packs come complete with chequered cloth, plates, flatware, wine-glasses, a bottle of your wine of choice, a thermos of espresso and fresh sandwiches. GiNa: 7a Via San Sebastionello; tel: 06-678 5201; www.ginaroma.com.

RIGHT: Giardino del Lago. **BELOW:** hunting and war scenes on a gilded silver bowl, Museo Etrusco di Villa Giulia.

charge Flaminio
3, 19, 231, 926

To the west of the modern art gallery is Rome's Museum of Etruscan Art. It is housed in the Villa Giulia, a splendid late Renaissance palace built as a summer villa for Julius III between 1551 and 1553. The museum gives a unique insight into the life and art of the enigmatic pre-Roman civilisation of the Etruscans. Among the many outstanding exhibits are the sweet 6th-century BC sarcophagus of a married couple – *degli Sposi* – from the excavations in Cerveteri, and a 6th-century bronze statue of Apollo of Veio. These and other pieces form one of the finest collections of Etruscan art in the world, rivalled only by that of the Vatican.

Some of the collection is on show in the restored, 16th-century Villa Poniatowski nearby. Once part of the Villa Giulia complex, it was renovated in the early 19th century by the Polish Prince Stanislao Poniatowski.

The zoo (Bioparco) ⓫

Piazzale del Giardino Zoologico; www.bioparco.it 06-360 8211
Apr–Oct 9.30am–6pm, Nov–Mar 9.30am–5pm charge Flaminio
bus: 52, 53, 217, 360, 910, 926; tram: 3, 19

The road leading uphill to the left ends at the entrance to the zoo, or Bioparco, its official eco-friendly name. In the past the zoo had a reputation for being neglected, but in recent years there have been some worthy and fairly successful attempts to phase out the caging of exotic animals and keep other specimens in more humane, purpose-built environments that more closely resemble their natural habitats.

Galleria Borghese ⓬

5 Piazzale del Museo Borghese; www.galleriaborghese.it 06-32810
Tue–Sun 9am–7pm, controlled entry every two hours on the hour until 5pm, by reservation only
charge 5, 19, 52, 53, 88, 116, 204, 217, 910, 926

In the eastern corner of the park, one of the world's great private art collections is housed in the Casino Borghese, built as a summer home for the worldly, pleasure-loving Cardinal Scipione Borghese between 1613 and 1615. The cardinal was a great patron of the arts and laid the

Recommended Restaurants, Bars & Cafés on page 197

basis for the remarkable collection of paintings and sculptures on view today *(see pages 198–9)*.

NORTHEAST OF THE CITY

To the northeast *(see map on page 190)*, **Via Salaria** crosses the suburbs and leads out to the Sabine Hills, and onward to the Adriatic coast. This old Roman road is named after the salt *(sale)* which was transported into Rome from the sea and through the hills. Just before the Salaria Bridge (1874) is the hill of Monte Antenne, where the Sabine settlement of the Antemnae is said to have stood. It is here that the Romans, under Romulus, supposedly kidnapped the Sabine women to populate their growing empire. Via Salaria was an important street and, in the early years of Christianity, many churches and catacombs were built here.

Catacombe di Priscilla ⓭

430 Via Salaria; web.tiscali.it/catacombe_priscilla 06-8620 6272 Tue–Sun 8.30am–noon, 2.30–5pm, closed in August charge 63, 86, 92, 310

Entered through the cloister of a Benedictine monastery, the 13km (8-mile) network of catacombs evolved between the 1st and 4th centuries. Seven early popes and numerous martyrs were buried here, hence the high-quality frescoes and stucco decorations. The catacombs extend under the park of Villa Ada, now the Egyptian Embassy but formerly Victor Emmanuel II's hunting lodge. It is surrounded by a beautiful park which is open to the public.

Quartiere Coppedè ⓮

To the east of Via Salaria, just off Piazza Buenos Aires, is the fashionable Quartiere Coppedè, a residential area named after a Florentine architect

KIDS

If you've children in tow, two good places to know about are the zoo *(see page 192)* and the nearby Explora Museum (82 Via Flaminia; tel: 06-361 3776), a science museum full of interactive displays to keep them amused.

ABOVE LEFT: outside the zoo. **ABOVE:** the *Good Shepherd* mosaic in the Catacombe di Priscilla. **BELOW:** the Galleria Borghese.

On the other side of Villa Ada is the chic residential area of Parioli, where the main attraction is Rome's first mosque. Built in 1992, it serves a Muslim population of 100,000 and is the largest mosque in Europe to date. Noted for its modern feel and contextual design, the mosque sits on over 3 hectares (7½ acres) of verdant park space, and its interior follows a forest motif. To reach the mosque, take the local Viterbo-bound train to Acqua Acetosa (Campi Sportivi).

RIGHT: decorated housefront in the Quartiere Coppedè. **BELOW:** Villa Torlonia.

who designed many buildings here between 1921 and 1926, using Art Nouveau-inspired motifs. Of particular interest is Piazza Mincio, a square with an unusual fountain of frogs that Gabriele d'Annunzio described as "a genuine disgrace to Rome". Coppedè, whose buildings were the last notable architecture of pre-Fascist Rome, intended this square to show a harmony between the individual details of each house and the great tradition of Florentine craftsmanship.

MACRO ⓯

✉ 54 Via Reggio Emilia; www.macro.roma.museum ☎ 06-0608 ⏲ Tue–Sun 9am–7pm Ⓔ charge 🚌 3, 19, 36, 38, 60, 62, 80, 84, 490, 491, 495

At the beginning of Via Nomentana, set in a former Peroni brewery, is the Museo d'Arte Contemporanea di Roma (MACRO). One of two sites (the other is in Testaccio, *see page 217*), it houses artworks by the key figures in Italian contemporary art. There is also a café and museum shop on site.

Villa Torlonia ⓰

✉ 70 Via Nomentana; www.museivillatorlonia.it ☎ 06-0608 ⏲ 1 Apr–30 Sept Tue–Sun 9am–7pm, Mar and Oct 9am–5.30pm, 1 Nov–28 Feb 9am–4.30pm Ⓔ charge 🚌 36, 60, 84, 90

Further east, on Via Nomentana, the Villa Torlonia was the last great villa built in Rome. In the early 19th century, the aristocratic Torlonia family contracted French architect Valadier to design the villa, which had a small lake, guesthouse, sports field and Temple of Saturn. The splendid

Recommended Restaurants, Bars & Cafés on page 197

three-storey residence, the Casino Nobile, was Mussolini's home from 1924 until 1943 (his rent was 1 lira a month). It was then occupied by Allied Forces, who used it as a military command base, but after the war it was left to disintegrate.

Following 50 years of neglect the palace has been restored to something of its former glory, and was opened to visitors in 2006. The rooms are lavishly decorated – the chandeliered ballroom is the grandest – though furnishings are sparse, as so much was looted or destroyed. You can also visit the network of bunkers Mussolini had built in case of air raids or gas attacks.

While you're in the Villa Torlonia grounds, the **Casina delle Civette** (Owl House) is also worth a visit. The Swiss chalet-style residence was built in 1840 and restored in the 1920s in the Art Nouveau style, with stained-glass windows featuring idyllic scenes of flora and fauna.

Nearby, a small medieval building houses Technotown (Tue–Sun 9am–7pm, www.technotown.it), a hands-on science and technology museum designed for 11–15-year-olds. See website for events and special activities.

Sant'Agnese fuori le Mura ⓱

349 Via Nomentana; www.santagnese.net 06-8620 5456 church: daily 7.30am–noon, 4–7.30pm, catacombs and mausoleum: daily 9am–noon, 4–6pm charge for catacombs 30, 60, 84, 90, 93

Continuing down Via Nomentana, you come to Sant'Agnese fuori le Mura, an important early Christian church built over the site of the tomb of St Agnes (martyred in AD 304) in the mid-4th century by Princess Costantina, daughter of the Emperor Constantine. It was rebuilt by Pope Honorius I in the 7th century. The relics of St Agnes are housed in the high altar. Every 21 January, the saint's day, two lambs are blessed and shorn to make woollen robes for the Pope.

The adjoining catacombs are remarkably well preserved. The nearby church of St Costanza, built as Constantina's own mausoleum, contains some interesting 4th-century mosaics depicting scenes of the *vendemmia* (grape harvest).

An old Peroni brewery is now home to Rome's contemporary art collection.

FLAMINIA

Northern Rome is connected to the city by the Via Flaminia, which begins at Piazza del Popolo and continues in a straight line all the way to the historic Ponte Milvio *(see below and page 196)*, a Roman footbridge which offers wonderful views of the Tiber. From here it's a short walk to the Foro Italico sports centre, one of the most intact examples of Fascist-era architecture in the city.

Foro Italico ⓲

The Foro Italico sports complex was designed for Mussolini in the late

BELOW: lovers on Ponte Milvio.

The Love-Locks of Ponte Milvio

The ancient bridge of Ponte Milvio has become a pilgrimage site for lovers who seal their *amore* in a ritual of fixing a padlock to the bridge's lamp-posts, throwing the key over their shoulders into the river. The love-lock tradition started in 1992, with the publication of Federico Moccia's romantic novel *Tre Metri Sopra Il Cielo* (Three Metres Above The Sky). In the story, two teenagers of different backgrounds use the padlock ritual to promise each other eternal love on the bridge. Since then, hundreds of youngsters have sought to emulate the famous couple. In 2006, politicians began wondering whether it was acceptable that such historic lamp-posts –designed in 1805 by architect Valadier– should bear the weight of over a thousand padlocks. A political battle between the pro-padlock 'romantics' and the anti-padlock art-conscious ensued. In 2007, two of the lamp-posts bent over and collapsed, so the city hall added metal racks to make room for future padlocks.

Ponte Milvio is one of Rome's oldest bridges. Dating back to 2 BC, it is one of only three bridges that stood in the ancient city. It was the site of the great battle between rivals for the Imperial crown: Constantine and Maxentius. On the eve of the battle in AD 312 Constantine had a vision of Christ, and converted to Christianity. He went on to win the battle and turn the Roman Empire to Christianity.

ABOVE RIGHT: Museo Nazionale delle Arti del XXI Secolo. **BELOW:** a modern Olympian at the Foro Italico.

1920s by prominent architect Enrico del Debbio. This district was formerly dominated by the **Stadio dei Marmi**, built in the style of a Greek stadium and surrounded by 60 marble figures of athletes in heroic poses. Today, it is dwarfed by the **Stadio Olimpico**, the huge football and athletics stadium immediately behind it, with capacity for 80,000 spectators. This is where the opening ceremony of the 1960 Olympics took place, and, when the World Cup was held here in 1990, the stadium was extended into the Monte Mario behind it.

The stadium now hosts football matches most Sundays during the season, and is the venue for much passion and excitement – and also, unfortunately, violence when the two home teams, AS Roma and SS Lazio, come together in a match.

The Foreign Ministry, the Farnesina, stands on an empty patch east of the stadium.

The Auditorium ⓳

30 Viale Pietro de Coubertin; www.auditorium.com 06-8024 1281 Flaminio, then tram 2 53, 217, 231, 910

Back on the south side of the Tiber, just north of the Parioli district and east of Flaminio, is the largest arts complex of its kind in Europe. The state-of-the-art Auditorium Parco della Musica designed by Genoese architect Renzo Piano opened in 2002. The huge venue is set in open parkland, with a 7,600-seat capacity spread over three concert halls. It has a large outdoor amphitheatre and even incorporates a ruined Roman villa, unearthed during construction. The "city of music" offers an excellent programme of international music and dance. See the website for up-to-date details.

MAXXI ⓴

4A Via G. Reni; www.maxxi.beniculturali.it 06-3210 1836 Tue–Sun 11am–7pm, Thur 11am–10pm charge Flaminio, then tram 2 19, 53, 217, 225, 910

Just across Via Flaminia, west of the Auditorium, stands the brand-new Museo Nazionale delle Arti del XXI Secolo (MAXXI). The art complex designed by Anglo-Iraqi Zaha Hadid was inaugurated in May 2010. As the architect said, it resembles 'curves unwinding like a ribbon in space', and houses a centre for contemporary art and architecture subdivided into five spaces for permanent collections, site-specific installations and special events. ❑

BEST RESTAURANTS, BARS AND CAFÉS

Restaurants

Price includes dinner and a half-bottle of house wine:
€ = under €25
€€ = €25–40
€€€ = €40–60
€€€€ = more than €60

Cantina Cantarini

✉ 12 Piazza Sallustio ☎ 06-485 528 ◷ L & D Mon–Sat. **€€** [p336, B2]

A high-quality family-run trattoria where the price is still right. Dishes are meat-based the first part of the week, fish-based Thur–Sat.

Casina Valadier

✉ Pincio Gardens, Villa Borghese ☎ 06-6992 2090 ◷ L & D daily. **€€–€€€** [p335, E2]

The service can be indifferent and the quality of the food is not necessarily reflected in the price, but you might be prepared to risk it just to enjoy the location *(pictured below)*.

Al Ceppo

✉ 2 Via Panama, Parioli ☎ 06-841 9696 ◷ L & D Tue–Sun. **€€–€€€** [off map p336, A1]

A class act with impeccable and imaginative food, a vast wine list and home-made sweets.

Girarrosto Fiorentino

✉ 46 Via Sicilia ☎ 06-4288 0660 ◷ L & D daily. **€€–€€€** [p336, A2]

An island of reliability in a sea of tacky venues. The service is faultless, and wall-hangings give it a pleasantly dated look. All the classic Roman dishes are on offer, along with some Florentine specialities, including wonderful T-bone steaks.

La Mantia

✉ 50 Via Veneto (Majestic Hotel) ☎ 06-421 441 ◷ L & D Mon–Sat, D only Sun. **€€€** [p336, A3]

A chic glassed-in hotel restaurant with neoclassical interiors, a romantic terrace and a spectacular view over Via Veneto. Filippo La Mantia, one of Italy's most popular star chefs, prepares exquisitely elaborate dishes inspired by the cuisine of his native Sicily, revisited with creative touches and innovative ingredient combinations.

Papà Baccus

✉ 36 Via Toscana ☎ 06-4274 2808 ◷ L & D Mon–Fri, D only Sat. **€€€** [p336, A2]

Renowned for its attentive service and Tuscan cuisine. Meat features heavily, but there are fish and vegetarian options too.

La Terrazza dell'Eden

✉ 49 Via Ludovisi ☎ 06-478 121 ◷ L & D daily. **€€€€** [p336, A2]

One of the capital's top restaurants, with a panoramic terrace that's as much of a draw as the food; try the risotto with melted taleggio and aubergine. The extensive wine list (650 bottles to choose from) is another mark in its favour.

Bars and Cafés

The recently revamped **Doney** (145 Via Veneto) harks back to *Dolce Vita* glamour. A good bet for everything from breakfast to dinner, cocktails and aperitifs.

Caffè delle Arti (73 Via Gramsci) in the Villa Borghese's National Gallery of Modern Art is touted as the finest museum café in Italy. It has a beautiful terrace and a fine interior. The restaurant is open in the evenings, and also serves Sunday brunch.

ReD (12 Viale Pietro de Coubertin). The Auditorium's designer restaurant-bar is all sweeping lines and elegant aesthetics, with red being the predominant colour. Stop by for one of the city's chicest cocktails.

Galleria Borghese

Legacy of an art-loving cardinal, this is one of the finest collections of paintings and statuary in Rome

The Galleria Borghese is housed in an early 17th-century *palazzina* built for Cardinal Scipione Borghese. The cardinal was a great patron of the arts and laid the basis for the remarkable collection of paintings and sculptures on view today. Between 1801 and 1809 the sculpture collection was severely depleted, when more than 500 pieces were sold to Napoleon. These now make up the Borghese Collection of the Louvre in Paris, but there are still some marvellous pieces on show.

The cardinal was an early patron of Bernini, and the villa contains some of his best work, including his dramatic statue of *David*, caught just as he is about to release his slingshot *(above)*, *Apollo and Daphne* and *Pluto and Persephone*.

Scipione was one of the few cardinals to appreciate Caravaggio, and the collection includes several of his paintings, alongside works by other great Italian masters including Raphael, Correggio, Titian, Perugino, Lotto, Domenichino, Giorgione, Dossi and Bassano, as well as by Rubens and Cranach, among others.

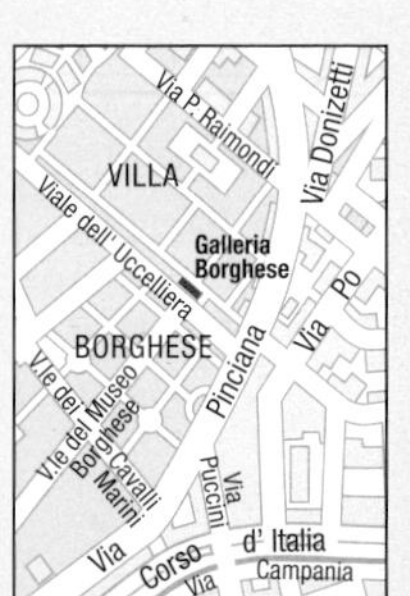

The essentials

5 Piazzale del Museo Borghese
06-32810
Tue–Sun 9am–7pm; entrance every two hours on the hour until 5pm; visits limited to two hours
charge
5, 19, 52, 53, 88, 116, 204, 217, 910, 926

Top: Titian's *Sacred and Profane Love*, *c.*1515, made for an aristocratic wedding, is loaded with symbolism. **Above:** Raphael's celebrated *Deposition*, 1507.

Right: *David and Goliath*, by Caravaggio, 1606. The head of Goliath is a self-portrait, said to be a sign of contrition by the artist for the murder he had recently committed.

THE PATRON'S PALACE

The Casino Borghese was built as a summer house for the pleasure-loving cardinal Scipione Borghese between 1613 and 1615. As a close associate of the Pope, he entertained many high-profile guests in his *palazzina*. The ancient statuary and the building itself, modelled on the classical villa, recalled the glories of Imperial Rome, and with the precious art collections on display, were a forceful demonstration of the cardinal's power.

In his will, he stated that the villa and grounds should never be separated. In 1902, the entire Villa Borghese estate was bought by Umberto I of Italy and presented by him to the city.

ABOVE: the gleaming Galleria Borghese is made of creamy white travertine which reflects the light.

BELOW: one of the highlights of the collection is the sensual statue of Pauline Bonaparte by Canova. The 19th-century femme fatale, whose conquests in the bedroom matched her brother's on the battlefield, was appropriately sculpted as Venus Victrix. When asked how she could possibly have posed so scantily dressed, she replied, "The studio was heated."

RIGHT: *Venus and Cupid with a Honeycomb*, by German painter Lucas Cranach the Elder (1531).

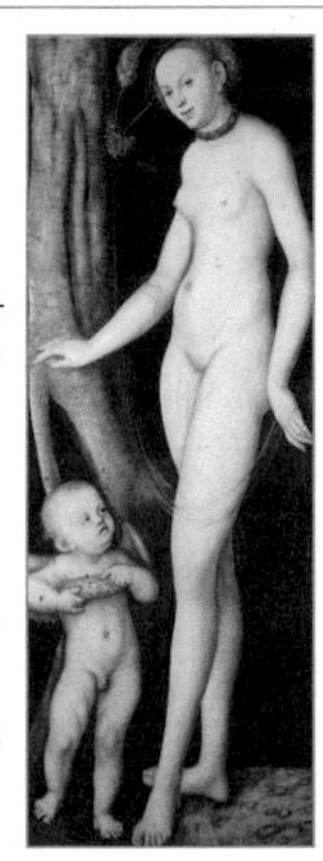

Recommended Restaurants, Bars & Cafés on pages 208–9

TRASTEVERE AND THE GIANICOLO

Rome's traditional working-class district "across the Tiber" has always stood apart from the rest of the city. Although it is now the gentrified turf of bourgeois Romans and expats, Trastevere retains a special charm. Rising behind it, the Gianicolo hill offers some of the best views of the city

Main attractions

SANTA MARIA IN TRASTEVERE
MUSEO DI ROMA IN TRASTEVERE
SAN FRANCESCO A RIPA
PORTA PORTESE FLEA MARKET
SANTA CECILIA IN TRASTEVERE
VILLA FARNESINA
PALAZZO CORSINI
ORTO BOTANICO
PIAZZALE GARIBALDI
BRAMANTE'S TEMPIETTO
VILLA PAMPHILI PARK

Across the river *(trans Tiberim)* from the Centro Storico lies Trastevere. The area has a long history as the residence of outsiders: in Roman times it was settled by sailors, foreign merchants and a large Jewish community which later moved across the river. Over time, Trastevere's separation from the rest of the city resulted in the development of its own customs, traditions and dialect.

For centuries, the *Trasteverini* considered themselves to be *i romani di Roma*: Rome's Romans – a cohort of proud working men and women who faced life with a quick-witted sardonic joy. The energy of life on the streets of *er core de Roma* – the heart of Rome – nurtured some of the city's great artistic talent. The actor Alberto Sordi turned Trastevere's backstreets dialect into his comedy trademark. Inventor of the Spaghetti Western, Sergio Leone, grew up in Viale Glorioso, and his neighbourhood school was also the Alma Mater to film-music maestro Ennio Morricone.

But the old *Trasteverini* are a dying breed. After the war, the area's down-at-heel charm attracted gentrifying expats and middle-class Romans. Inhabitants with roots going back generations departed for housing on Rome's periphery. The new *Trasteverini* are more likely to be artists, actors and film stars in residence.

Fortunately, Trastevere has kept some of its idiosyncracies, even if many of the old *trattorie* and *osterie* have given way to pizzerias, pubs and trendy wine bars. During the day, it is left to its sleepy self: residents exercise dogs and do their daily shopping, while children play and the elderly sit outside their houses. In the evening,

LEFT: the mellow shades of a Trastevere street. **RIGHT:** graffiti is inescapable in Rome and prolific in Trastevere.

ABOVE: Santa Maria in Trastevere and a detail from the interior mosaic.

the streets and squares are packed with locals and tourists, who flock here to eat, drink or stroll among stalls selling ethnic jewellery, and fortune-tellers shuffling their cards.

One major blot on this appealing landscape is the amount of graffiti scrawled across walls and doors. Also late-night drunk and disorderly behaviour, something until recently unheard of in Rome, is on the increase in and around the main square. Locals are campaigning hard for the mayor to address these social problems and for stronger policing in the area.

PIAZZA SANTA MARIA IN TRASTEVERE

This cobbled square is the throbbing heart of the neighbourhood and is one of the most charming piazzas in Rome. There's a steady ebb and flow of tourists and locals whiling away their time in the cafés or sitting on the steps of the **fountain** (1692) around which musicians perform in summer.

Santa Maria in Trastevere ❶

Piazza Santa Maria in Trastevere
daily 7.30am–8pm free
bus: 8, 780, tram: H

The piazza is named after the basilica on its eastern side, one of the oldest churches in Rome and one of the first to be dedicated to the Virgin. It was founded in the 3rd century, and rebuilt in the 12th century, although the portico was added in 1702. The 12th- and 13th-century mosaics, both inside and outside the church, are spectacular, and it is worth taking a

Trastevere and the Gianicolo

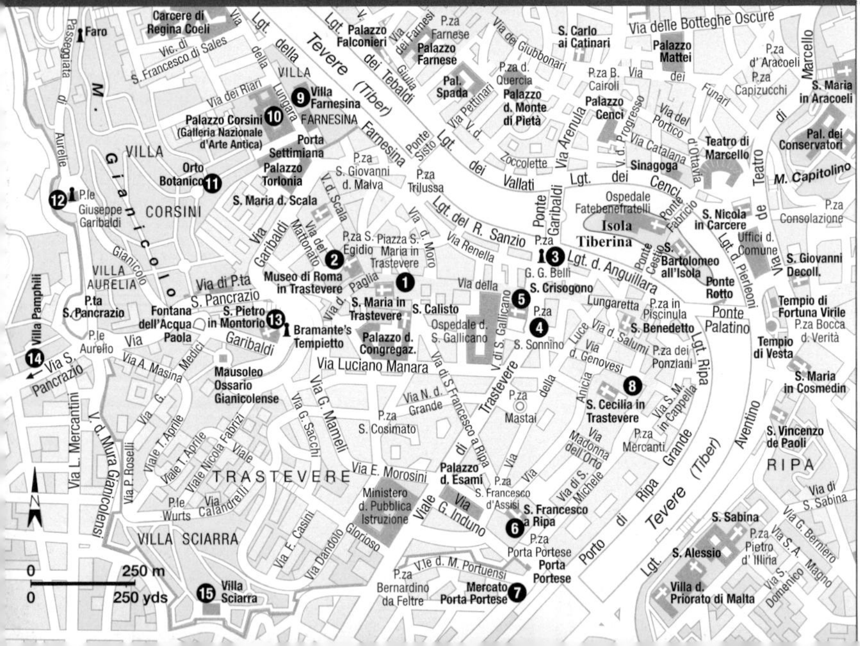

pair of binoculars to enjoy their details. *The Life of the Virgin* series is by Cavallini (1291). Also worthy of note are the 21 granite columns which divide the nave from the aisles. These were taken from classical buildings including the Baths of Caracalla *(see page 227)*.

Museo di Roma in Trastevere ❷

1B Piazza Sant'Egidio 06-0608
Tue–Sun 10am–8pm free
bus: 8, 780, tram: H

Northwest of the square, this small museum, housed in a beautifully restored Carmelite convent, is dedicated to Roman folklore. The exhibition on the upper floor begins with a collection of watercolours by Ettore Roesler Franz (1845–1907), known as "Lost Rome". They present a rose-tinted Rome as it was before the urban restructuring of the 1870s, through romantic scenes of daily life in and around the Tiber.

At the far end of the floor is a series of life-size reconstructions of Roman life in the 18th century, and a room chock-full of objects from the studio of popular Trastevere poet Carlo Alberto Salustri (1871–1950), known as Trilussa (he is also remembered in a statue that graces the **Piazza Trilussa**).

The staircase features casts of the so-called "Talking Statues" *(see page 162)*. The ground floor of the museum is used for temporary exhibitions, often focusing on photography and new media.

The atmosphere is more brisk and businesslike in **Piazza San Cosimato** to the south, where the daily food market is surrounded by grocers, bars, restaurants and a hospital.

FOOD

Brush up on your bad language and visit La Parolaccia restaurant (3 Vicolo del Cinque; Mon–Sat), where food is served accompanied by bawdy language (the restaurant's name means swear word) and a brusque but entertaining Roman manner.

LEFT: Caffè del Moro is a historic meeting place. **BELOW LEFT:** busker in Piazza Santa Maria. **BELOW:** the facade of Santa Maria in Trastevere.

Trastevere was the site of Rome's notorious old prison, the Carcere Regina Coeli. In the 18th century, women would pay "prison singers" to sing their messages from the piazza, which their incarcerated loved ones could hear from inside.

Viale di Trastevere

Like every old quarter of Rome, Trastevere had to make sacrifices when the capital started expanding after 1870. Many historic buildings and streets were destroyed in order to make way for the **Viale di Trastevere**, a broad boulevard that cuts through the patchwork of Trastevere's little streets. At its northern end, on the banks of the Tiber, is **Piazza G.G. Belli** ❸, named after the much-loved 19th-century Roman dialect poet, Giuseppe Gioacchino Belli (1791–1863) whose statue stands here.

Behind Piazza Belli is **Piazza Sidney Sonnino** ❹. The Torre degli Anguillara, the last of many towers that once guarded Trastevere, is marked with a plaque commemorating Dante's stay here in 1300. The nearby church of **San Crisogono** ❺ (daily 8–11.30am and 4–7.30pm) was built over one of the oldest sites of Christian worship in Rome, dating from the 3rd century. The facade is a 17th-century copy of the medieval original. Inside are remains of a 5th-century basilica.

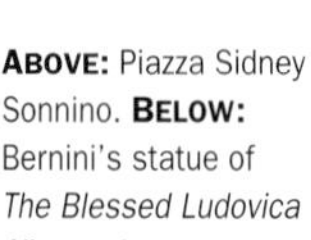

ABOVE: Piazza Sidney Sonnino. **BELOW:** Bernini's statue of *The Blessed Ludovica Albertoni.*

San Francesco a Ripa ❻

Piazza di San Francesco d'Assisi
daily 7am–noon, 4–7.30pm free
bus: 8, 780, tram: H

On the south side of the Viale di Trastevere lies the church of San Francesco a Ripa. Dedicated to St Francis, who stayed in a convent near here, it contains a powerful late work by Bernini, the statue of *The Blessed Ludovica Albertoni*. From a wealthy family, she spent her fortune and ruined her health caring for the poor.

Renowned for her religious ecstasies, she became known as a miracle-worker and, it was said, had the gift of levitation. Her ecstatic expression is reminiscent of his more famous statue of St Teresa in Santa Maria della Vittoria *(see page 187)*.

Porta Portese

The church is not far from **Porta Portese**, a gateway built by Urban VIII on the site of the ancient Porta Portuensis. Rome's cheap and cheerful **flea market** ❼ is held here on Sunday mornings *(see opposite)*.

Santa Cecilia in Trastevere ❽

22 Piazza di Santa Cecilia Mon–Sat 9.30am–1pm, 4–6.30pm, Sun 11.30am–12.30pm and 4–6.30pm, crypt: Mon–Sat 9.30am–12.30pm, 4–6.30pm, Sun 11.30am–12.30pm
free bus: 8, 780, tram: H

Nestling in a quiet and secluded part of Trastevere, this church is dedicated to the martyr St Cecilia, traditionally regarded as the inventor of the organ and the patron saint of music. Condemned to death for her faith in 230, she was to have been executed by means of suffocation, but when this failed, an executioner was despatched to behead her. She survived three strokes of the axe, living for a further three days and converting 400 pagans before she finally died. In 1599, her tomb was opened and her body, in a semi-foetal position, was found in a miraculous state of preservation. The artist, Maderno, made a beautiful statue of the saint which can be seen beneath the high altar.

VIA DELLA LUNGARA

Via della Scala leads from Piazza Sant'Egidio to the **Porta Settimiana**, a gate erected by Emperor Septimius Severus and replaced by Pope Alexander VI in 1498. From here Via Garibaldi climbs to the Gianicolo *(see page 206)*. This route was used in the Middle Ages by pilgrims en route to the Vatican, before the building of the *"retifili"* – the long, straight roads built by the Renaissance popes. The longest of these is Via della Lungara, laid out in the early 16th century to connect Trastevere with the Borgo. It's a short walk from the Porta Settimiana along Via della Lungara to the Villa Farnesina, a Trastevere gem.

Villa Farnesina 9

230 Via della Lungara 06-6802 7268 Mon–Sat 9am–1pm charge 125

This sumptuous villa was built between 1508 and 1511 for the fabulously wealthy papal banker, Agostino Chigi. Renowned for his lavish banquets, Chigi was also a

Rome's most famous flea market is Porta Portese *(see opposite)*, held on Sunday 7am–2pm on Via Portuense and adjacent streets between Via Ettore Rolli and Porta Portese. Go early if you want to get the bargains and avoid the crowds.

LEFT: Villa Farnesina. **ABOVE:** puppets for sale at Porta Portese. **BELOW:** Raphael's *Triumph of Galatea*, Villa Farnesina.

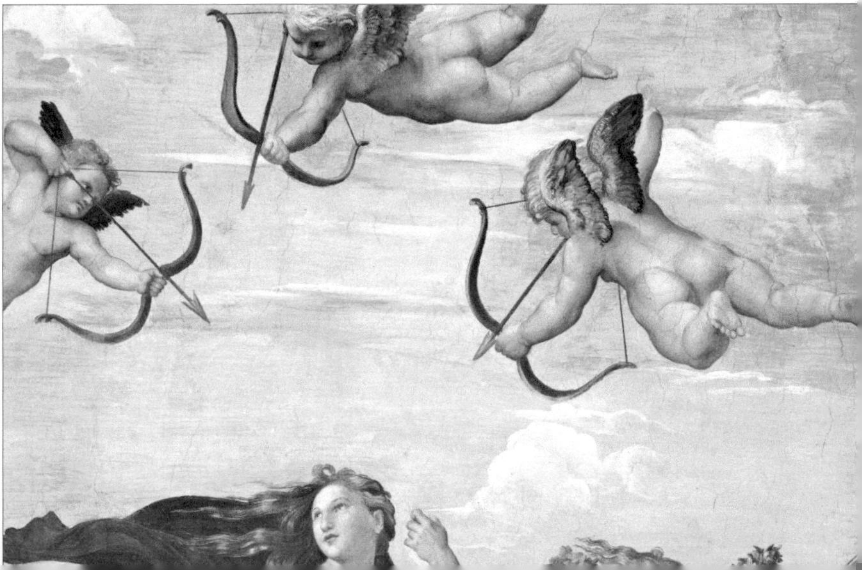

KIDS

The Piazza Garibaldi is home to a puppet theatre. It opens daily at 4pm, and has entertained children for decades. Please give generously, as it survives on donations from the public.

The 115 goes up the Gianicolo hill.

BELOW RIGHT: Piazzale Garibaldi.

noted patron of the arts and had his villa decorated with a series of beautiful frescoes by some of the best artists of the time. The highlights of the downstairs rooms are Raphael's sensual *Triumph of Galatea* and *Three Graces*. Upstairs is a fine *trompe l'œil* depicting contemporary views of Rome by Peruzzi, and Sodoma's magnificent *Wedding of Roxanne and Alexander*.

Palazzo Corsini ⑩

✉ 10 Via della Lungara; www.galleriaborghese.it/corsini ☎ 06-6880 2323 ⏲ Tue–Sun 8.30am–7.30pm Ⓔ charge 🚌 125

Built in the 15th century for a wealthy cardinal, this *palazzo* opposite the Villa Farnesina now houses part of the **Galleria Nazionale d'Arte Antica** collection, which includes works by Fra Angelico, Rubens, Van Dyck, Caravaggio and Luca Giordano, whose *Christ among the Doctors* is one of the collection's key works. (The rest of the collection is in Palazzo Barberini, *see page 120*).

Orto Botanico ⑪

✉ 24 Largo Cristina di Svezia ☎ 06-4991 7140 ⏲ Mon–Sat 9.30am–6.30pm in summer, until 5.30pm in winter Ⓔ charge 🚌 125

Originally part of the Corsini palace grounds, the botanical gardens are now open to the public. There are about 7,000 plants on display, including a scented garden for the blind and a collection of medicinal herbs. On the slopes up to the Gianicolo is a series of tiered fountains.

THE GIANICOLO

The Gianicolo (Janiculum hill) is climbed from Trastevere via the long and winding Via Garibaldi. The hill was the site of one of Italy's decisive battles for independence, when in 1849 Garibaldi and his army defeated French troops sent to restore papal rule. At noon, a cannon blast sounds to commemorate the struggle for liberation.

Piazzale Garibaldi ⑫

You can either walk or hop on a bus (115 or 870) up the hill to Piazzale

Bramante's Tempietto

When the centre of the Renaissance shifted from northern Italy to Rome at the end of the 15th century, the atmosphere of the Eternal City gave the architects of the day fresh impetus to rediscover the styles and motifs of antiquity. Donato Bramante had learnt his trade in the north and moved to Rome in 1499. His Tempietto di San Pietro in Montorio (1502) is the first monument of the High Renaissance style. It possesses a gravity all of its own – not surprising, considering its location: it marks the spot that was believed to be the site of St Peter's crucifixion. On closer inspection, you will notice there is very little surface decoration, and the colonnade is also unadorned. Too small to fit a congregation (5 metres/15ft in diameter), the circular temple supports a classical entablature, which lends further weight and severity. These features, combined with the perfect classical proportions, make the Tempietto a brilliant homage to antiquity.

Map on page 202

Recommended Restaurants, Bars & Cafés on pages 208–9

Garibaldi. The broad square is dominated by an **equestrian monument** to the freedom-fighter, while further north is another for his wife, the intrepid Anita, represented as an Amazon. Views from the terrace are magnificent.

Via Garibaldi

If you're catching the bus up to the Piazzale it's worth jumping off on the way up at the church of **San Pietro in Montorio**, with works by Vasari, del Piombo and Bernini, but most importantly **Bramante's Tempietto** ⓭ (daily 8.30am–noon and 3–4pm; free), one of the gems of the Renaissance *(see box left)*. During the bloody fighting that took place in 1849, the wounded were brought into the church, which was right next to the battlefield. A commemorative plaque on the outside of the church, with a French cannonball stuck to it, marks the event.

A little further uphill stands the **Fontana dell'Acqua Paola**, a fountain commissioned in 1612 by Pope Paul V to grace the end of an ancient aqueduct built by Trajan.

FURTHER AFIELD

Southwest of Trastevere lies the green and well-heeled **Monteverde Vecchio** residential zone, built in the late 19th and early 20th centuries. This is one of the most desirable places in Rome to live. Here also is the vast **Villa Pamphili park** ⓮ (entrance on Via di San Pancrazio; dawn–dusk; bus 115, 710, 870 to Piazzale Aurelio), the largest green space in Rome, with undulating terrain, fields, picturesque walkways, pine forests, fountains, lakes and gardens, a theatre museum, a bistro and pony hire.

The basilica of **San Pancrazio** (Piazza San Pancrazio; Mon–Sat 8.30am–noon; bus 75) was founded in the 6th century on the burial site of a young Roman martyr, who was beheaded for his faith in 304. Underneath the church are the **catacombs of San Pancrazio** (currently closed for restoration).

Not far to the east is another, far smaller but beautifully designed park and house, the **Villa Sciarra** ⓯ (currently closed for renovation). The park boasts botanical plants and statues of mythological figures. ❑

Opposite the church of San Pietro in Montorio, a striking white monument is Mussolini's tribute to the heroes of the Risorgimento (1848–70). On it is written the slogan "Roma o morte" *(Rome or death), Garibaldi's famous war-cry uttered on this spot.*

BELOW sunset view from Piazzale Garibaldi.

BEST RESTAURANTS, BARS AND CAFÉS

Restaurants

Price includes dinner and a half-bottle of house wine:
€ = under €25
€€ = €25–40
€€€ = €40–60
€€€€ = more than €60

Antica Pesa

18 Via Garibaldi 06-580 9236 L & D Mon–Sat. **€€€** [p338, C2]
This historic restaurant serves up all the usual Roman classics, along with some surprises: try the ravioli with white truffles, or steak with strawberries and balsamic vinegar. Booking advised.

Antico Arco

7 Piazzale Aurelio 06-581 5274 D daily. **€€€** [p338, B2]
Excellent restaurant on the Gianicolo hill, with a mix of traditional and innovative dishes. The speciality is risotto with a Piedmontese cheese. Closed two weeks Aug.

Asinocotto

48 Via dei Vascellari 06-589 8985 L & D Tue–Fri, D only Sat–Sun, L only Mon. **€€€** [p339, D2]
Small, typical Trastevere trattoria offering refined and creative cuisine (gnocchi with peppers and mint, veal liver in raspberry vinegar). Gay-friendly and gay-owned.

Bir & Fud

23 Via Benedetta 06-589 4016 D daily. **€–€€** [p339, C1]
A high-end pizzeria with a passion for quality ingredients. Choose from a large selection of fried antipasti and more than 100 labels of local and international beers, mainly from small, family-run breweries.

Checco er Carettiere

10–13 Via Benedetta 06-580 0985 L & D daily. **€€–€€€** [p338, C1]
A pleasant outdoors section and a steadfast Roman menu of fish and meat make this a sure bet. Sweets and ice cream are home-made.

Il Ciak

21 Vicolo del Cinque 06-589 4774 D only Tue–Thur, L & D Fri–Sun. **€€** [p338, C2]
Game hanging in the windows testifies that this is a meat-eating venue. Dishes based on hearty Tuscan recipes and served with the house Chianti.

La Cornucopia

18 Piazza in Piscinula 06-580 0380 L & D Wed–Mon. **€€** [p339, D2]
Specialising in fish dishes, this restaurant's other selling point is its lovely garden, which is a pleasant place for dinner in the summer months.

Enoteca Ferrara

41 Piazza Trilussa 06-580 3769 D only daily. **€€–€€€** [p339, C1]
Minimalist decor and creative menu with organic ingredients. Comprehensive wine selection (850 labels). Light snacks or full meals. Reservations essential at weekends.

La Fraschetta

134 Via S. Francesco a Ripa 06-581 6012 L & D Wed–Mon, D only Tue. **€** [p339, C2]
Simple pizzeria and trattoria menu served with house wine in a jovial atmosphere.

Alle Fratte di Trastevere

49–50 Via delle Fratte di Trastevere 06-583 5775 L & D Thur–Tue. **€€** [p339, C2]
A family-run, authentic Trastevere trattoria serving up Roman dishes with Neapolitan touches – try the oven-roast sea bream. In summer, request one of the few outside tables.

Glass Hostaria

58 Vicolo del Cinque 06-5833 5903 D only Tue–Sat. **€€€** [p338, C2]
Ultra-modern Glass offers creative Italian cuisine and attentive service. Though the cutting-edge design

LEFT: Trastevere has a wide choice of pizzerias.

won't be to everyone's taste, it does make a change from Trastevere's predominantly red-checkered-tablecloth, trattoria decor.

Jaipur

✉ 56 Via di San Francesco a Ripa ☎ 06-580 3992 ⓒ L & D Tue–Sun, D only Mon. €€ [p339, C2]

If you just can't face another pizza, Jaipur is one of the city's best Indian restaurants, with friendly service and a great selection of tandoori dishes. Particularly strong on vegetarian options.

Le Mani in Pasta

✉ 37 Via de' Genovesi ☎ 06-581 6017 ⓒ L & D Tue–Sat. €€ [p339, D2]

Inviting and friendly restaurant serving meat and fish carpaccios; home-made pastas are cooked in myriad different ways. No menu, but the prices are reasonable. Booking advised. Closed three weeks Aug.

Panattoni

✉ 53 Viale Trastevere ☎ 06-580 0919 ⓒ D only Thur–Tue. € [p339, D2]

Not the most inspiring of interiors, but a Rome classic for its thin crusty pizzas, large antipasti buffet, low prices and its quicker-than-lightning, brusque Roman service.

Paris

✉ 7a Piazza San Calisto ☎ 06-581 5378 ⓒ L & D Tue–Sat; L only Sun. €€€ [p339, C2]

Reliably excellent traditional Roman-Jewish cuisine, such as golden deep-fried vegetables and *coda alla vaccinara* (braised oxtail with tomatoes, celery and white wine) characterises this eaterie. Small outdoor eating area. Closed for three weeks in Aug.

Dar Poeta

✉ 45–46 Vicolo del Bologna ☎ 06-588 0516 ⓒ D only daily. € [p338, C2]

Pizzas made with a blend of yeast-free flours which creates an incomparably fluffy base. Tasty toppings. No reservations.

Rivadestra

✉ 7 Via della Penitenza ☎ 06-6830 7053 ⓒ D only Mon–Sat. €€–€€€ [p338, B1]

This fairly new "concept restaurant" bases its menu around fresh, seasonal ingredients. Its predominantly Roman flavours are spiced up with the odd Oriental touch.

Spirito Divino

✉ 31a/b Via de' Genovesi ☎ 06-589 6689 ⓒ D only Mon–Sat. €€ [p339, D2]

History permeates this restaurant which stands atop the remains of a synagogue and an ancient Roman house. Classic dishes, many based on recipes used in Ancient Rome. The wine list is international and has won plaudits.

Trattoria degli Amici

✉ 5 Piazza Sant'Egidio ☎ 06-580 6033 ⓒ L & D Mon–Sat. €€ [p338, C2]

This restaurant gives work experience to mentally and physically handicapped people. There's a friendly atmosphere, hearty Roman cooking and great value for money. Popular so book ahead. Closed throughout Aug.

Da Vittorio

✉ 14a Via di San Cosimato ☎ 06-580 0353 ⓒ D daily. € [p339, C2]

One of Trastevere's most popular pizzerias, Da Vittorio serves up delicious Neapolitan-style pizza: try the house special Vittorio, with a classic topping of mozzarella, tomato and basil. Great atmosphere and good value.

Bars and Cafés

The perfect place for a pre-dinner cocktail or a post-dinner drink is **Ombre Rosse** (12 Piazza Sant'Egidio). In a scenic piazza, it has a lively atmosphere and is open all day every day (except Sunday morning).

A retro feel, a fabulous position between Trastevere and Gianicolo, and plenty of outdoor space have turned **Baretto** (27F Via Garibaldi) into a popular pre- and post-dinner stopover. Live music and film screenings in summer.

Freni e Frizioni (4–6 Via del Politeama) is a buzzy bar open for breakfast, lunch and dinner, but is most popular for aperitifs in the early evening, when the crowds spill out onto the piazza outside.

Bar San Calisto (3–4 Piazza San Calisto) is small and plain but nevertheless pulls in an incredibly mixed crowd. Its chocolate ice cream and hot chocolate in winter are deservedly famous.

Stardust (4 Vicolo de' Renzi) is open late, and attracts an arty, trendy crowd.

The ever-popular **Friends Art Café** (34 Piazza Trilussa), open all day long until late at night, is a good place for a quick bite or an expertly mixed cocktail.

On the scenic Gianicolo hill, the **Caffè del Gianicolo** (5 Piazzale Aurelio) is a simple bar where light snacks and fruit-shakes can be consumed indoors and out.

The best-priced café in lovely Piazza Santa Maria is **Caffè di Marzio** (15 Piazza Santa Maria in Trastevere). Excellent opportunities for people-watching.

Recommended Restaurants, Bars & Cafés on pages 218–19

AVENTINO AND TESTACCIO

The most southerly of Rome's hills, the Aventine has always been a tranquil and sought-after residential area. It is also home to a number of religious shrines. Testaccio, once a busy working river port, is still one of the city's most down-to-earth and genuinely Roman districts

Main attractions

SANTA SABINA
PIAZZA DEI CAVALIERI DI MALTA
PIRAMIDE DI CAIO CESTIO
PROTESTANT CEMETERY
TESTACCIO
MATTATOIO
CENTRALE MONTEMARTINI
GARBATELLA
SAN PAOLO FUORI LE MURA
EUR

The Aventine Hill is now one of the most desirable places in which to live in Rome, a tranquil oasis conveniently close to the city centre. Considered the "Sacred Mount" in ancient times, it is the site of pagan temples and of some of Rome's earliest Christian churches.

For centuries, the Aventine lay outside the city walls. It remained virtually uninhabited until 494 BC when the plebeians retreated here to organise the first general strikes against patrician rule. During the latter years of the Republic, it was the residence of foreign merchants and nouveau riche plebeians.

By the Imperial era, the hill had moved right up the social scale. The aristocracy moved in and built magnificent temples and luxury villas on it. In subsequent centuries, several churches were built on the ancient sacred sites. Today, the Aventine remains a well-to-do neighbourhood.

THE AVENTINE HILL

High on the hill is the **Parco Savello**, the gardens once surrounding the 12th-century residence of the noble Savello family. Today the park is a peaceful destination for walks or picnics, lined with orange trees and overlooking St Peter's dome which, thanks to an optical illusion, appears farther away as you move towards it from the park's entrance.

Santa Sabina and Sant'Alessio ❶

Piazza Pietro d'Illiria daily 7am–1pm, 3–7pm free 81, 122, 160, 175, 628, 715

The gardens flank the early Christian basilica of Santa Sabina, skilfully

LEFT: the Pyramid of Caius Cestius – a touch of Egypt in the heart of Rome.
RIGHT: siesta time in the Parco Savello.

A Maltese cross in Piranesi's Piazza dei Cavalieri di Malta.

RIGHT: ceiling detail, Sant'Alessio.

restored to its near-original state in 1936. It was built in the 5th century by a priest from Dalmatia, Peter of Illyria, on the site of the house of a martyred Roman matron called Sabina. The broad nave is lined with elegant Corinthian columns, relics of a temple which once stood here. The west door, made of cypress wood, is as old as the church; its carved panels depict biblical scenes, including the earliest known representation of the Crucifixion.

Next door, the church of **Sant' Alessio** has a fine Romanesque *campanile* (belltower). A pretty courtyard leads into a Baroque interior with a gilt-covered relic of a staircase, beneath which St Alexis is said to have lived and died.

The Knights of Malta

From here, Via Santa Sabina leads into **Piazza dei Cavalieri di Malta** ❷. The square is named after the ancient chivalric order founded in 1080 as

Aventino, Testaccio and Garbatella

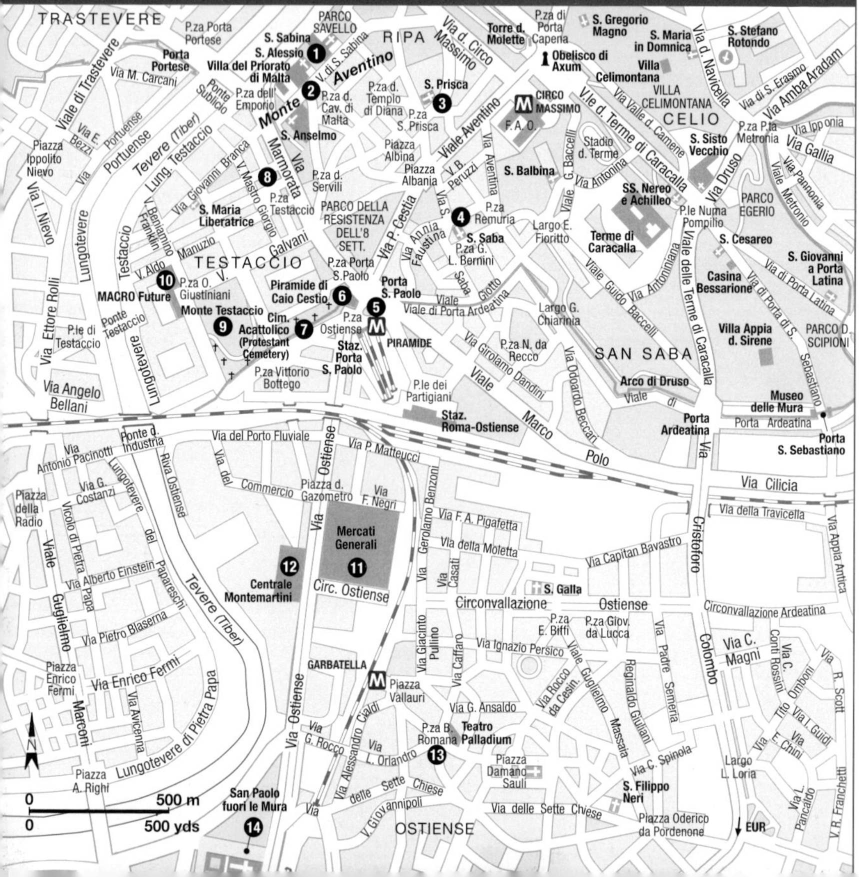

Recommended Restaurants, Bars & Cafés on pages 218–19

the Hospitallers of St John to run a hospital for pilgrims in Jerusalem. The Hospitallers became a powerful military order, based in Malta until they were expelled by Napoleon in 1798. The Knights of Malta have been based in Rome ever since.

The square was designed by the 18th-century engraver Piranesi and has heraldic symbols containing allusions to the military prowess of the knights. Piranesi was also responsible for the monumental gate to the **Priorato di Malta**, the residence of the Grand Master of the order.

Santa Prisca and San Saba

Down the hill and to the northeast is the church of **Santa Prisca** ❸ (11 Via di Santa Prisca; daily 8.30am–noon 4.30–6.30pm), said to occupy the site of a 3rd-century house belonging to Prisca and Aquila, who invited St Peter to dine here. Beneath the church are the remains of a *mithraeum*, a grotto to the ancient god Mithras.

Further down the hill you come to the Viale Aventino, which divides the main Aventine Hill from the smaller one known as *Il Piccolo Aventino*. On the right are remnants of the city walls dating from the 4th century BC.

Across Piazza Albani, Via San Saba leads to the pretty 10th-century church of **San Saba** ❹ (20 Piazza G. Bernini; daily 8am–noon, 4–7.10pm), founded in the 7th century by exiled Palestinian monks. Ancient sculptural fragments are displayed in its portico, and the interior has some Cosmatesque work and remains of a 13th-century fresco of St Nicolas.

This door leads to the gardens of the Priorato di Malta. Peek through the keyhole for an unusual view of the dome of St Peter's framed by a tree-lined avenue.

LEFT: in conversation outside Sant'Alessio.
BELOW: view of the Tiber from the Parco Savello.

The ashes of Romantic poet Shelley are in the Protestant Cemetery. He drowned off the coast of Viareggio and was cremated in the presence of Lord Byron. His heart, however, was snatched from the pyre and was buried alongside Mary Shelley in an English churchyard.

ABOVE: Porta San Paolo and the Piramide di Caio Cestio. **BELOW:** the moving inscription on Keats' tomb.

PIRAMIDE

Originally called the Porta Ostiense, because it marked the beginning of the road to Ostia, **Porta San Paolo** ❺ is one of the best-preserved of the ancient city gates. It was renamed after St Paul who entered Rome through it. Impressive though the gateway is, it is overshadowed by the **Piramide di Caio Cestio** ❻, the tomb of a vainglorious Roman officer, Gaius Cestius, buried here in 12 BC.

Protestant Cemetery ❼

✉ 6 Via Caio Cestio; www.protestantcemetery.it ☎ 06-574 1900 🕒 Mon–Sat 9am–5pm € free Ⓜ Piramide 🚌 3, 23, 30, 60, 75, 175, 280

Adjoining the pyramid is Rome's **Cimitero Acattolico**, known in English as the Protestant Cemetery. Romantic poets Shelley and Keats (the latter dying in a house overlooking the Spanish Steps), and the son of the German writer Goethe are buried here. The cemetery is perhaps more properly regarded as the burial place of non-Catholics rather than just foreigners, and it also contains the graves of a number of prominent Italians, including Antonio Gramsci, founder of the Italian Communist Party.

TESTACCIO

Testaccio, the area west of Porta San Paolo, doesn't feature on most tourist itineraries, but it's worth a visit if you want to experience a genuine Roman working-class district, before it goes the way of Trastevere and gentrification changes its character for good.

By the Middle Ages Testaccio had largely been abandoned, and wasn't developed into a residential area until the end of the 19th century when rows of low-cost tenement blocks with internal courtyards were built to house the workers. Many of these so-called *case popolari* are still rent-controlled working class residences, though the influx of a new generation of more moneyed residents drawn to the fashionable district is driving property prices up.

Testaccio is now one of the most culturally active areas in Rome, with theatres, a cinema, a music school and some of the liveliest nightlife in town. Many of the old wine cellars have been transformed into clubs and late-night bars.

Piazza Testaccio ❽

Despite its ongoing gentrification, Testaccio still retains something of an authentic working-class appeal. The boisterous daily produce market in Piazza Testaccio is a testimony to this.

To the south lies **Via Galvani,** home to some trendy minimalist

restaurants serving fusion cuisine. Galvani leads to Monte Testaccio, which is bounded by **Via di Monte Testaccio**, an uninhabited, quasi-rural lane that is best visited at night when its clubs, bars and restaurants, housed in unlikely looking warehouses and low buildings, really get going.

Monte Testaccio ❾

The heart of the district is the 35-metre (105ft) -high Monte Testaccio, or "Hill of Shards", which gets its name from the broken bits of amphorae that can be found here. Testaccio was basically an ancient landfill site. The amphorae used to transport oil and wine were dumped here once their contents had been unloaded in the warehouses of the Republican port which lined the Tiber between Ponte Testaccio and Ponte Aventino. Today the mound is closed to the public, but you can arrange guided visits through the Comune di Roma Archaeological Tourism (tel: 06-6710 3819). Views of the Tiber valley from the top are splendid.

MATTATOIO

Between Monte Testaccio and the river lies the Mattatoio, the city's former slaughterhouse dating from 1891, when the cattle market was moved here from Piazza del Popolo. For decades, the Mattatoio was the main source of revenue for Testaccio, but in 1975 it was pensioned off when a modern "meat centre" was built outside the city. Today, the buildings house a contemporary art gallery (*see page 61*), the university's architecture department and a farmers' market on Sundays.

Another section is home to **Villaggio Globale** (entrance on Lungotevere Testaccio; tel: 06-5730 0329), an alternative arts venue with live music acts, drawing a young, punky crowd.

TIP

Several of the clubs and restaurants built into Monte Testaccio offer a view of the amphorae shards at their lower levels. One of the finest displays can be seen in the back room of Ketumbar (24 Via Galvani; www.ketumbar.it; tel: 06-5730 5338). The oriental-inspired fusion restaurant and bar attracts a hip crowd, and the food is a welcome break from everyday Italian.

LEFT: detail from the terraces of stacked amphorae. **BELOW:** the Volpetti delicatessen in Testaccio.

EUR

The stark district was Mussolini's attempt to build a city fit for Fascists. Today it is a sought-after residential neighbourhood

The rather clumsy acronym EUR stands for the Esposizione Universale di Roma (Universal Exhibition of Rome), which was to have been held in 1942 to mark the 20th anniversary of Mussolini's accession, but because of the war it never took place. The slightly hilly site, south of San Paolo, was intended to form an impressive entrance to a new town extending all the way to Ostia. But by the time the Fascist regime was over, only two palaces on either side of Via Cristoforo Colombo had been built.

A start had been made on **Palazzo della Civiltà del Lavoro** (Palace of the Civilisation of Labour), popularly known as the "square Colosseum". Piacentini's plans for the new town combined monumental grandeur and a repetitive motif: square pillars, square ground plans and square roofs. The buildings radiate a cold beauty that is all the more striking because, in the city's centre, nothing is rarer than a straight line. After the war, Mussolini-style architecture gave way first to glass facades and reinforced concrete, and then to post-modernism. The result is a largely unplanned mishmash of styles.

But it is not all modern. There is a reminder of Ancient Rome in the form of the **Abbazia delle Tre Fontane**, the 8th-century abbey on the northeast slope of the EUR hill, reached by a path from the sports ground on Via delle Tre Fontane. This is where St Paul was reputedly beheaded *(see page 218)*.

Museums are EUR's main attraction. The **Museo Nazionale Preistorico-Etnografico Luigi Pigorini** (www.pigorini.arti.beniculturali.it; daily 10am–6pm; admission charge) on Piazza Marconi has a large collection of prehistoric artefacts. Next to it, the **Museo Nazionale delle Arti e Tradizioni Popolari** (www.popolari.arti.beniculturali.it; Tue–Sat 9am–6pm, Sun 9am–8pm) presents a lively portrayal of Rome's social history (though everything is labelled in Italian).

Opposite, the **Museo dell'Alto Medioevo** (Tue–Sat 9am–2pm) houses valuable medieval collections, but the most interesting of all is the **Museo della Civiltà Romana** (10 Piazza G. Agnelli; www.museociviltaromana.it; Tue–Sat 9am–2pm, Sun 9am–1.30pm), which chronicles every aspect of Ancient Roman life.

Every summer, the area surrounding the lake hosts Europe's longest-lasting outdoor gay festival, open every night from June to August with three dance floors, bars, restaurants, a theatre and market stands (www.gayvillage.it). Another good place for cooling off is the open-air **swimming pool** (20 Viale America, www.piscinadellerose.it).

The quickest way to reach EUR is by metro on the B line, but there are many bus services from the city centre. ❑

LEFT: Palazzo della Civiltà del Lavoro, symbol of EUR.
ABOVE: macho Mussolini statuary.

Recommended Restaurants, Bars & Cafés on pages 218–19

MACRO Future ⑩

✉ 4 Piazza Orazio Giustiniani, www.macro.roma.museum ☎ 06-0608 ⏲ open for exhibitions only Tue–Sun 4pm–midnight € free 🚇 Piramide 🚌 bus: 23, 30, 75, 95, 280, 673, 716, tram: 3

This is one of two sites occupied by the Museo d'Arte Contemporanea di Roma (*see page 194*). This gallery hosts impressive art shows and installations, often in collaboration with the big guns on the contemporary art scene, including MoMa and PS1.

SOUTH OF THE CENTRE

First impressions of **Ostiense**, a former industrial district south of Testaccio, are not favourable. But for those interested in discovering the face of modern Rome, it's worth delving beneath the grubby surface of this up-and-coming young area. Bars, restaurants and clubs are mushrooming in the streets around **Via Ostiense**.

Rome's former wholesale food market, the vast **Mercati Generali** ⑪ is undergoing a Covent Garden-style make-over led by Dutch architect Rem Koolhaas, who is transforming the area into a state-of-the-art shopping and leisure district.

Centrale Montemartini ⑫

✉ 106 Via Ostiense; www.centrale montemartini.org ☎ 06-0608 ⏲ Tue–Sun 9am–7pm € charge 🚇 Garbatella 🚌 23, 271, 769

Just a 10-minute walk from the Piramide di Caio Cestio is Ostiense's main attraction. What began as a temporary solution to the overcrowding of the Capitoline Museums has become a delightful landmark museum. Four hundred pieces of Roman sculpture are on permanent display in a converted electricity power plant. The juxtaposition of statues with machinery, tubes and furnaces makes this a highly unusual venue. The occasional live jazz performance adds a classy soundtrack.

Garbatella

On the other side of Via Ostiense is the vibrant working-class neighbourhood of Garbatella (Metro B Garbatella, exit left side), worth visiting both for its old-Rome authenticity and for the architecture. The area was conceived and constructed in the 1920s during the post-WWI building boom. First intended for city workers and immigrants, the quarter was modelled on the English "garden city", which laid out two or three-storey buildings in plots with plentiful gardens and gathering space, in the

The inhabitants of Testaccio are said to be the most loyal supporters of the Roma football team.

LEFT: street art in Ostiense. **BELOW:** Centrale Montemartini.

St Paul was martyred in AD 67 at Aquae Salviae, about 3km (2 miles) from San Paolo fuori le Mura. Legend relates that when he was beheaded, after having converted one of Nero's favourite concubines, milk instead of blood flowed from his veins.

ABOVE: Teatro Palladium.

hopes that newcomers to the city would thrive among their Roman neighbours in communal harmony. The architects in charge of the project, Sabbatini and Giovannoni, added character to what might otherwise have been run-of-the-mill housing projects, with balconies, chimneys, floral embellishments and arches.

Piazza Bartolomeo Romano ⓭, one of the neighbourhood's most characteristic squares, is home to the **Teatro Palladium** (www.teatro-palladium.it; tel: 06-5733 2768). Today the arts centre stages international music and dance performances, and participates in the prestigious multimedia RomaEuropa Festival (www.romaeuropa.net).

San Paolo fuori le Mura ⓮

✉ 190 Via Ostiense ☎ 06-6988 0800 ⌚ daily 7am–7pm € free 🚇 San Paolo 🚌 23, 128, 271, 670, 707, 761, 766, 769, 770

In an unappealing site between Via Guglielmo Marconi and the Tiber stands San Paolo fuori le Mura, one of Rome's four patriarchal basilicas.

Built on the site of St Paul's tomb, it was once the most glorious church in Rome, but it was sacked by Saracens, then in 1823 almost completely destroyed by a fire. It may have lost much of its ancient splendour, but it's impressive nonetheless. Remnants of the original basilica include a set of doors dating back to the 11th century, engraved with stories from the Bible, and a Gothic tabernacle by Arnolfo di Cambio, rising over the high altar.

The 13th-century mosaic in the apse depicting Christ and Saints Peter, Paul, Andrew and Luke, was the work of Venetian craftsmen sent to Rome by the Doge. The cloisters are among the most beautiful in Rome.❑

BEST RESTAURANTS, BARS AND CAFÉS

Restaurants

Price includes dinner and a half-bottle of house wine:
€ = under €25
€€ = €25–40
€€€ = €40–60
€€€€ = more than €60

Addo' Masto 2
✉ 119 Via Ostiense ☎ 06-574 6372 ⌚ L & D Tue–Sun. **€–€€** [p339, E4, off map]
Though their speciality is Neapolitan-style pizza, the family that owns this restaurant near Ostiense Station also offer a range of well-executed fish and seafood dishes.

Agustarello
✉ 100 Via G. Branca ☎ 06-574 6585 ⌚ L & D Mon–Sat. **€€** [p339, D4]
This restaurant specialises in cooking with the "poor" ingredients that this area – one of the city's most authentic – is famous for: *coda alla vaccinara* (oxtail in a tomato-based stew), tripe and the like.

Le Bistrot
✉ 160 Via delle Sette Chiese ☎ 06-512 8991 ⌚ L & D Mon–Fri, L only Sat. **€€–€€€** [p339, E4, off map]
A little way from Testaccio in villagey Garbatella, this cosy restaurant offers a variety of vegetarian dishes; the menu is split between pasta and dishes with a French slant.

Bucatino
✉ Via della Robbia 84 ☎ 06-574 6886 ⌚ L & D daily. **€** [p339, D4]
Bucatini alla amatriciana is the dish that gave the name to this trattoria specializing in authentic Roman cuisine. The interiors remain unchanged since the 1960s, with wood-panelled walls and wooden tables. Service is fast (sometimes even too fast) and the evenings are loud and definitely informal – and people keep coming back.

Cantina Castrocielo
35 Viale degli Astri 06-520 4979 D only Tue–Sat. €€ [p339, D4, off map]
More than just a wine bar, the menu at this *enoteca* in EUR includes a wide range of dishes for a complete dinner. Apart from the usual (but delicious) cold platters, Castrocielo serves ravioli with parmesan, and meat stews. Wine lovers have a wealth of labels to choose from.

Checchino dal 1887
30 Via di Monte Testaccio 06-574 6318 L & D Tue–Sat. €€€ [p339, D4]
Typical Roman cuisine, excellently prepared. Known throughout the city. Booking advisable. Closed Aug.

Città dell'Altra Economia
Largo Dino Frisullo 33 3418 7870 L & D Tue–Sun. €–€€ [p339, C4]
Situated in the eco-space of the former slaughterhouse, this trattoria serves simple dishes made with organic ingredients from local producers. Try the small selection of natural wines and beers.

Estrobar
20 Via P. Matteucci 06-5728 9141 D only daily. €€€ [p339, D4]
This classy restaurant within the designer Abitart hotel has an arty theme. Exhibitions of young artists' work provide a suitable backdrop for the sophisticated menu. There's also a tasting menu.

Da Felice
29 Via Mastro Giorgio 06-574 6800 L & D Mon–Sat, L only Sun. €€ [p339, D4]
A Testaccio institution, this bustling restaurant serves up classics of Roman cuisine such as roast lamb with rosemary potatoes. Closed three weeks Aug.

Ketumbar
24 Via Galvani 06-5730 5338 D only daily. €€–€€€ [p339, D4]
Sleek, minimalist interior. Food might include sushi, nasi goreng and braised tuna fillets with parmesan wafers. Music gets louder as the evening wears on.

Manali
108 Viale Avignoni 06-8992 7741 L & D Mon–Fri, D only Sat. €€ [p339, D4, off map]
This pleasant, airy restaurant near the lake in EUR offers creative Mediterranean cooking, using seasonal ingredients. Home-made desserts include a delicious white chocolate mousse *cannolo*.

Osteria degli Amici
Via Zabaglia 25 06-578 1466 L & D Wed–Mon. €€ [p339, D4]
This youthful and welcoming *osteria* is the brainchild of two friend-gourmands, offering Roman specialties prepared with creativity. In summer, book in advance to be seated outside.

Remo
44 Piazza S. Maria Liberatrice 06-574 6270 D only Mon–Sat. € [p339, D4]
One of the best pizzerias in the area, with good starters. No booking.

Satollo
22 Via Rubattino 06-5728 9587 D Mon–Fri, L & D Sat. €€€ [p339, C3]
The menu is creative and audacious, and the chef only uses top quality ingredients. But people don't just come here for the food: the atmosphere is trendy, and many of the design objects on display are for sale.

Tuttifrutti
3a Via Luca della Robbia 06-575 7902 D only Mon–Sat. € [p339, D4]
Hidden down a side street is this friendly, charming restaurant. The menu changes on a daily basis but always contains Italian classics such as *cacio e pepe* (pasta and baked lamb). Closed two weeks Aug.

ABOVE: Estrobar at the Abitart hotel.

Bars and Cafés

Oasi della Birra (38 Piazza Testaccio) is a popular meeting spot for young Romans, with a choice of more than 500 beers from all over the world.

For an espresso, cappuccino or light lunch head to trendy **Il Seme e la Foglia** (18 Via Galvani).

Doppio Zero (68 Via Ostiense) is a fairly new, chic café which offers light meals and snacks, as well as a selection of delicious cakes at tea-time.

For more of the latter, try also **Andreotti** (54b Via Ostiense), a historic *pasticceria*, where they'll not only serve you a perfect cappuccino, but also beautifully wrap up any pastries you want to take with you.

Recommended Restaurants, Bars & Cafés on page 227

CELIO AND SAN GIOVANNI

The Lateran, on the eastern extremity of the Caelian Hill, was the centre of the Catholic Church until the Papacy was transferred to the Vatican in the 14th century. Slightly off the beaten track, this area is packed with striking ancient monuments and churches steeped in history

When the Lateran Palace was the seat and residence of the popes (from the 4th century until the papacy's temporary move to Avignon in 1309), the Lateran was the centre of the Catholic Church. On the return of the papacy to Rome in 1377, the Pope's official residence was moved to the Vatican, but the Lateran remained an important centre for the Church – popes were still crowned here until 1870.

PIAZZA DI SAN GIOVANNI

At the heart of the Lateran district is **Piazza di San Giovanni**, flanked by the **Palazzo Lateranense** (Lateran Palace; closed to public). The original papal residence, founded in the 4th century, was damaged by fire and fell into ruin. In 1586, Pope Sixtus V commissioned Domenico Fontana to build a new palace as a papal summer residence, though it was never used as such. Fontana's Baroque palace now houses the offices of the diocese of Rome (of which the Pope is bishop). It was the site of the historic meeting that led to the 1929 Lateran Treaty, which established the current boundaries of the Vatican and stabilised its relationship with the Italian state.

LEFT: Baths of Caracalla.
RIGHT: San Giovanni in Laterano.

San Giovanni in Laterano 1

4 Piazza San Giovanni in Laterano 06-6988 6433 daily 7am–6.30pm free San Giovanni 3, 16, 81, 85, 87, 117, 186, 218, 590, 650, 714, 810, 850

Next to the palace stands the mighty **San Giovanni in Laterano**, the "mother of all churches" and the first Christian basilica in Rome, founded by Constantine the Great. The church has stood here since 313, but it has burnt down twice and

Main attractions

- SAN GIOVANNI IN LATERANO
- SCALA SANTA
- SANTI QUATTRO CORONATI
- SAN CLEMENTE
- PARCO DEL CELIO
- SANTA MARIA IN DOMNICA
- SANTI GIOVANNI E PAOLO
- THE BATHS OF CARACALLA

The ancient bronze doors of San Giovanni in Laterano.

ABOVE RIGHT: detailed gold mosaic in the apse of San Clemente.

been rebuilt several times. As a result, it is a mixture of styles from the exquisite 4th-century baptistery to the majestic Baroque interior.

The east facade, through which you enter, is the work of Alessandro Galilei (1732–5), but it was Fontana who designed the north facade, when he was rebuilding the Lateran Palace.

The central doorway has the original bronze doors taken from the Roman Curia of the Forum. The facade is crowned by 15 huge statues of Christ and the Apostles, visible for miles around. Most of the marble-clad interior is the result of remodelling by Borromini (1646), but some of the works of art and church furnishings are far older. They include a fragment of fresco attributed to Giotto (1300) and a 14th-century Gothic baldacchino from which only the Pope is allowed to celebrate Mass. The nave's gilded wooden ceiling was completed in 1567. Other features of note include the Baroque frescoes and reliefs of the transept, and the peaceful 13th-century cloisters *(see margin, right)*.

The Baptistery

The **Battistero Lateranense** (Baptistery; daily 7.30am–12.30pm and 4–6.30pm; free) was part of the original complex, built by Constantine around 320; it was rebuilt in its present octagonal shape in the 5th century. In the earliest days of Christianity, all Christians were baptised here. The chapels of San Giovanni Evangelista (St John the Evanglist) and Santi Rufina e Secunda (the

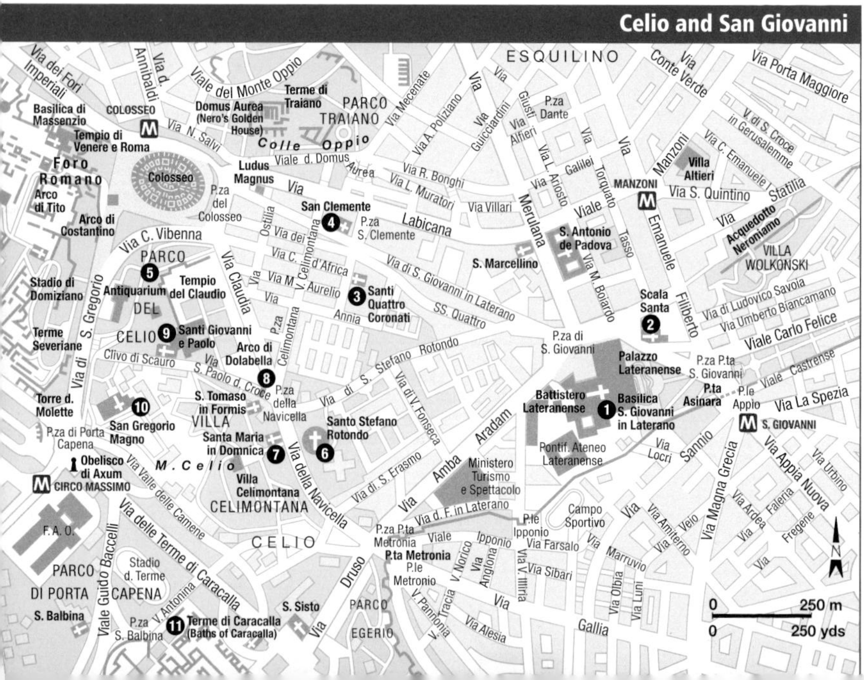

Celio and San Giovanni

Recommended Restaurants, Bars & Cafés on page 227

original entrance) contain a series of exquisite 5th-century mosaics.

Standing 30 metres (100ft) high, the **obelisk** on the square is the tallest and oldest in Rome; it honours the Pharaoh Tutmes III and once stood in the Circus Maximus.

Scala Santa ❷

Piazza San Giovanni in Laterano daily 6.15am–noon, 3–6pm, Mass at 6pm free San Giovanni *see page 221*

Across the street from the Lateran Palace is the entrance to the Scala Santa, said to be the stairs that Christ ascended when he was tried by Pontius Pilate. Brought to Rome from Jerusalem by Constantine's mother, Helena, they are protected under a layer of wood, but you still have to mount them on your knees, and the devout (who arrive in bus loads) do so slowly, stopping on each of the 28 steps to pray.

You can cheat and walk up one of the side staircases to the **Sancta Sanctorum** (Holy of Holies; tel: 06-772 6641; Mon–Sat 6.30am–noon and 3–6pm; admission charge), where there is a painting of Christ – said to be the work of St Luke and an angel.

Santi Quattro Coronati ❸

20 Via dei SS Quattro daily 9am–noon, 4.30–6pm free 85, 87, 117, 571, 810, 850

Originally part of the fortress that protected the Lateran Palace, the "Four Crowned Saints" belongs to a community of silent Augustine nuns.

TIP

The cloisters (daily 9am–6pm) of San Giovanni in Laterano are a high spot of any tour of the basilica. Completed around 1230, they are the work of father-and-son team Jacopo and Pietro Vassalletto, supreme masters of the Cosmatesque school of mosaic work. Note how the columns are inlaid with chips of coloured glass and marble, which were plundered from ancient remains.

LEFT: Santi Quattro Coronati. **BELOW:** Scala Santa draws penitent pilgrims.

Cross, which she found at the same time as the Scala Santa.

San Clemente ❹

✉ Via dei SS Quattro; www.basilicasanclemente.com ☎ 06-774 0021 🕒 Mon–Sat 9am–12.30pm, 3–6pm, Sun 10am–6pm 💰 free; excavations admission charge 🚇 Colosseo 🚌 60, 75, 85, 87, 117, 571, 810, 850

ABOVE: San Clemente. **BELOW:** Persian god Mithras. **BELOW RIGHT:** the ceiling of San Clemente.

The present church, built over the remains of a much larger 4th-century edifice, dates from the 11th century.

You can ring a bell and ask a kind-hearted nun to give you the key so you can see into the beautiful 12th-century cloisters, with slender columns and a fountain, or to the **Chapel of San Silvestro**. This 13th-century chapel contains an endearing fresco illustrating the conversion of Constantine to Christianity by St Sylvester (who was Pope at the time). You can see the emperor suffering from what looks like the advanced stages of a skin disease, then travelling to Rome to be cured by the Pope. A mosaic depicts St Helena's discovery of the True

The basilica of **San Clemente** is one of Rome's most fascinating churches, with some of the finest mosaics and frescoes in the city. Run by an order of Irish Dominicans, it is in fact two churches, one built on top of the other, beneath which lie still earlier remains. The present church dating from the 12th century is built in basilica form with three naves divided by ancient columns. In the apse is a beautifully detailed mosaic depicting the cross as the Tree of Life nourishing all living things. Against a background of brilliant gold, the crucified Christ is depicted in jewel-like blues, reds and greens.

In the **Chapel of St Catherine** are some lovely early Renaissance

Mithras

Mithraism was a mystery religion which came from the Eastern Mediterranean in the 2nd century BC and was practised throughout the Roman Empire from the 1st century BC to the 5th century AD. It is difficult to unravel the exact workings and beliefs of Mithraism as the rituals were the secret of its exclusively male members. It was particularly popular with the army, with followers of the cult enduring severe ordeals, involving heat, cold and hunger. One ritual involved being locked in a coffin for several hours. Worship took place in a temple or *mithraeum* – a cave constructed to resemble Mithras' birthplace.

One extraordinary aspect of Mithras is the similarity with the life of Christ. Mithras' birth was over the winter solstice, he became a travelling teacher who performed miracles, had 12 disciples, was called the Good Shepherd and the Messiah, had a last supper, was buried in a tomb, rose three days later on Sunday, and was celebrated once a year in the spring.

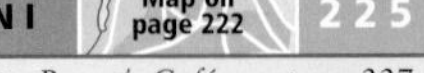

Recommended Restaurants, Bars & Cafés on page 227

frescoes of the life of St Catherine of Alexandria by Masolino (1383–1447) and Masaccio (1401–28). You can see Catherine praying while the wheel to which she was strapped and tortured to death is prepared.

To the right nave a staircase leads down to a 4th-century church, with fine 11th-century frescoes of miracles being performed by St Clement, the fourth pope.

Temple of Mithras

An ancient stairway leads deeper underground to a Roman alley and a maze of damp corridors and eerie chambers. Down here is the earliest religious structure on the site, a 2nd-century **Temple of Mithras**, dedicated to the Persian god whose cult spread to Rome *(see box opposite)*.

THE CELIO

The Celio (Caelian Hill), incorporated into the city in 7 BC when the defeated citizens of the rebellious city of Alba lived there, is one of the seven classical hills of Rome. Today it's home to Villa Celimontana, surrounded by a pleasant park.

Parco del Celio ❺

Sprinkled with ancient ruins and some fine early medieval churches, Villa Celimontana was once a vineyard, and was bought by the Mattei family in the 16th century, who turned it into gardens and an art gallery. The villa is now a public park – a calm sanctuary of greenery and birdsong in a chaotic city. There are two entrances; the main gateway is on Piazza della Navicella.

A short driveway leads to the villa building, which is now the home of the Italian Geographical Society. To the left of the building are some winding pathways, a pristine lawn, and views over southern Rome and the Baths of Caracalla. To the right of the main building is a charming sloping area planted with trees and offering plenty of picnic spots. The park is often home to art exhibitions and special events; in the summer a series of evening jazz concerts is held here.

On the southeastern edge of the park is the 5th-century church of **Santo Stefano Rotondo** ❻ (tel: 06-421 199; Tue–Sat 9.30am–12.30pm and

Pony rides are available in the Parco del Celio, which also has a children's playground.

BELOW: tranquil Parco del Celio.

The ancient Arco di Dolabella was incorporated into Nero's aqueduct.

2–5pm, Sun 9.30am–12.30pm; bus no. 117), one of the few remaining circular churches in the city. The soft natural light that filters through its windows reveals gruesome 16th-century frescoes of martyred saints by Pomarancio.

Santa Maria in Domnica ❼

✉ 10 Via della Navicella ☎ 06-7720 2685 ⏲ daily 9am–noon, 3.30–6pm 🚌 81, 673

On the other side of Via della Navicella is the 9th-century church of Santa Maria in Domnica. In the apse is a magnificent mosaic of the Virgin and Child surrounded by saints and angels in a garden of paradise – the man on his knees at the Virgin's feet is Pope Paschal I, who commissioned the mosaic.

Turn left outside the church to reach Via di San Paolo della Croce, which is straddled by the dramatic 1st-century **Arco di Dolabella** ❽, part of Nero's great aqueduct *(see page 113)*. Next to the arch, the gateway of **San Tommaso in Formis** is decorated with a 13th-century mosaic showing Christ with two freed slaves, one black and one white.

ABOVE RIGHT: mosaic of Virgin and Child with Pope Paschal I in the church of Santa Maria in Domnica. **BELOW:** the Baths of Caracalla.

Santi Giovanni e Paolo ❾

✉ 13 Piazza Santi Giovanni e Paolo ☎ 06-700 5745 ⏲ daily 8.30am–noon, 3.30–6pm € free 🚇 Circo Massimo 🚌 60, 75, 81, 175, 673

The Via di San Paolo della Croce leads to the church of Santi Giovanni e Paolo. The first church here was built in the 4th century, but the present one is mainly 12th-century, with an early 18th-century interior. The 13th-century belltower was built into the remains of a temple of Claudius. The church also gives access to the remains of houses dating back to the 1st century AD (13 Via Chiavio di Scauro; Thur–Mon 10am–1pm and 3–6pm; admission charge).

San Gregorio Magno ⑩

1 Piazza di San Gregorio Magno 06-700 8227 daily 9am–1pm, 3–7pm free Circo Massimo 60, 75, 81, 175, 271, 673

Another noteworthy church in this area is the 17th-century **San Gregorio Magno**. Founded by St Gregory in the 6th century, the church is run by Benedictine monks. Inside, the medieval chapels of Santa Barbara and Sant'Andrea are of particular interest, the latter with frescoes by Guido Reni and Domenichino. The chapel of St Sylvia dates from the 17th century.

The Baths of Caracalla ⑪

52 Viale delle Terme di Caracalla; www.pierreci.it 06-3996 7700 Tue–Sun 9am until one hour before dusk, Mon 9am–2pm charge Circo Massimo 160, 628

In AD 212 these were the most luxurious baths in Rome and the city's largest until the completion of the Baths of Diocletian a century later. In their heyday, these baths could accommodate 1,600 people. Visitors could enjoy the use of libraries and lecture rooms, a gymnasium and a stadium, quite apart from the complex of saunas and pools.

The interior was sumptuously decorated with marble, gilding and mosaics. The unearthed statues are now scattered among various collections, but the buildings are still impressive, their vaults rising 30 metres (100ft). ❑

The remains of the *caldarium* (hot room) in the Terme di Caracalla is used to stage the Teatro dell' Opera's annual outdoor opera and ballet festival in July and August (www.opera roma.it).

LEFT: fragments of mosaic are scattered around the Baths of Caracalla.

BEST RESTAURANTS, BARS & CAFÉS

Restaurants

Crab

2 Via Capo d'Africa 06-7720 3636 L & D Tue–Sat, D only Mon. **€€€** [p340, B2]
A reputable but expensive seafood restaurant with the best oysters in town, as well as every kind of crustacean and mollusc imaginable.

I Clementini

106 Via San Giovanni in Laterano 06-4542 6395 L & D daily. **€** [p340, B2]
Service is friendly and the food is traditional at this old neighbourhood trattoria. Try the *pasta ai clementini* (garlic, hot pepper and cherry tomatoes), or good old classics like carbonara and *amatriciana*.

Isidoro

59a Via San Giovanni in Laterano 06-700 8266 L & D Sun–Fri, D only Sat. **€–€€** [p340, B2]
Fifty pasta first courses, most of which are suitable for vegetarians, although on Fridays many are fish-oriented. You can ask to try several different varieties of pasta on one plate.

Ai Tre Scalini

30 Via dei SS Quattro 06-709 6309 L & D Tue–Sun. **€€** [p340, B2]
Modern, inviting decor and convenient for the Colosseum. Equally strong on meat, fish and pasta. If it's too hot outside, try one of the naturally cool rooms on the lower level.

Bars and Cafés

Sitting at the rooftop bar of **Hotel Gladiatori** (125 Via Labicana) gives you an unparalleled view of the Colosseum. A charming place for an atmospheric *aperitivo*.

The lively **Shamrock** (26d Via Capo d'Africa) offers Guinness on tap and reasonable pub food.

Price includes dinner and a half-bottle of house wine. ***€€€€** = more than €60, **€€€** = €40–60, **€€** = €25–40, **€** = under €25.*

RISTORANTE

Recommended Restaurants, Bars & Cafés on pages 236–7

MONTI AND ESQUILINO

This sprawling area centres on the Esquiline and Viminal hills that lie between the Colosseum and Stazione Termini. Wander the streets of bohemian Monti and multicultural Esquilino, take in the artworks and mosaics of their many fine churches, and visit a stunning collection of Roman antiquities

Main attractions

- SANTA MARIA MAGGIORE
- SANTA PRASSEDE
- SAN PIETRO IN VINCOLI
- MUSEO NAZIONALE D'ARTE ORIENTALE
- TERME DI DIOCLEZIANO
- PALAZZO MASSIMO ALLE TERME
- STAZIONE TERMINI
- SANTA CROCE IN GERUSALEMME
- SAN LORENZO
- SAN LORENZO FUORI LE MURA

In ancient times Monte Esquilino, the largest of Rome's seven hills, was the site of communal burials for slaves and executed prisoners. Emperor Augustus transformed the area into an aristocratic residential zone with palatial villas and idyllic gardens. Maecenas, a rich bon vivant and Augustus' lifelong friend, built himself a luxury villa on the hill, and Virgil and Horace also had homes here. Nero built his magnificent Domus Aurea *(see page 112)* on the Oppian Hill (Colle Oppio), which was later incorporated into the foundations of Trajan's Baths. Pope Sixtus V's magnificent villa stood on the site of what is now Termini Station. While the wealthy lived in luxury on the breezy summit, the foot of the hill was occupied by the slums of the densely populated Suburra district.

Many of the ancient palaces and villas of the area were cleared or built over to make way for the boulevards flanked by stately *palazzi* built after Unification in 1870.

MONTI

These days traffic thunders along Via Nazionale and Via Cavour, two characterless thoroughfares intersecting the area, but between the lower end of them is a cluster of pretty, narrow, cobbled streets lined with bars, restaurants and boutiques, which make up the heart of the trendy bohemian Monti district. To the east, centred around the faded splendour of Piazza Vittorio, lies the Esquilino quarter, now the capital's prime multicultural district, with many shops and restaurants owned and run by North Africans, Indians and Chinese.

The western side of the Esquiline Hill known as Rione Monti or simply

LEFT: streets of Monti.
RIGHT: Termini Station.

If you are in the area on 5 August, head for Santa Maria Maggiore, where the Festa della Madonna delle Neve is celebrated. Thousands of white flower petals cascade down from the roof of the church, commemorating the legendary summer snowfall on the Esquiline Hill.

called Monti, is now a lively district popular with artists, artisans and boutique-owners, and has a number of notable churches.

Santa Maria Maggiore ❶

✉ Piazza Santa Maria Maggiore; www.vatican.va ☎ 06-6988 6800 ◷ daily 7am–7pm € free 🚆 Termini 🚌 C3, 16, 70, 71, 360, 649

According to legend, in August of AD 352, following a vision of the Virgin Mary, Pope Liberius witnessed a snowfall on the summit of the Esquiline Hill. To commemorate the miracle he built the basilica of Santa Maria Maggiore.

The church is the only one of the four patriarchal basilicas in Rome to have retained its paleo-Christian structures. The 18th-century Baroque facade gives no indication of the building's true antiquity, but step inside and its venerable origins become apparent. The striking gilded coffered ceiling and elaborate chapels are 16th- and 17th-century additions, but the mosaics that decorate the triumphal arch and the panels high up on the nave walls are the original 5th-century ones. To the right of the main altar is the burial place of Bernini, Rome's Baroque genius.

Santa Prassede ❷

✉ 9 Via Santa Prassede ☎ 06-488 2456 ◷ daily 7.30am–noon, 4–6.30pm € free 🚆 Termini 🚌 C3, 16, 70, 71, 360, 649

South of Santa Maria Maggiore lies **Santa Prassede**, built by Pope Paschal I in the 9th century. He commissioned mosaic-workers from Byzantium to decorate the apse, the triumphal arch and the chapel of San Zeno, reintroducing an art that had not been practised in Rome for three centuries – with stunning results.

Monti and Esquilino

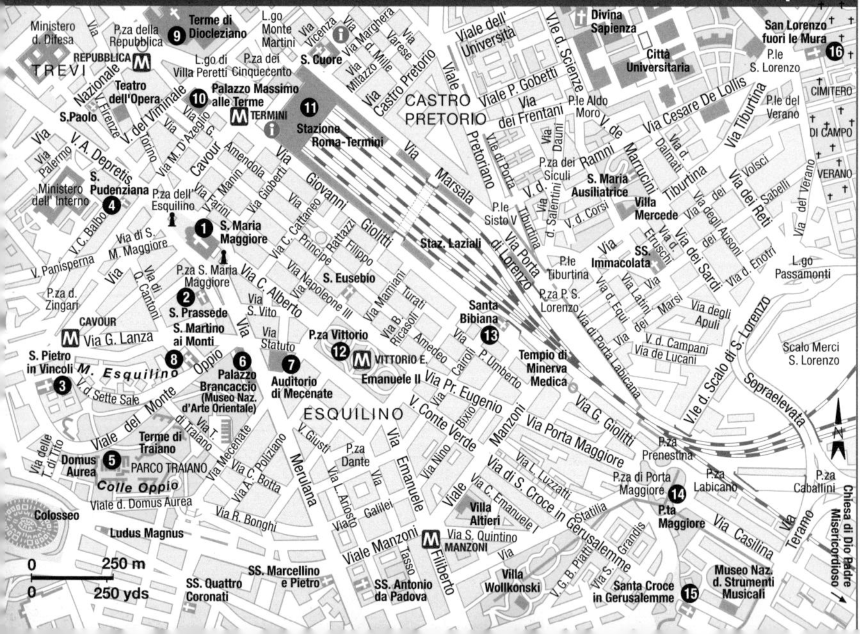

San Pietro in Vincoli ❸

✉ 4 Piazza di San Pietro in Vincoli ☎ 06-488 2865 ⏲ daily 8am–12.30pm, 3–7pm (6pm in winter) € free Ⓜ Cavour 🚌 C3, 16, 70, 71, 75, 84, 117

From Piazza dell'Esquilino, in front of Santa Maria Maggiore, the busy Via Cavour descends the hill towards the Forum. Halfway down, a steep flight of steps leads to Via delle Sette Sale and San Pietro in Vincoli.

The church of St Peter in Chains was founded in the 5th century as a shrine for the chains said to have bound St Peter during his imprisonment in Jerusalem. They are preserved beneath the high altar in a bronze-and-crystal reliquary. Over the centuries the church was rebuilt and restored many times, but the ancient Doric columns lining the nave remained. The church is also home to Michelangelo's monumental *Moses*, part of the unfinished tomb that the artist was preparing for Pope Julius II.

Offbeat Monti

The cobblestone streets between Via Cavour and Via Panisperna are lined with artisans' shops, funky clothes shops, cool bars and ethnic restaurants. This area retains traces of its medieval past, as well as an intimate villagey atmosphere. Here you'll find some of the most interesting boutiques and workshops in town.

Just off Via Panisperna is the beautifully restored Piazza degli Zingari, where gypsy *(zingari)* caravans once congregated. From the square, Via Urbana leads to the church of **Santa Pudenziana** ❹ (8.30am–noon and 3–6pm), built over a house where St Peter allegedly stayed. Dating from the 4th century, its apse is decorated with one of the earliest known Christian mosaics.

OPPIO

The **Oppian Hill**, site of Nero's legendary Golden House – the **Domus Aurea** ❺ *(see page 112)*, is now an ill-kempt park strewn with rubbish and home to lots of stray cats, but there are some lovely views of the Colosseum from up here, and it's pleasant to get away from the bustle of the city. Cutting through this area is the busy Via Merulana.

Museo Nazionale d'Arte Orientale ❻

✉ 249 Via Merulana ☎ 06-469 748 ⏲ Tue, Wed and Fri 9am–2pm, Thur, Sat and Sun 9am–7.30pm € charge Ⓜ Vittorio E. 🚌 C3, 16, 714

Steep steps link San Pietro in Vincoli with Via Cavour.

LEFT: bar in Monti. **BELOW:** Santa Maria Maggiore.

TIP

The Museo Nazionale Romano's collection of classical Roman art and statuary is contained in four different sites: the Terme di Diocleziano and Palazzo Massimo alle Terme near the station, Palazzo Altemps by Piazza Navona and Crypta Balbi near the Jewish Ghetto. A €7 museum card, valid for three days, covers all four sites.

The 19th-century Palazzo Brancaccio houses the Museum of Oriental Art, a small but impressive collection ranging from 6,000-year-old Middle Eastern pottery to 18th-century Tibetan fans and ancient artefacts from the Swat culture in Pakistan. The museum also includes sections on Nepal, India, China, Japan, Korea and southeast Asia. In the gardens are remains of Nero's water cistern, the Sette Sale, built for his private house and used to feed Trajan's Baths.

Further along Via Merulana is the **Auditorio di Mecenate** ❼ (visits must be booked in advance, tel: 06-0608; admission charge), dating from 30 BC and believed to be the *nymphaeum* of Maecenas' villa. Inside are the remains of frescoes depicting garden scenes, birds and small figures.

Follow Viale del Monte Oppio downhill to the 8th-century **San Martino ai Monti** ❽ (7.30am–noon and 4–7pm), a damp, dark church dotted with mosaic remnants and classical statuary.

ABOVE RIGHT: Santa Pudenziana. **BELOW:** boutique in Monti.

ESQUILINO

In many cities the area around the main train station is scruffy and insalubrious, and Rome is no exception to this, with Termini Station surrounded by shabby apartments and run-down hotels. The city council claims that Esquilino is undergoing a "renaissance", which may not be evident as yet, but it certainly deserves one as there is plenty to see.

Terme di Diocleziano ❾

79 Via Enrico de Nicola; www.archeorm.arti.beniculturali.it 06-3996 7700 Tue–Sun 9am–7.45pm charge Termini 36, 40, 64, 170

At the northern end of Piazza della Repubblica are the remains of the Baths of Diocletian, one of the four sites of the Museo Nazionale Romano. Early in the 4th century, these baths – then the largest and most beautiful of the city's 900 bath-houses – were a buzzing centre of social activity. They fell into ruin after the aqueduct that fed them was destroyed by invading Goths.

In the 16th century, the church of **Santa Maria degli Angeli** (www.santamariadegliangeli roma.it; tel: 06-488 0812) was built inside the *tepidarium* (warm bath) to a design by Michelangelo. The interior exploits the massive vaulting of the ancient building to dramatic effect. Highlights include a painting by Domenichino of the *Martyrdom of St Sebastian* and an elaborate time-piece on the nave floor.

Recommended Restaurants, Bars & Cafés on pages 236–7

The splendid **Aula Ottagona** (Octagonal Hall, currently undergoing restoration work) round the corner is an integral part of the immense structure of the baths, in which sculptures from the museum collection are displayed.

Palazzo Massimo alle Terme ⑩

1 Largo di Villa Peretti 06-3996 7700 Tue–Sun 9am–7.45pm charge Termini all buses to Termini

On Piazza dei Cinquecento is the imposing Palazzo Massimo alle Terme, the main site of the Museo Nazionale Romano's museum quartet, where you'll find the most important part of its vast collection of Roman antiquities. There's a stunning array of statuary on the ground floor from the Republican Age (2nd–1st century BC) to the late Imperial Age (4th century AD), but best of all are the splendid floor mosaics and wall paintings from the houses of wealthy Romans, seen at their best in the delicate frescoes from the Villa di Livia, the house of Augustus' wife that once stood on the Via Flaminia. The frescoes decorated the dining room and depict a garden paradise.

Stazione Roma Termini ⑪

On the other side of the piazza is one of the few successful pieces of post-war architecture, the graceful ticket hall of **Stazione Termini**, designed by Angiolo Mazzoni. Its undulating roof echoes the remains of the Servian Walls which are visible through long glass windows. Uncovered during the building of the first station in 1867, they are believed to date from the reign of Servius Tullius (6th century BC). The

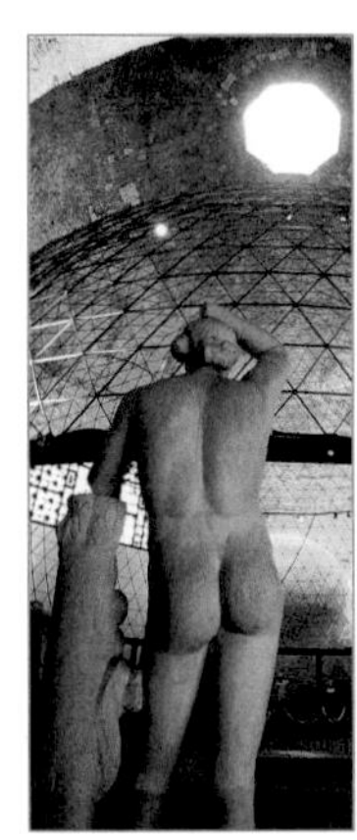

Aula Ottagona houses some exquisite pieces of early Roman sculpture.

LEFT: mosaic detail in the Palazzo Massimo alle Terme.
BELOW: Terme di Diocleziano.

FOOD

The monks and friars at the church of Santa Croce in Gerusalemme run a small kiosk that sells organic jam, honey and excellent chocolates.

revamped station now offers a vast selection of services including a shopping centre, an excellent art gallery (by platform 24), a gym, restaurants, a post office, a church and a medical centre.

Towards Porta Maggiore

Directly south of the station is **Piazza Vittorio Emanuele II** ⓬. Built in the late 19th century to accommodate government ministries, it features one of the longest colonnades in Europe. A food market runs off the piazza on Via Ricasoli (Mon–Sat 7am–3pm).

Several blocks east is the church of **Santa Bibiana** ⓭ (154 Via Giolitti; 7.30–10am and 4.30–7.30pm). Small enough to seem like a private chapel, it is one of Bernini's first architectural projects.

Heading south on Via Giolitti, you pass the romantic remains of the 4th-century **Tempio di Minerva Medica**, a landmark if you arrive by train. To the southeast is **Porta Maggiore** ⓮, a wonderfully preserved 1st-century gate which also served as an aqueduct. You can still see the channels that carried the water. In 1917, a 1st-century underground basilica was discovered here, but it is not open to the public.

ABOVE: interior of Stazione Termini. **BELOW:** bust of Marcus Aurelius.

Santa Croce in Gerusalemme ⓯

12 Piazza Santa Croce in Gerusalemme 06-701 4769 daily 7am–1pm, 2–7pm charge bus: 81, 85, 87, 571, 649, tram: 3, 5, 14

South of Porta Maggiore, along Via Eleniana, is the splendid white facade of Santa Croce in Gerusalemme, which was established in AD 320 by St Helena, Emperor Constantine's mother, to house fragments of the True Cross and other relics that she acquired on a visit to the Holy Land.

Next door, the **Museo Nazionale degli Strumenti Musicali** (www.museostrumentimusicali.it; admission charge; Tue–Sun 8.30am–7.30pm) has some 3,000 pieces documenting musical history from antiquity to the 19th century.

Surrounding the church and the museum are the remains of the 3rd-century **Anfiteatro Castrense**. The section along Via Castrense is particularly well preserved.

Recommended Restaurants, Bars & Cafés on pages 236–7

EASTERN SUBURBS

East of the railway tracks, beyond the ancient Porta Tiburtina, lies the densely populated area of **San Lorenzo**, known as the student area of Rome. Built to house workers in the 1880s, but with few amenities or public services, the area has a reputation for being a focus for left-wing unrest. Today it is one of the city's liveliest districts, its streets – named after Italic and Etruscan tribes – filled with restaurants, artisans' workshops and cultural diversity.

Nearby is the Città Universitaria, one of Europe's biggest universities, which was constructed in the 1930s in typical Fascist style: big, white and imposing.

San Lorenzo fuori le Mura 16

3 Piazzale del Verano 06-491 511 daily 7.30am–12.30pm, 3.30–7pm free bus: 71, 492, 649, tram: 3, 19

The area takes its name from the ancient basilica of San Lorenzo fuori le Mura (St Lawrence outside the Walls), which stands at the entrance to the vast Verano cemetery. One of Rome's first Christian places of worship, the basilica is made up of two churches joined together.

The raised apse is the nave of the Constantinian church erected in 330 (rebuilt in the 6th century with beautiful Corinthian columns); the 5th-century basilica next door forms the present nave. The two were joined together in the 8th century. The interior is decorated with early mosaics and some beautiful Cosmatesque work. To the right is the entrance to the pretty 12th-century cloister and underneath lies a labyrinth of catacombs. The church was badly bombed in World War II, but was soon restored to its former glory. ❑

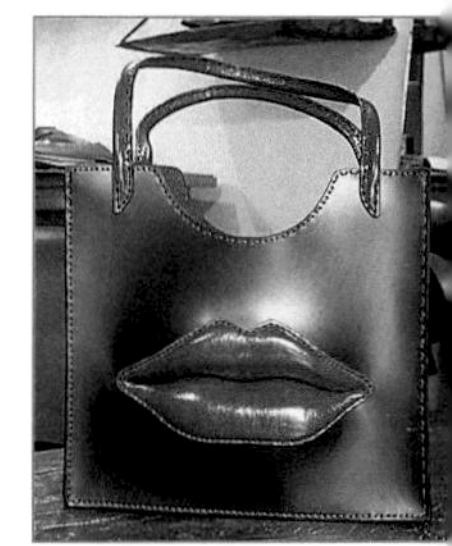

Artists' studios rub shoulders with cheap and cheerful restaurants in the student quarter of San Lorenzo.

LEFT: urban expression in San Lorenzo.
BELOW: Richard Meier's Jubilee Church (aka Chiesa di Dio Padre Misericordioso).

Tor Tre Teste

Rome's isolated eastern suburb of Tor Tre Teste has a church designed by Richard Meier which was inaugurated in 2003. The **Chiesa di Dio Padre Misericordioso** (www.diopadremisericordioso.it; 7.30am–12.30pm and 3.30–7.30pm) on Via Francesco Tovaglieri stands somewhat incongruously but majestically in the centre of a triangular site, with a public park on one side and several 10-storey apartment blocks on the others. Its three striking white shells of graduated height curve up and over the main body of the church. The stark white of the walls, a Meier trademark, creates a sensation of space and light. enhanced and amplified by the dizzying array of skylights and the walls of glass.

BEST RESTAURANTS, BARS AND CAFÉS

Restaurants

Price includes dinner and a half-bottle of house wine:
€ = under €25
€€ = €25–40
€€€ = €40–60
€€€€ = more than €60

Africa

✉ 26 Via Gaeta ☎ 06-494 1077 ⏲ L & D Tue–Sun. **€** [p336, B3]
Stewed dishes from Ethiopia and Eritrea which you scoop up with flat bread. Some vegetarian options.

Agata e Romeo

✉ 45 Via Carlo Alberto ☎ 06-446 6115 ⏲ L & D Mon–Fri. **€€€€** [p340, B1]
Despite their weekend closing and the fact that the kitchen shuts down at 10.30pm, this is still one of the city's best dining experiences. Highly creative dishes (for example, Irish cod served in four different ways and trench-seasoned cheese soufflé with pear sauce). Huge wine selection from its renowned cellar. Booking essential.

Gli Angeletti

✉ 3 Via Angeletto ☎ 06-474 3374 ⏲ D only daily. **€€** [p340, A1]
Enjoying a great location, overlooking a picture-postcard piazza, Gli Angeletti serves up tasty dishes such as tagliolini with red onion, pancetta and balsamic vinegar, and duck breast in a marsala sauce.

Baires

✉ 315 Via Cavour ☎ 06-6920 2164 ⏲ L & D daily. **€€** [p340, A1]
The meat comes directly from Argentina at this popular steakhouse. Empanadas, sirloin and entrecote are among the most popular dishes, and there's a wide selection of South American wines. Fixed-price salad lunch until 3pm.

Alle Carrette

✉ 14 Vicolo delle Carrette ☎ 06-679 2770 ⏲ D only Tue–Sun. **€** [p340, A1]
Here, tucked away in a little side street close to the Forum, is what many consider the best pizzeria in the area. There's a beer tavern feel to it and some outdoor seating.

Cavour 313

✉ 313 Via Cavour ☎ 06-678 5496 ⏲ L & D Mon–Sat, D only Sun. **€–€€** [p340, A1]
This attractive *enoteca* has an impressive 500 bottles on its wine list. Friendly staff are happy to advise on which of their platters of cheeses and cold meats pairs best with your chosen vintage.

F.I.S.H.

✉ 16 Via dei Serpenti ☎ 06-4782 4962 ⏲ L & D Tue–Sun. **€€€** [p340, A1]
A trendy fusion and sushi restaurant done up

in hi-tech style. The menu is fish-based only and divided into four sections – oriental, oceanic, Mediterranean and sushi/sashimi. The results are mostly very good. Limited dessert options, but that's not what people come for.

Formula Uno

✉ 13 Via degli Equi, San Lorenzo ☎ 06-445 3866 ⏲ D only Mon–Sat. € [p337, D4]

Genuine buffalo mozzarella on the pizzas makes this a cut above most pizzerias, and the fried *baccalà* (salt cod) is excellent.

Da Franco ar Vicoletto

✉ 1–2 Via dei Falisci, San Lorenzo ☎ 06-4470 4958 ⏲ L & D Tue–Sun. € [p337, D4]

A real neighbourhood trattoria with no frills, just lots of good and fishy food. Pick the set-price menu and the waiters will bring out dish after dish of seafood served with pasta or salad, or simply grilled, roasted or fried.

Il Guru

✉ 4 Via Cimarra ☎ 06-474 4110 ⏲ L & D daily. €€ [p336, A4]

To satisfy your need for something not pizza or pasta-based go to Guru, one of the most welcoming Indian restaurants in town. Choose various dishes from the classic tandoori or curry options or one of three fixed menus – vegetarian, fish or meat.

LEFT: tempting sushi at Hasekura restaurant.

Hang Zhou

✉ 33c Via San Martino ai Monti ☎ 06-487 2732 ⏲ L & D daily. € [p340, B1]

One of the better of the many Chinese restaurants in Rome, Hang Zhou offers a fixed menu or à la carte. Particularly good are the steam-cooked vegetable ravioli and the chicken with ginseng. The fried ice cream is delicious. Closed three weeks Aug.

Hasekura

✉ 27 Via dei Serpenti ☎ 06-483 648 ⏲ L & D Tue–Sat, D only Mon. €€€ [p336, A4]

A small, streamlined interior makes a classic Japanese setting for sushi, sashimi and tempura. At lunchtime you can choose from one of many *degustazione* menus priced at €15–35.

La Piazzetta

✉ 23a Vicolo del Buon Consiglio ☎ 06-699 1640 ⏲ L & D Mon–Sat. €€ [p339, E1]

A popular restaurant which, due to its small size, can get packed out. Fish and large portions of perfectly cooked pasta are polished off with enthusiasm, and the in-house puddings are excellent. Some seating in the medieval lane outside in summer.

Rouge

✉ 193 Via dei Sabelli ☎ 06-494 0863 ⏲ L & D Mon–Sat. € [p337, E4]

Non-matching, colourful tableware and chairs are their artful way to say "we are informal". This little restaurant boasts a hearty menu with Slavic influences (the chef is Serbian), and the menu changes every night, so consult the blackboard.

Said

✉ Via Tiburtina 135 ☎ 06-446 9204 ⏲ L & D Mon–Sat. €€ [p337, D4]

An old chocolate factory turned into a café and restaurant. While chocolate is the main reason people flock here (you can watch the maitres chocolatiers at work), this is also a great venue for a salad lunch, soup or a full Italian dinner.

Tram Tram

✉ 44 Via dei Reti, San Lorenzo ☎ 06-490 416 ⏲ L & D Tue–Sun. €€ [p337, D4]

A small, cosy trattoria. Pugliese specialities such as linguine with squid and porcini.

Trattoria Monti

✉ 13a Via San Vito ☎ 06-446 6573 ⏲ L & D Tue–Sat, L only Sun. €€ [p336, B4]

The owners are from the Marche region and the menu reflects this: home-made vegetable lasagne, chicken or rabbit in *potacchio* (with tomato, onion, garlic and rosemary), roast turkey with balsamic vinegar. There is fish on Friday, and the menu changes almost daily in this long and narrow, elegant trattoria. Closed for three weeks in Aug.

Bars and Cafés

Il Palazzo del Freddo di Giovanni Fassi (65–7 Via Principe Eugenio) is a Roman institution. Its huge, kitsch interior is filled with locals day and night (it's open until midnight) queuing to get their hands on some of the tastiest ice cream in the city. Their speciality is *gelato al riso* (rice ice cream).

For a decidedly more contemporary experience, which is worlds away from the multicultural area in which it stands, try the rooftop chill-out Zest bar of the luxury **Radisson Blu es. Hotel** (171 Via Filippo Turati). Here you can sip a cocktail as you lounge on leather sofas and look out onto the streamlined spectacle of Termini Station below.

There's a pool table, a piano and a TV screen for sporting events at **The Fiddler's Elbow** (43 Via dell'Olmata), a small Irish pub near Santa Maria Maggiore.

Recommended Restaurants & Bars on page 243

THE APPIAN WAY

Just outside the city walls the "Queen of Roads", begun in 312 BC, was an important part of Christian Rome. The old Appian Way is home to ancient monuments, catacombs and dramatic ruins

Main attractions
- MUSEO DELLE MURA
- VIA APPIA ANTICA
- DOMINE QUO VADIS
- FOSSE ARDEATINE
- CATACOMBS
- CIRCUS OF MAXENTIUS
- TOMB OF CECILIA METELLA

Rome's first great military road, the Via Appia Antica, initially led to Capua 200km (124 miles) away; by 191 BC it extended to Brindisi, the main port for Greece and the Eastern Empire, and was known as the *regina varium*, "Queen of Roads". As Roman law prohibited burial within the city walls, the Appian Way became lined with tombs, vaults and mausoleums. Later it became the site of the first catacombs built by the early Christians.

Although the Appian Way has suffered greatly throughout the centuries, with many of the monuments reduced to rubble, there is still lots to see, and it is a wonderful area to spend a day. You can hire bikes from the visitors' centre *(see box on page 241)*.

To Porta San Sebastiano

Once part of the Appian Way, the Via di Porta San Sebastiano passes through the **Parco degli Scipioni** ❶. At No. 9 is the **Sepolcro degli Scipioni** (closed for restoration work), the mausoleum of the powerful Scipio family. The first family member entombed here was L. Cornelius Scipio, a consul in 298 BC. By the middle of the 2nd century BC, the square tomb was full and an annexe was dug adjacent to it.

Nearby is the 1st-century AD Columbarium of **Pomponio Hylas** (visits by appointment only), which stored the cremated remains of those too poor to build their own tombs. Rich Romans often had *columbaria* built for their freedmen, but this was probably a commercial venture in which people bought a slot.

To go inside, make an appointment at the Museo delle Mura.

LEFT: Claudio aqueduct. **RIGHT:** fresco detail of an old woman and Saint Petronilla the Martyr, Catacombe di Domitilla.

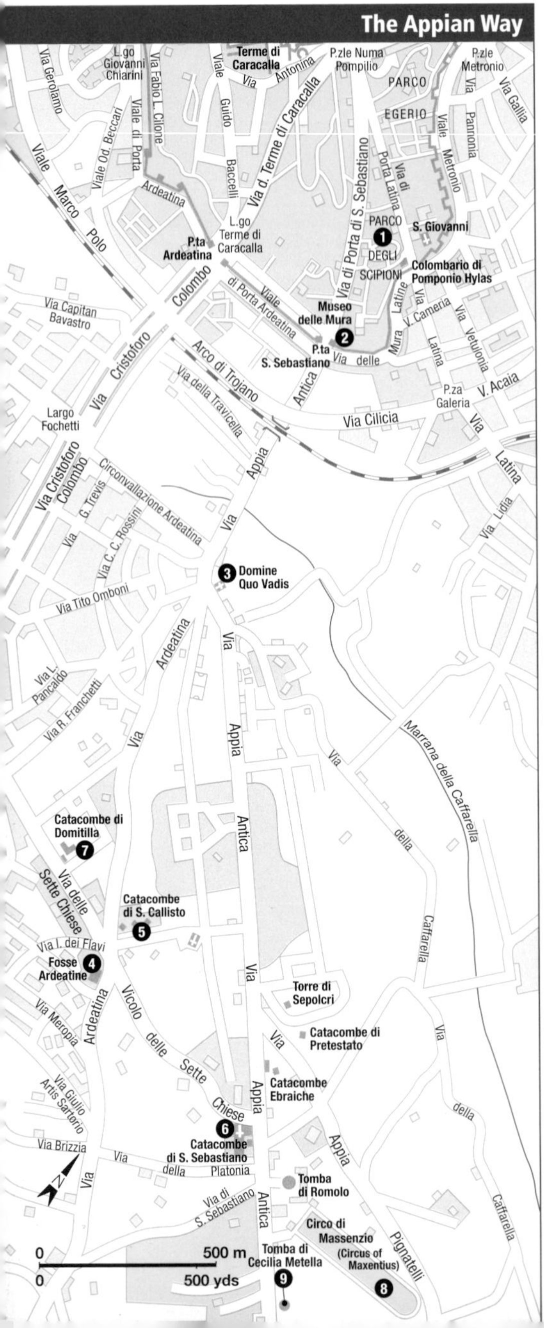

The Appian Way

1 Parco degli Scipioni
2 Museo delle Mura
3 Domine Quo Vadis
4 Fosse Ardeatine
5 Catacombe di S. Callisto
6 Catacombe di S. Sebastiano
7 Catacombe di Domitilla
8 Circo di Massenzio (Circus of Maxentius)
9 Tomba di Cecilia Metella

Museo delle Mura 2

☎ 06-0608 ⏱ Tue–Sun 9am–2pm
€ charge 🚌 118

Porta San Sebastiano is the largest and best-preserved of the gateways in the Aurelian Wall, and inside, the Museo delle Mura gives a detailed account of the building of the walls, once almost 20km (12 miles) long with 381 towers. In AD 403, their height was doubled – to 12 metres (40ft). They were then 3.5 metres (12ft) thick and had 18 gates. Older buildings were incorporated into the walls.

A walk along the top gives some idea of the view the Imperial legionaries had as they watched for barbarian armies. Today, however, there are concrete blocks in every direction, except towards Via Appia, where the Campagna is almost in its original state.

When the Via Appia was extended outside the city walls to Capua, it followed an existing route to the Alban Hills and was the major campaign path for the conquest of southern Italy. In 190 BC it was extended via Benevento to Brindisi,

connecting Rome with the eastern Mediterranean. When the Empire fell, the road decayed and was not used again until the time of Pius VI.

VIA APPIA ANTICA

Beyond the gate is Via Appia Antica. The first part, with the main monuments and sights, is not an entirely pleasant walk due to unrelenting traffic. About 1km (½ mile) down, on the left, is the church of **Domine Quo Vadis** ❸ ("Lord, where are you going?"), where the Apostle Peter, after escaping from a Roman prison, is said to have met Jesus. Jesus replied to Peter's question: "To let myself be crucified a second time."

Jesus is said to have left his footprints on the road and you can see a copy of the footprints on a marble slab inside the church (the original slab is preserved in the nearby basilica of San Sebastiano).

To the left of the church is the little Via della Caffarella, which leads into the Caffarella valley, a lovely stretch of Roman countryside, scattered with ruins, sheep and farmhouses. If you take the right fork at Domine Quo Vadis and head along Via Ardeatina, you come to **Fosse Ardeatine** ❹ (174 Via Ardeatina; tel: 06-678 3114; Mon–Fri 8.15am–3.15pm, Sat–Sun until 4.15pm), a moving memorial to the 335 Italians who were murdered on 24 March 1944, in revenge for an ambush by Resistance fighters in which 32 Nazi soldiers were killed. The victims had nothing to do with the attack, but were rounded up, shot and buried in a mass grave. After the war, their bodies were retrieved and reburied in sarcophagi in the mausoleum.

Catacombs

On the way back to Via Appia are the **Catacombe di San Callisto** ❺

The church of Domine Quo Vadis, built on the spot where St Peter is said to have met Jesus.

LEFT: Porta San Sebastiano. **ABOVE LEFT:** the Archeobus runs along the Appian Way. **BELOW:** the San Sebastiano catacombs are one of the most popular to visit.

Bikes and Buses

A hop-on hop-off minibus, the Archeobus, leaves daily from Piazza Venezia and goes the length of the Appian Way (www.trambusopen.com; tel: 06-684 0901; daily departures on the hour 10am–4.50pm; ticket purchased on board or online, and valid all day).

Alternatively, you can hire a bike from the visitors' centre (60 Via Appia Antica; www.parcoappia antica.org; tel: 06-513 5316; daily 9.30am–5.30pm; book ahead if in a group) or take a guided bike tour – the itinerary lasts about 2½ hours and winds through the Caffarella valley (daily) and along the Appian Way (Sundays and Bank Holidays). The best time to visit is on a Sunday or Bank Holiday, when traffic is restricted.

Signs and symbols in the catacombs:
Dove holding a twig – reconciliation between God and Man.
Anchor – sign of hope.
Fish – symbol of Christ (the initial letters of the Greek word for fish make the phrase "Jesus Christ, God's Son, Saviour").
Dolphin – coming to save the shipwrecked, Jesus the Saviour.
Jonah and the Whale – the Resurrection.

(Thur–Tue 9am–noon and 2–5pm; *see page 245*). In the **Cripta dei Papi** (Crypt of the Popes), inscriptions of at least 10 bishops of Rome from the 3rd and 4th centuries have been discovered. Among them is the first documented use of the title "Pope" for the bishop of Rome (from AD 298).

Also open to the public are the **Catacombe di San Sebastiano** ❻ (Mon–Sat 9am–noon and 2–5.30pm; *see page 245*), the first of the underground burial sites to be so called due to its proximity to a cave (from the Greek *kata*, near, and *kymbas*, cave), and the **Catacombe di Domitilla** ❼ (Wed–Mon 9am– noon and 2–5pm; *see page 245*), one of the largest catacombs in Rome. Contrary to popular belief, the catacombs were not used for worship, nor for hiding in during times of Christian persecution; the excavated rooms were used for simple funeral ceremonies.

Among the rows of shelves for the dead are a lot of small "tombs", used for the tragically high number of infant deaths, and some particularly large or imposing ones, usually belonging to martyrs who were reburied in Roman churches in the Middle Ages. Further along Via Appia, at No. 119a, are the Jewish catacombs of Vigna Randanini. To visit them you need to seek permission from the Comunità Ebraica in Rome.

Circus of Maxentius ❽

✉ 153 Via Appia Antica ☎ 06-0608
🕒 Tue–Sat 9am–1.30pm € free
🚌 660

Also worth seeing are the **Circo di Massenzio**, built by the Emperor Maxentius, and the **Mausoleo di Romolo**, both from around AD 310. The Circus was used for chariot races and could seat 10,000 spectators. Maxentius' Imperial palace,

RIGHT: the colossal tomb of Cecilia Metella.
BELOW: Circo di Massenzio.

Recommended Restaurants & Bars listed below

Villa di Massenzio, is nearby (opening times as above).

The tomb of Cecilia Metella 9

161 Appia Antica, www.pierreci.it 06-3996 7700 daily 9am–4.30pm (closing time varies according to season) charge 660

The tomb of Cecilia Metella was built around 50 BC for the daughter of Quintus Metellus Creticus, conqueror of Crete. She was later the wife of Crassus, son of the famous member of the Triumvirate of Caesar's time. During the 14th century the tomb was incorporated into a fortress and crenallations added by the Caetani family, relatives of the Pope, who used to boost the family coffers by extracting tolls from passers-by.

After this, the Via Appia is far more rural, sparse and quiet, with overgrown ruins, fabulous gated modern villas and shady trees. The remains of tombs built by the great families of Rome dot the roadside. To the east, you can see the dramatic arches of the Claudio aqueduct, one of 11 that supplied Rome with water at the height of its power.

Beyond the crossing with Via Erode Attico, the remains in the farmland to the left are those of the 2nd-century AD **Villa dei Quintili** (1092 Via Appia Nuova; www.pierreci.it; Tue–Sun 9am–7pm, times do vary). If you look closely, you can see a *nymphaeum* and aqueduct arches. Finally, where Via Appia joins the road that leads back to Via Appia Nuova is **Casale Rotondo**, a late 1st-century BC tomb, with a farmhouse sitting on top. ❑

TOP AND ABOVE: on Sundays the Via Appia Antica is popular with runners and cyclists.

RESTAURANTS & BARS

Restaurants

L'Archeologia
139 Via Appia Antica
06-788 0494 L & D Wed–Mon. **€€–€€€**
Set in a 16th-century house with a beautiful outdoor area and ancient ruins on view. Fresh fish daily. Excellent wine cellar in an old catacomb.

Cecilia Metella
125–129 Via Appia Antica
06-513 6743 L & D Tue–Sun. **€€–€€€**
Just across from the catacombs of San Sebastiano, this could easily have been a tourist trap but isn't. Good cooking, and a delightful terrace.

Hostaria Antica Roma
87 Via Appia Antica
06-513 2888 L & D Tue–Sun. **€€€**
This charming restaurant's garden features ancient Roman ruins. Specialities include gnocchi with clams and a succulent beef fillet with truffles. A tasting menu of ancient recipes is available on Tuesdays and Thursdays.

Ar Montarozzo
4 Via Appia Antica
06-7720 8434 L & D Tue–Sun. **€€€**
A lovely restaurant with garden for alfresco eating and a predominantly fishy menu – try the risotto with asparagus tips and prawns. All the usual Roman classics are here, too, and there's an extensive wine list, with 300 bottles.

Bars

Bar Appia Antica (on the corner of Via Appia Antica and Via Cecilia Metella; closed Mon) is a good place for a restorative coffee and a snack, before or after a brisk walk along the Appian Way's famous but sometimes wearying cobblestones.

Price includes dinner and a half-bottle of house wine. €€€€ = more than €60, €€€ = €40–60, €€ = €25–40, € = under €25.

Relics of the Catacombs

"A desert of decay, sombre and desolate; and with a history in every stone that strews the ground" – Charles Dickens

For health reasons and habit, the Romans buried their dead outside the city walls; the Appian Way is lined with the tombs of Romans, Christians and Jews – and, for the less wealthy, catacombs, whose labyrinthine galleries contain niches *(loculi)* built into the tufa rock.

While Christian and Jewish practice was burial of the body, Romans believed in cremation, with the ashes buried in an urn. Christian bodies, embalmed or shrouded in linen, were placed on ledges in the walls, sealed beneath marble slabs on the floor or interred in family vaults *(cubicula)*.

The Christianisation of Rome led to the cult of the early martyrs, with pilgrimages and renewed interest in the catacombs. The frescoed interiors are adorned with Christian symbols or graffiti, from a dove, fish or anchor to acanthus leaves and vines. While some are mossy and mouldering, the weather-worn tombs make an impressive proclamation of faith. Today, the Via Appia is an inspired or desolate scene, depending on one's mood.

Above: the Last Supper fresco in the catacombs of St Callistus. Founded around the middle of the 2nd century AD, they are part of a huge complex of galleries, 19km (12 miles) long and more than 20 metres (66ft) deep. Callistus was the deacon in charge of the cemetery; he was born a slave and became Pope before dying as a Christian martyr in 222. These catacombs were only discovered in 1850.

Left: skulls and fragments of engravings in the catacombs of St Callistus.

MAIN PICTURE: this chamber, called the Hypogeum, is part of an underground tomb or *ipogeo*. These were often frescoed, depicting pagan scenes such as funerary feasts or blood sacrifice. Henrik Ibsen enjoyed lying among the tombs. **ABOVE:** many Jews converted to Christianity, but those who kept their faith were buried separately in the Jewish Catacombs.

SUBTERRANEAN SCENE

Three of the largest Roman underground burial sites are to be found in the vicinity of the Appian Way:

- **Catacombe di San Callisto** (110 Via Appia Antica; tel: 06-5130 1580; Thur–Tue 9am–noon and 2–5pm; admission charge; bus no. 218). Rome's first official Christian cemetery encloses the crypts of many early popes and saints.
- **Catacombe di San Sebastiano** (136 Via Appia Antica; tel: 06-785 0350; Mon–Sat 9am–noon and 2–5.30pm; admission charge; bus nos 118, 218, 660). Three exquisitely preserved mausoleums and miles of subterranean galleries over four levels.
- **Catacombe di Domitilla** (282 Via delle Sette Chiese; tel: 06-511 0342; Wed–Mon 9am–noon and 2–5pm; admission charge; bus nos 714, 218). One of the earliest images of Christ as the Good Shepherd features among its sublime frescoes.

The following are in the northeast of Rome:

- **Catacombe di Priscilla** (430 Via Salaria; tel: 06-8620 6272; Tues–Sun 8.30am–noon and 2.30–5pm, closed in August; admission charge; bus nos 63, 86, 92). In the 3rd and 4th centuries, these catacombs were the preferred resting place of the upper classes.
- **Catacombe di Sant'Agnese** (349 Via Nomentana; tel: 06-8620 5456; Mon–Sat 9am–noon and 4–6pm, Sun and religious holidays 4–6pm; admission charge; bus nos 36, 60).

TOP RIGHT: this fresco, a particularly delicate tomb decoration, is in the catacombs dedicated to the Roman soldier who became a Christian martyr (San Sebastiano).

BELOW: underground Rome has more to offer than catacombs. This 1st-century Temple of Mithras, dedicated to a polytheistic Persian cult, lies below San Clemente. In a relief, Mithras is depicted slaying a bull, the symbol of fertility.

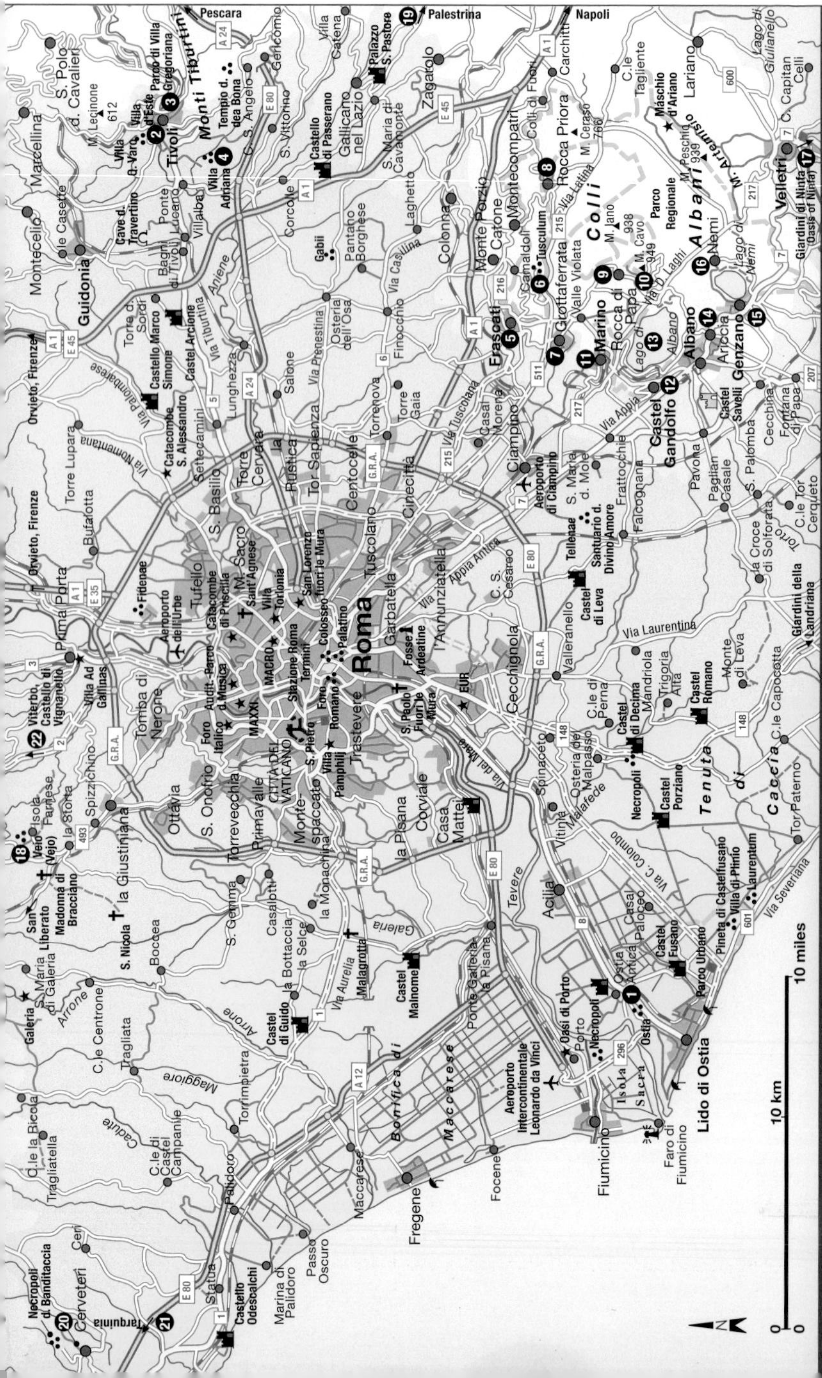

Excursions from Rome

EXCURSIONS FROM ROME

All roads may lead to Rome, but it's worth considering going in the opposite direction to explore the fertile, hilly areas, Etruscan and Roman sites, and Renaissance villas and gardens, all within easy reach of the capital

Given that more than 20 million tourists pour into Rome each year, it's surprising that so few find their way into the Roman hinterland. The region of Lazio remains relatively unexplored, but has plenty to offer. As with any major metropolis, the area immediately around the capital doesn't instantly give way to a pastoral idyll. The shift from suburban sprawl and industrial development to rolling countryside is gradual. However, there are some delightfully picturesque pockets and landmarks to discover, all within easy reach of the city.

The Pope is not alone in choosing the gentle, wine-producing hills of the Castelli Romani south of Rome for his rural retreat. During the sweltering summers and at weekends Romans leave the capital in droves to indulge in the region's excellent food and wine – a favourite Italian pastime – lounge around its lakes and enjoy the scenery. Sun-seekers head for convenient Lido di Ostia, but the resort of Fregene, north of the Tiber, has more cachet. The most scenic stretches of beach, however, are a lengthier drive away at the southern end of the Lazio coast.

Ostia Antica, Hadrian's Villa and the Etruscan graves of Cerveteri draw romantics to their ruins. Lake Bracciano appeals to escapists, walkers, golfers and riders. Villa d'Este, with its pleasure palace and water gardens dominating the town of Tivoli, is a favourite spot for picnickers.

The chapters in this section cover the most popular day-trip destinations, though some places may tempt you into an overnight stay (recommended hotels are listed in the Travel Tips section at the back of this book).

Most of the destinations are accessible by bus or train, but a hire car will give you much more flexibility and enable you to explore Lazio's countryside and coast at your leisure. ❑

PRECEDING PAGES: the ruins of Hadrian's Teatro Marittimo, Villa Adriana.

Recommended Restaurants on page 255

OSTIA ANTICA

The evocative ruins of the Roman town of Ostia, surrounded by pines and flat coastal plains, make a good excursion from the dusty hustle and bustle of Rome. For a sun, sea and sand break, bypass the Lido di Ostia and head for Fregene or explore Lazio's more scenic southern beaches

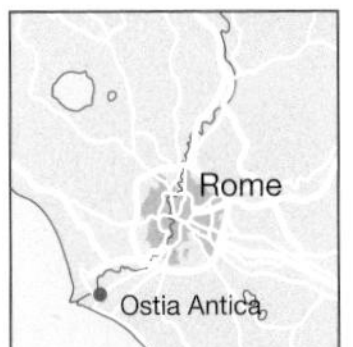

Main attractions

OSTIA ANTICA
LIDO DI OSTIA
FREGENE
ANZIO AND NETTUNO
MEDIEVAL OSTIA

According to legend, King Ancus Marcius founded a port town in the 7th century BC and named it **Ostia** ❶ after the *ostium* or mouth of the Tiber. However, the archaeological evidence dates only to the second half of the 4th century BC, when fortifications were built around the town. Rome was very dependent on this one connection with the sea, because all its essential commodities – especially grain – were transported from Ostia along the **Via Ostiense**. It also became the main base of the Roman fleet in around 300 BC, and by the Imperial era had become a major city, with a population of about 80,000.

Rome's dependence on Ostia was good news for the port's inhabitants. The trade of imported goods from the West and East brought the local population wealth and luxury. The town even had special status, with the male inhabitants being freed from military service. There was also money to be made from holidaymakers. On hot summer days, when the stone streets of Rome practically blazed, Romans fled to the seaside resort.

However, when Emperor Augustus transferred the Roman naval base to Misenium, Ostia felt the loss of the free-spending sailors and all the associated trade. For a while, it remained the unloading point for the grain ships and, in AD 41–54, Claudius had new docks built, but the beginning of the end of Ostia was already evident – the harbour was silting up. Not even a new harbour basin – now the airport of Fiumicino – that was dug on the orders of Trajan (AD 98–117) could stop this process. The coastline gradually moved west, and today Ostia is several kilometres from the sea.

LEFT: the Capitolium Curia, Ostia Antica.
RIGHT: beach huts at the Lido di Ostia.

Part of the well-preserved mosaic in the Baths of Neptune.

Mass exodus

Ostia's prosperity peaked in the early 2nd century, but its decline was steady and relentless. Emperor Constantine's decision to move the capital of the Empire to Constantinople in the 4th century, continual pirate attacks and, in the early Middle Ages, the threat of Saracen invasions, meant that Ostia's population was forced to leave their homes. Soon, the only inhabitants left were malarial mosquitoes.

At that time, the coastline was about 4km (2 miles) further inland than it is today. Luckily for archaeologists, the city was never repopulated, and it has been very well preserved under a bed of sand. Although the ruins were quarried for building materials in the Middle Ages, about two-thirds of the Roman town can now be seen, thanks to extensive archaeological excavation.

Since the 19th century, when excavations began under Popes Pius VII and Pius IX, this archaeological treasure house has been systematically laid bare. The better finds are on display in Rome's museums.

OSTIA ANTICA

06-5635 8003 Tue–Sun Apr–Oct 8.30am–7.30pm, Nov–Mar 8.30am–4/5pm charge Ostia Antica/Scavi

Among the umbrella pines and wild flowers of the ancient site are the remarkably well-preserved remains of warehouses, shops, baths and barracks, temples and theatres. They give as good an insight into the everyday urban life of ancient Rome

RIGHT: one of few statues left *in situ* – most of the finds are in museums.
BELOW: evocative ruin.

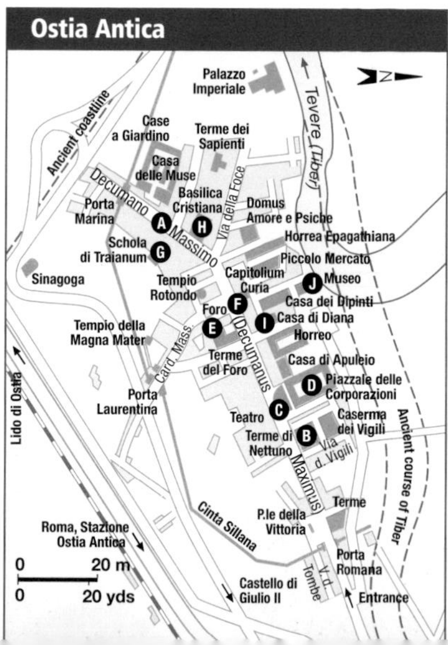

Recommended Restaurants on page 255

as the Forum, or even Pompeii. From the entrance, visitors follow the **Decumanus Maximus** Ⓐ, the same main road used by the Ancient Romans, which leads through the city centre. Worth noting en route are the **Terme di Nettuno** Ⓑ (Baths of Neptune), named after their glorious mosaic floor, and the **Teatro** Ⓒ (Theatre), which warrants a visit for the splendid views offered by its upper tiers. Underneath these tiers there would have been taverns and shops. Beside the theatre, three large masks have been mounted on tufa columns – they were originally part of the Theatre's decoration. In summer months, the Theatre is used to stage plays and concerts.

Also well worth looking at are the stalls in the **Piazzale delle Corporazioni** Ⓓ (Square of the Guilds), where lovely floor mosaics preserve the insignias of the various guilds, most of which were associated with the fitting and supplying of ships.

The Forum

The Decumanus Maximus leads to the **Foro** Ⓔ (Forum), where citizens congregated and justice was dispensed by city officials, and the **Capitolium Curia** Ⓕ, Ostia's largest temple, which was dedicated to Jupiter, Juno and Minerva. Beyond is the **Schola di Traianum** Ⓖ (School of Trajan), formerly the headquarters of a guild of merchants, and the **Basilica Cristiana** Ⓗ (Christian Basilica).

The workers of Ostia lived in *insulae*, Roman apartment blocks that were three or four storeys high. The **Casa di Diana** Ⓘ (House of Diana), near the Forum, is one of the

The Pontin archipelago is a group of volcanic islands just off the coast of Lazio. Ponza is the largest and best-equipped with hotels and restaurants, and is a popular weekend getaway with Romans. A trip to this picture-postcard island is a relaxing way to round off a Roman holiday. There's a regular ferry service from Anzio, the nearest port to Rome, and the journey time is about 70 minutes. For more information visit www.ponza.com.

ABOVE LEFT: one of a trio of theatrical masks. **BELOW:** the Theatre, still used to stage occasional summer performances.

Lazio Beaches

Sunseekers should avoid Ostia and head instead for the cleaner beaches a little further afield

Lido di Ostia, just half an hour by train from Piramide metro station, and the surrounding beaches are the most popular, and locals start descending on them at weekends in their hundreds of thousands from late May or early June. This cannot be attributed to the cleanliness of the water or the charm of modern Ostia, but to its convenience as the nearest seaside resort to Rome and the fact that it is packed with *stabilimenti* (amenities) and a rather chaotic nightlife.

It is worth bearing in mind that Italian beaches are organised around *stabilimenti balneari*, bathing establishments, which increasingly offer far more than clean toilets, deckchairs, sunloungers and umbrellas for hire (for a daily fee). Since many holidaymakers spend their whole day there, the complexes have increased their services, and many now offer sporting equipment for hire, host children's activities, put on courses for adults and children, and have cafés which may include full-blown restaurants.

A more upmarket alternative to Lido di Ostia is **Fregene**, north of the Tiber, about 40km (25 miles) west of Rome. Once the glamorous retreat of the *Dolce Vita* set, this appealing resort, backed by a pine wood and luxury villas, is fashionable again (although the water quality is not the best). It's an hour's journey by bus from Lepanto metro station or by train from Termini to Maccarese, then bus to nearby Fregene.

Another alternative some 10km (6 miles) south of Ostia is the sand dunes of **Capocotta**. A once-infamous nudist beach (a small, respectable and predominantly gay section, known as Il Buco, remains, just beyond the gates, going towards Torvaianica), it has cleaned up its act and is now run by a Rome City Council-backed consortium which offers free *stabilimenti*. Located behind several gates, which close at about 7.30pm, this stretch of coastline is clean, well kept and of some natural beauty, since it is located within the protected Parco del Litorale Romano. Take the Roma–Lido di Ostia train from Piramide metro station but get off at Cristoforo Colombo, the last stop. Here you can hire a bike and pedal down the coast, or wait for the "Mare 2" shuttle bus.

Further south, **Anzio** and **Nettuno** are two nostalgic port towns with hotels, restaurants, seafront cafés and boutiques. For a heady mix of antiquity and sunbathing, head to the beach at Villa di Nerone, to which you can walk or cycle with ease from the centre of Anzio. Here you can sunbathe in full view of the remains of Nero's palace. Trains to Anzio and Nettuno leave regularly from Roma Termini.

For the first really clean water and large sandy beaches south of Rome you will have to go a bit further, to **Sabaudia** (direct buses leave from the EUR Fermi metro stop), or the ancient Roman port of **Sperlonga** (about halfway between Naples and Rome). ❑

ABOVE: bathing establishment in Ostia.
LEFT: find long sandy beahces at Sperlonga.

Recommended Restaurants below

smarter ones and is well preserved. It had a balcony on the second floor, its own private bathhouse and a central courtyard where there was a cistern to collect water.

An interesting insight into the sort of housing used by ancient Romans, it also incorporates a tavern on the ground floor, complete with a marble counter on which customers were served their sausages and hot wine (sweetened with honey), as well as ovens, storage facilities, and a beer garden for outdoor drinking.

The Museum

North of the Casa di Diana, a Renaissance building houses the **Museo** ❶. Originally built for storing salt from the nearby salt pans, today the excavation museum contains a collection of sculptures, tools, mosaics, sarcophagi and a variety of other finds from the site, which help to build a picture of daily life in Ostia.

Medieval Ostia

Before heading either back to Rome or on to the beaches of Ostia, while here don't miss the opportunity to visit the medieval town of Ostia.

Developed around the ruins of Gregoriopolis, a fortified citadel built on the orders of Pope Gregory IV between 827 and 844, Ostia was a medieval village within defensive walls; its inhabitants worked in the nearby salt pans.

After it had been destroyed by invading forces in 1408, Martin V built a defensive tower against the barbarians and Saracens. This tower became the centre of a castle built by Pontelli later in the same century for the future Pope Julius II, then a cardinal. However, the attacks continued and, together with the silting-up of the river and a huge flood in the 16th century, drove the inhabitants away.

You can visit the **Castello di Giulio II** (16 Piazzale della Rocca; tel: 06-5635 8024; Tues–Sun 10am–noon, also 3–5pm Tues and Thur; free) as the castle is now known. It has some interesting features, such as scarped curtain walls, which were innovative at the time, but became commonplace in the 16th century.

You can also see the fortress's museum, its church, Santa Aurea, and the Palazzo Episcopale, official residence of the bishop of Ostia. The latter houses some notable frescoes by Peruzzi. ❑

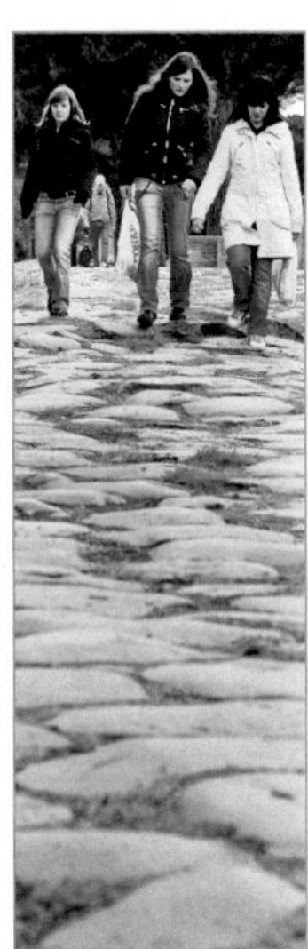

On the Decumanus Maximus.

LEFT: fisherman in Anzio.

BEST RESTAURANTS

Ristorante Il Monumento

✉ 8 Piazza Umberto I
☎ 06-565 0021 Ⓒ L & D Tue–Sun. **€€–€€€**

Close to one of the entrances to the medieval town of Ostia, this restaurant offers a great selection of fish dishes – the house special is spaghetti with shellfish and squid. Carnivores are well provided for with classic Italian dishes such as chicken with white wine, rosemary and garlic.

Price includes dinner and a half-bottle of wine. ***€€*** *= €25–40,* ***€€€*** *= €40–60.*

Lo Sbarco di Enea

✉ 675 Via dei Romagnoli
☎ 06-565 0034 Ⓒ D Mon–Thur, L & D Fri–Sun. **€€€**

Right next to the entrance to the ruins, this reliable fish restaurant is perennially popular. The new pizzeria next door, under the same ownership, is a more economical option.

TIVOLI

Pressed against a hillside with commanding views of the plains below, this small workaday town was once home to Roman emperors and Renaissance aristocrats. The historic villas people flock to Tivoli to visit are testament to its glory days as a retreat for the rich

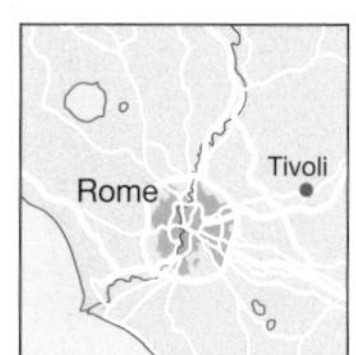

Main attractions
VILLA D'ESTE
VILLA GREGORIANA
VILLA ADRIANA

Tivoli is one of many towns set in the hills outside Rome that has long served as a getaway for Romans during the hot summer months. The town itself would be unremarkable, but for its famous villas and gardens which make it a popular attraction and a worthwhile day trip. The Renaissance Villa d'Este, of Tivoli fountains fame, and the Villa Gregoriana park are within the town, while the impressive remains of Hadrian's Villa are a couple of kilometres south of it. Tivoli is about 31km (19 miles) east of Rome.

If you're driving, take the A24 Roma–L'Aquila motorway and exit at Tivoli e Castel Madama. Alternatively, trains for Tivoli depart from Stazione Tiburtina, or you can take a bus (journey time approximately 45 minutes) from Ponte Mammolo station on metro line B.

VILLA D'ESTE ❷

1 Piazza Trento, Tivoli; www.villadestetivoli.info 077-433 2920 Tue–Sun 8.30am–1 hr before sunset charge Tivoli

The Villa d'Este – a UNESCO world heritage site – is a big tourist draw. The villa itself is worth a visit, with its beautiful frescoes, but the main reason people come here is to see the wonderful fountains and waterworks.

Originally a Benedictine convent, the building was converted into the Governor's Palace in the 13th century. In 1550, Cardinal Ippolito d'Este, son of Lucrezia Borgia and grandson of Pope Alexander VI, was elected governor. He immediately set about renovating the villa and its gardens, to turn it into something befitting his aspirations to the papacy. Ippolito commissioned Pirro Ligorio to design

LEFT: a fresco in the Villa d'Este.
RIGHT: oval fountain in the villa gardens.

the grounds. Ligorio, who had studied the nearby Hadrian's Villa, excavated the hillside, laid it out in terraces and built an aqueduct and underground canal, fed by the river Aniene, to supply the extensive waterworks. The gardens took seven years to complete, and their beauty and ingenuity created the desired impact.

Ippolito d'Este never did make pope, but he did leave a memorial to himself in the fountains, which have delighted visitors for centuries and served to inspire waterworks all over Europe. After the decline of the Este family, the Habsburgs inherited the villa, but they were poor caretakers. After World War I, the Italian State took it over and began the long task of its restoration.

On summer weekends, the Villa d'Este extends its opening times until midnight for visitors to enjoy the spectacle of the fountains beautifully floodlit. Visit the website for current dates.

Above and Right: Avenue of a Hundred Fountains.
Below: view of the "Rometta" fountain and the plains below Tivoli.

The gardens

A walk through the terraced gardens, geometrically laid out with more than 500 fountains, is a delight. The first glimpse you get of the gardens is from the upper terrace, which offers a wonderful vista of the lawns, fountains and walkways that fan out from the central axis which runs down the hill. The café here is a good spot to relax and take in the view of the gardens and the valley below.

As you wend your way from top to bottom, the main fountains to look out for include the **Viale delle Cento Fontane** (Avenue of a Hundred Fountains), a row of close-set pipes that spray water into the air, which terminates at one end with the

Recommended Restaurants & Bars on page 261

Fontana dell'Ovato (Oval Fountain) decorated with nymphs, and at the other with the **Rometta** (Little Rome), a minature representation of Roman landmarks. Halfway along is the **Fontana dei Draghi** (Fountain of Dragons), made in honour of Pope Gregory XIII, who was once a guest here, and whose papal insignia included a dragon.

One of the most inventive of these playful creations was the **Fontana dell'Organo Idraulico** (Fountain of the Hydraulic Organ), designed with an elaborate water-operated organ. Recently restored, it can be seen in operation every two hours from 10.30am. Notice the two upper reliefs portray Apollo and Orpheus playing the lyre and the violin. The **Fontana della Civetta e degli Uccelli** (Fountain of the Owl and the Birds) was another ingenious invention, designed to reproduce the screech of an owl and birdsong through water power (daily demonstrations every two hours from 10am).

One word of warning: avoid the temptation to drink or touch the water – it comes from the sewers.

Parco di Villa Gregoriana ❸

Largo Sant'Angelo; www.villagregoriana.it 06-3996 7701 Tue–Sun Mar and mid-Oct–end Nov 10am–2.30pm, Apr–mid-Oct 10am–6.30pm, Dec–Feb by appointment only charge Tivoli

Tivoli's watery attractions don't all flow in the Villa d'Este. The town is full of ancient remains of temples and other buildings – some (such as the Temple of Vesta) are extremely well preserved, while others have been incorporated into medieval churches.

Not far from the Temple of Vesta is the entrance to the recently restored Villa Gregoriana, a dramatic and steep wooded park set in a rocky gorge. It was created in 1835 at the request of Pope Gregory XVI, whose aim was to avert frequent flooding of the town by diverting the flow of the River Aniene here.

Steep paths lead down to the villa's galleries, terraces and belvederes, from which visitors can admire the great waterfall and the nearby grottoes, both natural and artificial.

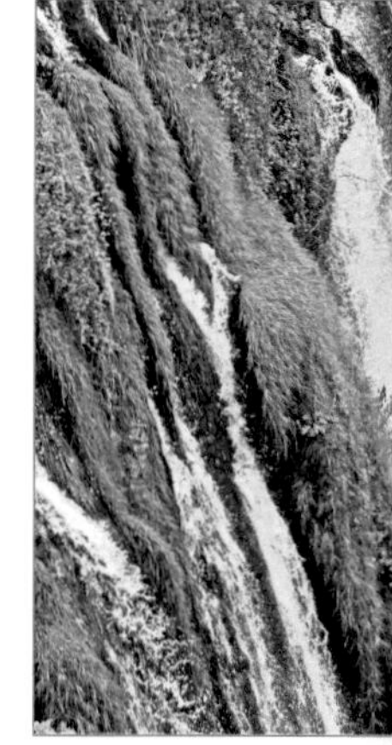

The 100-metre (300ft) -high Grande Cascata is fed by the River Aniene.

BELOW: the Tempio di Vesta overlooks the Parco di Villa Gregoriana in the gorge below.

There is a café just outside the site of Hadrian's Villa, but you might want to consider packing a picnic. There are plenty of benches and shady spots amid the olive trees to sit and enjoy lunch among the ruins.

VILLA ADRIANA ❹

Via Tiburtina, 6km (4 miles) southwest of Tivoli daily 9am–1 hr before sunset charge Tivoli and bus CAT no. 4 Cotral bus from Ponte Mammolo, direction Via Prenestina

Even more impressive than the Villa d'Este are the ruins of Hadrian's Villa, the most magnificent country residence of Imperial times.

When Rome was flourishing, Tivoli (ancient Tibur), in the foothills of the Sabine Hills, was a favoured retreat for wealthy citizens. Among the frequent guests at their splendid villas were Horace, Catullus, Maecenas, Sallust and Emperor Trajan.

In AD 117, Hadrian started to build a luxurious refuge for himself at the foot of the hill on which Tivoli stands. The emperor was a skilled architect (he was the creator of the Pantheon), and his plan was to reconstruct the monuments that had most impressed him on his travels through the Empire, particularly in Greece and Egypt. Another innovation was his idea of scattering the individual buildings over the 60 hectares (148 acres) of the park, rather than grouping them in a central complex. All the buildings were connected by covered walkways and underground passages *(cryptoportici)*, to protect against the weather.

ABOVE RIGHT: archway in the thick boundary walls.
BELOW: the Canopus, Villa Adriana.

Just before entering the ruins, take a look at the model reconstruction of the villa, which gives a good impression of the sheer scale and splendour of Hadrian's grand design.

Beautiful imitations

One of the most noteworthy structures is the colonnaded garden court, known as the **Pecile**, a reproduction of the Stoa Poikile Hadrian had seen in Athens. The surrounding wall, 230 metres (760ft) long, has survived on the north side, as has a basin in the centre. On the inner side stood a covered, pillared entrance.

One of the most outstanding buildings to survive is the **Teatro Marittimo** (Maritime Theatre), a circular building with a columned porch, inside which a circular moat surrounded an island that was reached by two wooden swing bridges. On the island stood a miniature villa where the emperor could relax in safety and privacy.

Between the Pecile and Maritime Theatre, the remains of a great dome that once covered the **Terme** (Baths) demonstrate the very high architectural standards that were employed.

The most ambitious of Hadrian's replicas was the **Canopus**, a copy of the famous Temple of Serapis near Alexandria in Egypt. A 15km (10-mile) canal, lined with luxury residences and statues, led from the River Nile to the Temple. Hadrian tried to imitate the scenario by creating a 119-metre (390ft) -long canal, by the side of which stood marble architraves and copies of Egyptian statues.

The southern bank was originally occupied by a copy of the Serapis shrine, but all that remains is a large niche in the rock and a big chunk of rock lying in the water basin.

Excavations of the villa, first carried out to obtain marble, have turned up more than 300 statues, as well as friezes, frescoes and mosaics. The museum near the Canopus displays various minor finds, but the majority of statues and other finds are now on display in museums throughout the world.

Hadrian didn't enjoy his Imperial palace for long – he died only four years after it was completed. ❑

Relaxing in the shade of the olive trees that line the Pecile basin.

LEFT: reclining statue near the Canopus. **BELOW:** the terrace café at Villa d'Este.

BEST RESTAURANTS AND BARS

Restaurants

Adriano

✉ 2 Largo M. Yourcenar
☎ 0774-382 235 ⌚ L & D daily. **€€€**

Located right next to the entrance to Hadrian's Villa, this restaurant has a large, shady terrace as well as a more formal indoor dining area. The creative menu might include dishes such as courgette-flower risotto, and ricotta and spinach-stuffed ravioli. Also has a few rooms.

Ristorante Sibilla

✉ 50 Via della Sibilla
☎ 0774-335 281 ⌚ L & D Tues–Sat, L only Sun. **€€€**

A few minutes from Piazza Garibaldi, Tivoli's central square, this historic restaurant has hosted popes, kings and emperors – but the charming staff are welcoming to all, and the menu of classic Italian dishes won't disappoint. The shady terrace, with its views of nearby Villa Gregoriana, is a lovely spot in warm weather.

Bars

Admire the view of the Tivoli fountains and gardens from the café on the upper terrace of the Villa d'Este *(pictured right)*.

Price includes dinner and a half-bottle of house wine.
***€€€€** = more than €60 ,*
***€€€** = €40–60, **€€** = €25–40,*
***€** = under €25.*

GREEN RETREATS

Lazio has many hidden gardens, both formal and wild. These peaceful retreats offer respite from the city's hustle and bustle

A trip out of the city in search of the region's little-explored gardens is a welcome antidote to a hectic sightseeing schedule and the weight of all that history. Options range from densely flowered oases such as the Giardini della Landriana and wild, medieval Ninfa, to wildlife sanctuaries such as the peaceful Oasi di Porto and fairytale gardens like the fountain-filled Villa d'Este and the Castello di Vignanello. Gardens generally open to the public from April to October, to coincide with the flowering season. Some gardens put on special events to showcase the plants in bloom; the most popular are the springtime flower shows at the Giardini della Landriana.

All the gardens illustrated here are within easy reach of Rome, and make good day-trip destinations for those willing to hire a car; if you're reliant on public transport, Villa d'Este and the Oasi di Ninfa are just a short train ride away.

If you've got kids to entertain, visit the Park of Monsters in Bomarzo. Created in 1552 for Pier Francesco Orsini as a memorial for his beloved late wife, the garden contains giant sculptures such as the huge boulder carvings of an ogre whose mouth you walk in, whales, dragons and Sleeping Beauty. Open 8am–sunset year-round, tel: 07-6192 4029, www.parcodeimostri.com.

ABOVE LEFT: GIARDINI DELLA LANDRIANA

These gardens, designed by English landscape architect Russell Page (1906–85), are distinctive for their orderly, geometric design: the grounds are divided into 30 "rooms" separated by hedges and paths. Don't miss the Valley of the Roses: hundreds of varieties bloom in romantic disarray across the hillside overlooking the lake, in beds bordered by thyme, lavender and clove pinks, interspersed with slim cypresses.

Open weekends and public holidays Apr–May 10am–noon and 3–6pm, first and third Sunday of June, July, September and October 10am–noon and 4–7pm. By car, take the Via Pontina out of Rome until the Campo di Carne exit. Follow Via Campo di Carne until you reach the gardens at No. 51. Call in advance as opening is weather-dependent, tel: 06-9101 4140.

LEFT: OASI DI NINFA

A bustling, prosperous city in medieval times, Ninfa was all but destroyed in a bloody civil war in 1382. Derelict for centuries, its ruins were restored and botanical species planted in the 1920s. Ninfa has retained its otherworldly appeal: plants and trees grow unchecked amid the moss-covered parapets and crumbling towers.

Open April–October, the first Saturday and Sunday of the month, and the third Sunday April–June. Take a regional train from Stazione Termini to Latina Scalo (30 min), then a taxi from the station for around €15.

RIGHT: VILLA D'ESTE

The grounds of the magnificent Villa d'Este in Tivoli are dotted with water features, from dramatic, gushing waterfalls to musical fountains, nymphaeums and grottoes. See it dramatically illuminated at night if you get the chance. *For more information see page 257.*

Open Tuesday–Sunday 8.30am–one hour before sunset; evening visits mid-June to mid–September Friday–Saturday 9pm–midnight. Take the train from Stazione Tiburtina to Tivoli; Villa d'Este is at 1 Piazza Trento, just off the main square.

LEFT: SAN LIBERATO

This magical garden lies 40km (25 miles) north-west of Rome, overlooking Lake Bracciano. It is full of exotic specimens such as Japanese cherries and tulip trees, and has a delicate, manicured rose garden. Open by appointment only, tel: 06-998 8384. By car, take the GRA ring road out of Rome (exit 5, Cassia Veientana towards Viterbo). Take the Trevignano-Mazzano exit. At Trevignano take the Settevene-Palo road to Bracciano until you reach the gardens at No. 33.

LEFT: CASTELLO DI VIGNANELLO

This beautiful villa has been owned by the aristocratic Ruspoli family for centuries. Ottavia Orsini, an ancestor of the Ruspolis, can be credited with the garden's creation, widely regarded as one of the most beautiful Italian parterres. The perfectly rectangular space is subdivided by mixed hedges of bay, laurel and box; the boxes-within-boxes form patterns, tracing the initials of their creator in the central beds.

Open April–October Sundays and holidays, 10.30am–1.30pm and 3–6pm. Take the GRA ring road out of Rome (exit 5, Cassia Veientana towards Viterbo). At Monterosi take the Cimina road, then continue towards Vignanello, following signs to the castle.

LEFT: OASI DI PORTO

Surprisingly peaceful considering it's just over 1km (½ mile) from Fiumicino Airport, this nature reserve is worthy of a visit. A vast lake makes an ideal habitat for migratory birds, and the surrounding parkland is dominated by imposing Roman pine trees, oaks and poplars. Guided tours by horse-drawn cart can be organised; call 06-588 0880 for details.

Open mid-October to mid-June, Thursday and Sunday 10am–4pm. From Rome, take the Roma–Fiumicino motorway, pass the airport exit and follow the viaduct towards Ostia. Take the first right to Fiumicino, then immediately left onto Via Portuense; the entrance to the Oasi is 3km (2 miles) along the road.

Recommended Restaurants on page 271

CASTELLI ROMANI

For a leisurely country drive through towns and villages famous for their food and wine, hire a car and tour this group of small towns southeast of Rome – a popular weekend retreat for the city's inhabitants

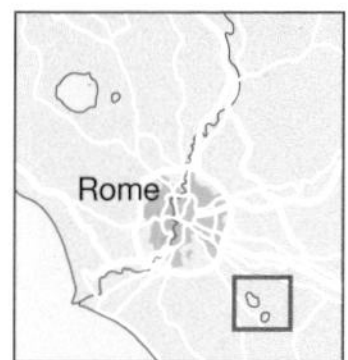

Southeast of Rome lie the Colli Albani, a group of volcanic hills which form a vast horseshoe shaped crater 60km (37 miles) in circumference. Within this giant horseshoe are a number of smaller craters, two of which contain the beautiful lakes of Nemi and Albano.

Thirteen towns in the Alban Hills are known collectively as the "Castelli Romani" (Roman Castles). The name stems from the fact that they evolved around the feudal castles of Roman patrician families who sought refuge here when anarchy ruled in Rome. The Castelli are best explored by car, though they can be reached by Cotral buses which depart from the car park at Anagnina station at the end of metro line A. Frascati is reached by car on Via Tuscolana; Castel Gandolfo, Albano and Ariccia by Via Appia Nuova. Lake Albano, Marino, Genzano and Nemi are reached by Via dei Laghi, which leaves Via Appia Nuovo just south of Ciampino Airport.

FRASCATI 5

Frascati, which takes its name from the thatch *(frasche)* used to roof its huts, turned from a small settlement into a town in 1197, when the ancient city of Tusculum was destroyed and its population settled here. During World War II, it was seat of the German High Command and suffered heavy damage from Allied bombing, which left much of the town destroyed. Many of its historic buildings, including several churches, were rebuilt after the war.

Frascati is the nearest of the Castelli Romani, only 21km (13 miles) away from Rome. One of the best times to visit is in October,

Main attractions

FRASCATI
TUSCULUM
GROTTAFERRATA
ROCCA DI PAPA
MONTE CAVO
MARINO
CASTEL GANDOLFO
GENZANO
NEMI
OASI DI NINFA

LEFT: Castel Gandolfo and Lago di Albano.
RIGHT: spring blooms in the Oasis of Ninfa.

In June hydrangea producers come to Frascati from all over Italy to compete in the lovely hydrangea festival. July and August are also eventful with food and wine festivals, theatre performances and concerts, and a celebratory gathering of vineyard-owners and farm labourers.

when the grape harvest begins; a *frasca di lauro*, a laurel twig, is displayed; the smoke of the first wood fires mixes with the sweet scents from the vineyards, and a fat, fresh *porchetta* (whole-roast pig stuffed with aromatic herbs, for which the region is known) lies on the counter of every *alimentari* (local grocery).

Wine and *porchetta*

The town's trademark is its wine – a light, quaffable wine with a faint, refreshing prickle – which is a product of the rich volcanic soil. In Italy, Frascati is drunk mostly by the *Frascatani* themselves. Much of the stuff on sale in supermarkets bears little relation to the drink served in the *cantine* (wine shops or bars), which ranges from pale to dark yellow.

Most of the exported wine comes from neighbouring towns and villages rather than Frascati itself, but the reason it is so poor is that most is based on the rather bland Trebbiano grape: only the better producers – Fontana Candida and Colli di Catone (especially Colle Gaio) – use Malvasia. For more information on

wine producers and wine tours and tastings in Frascati, visit the tourist office on Piazza Marconi.

Begin with a walk around town, starting at **Piazza San Pietro**. From here, go through the little *galleria* (walkway) next to the cinema to **Piazza del Mercato**, where there is a closed produce market and plenty of stalls where you can get a good sandwich bursting with *porchetta*. Go left past the market and you will find several wine shops and bars in **Via Regina Margherita** and further on in **Piazza del Olmo**, that allow customers to bring *cibo proprio* (their own food).

ABOVE RIGHT: a flask of Frascati in a backstreet *cantina*. **BELOW:** Piazza del Mercato, Frascati.

Frascati villas

Frascati is not only famous for its wine, but also for its palaces and gardens. Next to the bus station is the park of **Villa Torlonia**, originally part of a 16th-century estate that was bombed in World War II. Now only the gardens, and the striking Teatro delle Acque (Theatre of the Waters) fountain designed by Carlo Maderno, remain.

Standing majestically above the town, with commanding views of the surrounding countryside and, on a clear day, Rome, is the **Villa Aldobrandini**. Built in 1602 for Pietro Aldobrandini, a nephew of Pope Clement VIII, the villa is still occupied by the Aldobrandini family and closed to the public, but you

Recommended Restaurants on page 271

can visit the grounds (Mon–Fri 9am–1pm and 3–5pm, until 6pm in summer; permits are available from the tourist office on nearby Piazza Marconi; tel: 06-942 0331; free).

Back down on the main square, the former stables of the villa have been sensitively restored and converted by Massimiliano Fuksas into a fabulous space for high-profile art exhibitions. **Le Scuderie Aldobrandini** (6 Piazza Marconi; www.scuderiealdobrandini.it; tel: 06-941 7195; Tue–Sun 10am–6pm, until 7pm on Sat) is also the new home for the Tuscolano Museum, displaying finds from the nearby ancient city of Tusculum.

TUSCULUM ❻

About 5km (3 miles) from the Villa Aldobrandini is the site of the ancient hilltown of Tusculum. The city of the Latins (founded, according to legend, by Telegonus, son of Circe and Ulysses) was a monarchy before it fell within Rome's sphere of influence in the 6th century BC.

Later, in 340 BC, the city participated in the revolt against the Romans. From the 10th to the 12th centuries, the counts of Tusculum ruled over it – as well as Rome. In 1191, the Romans destroyed the town as an act of revenge for its subjugation, and its inhabitants fled to Frascati. Few ruins remain, but the views from up here are splendid, and it's a nice spot for a picnic.

GROTTAFERRATA ❼

It's only a few kilometres from Frascati to **Grottaferrata**, known for its Greek Orthodox abbey. The **Abbazia di San Nilo** (128 Corso del Popolo; www.abbaziagreca.it; tel: 06-945 9309; daily 6am–12.30pm and 3.30pm–sunset; free) was founded in 1004 by Nilus, a monk from Calabria

Villa Aldobrandini's own organic Frascati is for sale on the premises.

LEFT: remains of the amphitheatre at Tusculum. **BELOW:** Villa Aldobrandini.

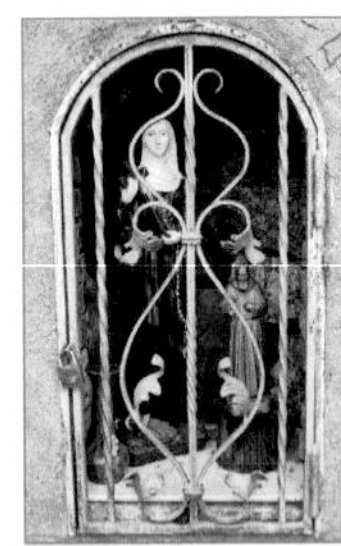

A shrine to the Virgin on Monte Cavo.

fleeing north to find a site safe from attack by Saracens. Under Byzantine rule, southern Italy had a large Greek minority, whose descendants survive today in a few remote areas.

The monastery was built on the remains of a sepulchre dating from the Republican era. The abbey church, **Santa Maria di Grottaferrata**, is decorated with some fine mosaics and has beautiful frescoes by Domenichino in the Cappella dei Santi Fondatori. On Sunday morning, Mass is celebrated according to the Greek Orthodox rite.

From here, you can see the cross atop the hill at **Rocca Priora** ❽, the highest town in the Castelli at 768 metres (2,520ft), which is often covered in snow in winter.

ABOVE RIGHT: entrance of the Abbey of San Nilo, Grottaferrata. **BELOW:** detail of a fresco by Domenichino, in the chapel dedicated to Saints Nilo and Bartholemew.

ROCCA DI PAPA ❾

The town of **Rocca di Papa** ("The Pope's Rock") lies a few miles away, on the northern flank of the **Monte Cavo**, the highest peak of the Alban Hills (949 metres/3,114ft). This attractive medieval town has a *quartiere bavarese*, named after the Bavarian mercenaries who were stationed here by Emperor Ludwig III in the 1320s. Rome is only a few miles away and yet the city, whose lights twinkle like glow worms below, couldn't seem more distant.

The wine of Monte Cavo is excellent, and a particularly delicious local speciality, the *sfogatelli* mushroom, is worth seeking out.

MONTE CAVO ❿

From Rocca di Papa, you may want to climb to the peak of **Monte Cavo**, following Via Sacra through the oak woods. The summit is a little disappointing because it is covered in hundreds of TV antennae. These stand over the remains of the ancient

Recommended Restaurants on page 271

shrine of Jupiter, worshipped by the 47 federated Latin cities, and a more recent monastery. Despite the antennae, the view is fantastic.

MARINO ⓫

Marino, another of the Castelli Romani noted for its wine, holds a celebrated wine festival each October. The town's fountains flow with wine, and there's plenty of wine tasting, eating and parading through the streets. The main square, **Piazza Matteotti** (named after the Socialist leader murdered by Mussolini) is dominated by the Fountain of the Moors, built in honour of the *condottiere* (mercenary admiral) of the papal fleet, Marcantonio Colonna, victor of the sea battle of Lepanto in 1571.

The **Madonna del Rosario** church is well worth a visit. Built in 1713, it is the most beautiful rococo church in Lazio.

CASTEL GANDOLFO ⓬

The pope's summer residence at Castel Gandolfo is beautifully situated 400 metres/1,300ft above the crater rim of Lago di Albano. This was the site of Alba Longa, the city founded by Aeneas. After a long struggle between Alba Longa and Rome, the latter won. Alba Longa was destroyed as a punishment for treachery, but the temples were spared. They are said to have occupied the exact spot of the papal villa.

The Holy See acquired Castel Gandolfo at the end of the 16th century, and in 1628 Pope Urban VIII commissioned Maderno to design a villa here. Completed by Bernini, the **Papal Palace** is linked by bridges and loggias to the other two pontifical villas, Villa Barberini and Villa Cybo. The gardens are closed to the public for security reasons. In summer, the Pope holds the angelus prayer at midday on Sunday on the **Loggia della Benedizione.**

Stendhal, Goethe and Gregorovius all had a high opinion of Castel Gandolfo, and modern Romans love it, too, particularly because it is so close to **Lago di Albano ⓭**. The clean water of this volcanic lake invites boating and swimming, but in the middle, where it is 170 metres (558ft) deep, there are dangerous currents. There is a delightful footpath, 10km (6 miles) long, around the lake. On Sunday, it is as crowded as the seaside.

To the southwest of the lake, the supposed tombs of the Horatian and Curatian families can be seen in **Albano Laziale** on the right-hand side of Via Appia Nuova, if you are travelling in the direction of Ariccia. The local park has remains of the **Villa of Pompey**.

Ariccia ⓮ itself contains a number of works by Bernini. He restored the **Palazzo Chigi** (which can be visited by guided tour; www.palazzochigiariccia.it; tel: 06-933 0053) and designed the church of Santa Maria dell'Assunzione and the pilgrim sanctuary of Santa Maria di Galloro. Like Frascati, the town is famous for its *porchetta*.

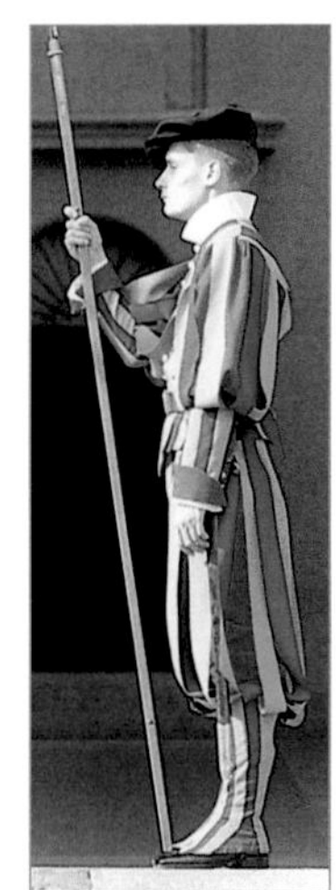

Swiss Guard on duty at the Papal Palace in Castel Gandolfo.

BELOW: Castel Gandolfo overlooking Lago di Albano.

Statue in the garden of Diana, Nemi.

GENZANO ⓯

Further along Via Appia Nuova, on the southeastern edge of the little crater-lake of Nemi, is the medieval town of Genzano, famous for its Flower Festival and its bread. The *Infiorata* takes place on the first Sunday after "Corpus Domini", usually in June, when the main street leading up to the church of **Santa Maria della Cima** is carpeted with holy pictures made from 5 tonnes of flower petals gathered by the townsfolk.

NEMI ⓰

Set on a spur of rock above the lake of the same name is Nemi, known for its *fragole di bosco* (wild strawberries) and the Strawberry Festival on the first Sunday of June, when free fruit is distributed. This unspoilt little village, surrounded by woods, was once home to a sacred shrine to the goddess Diana, in whose honour Caligula built two huge, ornate barges. These were sunk by the emperor's enemies and were only raised in the 1920s, then destroyed when the building they were kept in caught fire during an Allied air raid in 1944.

The **Museo delle Navi Romane** (15 Via Diana; tel: 06-939 8040; daily 9am–6pm; admission charge) displays one-fifth scale models of the Imperial boats, plus some of the decorative elements which survived and objects from Diana's sanctuary, the site of which can be visited on request.

OASIS OF NINFA ⓱

Southeast of the Castelli Romani, about 60km (38 miles) from Rome, the Oasi di Ninfa is one of the most evocative places in Lazio. If you are in a hire car and in the vicinity, a visit to these medieval ruins overgrown with exotic plants is worth considering. *For more information, see page 263.* ❑

ABOVE: Nemi's wild strawberries. **BELOW:** the lakeside town of Nemi.

BEST RESTAURANTS

Price includes dinner and a half-bottle of house wine:
€ = under €25
€€ = €25–40
€€€ = €40–60
€€€€ = more than €60

Castel Gandolfo

Ristorante Bucci

31 Via de Zecchini 06-932 3334 L & D Thur–Tues. **€€–€€€**

With great views of Lake Albano from its terrace, this family-run restaurant is strong on pasta dishes and meaty *secondi*.

Frascati

Da Una Cantina

8 Via Ottaviani 06-941 7379 D only Mon–Sat, L only Sun. **€–€€**

Situated in the heart of Frascati's Centro Storico. Chefs Mariella and Giacomo change the menu on a monthly basis according to what's in season; dishes are prepared using the freshest of ingredients. Has an excellent wine list. Booking is advised.

Genzano

Enoteca La Grotta

Via Belardi 31 06-936 4224 L & D Thur–Tue. **€€**

A small *enoteca*, situated along the road where the June flower show takes place, serves creative Mediterranean dishes.

Ristorante Pietrino e Renata

8 Via Cervi 06-939 1497 L & D Tue–Sun. **€€**

One of the best restaurants in the region, serving dishes made with seasonal ingredients. Specialities include zucchini flowers stuffed with mozzarella, fettuccine with chicken livers, papardelle with porcini mushrooms, and bean, barley and black cabbage soup. Good wine list.

Grottaferrata

La Briciola

12 Via D'Annunzio 06-945 9338 L & D Tue–Sat, L only Sun. **€€€**

A competent exponent of the hearty fare that the Castelli Romani hilltowns are known for: lamb stew and chickpea, barley and chestnut soup are typical dishes. Leave room for dessert, though: the pear and chocolate *millefoglie* is divine.

Marino

Al Cantuccio

3 Via G. Carissimi 06-938 8906 L & D Tue–Sun. **€–€€**

This friendly, family-run trattoria serves up excellent cooking at very reasonable prices. Try the outstanding beef tagliata with rosemary. Tables are set up on the pretty terrace in summer.

Trattoria la Credenza

4 Via Cola di Rienzo 06-938 5105 L & D Mon–Sat. **€€€**

Authentic Castelli cuisine such as *zuppa di baccalà e ceci* (salt-cod and chickpea stew), *coratella d'abbacchio* (lamb offal with artichokes) and *fagioli con le cotiche* (pork and beans).

Nemi

Il Castagnone

Diana Park Hotel, 44 Via Nemorense 06-936 4041 L & D Tue–Sat, L only Sun. **€€**

This family-run hotel restaurant offers classic Italian cuisine and great lake views from the summer dining terrace.

Rocca di Papa

La Longarina

1 Via dei Colli 06-949 5135 L & D Tues–Sun. **€€**

Surrounded by woodland, this restaurant is a tranquil place to sample the regional cuisine. Pasta dishes include the tasty fettuccine with porcini mushrooms and bacon. Meat is cooked on the grill in front of diners, with cuts generous enough to suit the hungriest of carnivores. The crispy pizza, cooked in a wood-fired oven, is also tempting.

ABOVE AND BELOW: deep-fried lamb chops prepared by Il Castagnone's chef.

Recommended Restaurants & Bars on page 279

ETRUSCAN TOWNS

The Etruscans built a series of cities, founded leagues and painted frescoed tombs in northern Lazio more than 2,700 years ago. The remains of these cities make for a fascinating archaeological excursion

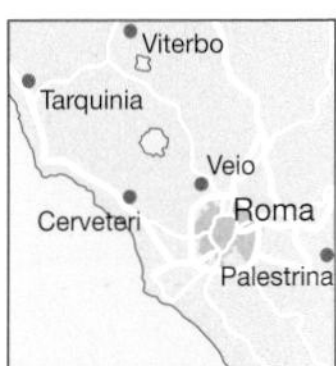

Main attractions
- **VEIO**
- **PALESTRINA**
- **CERVETERI**
- **TARQUINIA**
- **VITERBO**

There are many Etruscan settlements within Central Italy. This chapter highlights the most important ones in Lazio. Touring Etruria by car is probably the best way to take in the sites, though they can all can be reached by train from either Trastevere, Ostiense or Termini stations in Rome, or on a COTRAL bus from certain metro stations (ask at the tourist office for details).

Anyone whose curiosity is aroused by this mysterious and once powerful ancient race will find the well-preserved ruins of these archaeological sites fascinating. Some historical background will enhance the experience and help decode the ruins as well as the collections of Etruscan artefacts displayed in many city museums.

Etruscan origins

In about 800 BC, Etruscans settled on the west coast where Tuscany and Lazio are today. The origins of the Etruscans still puzzle scholars, but wherever they came from, they were a highly civilised people who had a hearty appetite for life. Hundreds of Etruscan tombs have survived, many with wall paintings depicting dancing, dinner parties and music-making. Other paintings show battle and hunting scenes. The Etruscans were also extremely skilled craftsmen, whose speciality was metalworking. Italy was rich in minerals, and trade in metal goods soon became the basis of an active urban society. Cities sprang up where previously there had only been simple villages.

Each Etruscan city supported itself by trade. Eager to obtain luxury goods from the Greek colonists, the Etruscans developed overland routes to reach the Greek cities. These cut straight through Latium, the plain

LEFT: Il Palazzo Papale, the jewel of Viterbo. **RIGHT:** a fine Etruscan fresco.

The Apollo of Veio, a masterpiece of Etruscan art, whose knowing, mysterious smile bears some resemblance to that of Leonardo's Mona Lisa.

BELOW: the 2,000-year-old Nile Mosaic in the Palazzo Barberini, Palestrina.

south of the Tiber occupied by Italian natives called Latins. One of their trading posts on the route south was a Latin village called Rome, originally only a cluster of mud huts. Under the influence of the Etruscans the settlement flourished. They drained the swamp that became the Roman Forum and built grand palaces and roads.

For 300 years, Etruscan kings ruled Rome, but by the 5th century BC their power was fading. The last king, Tarquin the Proud, was driven out when the Romans opted for a Republic. After this the Etruscans stayed north of the Tiber and their influence declined.

Veio ⓲

The Etruscan city closest to Rome, once the largest in southern Etruria, is Veio. Unlike other sites, where only tombs remain, the **Archaeological Area of Veio** (Località Isola Farnese, Via Riserva Campetti; tel: 06-3089 0116; Mon–Sat 9am–4pm, until 7pm in summer, Sun 9am–2pm; admission charge), which lies within the protected Parco di Veio (www.parcodiveio.it), includes parts of a swimming pool and the lower section of a temple. The striking Portonaccio sanctuary was located outside the city walls. Originally, it had a terracotta roof and was decorated with a series of larger-than-life statues of various gods. A block of tufa stone and an underground gallery are the only ruins left from this construction. The famous **statue of Apollo** *(pictured left)* dating from the 6th century BC was found in the temple dedicated to Minerva.

Palestrina ⓳

Ancient **Praeneste** (modern Palestrina) is one of the oldest towns of Latium (Lazio). According to myth, it was founded by Telegonus, son of Ulysses and Circe. The town was flourishing in the 8th century BC, but it wasn't until the 4th century that it became part of Rome. During the civil war between Marius and Sulla, Marius fled to Praeneste, which was besieged by Sulla's troops and eventually destroyed.

Sulla wanted to make amends and so ordered the reconstruction of the **sanctuary of Fortuna Primigenia**, the

Recommended Restaurants & Bars on page 279

mother of all gods. In the Middle Ages a new town rose on its ruins. In 1944 bombs destroyed part of the town, bringing the temple to light and prompting excavations.

The temple was one of the grandest of antiquity. It comprised a series of terraces on the slopes of Mount Ginestro connected by ramps. Adorned with statues and blazing with torches, the complex must have been an impressive sight, which could be seen from afar. The goddess Fortuna was worshipped in the upper part of the shrine. In the 16th century, a palace was built into this upper circle of the temple, occupied first by the patrician Colonna family and then by the Roman Barberini, who expanded it in the 1640s.

Museo Nazionale Archeologica di Palestrina

✉ 1 Piazza della Cortina ☎ 06-3996 7900 ⊙ daily 9am–8pm € charge

The Colonna-Barberini Palace now houses the Palestrina Museum, where countless busts and other local finds are on display, including the badly damaged remains of the statue of Fortuna. The Nile Mosaic on the top floor is the museum's prize exhibit. Dating from the 1st century BC, it shows, in detail, the Nile valley after the annual flood, a scene teeming with peasants, fishermen, priests, soldiers and animals.

Access to the excavated site (with a ticket bought from the museum) is

In the 17th century Praeneste changed its name to honour its most famous native son, Pierluigi di Palestrina, born here in 1525. His distinguished career as a composer included many years as an organist and choirmaster at St Peter's in Rome.

LEFT: Palestrina's 12th-century belltower. **BELOW:** the majestic entrance to the Palazzo Barberini which sits atop the site of Praeneste.

The best way to reach Cerveteri from Rome by public transport is to take the *regionale* (ie not an Inter-City or Eurostar) train to Pisa which stops at the town. Alternatively, a COTRAL bus leaves from Lepanto station on metro line A.

opposite the palace. The lower part of the shrine is buried beneath the old town of Palestrina which is enclosed within the temple's extensive walls. In the central **Piazza Regina Margherita** the Seminario incorporates the remains of the *area sacra*. Most archaeologists agree that this was the entrance to the **Oracle** – one of the most important of ancient times.

CERVETERI ⓴

Ancient remains, even older than those at Ostia, can be found near Cerveteri, where an Etruscan settlement called Kysry was established about 45km (28 miles) northwest of Rome and only 6km (4 miles) from the sea. In the 7th and 6th centuries BC, Kysry became one of the most powerful cities in Etruria, with a population of around 25,000. Revenue came mostly from rich ore deposits in the nearby Tolfa Hills, but there were also strong commercial ties with Hellenic lands, the influence of whose merchants made it the centre of a lively and sophisticated cultural life.

Kysry maintained good relations with its Roman neighbours. But eventually the barbaric strength of rising Rome wiped away what had been a refined and joyous civilisation. Under Roman rule the town became known as Caere. It grew steadily poorer, but was not abandoned until the Middle Ages, when the population then moved east to Ceri, renaming their abandoned town Caere Vetus, which evolved into Cerveteri.

ABOVE RIGHT: the 6th-century BC sarcophagus of a married couple, discovered in Cerveteri, can be seen in the Villa Giulia Etruscan Museum in Rome. **BELOW:** visiting the Cerveteri necropolis.

Necropoli della Banditaccia

✉ Via della Necropoli della Banditaccia, 2km (1¼ miles) from Cerveteri centre ☎ 06-994 0001 ⏲ Tue–Sun 8.30am–5.30pm Ⓔ charge

Nothing remains of the ancient town bar a few walls, but it is worth going to look at the excavation of Caere's necropolis on a hill, an atmospheric site with countless tombs carved into the soft tufa rock.

The oldest tombs (8th century BC) have a small circular well where the urns containing the ashes of the dead were placed. The first chamber-tombs, also cut into the stone and covered with rocky blocks and mounds *(tumuli)*, appeared as early as the 7th century BC. The noble Etruscans were either enclosed in great sarcophagi with their effigies on top, or laid out on stone beds in their chamber tombs. In the 6th and 5th centuries BC, the so-called cubic graves became common. These rectangular tombs were laid out in regular rows of streets, reflecting the social changes that had taken place in the city. By then, prosperity had spread to the lower classes and a

Recommended Restaurants & Bars on page 279

social levelling had taken place. From the 4th to the 1st century BC, the dead were buried in underground tombs called *hypogaea*, fairly plain by comparison to the earlier tombs.

The largest tomb in Cerveteri is the Tomba dei Rilievi *(see right)*. Other important tombs to look out for include the Tomba della Capanna, Tomba dei Dolii, Tomba dei Letti e dei Sarcofagi, Tomba dei Vasi Greci, Tomba della Cornice and Tomba degli Scudi e delle Sedie.

Museo Nazionale Cerite

✉ Palazzo Ruspoli, Piazza Santa Maria ☎ 06-994 1354 ⏲ Tue–Sun 8.30am–7.30pm € charge

Excavations of the tombs not already plundered (the Romans were the first collectors of Etruscan antiquities) revealed goods of gold, silver, ivory, bronze and ceramic. The vases show strong Greek influence as well as the excellent quality of Etruscan craftsmanship. Some of the objects found in the graves, including domestic implements, vases and terracotta lamps, are housed here in the 16th-century Palazzo Ruspoli. However, finds from Cerveteri are scattered as far afield as the British Museum, the Louvre in Paris, the Vatican's Museo Gregoriano and the Villa Giulia in Rome, which includes the famous sarcophagus of the married couple, the Sarcofago degli Sposi.

TARQUINIA ㉑

The Etruscan town of Tarquinia stood on a hill northwest of the picturesque medieval town bearing the same name. The town existed as early as the 9th century BC, but by the 8th and 7th centuries BC it was a rich and powerful city and became an active commercial and industrial centre. Its political supremacy extended over a vast area inland as far as the Cimini Mountains and Bolsena Lake.

Necropoli dei Monterozzi

✉ Zona Archeologica Via Ripagretta ☎ 0766 856 308 ⏲ Tue–Sun 8.30am–7.30pm € charge

The Necropolis di Tarquinia, together with that of Cerveteri, is the most important Etruscan burial site.

Cerveteri's most impressive tomb is the Tomba dei Rilievi, which belonged to a wealthy family. Dating from the 4th century BC, it has space for 32 bodies and is decorated with coloured reliefs depicting weapons, tools, household implements, musical instruments and furnishings.

BELOW LEFT: the 7th-century Tomba della Cornice, Cerveteri. **BELOW:** bucchero (Etruscan black pottery) vase from Cerveteri.

Cities for the Dead

Every Etruscan town or village had another "city for the dead" built outside its walls. For the Etruscans, life in the next world was just as important as life on earth – perhaps even more so, judging by the fact that dead were buried in larger spaces than the living inhabited. The Etruscans believed not only in the everlasting soul but in the survival, in some shape or form, of the human body after death, so the tombs had to be suitably equipped for the deceased to carry on living in the next world in the way he or she had become accustomed to living on earth. Accordingly, the dead were supplied with food and jewellery and surrounded with all the things that they had loved most when alive – even household furniture, such as beds and chairs, were carved out of the rock, giving a detailed impression of Etruscan everyday life. The most stunning necropolis, the Necropoli della Banditaccia *(see opposite)* can be found at Cerveteri off the main Civitavecchia road.

TIP

If you are exploring the area north of Rome by car, consider a trip to Lago di Bracciano, famous for fishing and watersports. In Bracciano, Castello Orsini-Odescalchi is worth visiting, but more idyllic is the medieval village of Anguillara on the lake's southern shores.

ABOVE: Tarquinia Museum. **BELOW:** shopping on Via di San Lorenzo, Viterbo. **BELOW RIGHT:** a pork butcher in Viterbo.

It stands on a hill south of the original town, occupying an area 5km (3 miles) long by 1km (⅔ mile) wide. Some tombs are painted with frescoes that are a precious document of Etruscan life, depicting banquets, dancing and musicians, athletics or gladiatorial fights, funeral processions, and even erotic scenes.

At any given time no more than 15 of the 6,000 tombs are accessible, as they are opened in rotation in an effort to preserve the delicate paintings. The Tomba della Caccia e della Pesca (530–20 BC), which shows some lively fishing and hunting scenes, and the Tomba del Cacciatore (the Tomb of the Hunter, 530–10 BC) are among the oldest. The Tomba delle Leonesse (Tomb of the Lionesses) shows a pronounced Greek influence. One of the best-known is La Tomba dell'Orco (4th century BC), which depicts a banquet attended by the prominent Surinna family.

Museo Nazionale Tarquinense

Palazzo Vitelleschi, Piazza Cavour
0766-856 036 Tue–Sun 8.30am–7.30pm charge

This museum in the atmospheric medieval town of Tarquinia houses one of the most important collections of Etruscan artefacts in Italy, most of which were discovered in the necropolis.

VITERBO 22

Viterbo's roots can be traced right back to the Etruscans. Crammed with medieval alleyways, porticoes, noble fountains and fine squares, alongside bustling streets lined with shops, cafés and restaurants, this characterful town, just 98km (60 miles) from Rome, is ideal for a day trip. The most notable of its many historic buildings is the 13th-century **Palazzo Papale**, a favourite residence of the popes. On the same square the

Recommended Restaurants & Bars listed below

Romanesque **cathedral of San Lorenzo** was built on top of an Etruscan citadel. The shop-lined **Corso Italia** leads to the **Piazza del Plebiscito**, dominated by the town hall and governor's palace. To the east the medieval **San Pellegrino quarter**, a labyrinth of narrow alleyways, arches and hidden corners, is the most atmospheric part of town.

Just outside the city wall, east of the centre, the **Museo Civico** (2 Piazza Crispi; tel: 0761-340 810; Tue–Sun 9am–7pm, until 6pm in winter; small charge) contains a collection of Etruscan finds such as sarcophagi with bas-reliefs, pottery urns and vases, and some bronze idols. There is also a small collection of paintings. Adjacent to the museum is the convent church of **Santa Maria della Verità**, worth visiting for its beautiful 13th-century cloister and the Mazzatosta chapel, frescoed by Lorenzo da Viterbo, a pupil of Piero della Francesca. ❑

Many of the most valuable finds from the sites covered in this chapter have been transferred to Rome. The most important Etruscan collections can be seen at the Villa Giulia *(see page 192)* and the Etruscan Museum in the Vatican *(see page 148)*.

ABOVE: the Papal Palace.

RESTAURANTS AND BARS

Cerveteri

Gola

✉ Via Settevene Palo Nuova ☎ 06-994 0672 ⏲ L & D Tue–Sun. **€€€**

Slightly out of town and conveniently located for exploring the Etruscan tombs, this restaurant is worth a trip just to try the great home-made pasta dishes and mainly fishy second courses.

Palestrina

Lo Schiribizzo

✉ 14 Piazza Garibaldi ☎ 06-953 7705 ⏲ L & D Tue–Sun. **€–€€**

This small trattoria serves both restaurant fare and pizza, but the latter, prepared in the view of diners and cooked in a wood-fired oven, are the main draw.

Tarquinia

Arcadia

✉ 6 Via Mazzini ☎ 0766-855 501 ⏲ L & D Tue–Sun. **€€–€€€**

This restaurant, right in the centre of historic Tarquinia, has a fish-based menu, an extensive wine list and charming staff. Closed in January.

Viterbo

Enoteca La Torre

✉ 5 Via della Torre ☎ 0761-226 467 ⏲ L & D Thur–Mon, D only Wed. **€€–€€€**

Located within the medieval walls of Viterbo, this upmarket restaurant rediscovers ancient local recipes, but with a modern twist. There's also a tasting menu, with each dish paired with a different local wine. The wine bar under the same management next door serves lighter dishes, such as platters of cheese and cold meats. Gourmet treats and wines and liqueurs of the region can be purchased at the attached shop. Closed end of July and August.

Price includes dinner and a half-bottle of house wine.
***€€€€** = more than €60,*
***€€€** = €40–60, **€€** = €25–40,*
***€** = under €25.*

IN HONOREM PRINCIPIS APOST PAVLVS V BVRGHESIVS ROMANVS PONT MAX AN MDCXII PONT VII

INSIGHT GUIDES

ROME

Travel Tips

TRANSPORT

GETTING THERE AND GETTING AROUND

Rome is easy to get to, but less easy to get around. Planes and trains deliver tourists to the city from all over the world with speed, efficiency and regularity. On arrival, however, brace yourself for a chaotic transport system – the bus network is hard to get to grips with, the metro coverage inadequate and driving a nightmare. The good news is that most places of interest in the city centre are within walking distance. A good map and comfortable walking shoes will be your best investment.

ABOVE: an ATAC bus.

GETTING THERE

By Air

Scheduled flights from around the world land at the main airport, **Aeroporto Leonardo da Vinci** in Fiumicino (tel: 06-65951; www.adr.it), about 30km (18 miles) southwest of Rome. The airport is served by most major national carriers, including Alitalia and British Airways. Along with several American carriers, Alitalia operates daily flights from New York and other US cities.

Charters fly in to **Ciampino Airport** (tel: 06-65951; www.adr.it), the city's second airport, about 15km (9 miles) southeast of the city.

Low-cost airlines easyJet and Ryanair are among many firms operating services to Ciampino *(for information on getting into the city from the airport, see pages 283–4).*

AIRLINES

Alitalia
Tel: 06-2222 (Rome)
Tel: 08714 241 424 (UK)
Tel: 800-223 5730 (USA)
www.alitalia.com

British Airways
Tel: 199-712 266 (Italy)
Tel: 0844 493 0787 (UK)
Tel: 1-800-AIRWAYS (USA)
www.britishairways.com

Continental
Tel: 06-6605 3030 (Italy)
Tel: 0845 607 6760 (UK)
Tel: 800-231 0856 (international destinations from USA)
www.continental.com

Delta
Tel: 848-780 376 (Italy)
Tel: 0845-600 0950 (UK)
Tel: 800-221 1212 (USA)
www.delta.com

easyJet
Tel: 899-234 589 (Italy)
Tel: 0871-244 2366 (UK)
www.easyjet.com

Ryanair
Tel: 899-018880 (Italy)
Tel: 0871-246 0000 (UK)
www.ryanair.com

By Train

Rome is well served by rail connections to the majority of major European cities, and the national railway, **Ferrovie dello Stato**, is efficient and relatively inexpensive. There are several categories: reservations are required (and included in the ticket price) for the Frecciarossa (Eurostar) and T-Biz, the fastest and most luxurious trains, and optional (but highly recommended) for the InterCity. You pay a supplement to use these lines, but they save time. Regional trains (called regionale or interregionale) are slower as they stop at many stations.

You should book a seat if you plan to travel by rail to towns outside Rome. Do this either at a travel agent *(agenzia di viaggio)* in the city, or in Stazione Termini, where there are plenty of easy-to-understand ticket machines. You can also book by credit card online (www.trenitalia.com) or by phone (tel: 892 021, no prefix; from landline phones only; 24-hours daily, press 2 to speak to an operator). You can then pick up your tickets at machines at Termini Station or on the train (ask for the "ticketless" option when booking). Both the website and phone service offer in-depth timetable information. If you're planning a lot of rail travel, it pays to look into various rail-pass offers at home and in Italy.

Train tickets are valid for two months after the date of issue, and must be stamped on the day you travel at one of the machines at the head of each platform, otherwise you will be fined. The only exception is Eurostar tickets, which always have a booking time printed on them.

Stazione Termini is the main railway terminal, the meeting point of the two metro lines and the main stop for many city buses. There is a tourist office opposite platform 24, and a hotel reservation booth opposite platform 20, as well as a luggage deposit, cafés, restaurants and fast-food joints, a bookstore, a telephone office and even an art gallery.

ABOVE AND BELOW: Termini Station, inside and out.

The official taxi rank is in front of the station. Do not be tempted by offers from unofficial cab drivers in the station interior.

By Coach

Most coaches arrive at the main terminus on Via Marsala next to Stazione Termini. If you are travelling on a COTRAL bus, the network which serves the Lazio region, you will arrive and depart from a metro stop: Lepanto and Ponte Mammolo for the north, Anagnina and EUR Fermi for the south, and Tiburtina for the east.

By Car

European (EU) driving licences are valid in Italy. Travellers from other countries normally require an international driving licence. Carry your licence, plus the vehicle registration and insurance (Green Card) documents with you when driving. If driving your own car, you may wish to take out extra insurance to cover home recovery in case of a breakdown.

Tolls are payable on motorways, including the A1. Pay in cash or with magnetic cards, available at service stations.

Motorists arriving in Rome from all directions will first hit the Grande Raccordo Anulare (GRA), the ring road. It is busy and can be alarming, but is usually the quickest way to reach one of the entry roads into the centre. During rush hour, however, there are frequently traffic jams.

The A1 Autostrada del Sole leads into the GRA from both north and south, as does the A24 from the east. If you arrive on the Via del Mare from the coast (Ostia), you can either switch to the GRA or continue straight on into the centre.

When leaving the GRA, follow white signs for the road you want (blue ones usually lead away from the centre). The city centre sign is a white point in a black circle on a white background.

GETTING AROUND

From the Airport

From Fiumicino, there are frequent train services to the city – every 15–30 minutes to Trastevere Station and every 30 minutes to Stazione Termini. Trains to Stazione Termini (the Leonardo Express) run from 6.37am to 11.37pm; the journey takes 35 minutes and the ticket

ABOVE: one of Rome's few remaining tram lines.

Bus Tours

ATAC's double-decker open-top service (the 110 Open) leaves every 10–15 minutes from Termini Station and tours the city's principal monuments. The service operates daily from 8.40am to 8.30pm, and the whole journey lasts about 2 hours. It's a hop-on, hop-off service, and tickets (€19) are valid for the whole day and for as many trips as you choose to make. A special night-time version of the tour departs at 9pm in summer and 8pm in winter. Tickets can be bought at the terminus in Piazza dei Cinquecento (or on board if you get on at one of the other 10 stops).

Archeobus is a small, eco-friendly minibus that serves the historic Appia Antica park. It departs on the hour from Termini Station between 10am and 4pm. The ticket (€8) is valid all day, and the route, which lasts roughly two hours, takes in the catacombs, the Appian Way, the tomb of Cecilia Metella and the Villa dei Quintili. Freephone for both buses: 800-281 281; www.trambusopen.com. A combined two-day ticket for both bus tours is also available (€28.50).

costs €11. If you're travelling to one of the suburban rail stations such as Trastevere, Ostiense and Tiburtina, take one of the trains bound for Orte, which run from 6.27am to 11.27pm; tickets cost €5.50. At night there's a COTRAL bus that leaves from the international arrivals terminus every 75 minutes bound for the Termini and Tiburtina railway stations. In 2006, the Rome authorities capped the taxi rates; a taxi from Fiumicino to the centre should cost no more than €40. If you suspect you are being fleeced, ostentatiously make a note of the driver's licence number and report any problems, tel: 066-7107 0721 or 06-0606.

From Ciampino, the best way to reach the centre is to take the Terravision, Schiaffini or SIT-busShuttle coaches which depart from outside the arrivals building and drop you off at Via Marsala, by Stazione Termini. The journey takes 40 minutes and tickets cost €4–6 one way and can be bought on board. Book online at www.terra vision.it, www.atral-lazio.it, or www.sitbusshuttle.it (at least 24 hours before departure) to be sure of a seat, or buy on the coach. There is at least one coach for every scheduled Ryanair and easyJet arriving or departing flight. Alternatively, taxi prices from Ciampino to the centre have been capped; a taxi into the centre should set you back no more than €30.

Orientation

It sometimes seems that all Roman roads lead to Piazza Venezia. This can produce traffic chaos, but from a visitor's point of view the square is a useful orientation point at the centre of ancient, medieval and modern Rome.

To the south of Piazza Venezia, the three roads, Via dei Fori Imperiali, Via di San Gregorio and Via delle Terme, thread between the greatest monuments of Ancient Rome to the Terme di Caracalla. Northwards, Via del Corso runs through the commercial heart of modern Rome to Piazza del Popolo. To the west, Corso Vittorio Emanuele II leads through the heart of medieval Rome and across the Tiber (Tevere) to St Peter's and the Vatican. Eastwards Via Nazionale, Piazza della Repubblica and Piazza del Cinquecento lead to Stazione Termini.

An easy and pleasant way to get an overview of the city is to walk or catch a bus up the Gianicolo (Janiculum hill) behind Trastevere. Alternatively, take the elevator (€7) to reach the top of the Vittoriano monument (Piazza Venezia).

Public Transport

Public transport is quite efficient and inexpensive, but overcrowded at peak hours. Tickets are available from bars, tobacconists and newspaper kiosks that display the

BELOW: a Roman's ideal city runaround.

ATAC (city bus company) emblem, and from vending machines in metro stations and bus terminals. Once validated in the metro turnstile or machine at the back of the bus, single-use tickets (BIT), costing €1, are good for unlimited bus or tram rides plus one metro ride, and last for 75 minutes after you first use them. One-day tickets (BIG), which cost €4, weekly tickets *(carta settimanale)*, which cost €16, and monthly tickets *(abbonamento mensile)*, which cost €30 and are only valid for the calendar month in which the ticket was bought, are also available.

Passengers caught without a ticket will be fined €51 on the spot. The amount doubles if you cannot pay immediately.

Buses and Trams

Bus and tram services run from 5.30am to midnight, with an all-night service on 22 bus lines, denoted by the letter "N" after the number. Bus and tram stops are clearly marked, and most list route numbers, the main destinations along each route and lines with night service.

Board buses at either the front or rear doors and stamp your ticket immediately. Ring the bell to request the next stop and exit through the centre doors.

The 40 Express is the quickest way to get from the station to the city centre and then St Peter's. Along with the 64 (a slower version of the 40 Express with more stops), it is one of the city's most popular bus routes, so watch out for pickpockets.

Five electric minibuses serve the narrow streets of the Centro Storico: the most useful are the 116 which passes through or alongside Campo de' Fiori, Piazza Farnese, Piazza Navona, the Pantheon and Piazza Barberini; the 119, which serves the area around Piazza del Popolo and Piazza di Spagna, and the 117, which goes from Piazza del Popolo to Basilica San Giovanni in Laterano.

Bus 81 runs from the Colosseum to Piazza del Risorgimento near the Vatican Museums. If you are visiting the catacombs, take bus 118 from the Piramide metro stop to the Via Appia. The No. 8 tramline links Largo Argentina in the centre to Trastevere and Monteverde in the west. From Piazza di Spagna to Stazione Termini, take metro line A. For the Colosseum, do the same and change at Termini to line B.

For information on trams, buses or the metro call freephone 800-431 784, Mon–Sat

BELOW: traffic cops have their work cut out in Rome.

CAR HIRE

Prices per day at all the major international firms start at approximately €60 for the smallest cars. Expect to pay a generous surcharge if you want unlimited mileage, and check exactly what is included in the insurance you are offered. All the major firms have offices at the airports and railway station, and most of them have online booking services as well as sections where you can work out how much the rental will cost. Avis, Europcar and Hertz probably provide the best cover, but Italy Rent, which also has an office at the airport, has the lowest rates. The main rental companies are:

Avis
Tel: 199-100 133
www.avisautonoleggio.it

Europcar
Freephone 199-307 030
www.europcar.it

Hertz
Tel: 199-112 211
www.hertz.it

Italy Rent
Freephone: 800-930 032
www.italyrent.it

Maggiore
Tel: 06-488 0049
www.maggiore.it

Several airlines also have an online car-hire booking service, though this is usually more expensive:

easyJet
Tel: +44-11-3388 3329; lines open 365 days a year for bookings.
www.europcar4easyjet.com

KLM Royal Dutch Airlines
Internet bookings only:
www.klm.com

Opodo (a company jointly owned by a number of European airlines)
Tel: +44-0871-277 0090
www.opodo.com

ABOVE: pleasure boat on the Tiber.

8am–8pm, or go to www.atac.roma.it, which has a useful route planner.

COTRAL runs regional buses that connect Rome to the airports, the rest of the province and the Lazio region (www.cotralspa.it).

Metro

The metro operates from 5.30am to 11.30pm and until 12.30am on Saturday night. The city is served by two metro lines (A and B), which intersect at Stazione Termini. There are only two lines because of the problems of circumnavigating the numerous unexcavated ruins underground. A third metro line is slowly being constructed, but it is likely to be years before it is operational.

Boats

The riverboat company Battelli di Roma organises tourist cruises lasting about an hour, with commentary, for €15. Romantic night-time cruises with dinner cost €50, and aperitivo cruises €35. Boats depart from Ponte Sant'Angelo and the Tiber Island (Isola Tiberina). Pleasure trips run daily every 30 minutes from 10am to 6pm, while dinner cruises only run Thursday–Saturday. Ask at the tourist information points for more details or contact Battelli di Roma, tel: 06-9774 5498.

Taxis

Licensed taxis are white and always have a meter. If you are approached inside railway stations or at the airport by someone muttering "Taxi, taxi," always refuse as they are likely to charge you far more than the official rate.

There are ranks outside Termini Station, outside both airports, and in many parts of the Centro Storico, such as Largo di Torre Argentina and Piazza Venezia. Otherwise you can always hail a taxi on the street as long as it has a light on, indicating it is free, or call one of the following radio taxi services – tel: 06-3570, 06-8822 or 06-4994.

Prices for licensed taxis are fixed and start with a minimum fee of €2.33. Surcharges are made for each large piece of luggage and for journeys after 10pm and on public holidays. By law every taxi should have a card (usually in the pocket of one of the front seats) listing the various rates and charges. Outside the city centre and beyond the Grande Raccordo Anulare (the ring road) the rate per kilometre also goes up.

Driving

Generally, a car is of little use within the city. Parking is hard to find, one-way systems are complex and much of the city centre is closed. Non-resident drivers are not allowed inside the city center's ZTL (Limited Traffic Zone) during the day and on some nights (mainly on weekends). Cameras at the entrance of the restricted area film licence plates, and cars without a permit will receive a fine each time they pass under the camera. The cameras are easily seen as they always come with an electronic sign that says whether access is open to everyone (*varco aperto*) or restricted (*varco chiuso*).

If you need to reach a hotel in a traffic-restricted area you must make arrangements with reception before arriving. Local drivers have a very personal set of rules and codes which allow for much flashing of lights, tooting of horns and rampant acceleration at what looks like vastly inopportune moments to anyone non-Roman. During the day most cars in the city centre obey the traffic lights. However, some of Rome's traffic lights are switched to flashing amber at night: this indicates caution, although not all drivers seem to understand this.

If you are not deterred by such problems or if you wish to make extensive trips out of town, you might want to hire your own vehicle *(see panel on page 285)*. Note that all cars are required by law to keep their low-beam lights on at all times on motorways and dual carriageways.

There is a large car park under Villa Borghese (entrance at the top of Via Veneto) and one on the Gianicolo hill near the Vatican called Terminal Gianicolo (entrance from Piazza della Rovere). Several of the four- and five-star hotels in the centre have their own garage or protected parking: ask when booking. Few two- or three-star hotels are able to help with parking.

Given the lack of parking spaces, it is not surprising that a lot of cars are towed away in Rome – over 10,000 a year – so if your car is no longer where you left it, this, rather than theft, may be the reason. The Ufficio

Rimozione of the traffic police (Vigili Urbani) will be able to tell you if this is the case. The fines you will have to pay to get your car back are high. Contact Vigili Urbani, 4 Via della Consolazione; tel: 06-67691 or 06-0606.

A lot of cars are clamped. If this happens to you, a note on the windscreen will give you the number to call.

If you think that your car has been stolen, you can report it at the nearest police station.

Breakdown Service

The Italian Automobile Association (ACI) provides an emergency breakdown service. If you need repairs, look in the Yellow Pages *(Pagine Gialle)* for the nearest mechanic *(Autofficine)*, or ask the ACI. ACI breakdown and information service, freephone: 803-116. ACI information, tel: 06-491 115.

Bicycles and Mopeds

Romans tend to cycle, if at all, on weekends away in Tuscany with their mountain bikes. However, on car-free Sundays you will see them darting along the Via dei Fori Imperiali. You can hire a bicycle by the hour, the day or the week. Riding in one of the parks is a pleasant alternative to the city streets.

The transport company recently launched a new public bike scheme called Roma'n'Bike, allowing you to borrow the city's bikes from various stands across the city. The procedure, however, is quite complicated and is designed for residents: you must first enrol and pay €30 deposit at the Trambus offices on Prenestina (call 800-43 1 784 or 06-57003), before charging an electronic "smartcard" which gives you access to the bikes.

Sundays are a good time to cycle along the Appian Way as traffic is restricted. You can rent a bike from the visitors' centre *(see page 241)*.

Bicycle and moped rental companies in the city include:

Bici & Baci
5 Via del Viminale
Tel: 06-482 8443 (mopeds also)

Collalti
82 Via del Pellegrino
Tel: 06-6880 1084

Touring Rome by moped or Vespa is not advisable for beginners or the nervous. You will need to show your licence when hiring a moped, and leave a deposit. Motorcycle rental companies include:

Happy Rent
3 Via Farini
Tel: 06-481 8185

Scooters for Rent
84 Via della Purificazione
Tel: 06-488 5485.

BELOW: cycling in Villa Borghese.

ABOVE: two wheels are better than four.

On Foot

In much of the city centre the best way to get around is on foot. Most of the main sights are within easy walking distance of each other, although there are some for which you may want to use public transport.

Some parts of the centre are for pedestrians only, such as the second half of Via del Corso, roughly from the Piazza San Silvestro to Piazza del Popolo and Piazza Navona. This pedestrianised area includes the section that goes from Largo Argentina past the Pantheon to the Parliament.

Moped riders in particular, but also some car drivers, often decide that they are exempt from this rule and drive along pedestrian zones.

Cross the road with confidence, staring down nearby drivers. If you wait timidly at a pedestrian crossing for the traffic to stop, you will spend the whole day there.

Most of the centre of Rome is reasonably safe, even at night, though the areas around Stazione Termini (particularly Via Giolitti) can be deserted and, despite recent improvements, are still rather seedy and should be avoided.

ACCOMMODATION

WHERE TO STAY

Even if Milan is the fashion capital par excellence, Rome can compete in cool hotels and old-school splendour. The peeling *pensione* of old has been supplanted by a wide choice of eclectic guesthouses. Diehard design junkies will find avant-garde interiors behind conventional façades. At the grander end of the scale, gracious, timeless hotels like Hotel de Russie retain their cachet. But for those not on an imperial budget there are plenty of welcoming guesthouses and family-run hotels, while self-catering apartments and bed and breakfasts are increasingly popular options.

Choosing a Hotel

The APT office *(see Tourist Information, page 317)* publishes an annual list *(Annuario Alberghi)* showing star categories, facilities and prices of all Rome hotels. This may be obtained from the Rome APT or through the Italian national tourist offices.

Hotels are rated by stars, but these ratings correspond to facilities and services, not to the quality, which is often disappointing compared with what you would expect from similarly rated hotels in other major European cities. Since many hotels are located in renovated medieval or Renaissance *palazzi* in the centre, the rooms and bathrooms can be a bit on the small side, and noisy, too.

There has been a recent explosion of designer and luxury hotels in Rome, which offer great views, memorable food, striking decor and often a health spa; prices are high, but deals can be found on their websites.

Bed & Breakfasts

The bed & breakfast sector in Rome is flourishing. Some offer the amenities of a hotel in noble *palazzi* for more competitive prices; others are nothing more than a private room in someone's home. The APT office on Via Parigi and tourist information points have full listings of registered establishments. The Bed and Breakfast Italia agency (tel: 06-687 8618; www.bbitalia.it) has hundreds of options in Rome, which it vets and awards with a crown system. The standard rates are posted on its website.

Self-catering

It's worth considering renting a self-catering apartment, especially if you're travelling as a group or family. Among the many operators in this field are Homes in Rome (tel: 06-3975 1474; www.homesinrome. com) and Roman Homes (www.romanhomes.com).

Hotel Areas

Rome offers countless places to stay, in every imaginable category. The following list gives a selection. The area around Piazza Navona, the Pantheon and Campo de' Fiori offers the best introduction to the city, since you are right in its medieval heart and within easy reach of most main sights. However, there are relatively few hotels in the area, and these tend to be booked up early. This area is always lively, and that means it is also noisy.

The Aventine Hill is quieter, although a little further out. The Via Veneto district has a number of large hotels at the higher end of the scale. It is a convenient location, although the area is no longer the fashionable centre. Around Piazza di Spagna there is a more varied selection.

The Monteverde district on Gianicolo Hill is dotted with turn-of-the-century villas, converted into welcoming guesthouses.

Many hotels can be found around Stazione Termini. This is not the most attractive area, but it is well connected with the rest of the city by public transport. A lot of the cheaper hotels are here, but there are a few in the middle and luxury ranges. The area south of the station is rather insalubrious and best avoided.

Hotels slightly out of the centre may offer more facilities, such as swimming pools and parking, and they are quieter.

Prices & Booking

Prices are high and do not always reflect what is on offer. A two-star can be as good if not better than a three- or even four-star. Expect to pay anything between €80 and €250 for a three-star (depending on the season), and don't expect views for less then €200.

High season is pretty much year-round in Rome, so book ahead. November to March and August are quieter and prices are lower. Bookings can be made online or by phone; sometimes a confirmation fax will be requested, as well as your credit card details. If you want to cancel, do it a few days in advance. Prices usually include breakfast, although it is rarely included in the luxury and five-star category. In bed & breakfast accommodation, guests typically pay €40–100 per night for a double room, but prices can go as low as €25 and as high as €200.

Accommodation Listings

Fontana di Trevi, Via Veneto & Villa Borghese

Aldrovandi Palace
15 Via Ulisse Aldrovandi
Tel: 06-322 3993
[off map p335, E1]
www.aldrovandi.com
This beautiful hotel near Villa Borghese has sumptuous rooms and suites, lush gardens, a spectacular outdoor pool and a restaurant run by a Michelin-starred chef. **€€€€€**

Aleph
15 Via di San Basilio
Tel: 06-422 901
[p336, A3]
www.aleph.boscolohotels.com
This stylish hotel has an intriguing "heaven and hell" theme, from its flame-red entranceway to its soothing "Paradise Spa". Bedrooms are inspired by 1930s design and have hi-tech touches. **€€€€€**

Ambasciatori Palace
62 Via Vittorio Veneto
Tel: 06-47493
[p336, A2]
www.ambasciatoripalace.com
Central and comfortable large hotel. Caters to a mainly business crowd, but the staff are friendly and efficient. **€€€€€**

Bernini Bristol
23 Piazza Barberini
Tel: 06-488 931
[p336, A3]
www.berninibristol.com
In an imposing building overlooking Piazza Barberini, this attractive hotel has elegant rooms, a spa and a prestigious restaurant, l'Olimpo. **€€€€**

Daphne Inn (A&B)
20 Via degli Avignonesi and 55 Via di San Basilio
Tel: 06-8745 0087
[p336, A3]
www.daphne-rome.com
This hotel in two locations excels in its level of service – friendly, knowledgeable staff, and laptops (one per floor) and mobile phones (one per room) are provided – an unexpected bonus in this price bracket. **€€–€€€**

Eden
49 Via Ludovisi
Tel: 06-478 121
[p336, A2]
www.hotel-eden.it
This is a discreet, elegant and ultra-refined hotel with excellent, unsnooty service and a prestigious roof garden restaurant. **€€€€€**

Fontana
96 Piazza di Trevi
Tel: 06-678 6113
[p335, E3]
www.hotelfontana-trevi.com
In a 13th-century monastery opposite the Fontana di Trevi. A tad pricey, but it has a beautiful rooftop breakfast room. **€€€–€€€€**

Jolly Vittorio Veneto
1 Corso Italia
Tel: 06-84951
[p336, A2]
www.jollyhotels.it
Modern, with all amenities, including conference rooms. Soundproofed. **€€€€**

BELOW: the Aleph.

Lord Byron
5 Via Giuseppe De Notaris
Tel: 06-322 0404
[off map p335, E1]
www.lordbyronhotel.com
Built into a former monastery, this small hotel has the atmosphere of a private club, and enjoys a serene location away from the city centre, in the well-heeled Parioli district. Sumptuous decor, and the restaurant is fabulous. **€€€€–€€€€€**

Parco dei Principi
5 Via G. Frescobaldi
Tel: 06-854 421
[off map p335, E1]
www.parcodeiprincipi.com
Two minutes' walk from Villa Borghese, this hotel is not in the thick of things, but a great choice if you want tranquillity and luxury. The excellent restaurant overlooks the park and the city. **€€€€€**

Residenza A
183 Via Veneto
Tel: 06-486 700
[p336, A2]
www.hotelviaveneto.com
A sleek grey colour scheme with contemporary art providing the odd splash of colour characterises this hotel. Rooms have a luxurious feel, with flat-screen computers and swanky bathrooms. **€€€–€€€€**

Residenza Cellini
5 Via Modena
Tel: 06-4782 5204
[p336, B3]
www.residenzacellini.it
With rooms that are unusually large for this price bracket, this hotel is deservedly popular. All bathrooms have jacuzzis or hydro-massage showers. **€€€**

Splendide Royal
14 Via di Porta Pinciana
Tel: 06-421 689
[p336, A2]
www.splendideroyal.com
Sweeping staircases, marble floors and dazzling chandeliers give this hotel a generous dose of *Dolce Vita* glamour. Ask for one of the rooms with views over nearby Villa Borghese. There's also a smart restaurant, Mirabelle, and a lovely rooftop terrace. **€€€€€**

Westin Excelsior
125 Via Vittorio Veneto
Tel: 06-47081
[p336, A2]
www.starwood.com
Part of the 1950s *Dolce Vita* scene, the Excelsior, fairly recently renovated, offers the ultimate in opulence and service. **€€€€€**

PIAZZA DI SPAGNA AND TRIDENTE

Hotel Art
56 Via Margutta
Tel: 06-328 711
[p335, E2]
www.hotelart.it
Set in a converted seminary, this upmarket hotel is a blend of old and new. The reception area is contained within two futuristic pods, and the sleek lounge area (an exercise in style over comfort) is laid out in the former chapel beneath frescoed, vaulted ceilings. **€€€€€**

Barocco
4 Via della Purificazione
Tel: 06-487 2001
[p336, A3]
www.hotelbarocco.com
Rooms at this charming, bijou hotel on a side street off busy Piazza Barberini are decorated with sumptuous fabrics and elegant furnishings. Try booking one of the superior rooms, as standard rooms tend to be on the small side. **€€€€**

Casa Howard (A&B)
18 Via Capo le Case
and 149 Via Sistina
Tel: 06-6992 4555
[p335, E3]
www.casahoward.com
Each of the 10 rooms in this stylish hotel has a different theme; those in the newer Via Sistina location all have en suite bathrooms and are slightly more luxurious. Turkish bath available at both sites. This is "*residenza*" accommodation: there is no reception – guests are given a set of keys. **€€€**

De Russie
9 Via del Babuino
Tel: 06-328 881
[p335, D2]
www.hotelderussie.it
This is Rome's original designer hotel, housed in a *palazzo* by Valadier. It is chic, modern and understated. The internal courtyard overlooking a tiered garden is magical, and the luxurious spa is one of the best in town. Ask for a room with a view of Piazza del Popolo. **€€€€€**

D'Inghilterra
14 Via Bocca di Leone
Tel: 06-699 811
[p335, E3]
www.royaldemeure.com
Old-fashioned and traditional, with unfussy service. The rooms, furnished with antiques, are cosy if on the dark side. Top-floor rooms are brighter and have terraces. Good position just off the Corso. **€€€€–€€€€€**

Fontanella Borghese
84 Largo Fontanella Borghese
Tel: 06-6880 9504
[p335, D3]
www.fontanellaborghese.com
This elegant hotel, once the residence of the noble Borghese family, is well located for shopping in the Piazza di Spagna and Via dei Condotti area. Rooms have beautiful old tiles or hardwood floors; those overlooking the internal courtyard are quieter. **€€€**

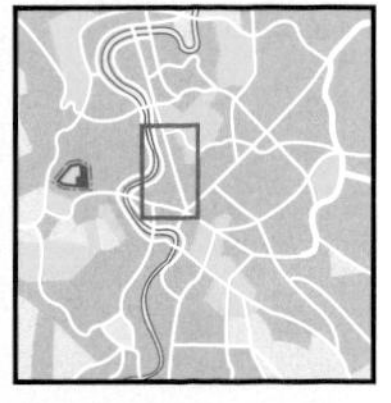

Gregoriana
18 Via Gregoriana
Tel: 06-679 4269
[p335, E3]
www.hotelgregoriana.it
This ex-convent has a striking Art Deco interior with a wonderful gold-and-black lift and original 1930s room numbers by the Russian fashion designer Erté. Near the Spanish Steps, it has only 22 rooms. **€€€**

Hassler
6 Piazza Trinità dei Monti
Tel: 06-699 340
[p335, E3]
www.hotelhasslerroma.com

ABOVE: the contemporary side of Hotel Art.

Situated above the Spanish Steps, this historic establishment is still one of Rome's most alluring luxury hotels, its olde-worlde glamour a real contrast with the sleek minimalism of some of the city's new 5-stars. The restaurant, with roof gardens and views over the city, is particularly beautiful. **€€€€€**

Inn at the Spanish Steps
85 Via dei Condotti
Tel: 06-6992 5657
[p335, E3]
www.atspanishsteps.com
A luxury boutique hotel right in the middle of shoppers' heaven. A sister hotel, the View at the Spanish Steps, along the same road at No. 95, is similarly luxurious, though slightly more pared-down in style. **€€€€€**

La Lumiere di Piazza di Spagna
72 Via Belsiana
Tel: 06-6938 0806
[p335, E3] www.lalumieredipiazzadispagna.com
On the corner with fashionable Via Condotti, this comfortable hotel offers spacious rooms and large, well-kept suites. The bathrooms are a bit small, but some have a jacuzzi. The terrace is especially pleasant. **€€€**

Locarno
22 Via della Penna
Tel: 06-361 0841
[p335, D2]
www.hotellocarno.com
Appealing Art Deco touches (the ornate cage lift alone is memorable), though some of the rooms have a slightly shabby feel. De luxe rooms in the new wing are lovely but cost more. Breakfast served in the garden or on the roof terrace when warm. Oodles of charm and class, and the location, two minutes from Piazza del Popolo, can't be beaten. Bicycle rental included in the price. **€€€**

Modigliani
42 Via della Purificazione
Tel: 06-4281 5226
[p335, E3]
www.hotelmodigliani.com
A lovely hotel with great views from top-floor rooms and a garden in an inner courtyard. Check the website for last-minute deals. **€€€**

Nazionale
131 Piazza Montecitorio
Tel: 06-695 001
[p335, D3]
www.nazionaleroma.it
This hotel has an impressive roster of illustrious past guests, Simone de Beauvoir and Jean-Paul Sartre among them. These days, the hotel more often hosts politicians and city types. **€€€€**

Hotel Panda
35 Via della Croce
Tel: 06-678 0179
[p335, E3]
www.hotelpanda.it
A rare budget option a stone's throw from the Spanish Steps, Panda's rooms, though small and pretty basic, have been attractively decorated, and some have wood-beamed ceilings. Book early. **€**

Portrait Suites
23 Via Bocca di Leone
Tel: 06-6938 0742
[p335, E3]
www.lungarnohotels.com
This boutique hotel has become a favourite with the fashion set – it's owned by the Italian couturier Ferragamo. Rooms are as stylish as you'd expect, and there's plenty of fashion memorabilia from the designer's archives. The decked terrace with underfloor heating and bar is a great place for an *aperitivo*. **€€€€€**

Regno
330 Via del Corso
Tel: 06-697 6361
[p335, E4]
www.hotelregno.com
More tranquil than you might expect for its location, Hotel Regno is a reliable mid-range option right in the centre of town. The rooms are pleasant despite the slightly outdated decor. **€€€€**

Hotel San Carlo
93 Via delle Carrozze
Tel: 06-678 4548
[p335, D3]
www.hotelsancarloroma.com
On a small street near Via Condotti, this hotel is a bit noisy, but the price is good considering the exclusive location. Try to book one of the rooms with a balcony. **€€**

Scalinata di Spagna
17 Piazza Trinità dei Monti
Tel: 06-679 3006
[p335, E3]
www.hotelscalinata.com
A small hotel in a beautiful town house at the top of the Spanish Steps. Breakfast on rooftop terrace in summer. Book early. **€€€–€€€€**

Suisse
54 Via Gregoriana
Tel: 06-678 3649
[p335, E3]
www.hotelsuisserome.com
This charming hotel near the Spanish Steps has a cosy, welcoming feel and is great value. Rooms are large, with sturdy wooden furnishings and classic decor. Breakfast is served in the rooms. **€€**

Valadier
15 Via della Fontanella
Tel: 06-361 1998
[p335, D2]
www.hotelvaladier.com
This family-run hotel is moments from the Spanish Steps. Rooms are grandly styled, with luxurious furnishings and marble bathrooms. **€€€€**

PRICE CATEGORIES

For a double room in high season:
€ = under €100
€€ = €100–180
€€€ = €180–260
€€€€ = €260–450
€€€€€ = over €450

THE VATICAN AND PRATI

Bramante
24 Vicolo delle Palline
Tel: 06-6880 6426
[p334, B3]
www.hotelbramante.com
Rooms at this charming hotel near St Peter's are elegantly furnished and quiet, and the small terrace is a pleasant place to unwind. **€€€**

Cavalieri Hilton
101 Via Cadiolo
Tel: 06-35091
[off map p334, A1]
www.romecavalieri.it
Luxury hotel situated on top of Monte Mario, just north of the Vatican. It is quiet and spacious, and offers amenities that more central hotels lack – tennis courts and indoor and outdoor swimming pools among them – as well as one of Rome's best restaurants (La Pergola) on the top floor, which spreads onto the terrace in summer. **€€€€€**

Colors
31 Via Boezio
Tel: 06-687 4030
[p334, C2]
www.colorshotel.com
Modern hotel on three floors, with individual rooms (with or without en suite bathroom), and dormitory accommodation. The newest rooms, on the third floor, are slightly more expensive but offer extras such as breakfast, satellite TV and air conditioning. There is a fully equipped kitchen should you want to cook, laundry facilities, a roof terrace and no curfew for dorm accommodation. The staff are very helpful. **€€€€**

ABOVE: Cavalieri Hilton.

Columbus
33 Via della Conciliazione
Tel: 06-686 5435
[p334, B3]
www.hotelcolumbus.net
On the main street leading up to St Peter's, this ex-monastery has retained some of its original features, including a large, vaulted dining room, frescoes, and a garden planted with orange trees where you can sit and dine in summer. This is a large, comfortable hotel with its own parking area. Prices go down a fair bit off season. **€€€€**

Dei Mellini
81 Via Muzio Clementi
Tel: 06-324 771
[p335, D2]
www.hotelmellini.com
Close to the river in Prati, a short walk from Castel Sant'Angelo and St Peter's, and just across the bridge from the Via del Corso and the Tridente shopping district. Rooms are spacious and elegant if a little old-fashioned. There is a pleasant rooftop terrace. Good facilities for the disabled. **€€€–€€€€**

Farnese
30 Via Alessandro Farnese
Tel: 06-321 2553
[p335, C2]
www.hotelfarnese.com
This upmarket four-star hotel occupies a grand old aristocratic residence. The attention to detail and period furnishings are what make it so special. The reception desk is a 17th-century altar from a deconsecrated church. The rooms are decorated with antiques, terracotta tiling, marble bathrooms and Murano lamps. The breakfast is excellent, and there is a pretty roof terrace. Lepanto metro station is nearby, and the hotel is within walking distance of St Peter's. **€€€€**

Franklin
29 Via Rodi
Tel: 06-3903 0165
[p334, A1]
www.franklinhotelrome.it
This modern hotel has airy, pleasant rooms, all with a musical theme. There are state-of-the-art CD players in all rooms, with an extensive collection of music for guests to borrow in the reception area, plus bicycles for guests' use, should you want to explore the Vatican on two wheels. **€€€€**

Gerber
241 Via degli Scipioni
Tel: 06-322 1001
[p334, C2]
www.hotelgerber.it
Rooms suffer slightly from floral overload but are comfortable and quiet. The hotel is close to the Vatican and has a pleasant terrace. Good value. **€€**

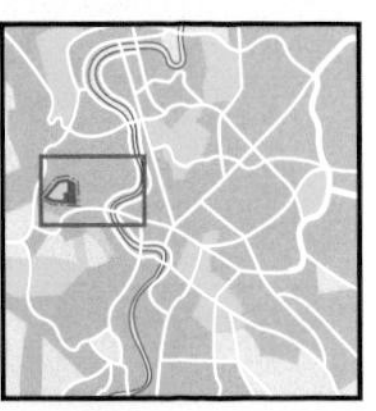

Orange Hotel
86 Via Crescenzio
Tel: 06-686 8969
[p334, B3]
www.orangehotelrome.com
Pleasing the five senses is part of the concept at the modern Orange Hotel. The new trendy boutique hotel is entirely decorated in orange and grey, and has a terrace with views of St Peter's. Ask for the junior suite with a bathtub in the bedroom and check the website for special offers. Has a private garage. **€€**

Ostello del Foro Italico
61 Viale delle Olimpiadi
Tel: 06-323 6267
[off map p334, B1]
www.aighostels.com
Advance reservations are strongly advised, as this 334-bed hostel is the only real hostel in Rome. It's open all year round, has a midnight curfew and is located some way out of the centre (but is accessible by bus). **€**

Sant'Anna
134 Borgo Pio
Tel: 06-6880 1602
[p334, B3]
www.hotelsantanna.com
Housed in a 16th-century building, this hotel has comfortable rooms with a slightly old-fashioned feel. Service is attentive and friendly. **€€€**

PIAZZA NAVONA AND THE PANTHEON

Abruzzi
69 Piazza della Rotonda
Tel: 06-679 2021
[p335, D4]
www.hotelabruzzi.it
Directly opposite the Pantheon, this hotel is not quiet in summer but all rooms have air conditioning and double glazing. Rooms are modest but clean, and almost all have breathtaking views of the Pantheon. There's no breakfast room, but breakfast – taken in a nearby café – is included. **€€€**

Due Torri
23 Vicolo del Leonetto
Tel: 06-6880 6956
[p335, D3]
www.hotelduetorriroma.com
A delightful hotel in a former cardinal's palace tucked away down a narrow cobbled street. Rooms are small and cosy; those on the top floor have terraces. Quiet by Rome standards. **€€€**

Grand Hotel de la Minerve
69 Piazza della Minerva
Tel: 06-695 201
[p335, D4]
www.grandhoteldelaminerve.com
Built within a 17th-century *palazzo* overlooking the lovely Piazza della Minerva. Vast areas of Venetian glass create spectacular public spaces. Rooms are large, and there are splendid views from the roof terrace. **€€€€€**

Navona
8 Via dei Sediari
Tel: 06-6830 1252
[p335, D4]
www.hotelnavona.com
This family-run hotel on the second floor of an attractive *palazzo* has a welcoming atmosphere. Rooms are fairly simple, but represent very good value for the area. **€€**

Raphael
2 Largo Febo
Tel: 06-682 831
[p335, D4]
www.raphaelhotelrome.com
A distinctive ivy-covered exterior, antique furnishings, artworks and stunning views. The Richard Meier-designed "executive" rooms on the third floor are sleek and modern, while the rest of the hotel has a classic feel. Some rooms don't quite live up to expectations, but facilities, rooftop restaurant, bar and views do. **€€€€**

Relais Palazzo Taverna
92 Via dei Gabrielli
Tel: 06-2039 8064
[p335, C4]
www.relaispalazzotaverna.com
Rooms at this guesthouse near the antiques shops of Via dei Coronari have stylish, modern decor with contemporary wallpaper and white-painted beams. Excellent value for this part of town. **€€€**

Santa Chiara
21 Via Santa Chiara
Tel: 06-687 2979
[p335, D4]
www.albergosantachiara.com
The Santa Chiara is in a large building behind the Pantheon with three wings, 96 rooms and three rooftop suites; its rooms are more luxurious than the price would suggest. Ask for a room with a terrace. **€€€–€€€€**

Sole al Pantheon
63 Piazza della Rotonda
Tel: 06-678 0441
[p335, D4]
www.hotelsolealpantheon.com
This 500-year-old hotel, a stone's throw from the Pantheon, has been renovated without spoiling the atmosphere. Front rooms have memorable views but are quite noisy. Quieter rooms overlook an internal courtyard. The decor is serene and fresh, with tiled floors, high ceilings and frescoes. **€€€€–€€€€€**

Teatro Pace 33
33 Via del Teatro Pace
Tel: 06-687 9075
[p335, D4]
www.hotelteatropace.com
This 17th-century building on a quiet, cobbled alley boasts a magnificent Baroque staircase (there's no lift) and high-ceilinged, wood-beamed rooms decorated in classic style. **€€€**

BELOW: the Raphael, with views of St Peter's from the rooftop restaurant.

PRICE CATEGORIES

For a double room in high season:
€ = under €100
€€ = €100–180
€€€ = €180–260
€€€€ = €260–450
€€€€€ = over €450

CAMPO DE' FIORI, THE GHETTO AND TRASTEVERE

Antico Borgo Trastevere
7 Vicolo del Buco
Tel: 06-588 3774
[p339, D2]
www.hotelanticoborgo.it
Though on the small side, rooms in this hotel are tastefully decorated, and have wood beams and tiled floors. Breakfast is served at nearby sister hotel the Domus Tiberina, on a piazza overlooking the river. €€

Arco del Lauro
27 Via dell'Arco de' Tolomei
Tel: 06-9784 0350
[p339, D2]
www.arcodellauro.it
This mini-hotel, with just four rooms, has recently opened in a quiet residential area in Trastevere. Rooms are decorated in a fresh, simple style. Breakfast is served in a nearby bar. €€

Barrett
47 Largo Torre Argentina
Tel: 06-686 8481
[p339, D1]
www.pensionebarrett.com
Located between Campo de' Fiori and the Pantheon, with large, comfortable rooms and big en suite bathrooms, this is one of the best-value hotels in Rome and has been run by the same family for 40 years. Breakfast is not included but can be arranged for an extra fee; alternatively, the area is full of cafés. No credit cards. €€

Campo de' Fiori
6 Via del Biscione
Tel: 06-6880 6865
[p339, C1]
www.hotelcampodefiori.com
A stone's throw from Campo de' Fiori, this recently renovated hotel has a beautiful terrace and intimate, individually decorated rooms with bijou en suite bathrooms. The hotel management also rents several apartments in the area. €€

Domus Tiberina
37 Via in Piscinula
Tel: 06-580 3033
[p339, D2]
www.hoteldomustiberina.it
The rooms are modest but undoubtedly comfortable and pretty, as they all have air conditioning, decorated yellow walls, and wooden-beams on the ceilings. The location is as Roman as can be, set in one of the quiet cobblestone alleys of Trastevere. €€

BELOW: tucked away down this quaint Trastevere alley is the lovely Santa Maria hotel.

Locanda Cairoli
2 Piazza Cairoli
Tel: 06-6880 9278
[p339, D1]
www.locandacairoli.it
Every room is different at this welcoming hotel, decorated with antique furnishings and modern paintings. The owners' objective was to create a real "home away from home", and this is the feeling you get the minute you walk in. Friendly and attentive service and free newspapers. €€€€

Pomezia
12 Via dei Chiavari
Tel: 06-686 1371
[p339, D1]
www.hotelpomezia.it
The rooms in this small hotel just off the Corso Vittorio Emanuele were renovated after the millennium, as were the reception and breakfast areas. They are basically furnished but comfortable, and all have en suite bathrooms with a power shower. There is a lift and a room equipped for people with disabilities. €€

Ponte Sisto
64 Via dei Pettinari
Tel: 06-686 3100
[p339, C1]
www.hotelpontesisto.it
Aside from its excellent, central location, this pleasant hotel offers elegant rooms and a peaceful, palm tree-lined courtyard. €€€€

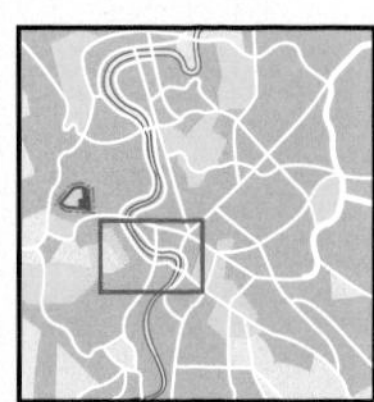

Residenza Arco de' Tolomei
27 Via dell'Arco de' Tolomei
Tel: 06-5832 0819
[p339, D2]
www.inrome.info
This beautifully decorated guesthouse on a quiet Trastevere street has just five rooms, three with terraces. Breakfast is a real event here, with home-made baked goods and jams served in a light-filled breakfast room. €€€

Residenza in Farnese
59 Via del Mascherone
Tel: 06-6889 1388
[p339, C1]
www.residenzafarneseroma.it
Rooms in this converted convent are spacious and attractive, some with original frescoes and hand-painted furniture. Ask for a room overlooking the gardens of Palazzo Spada or, on the other side, the magnificent French Embassy. €€€€–€€€€€

Ripa
3 Via degli Orti di Trastevere
Tel: 06-58611
[p339, C3]
www.ripahotel.com
Cutting-edge, clean and functional design characterise this hotel near the Porta Portese end of Trastevere. The Ripa is well located for Testaccio and Ostiense (the city's hippest

clubbing areas), the Aventine and Circus Maximus, and has all the usual extras to be found in this price range, including a fusion restaurant and its own trendy night-club (open Saturdays only). The street it's located in is a bit of an eyesore, however. €€€€

San Francesco
7 Via Jacopa de' Settesoli
Tel: 06-5830 0051
[p339, C3]
www.hotelsanfrancesco.net
This hotel benefits from being set back a little from the bustle of central Trastevere, and its rooms are a decent size and comfortable. There's also a stunning roof terrace where breakfast is served in warm weather. €€€

Santa Maria
2 Vicolo del Piede
Tel: 06-589 4626
[p339, C2]
www.htlsantamaria.com
Behind firmly closed gates in this quiet and typical Trastevere alley-way lies a refurbished 16th-century cloister. All the rooms are large and comfortable, with terracotta tiling and a view out onto a large, sunny central courtyard planted with orange trees. €€€

Smeraldo
9 Vicolo dei Chiodaroli
Tel: 06-687 5929
[p339, D1]
www.smeraldoroma.com
A good-value hotel in a central location in a narrow street between Largo Argentina and Campo de' Fiori. Its rooms are clean and comfortable, if a bit small, and some of those on the upper floors have lovely views over the rooftops. If these are booked up you can enjoy the views from the two roof gardens. Avoid the rooms overlooking the courtyard as they are on the gloomy side. €€–€€€

Sole
76 Via del Biscione
Tel: 06-6880 6873
[p339, C1]
www.solealbiscione.it
The main draw of this cosy hotel is its central location near Campo de' Fiori. It has quiet if basic rooms, a pretty inner garden and a small roof terrace offering lovely views of the domed church of Sant' Andrea della Valle. It's very popular, so book well ahead. There's no breakfast service, and no credit cards are accepted. €€

Teatro di Pompeo
8 Largo del Pallaro
Tel: 06-6830 0170
[p339, D1]
www.hotelteatrodipompeo.it
Built on the site of the ancient Theatre of Pompey (the remains of which can still be seen in the breakfast room), this is a charming, friendly hotel with comfortable, classically decorated rooms. €€€

Trastevere
24a–25 Via L Manara
Tel: 06-581 4713
[p339, C2]
www.hoteltrastevere.net
With clean, simple rooms overlooking the Piazza San Cosimato market square, this charming but down-to-earth little hotel, at the cheaper end of this price range, is a great deal for the area. €€

Villa della Fonte
8 Via della Fonte dell'Olio
Tel: 06-580 3797
[p339, C2]
www.villafonte.com
Five pleasant rooms make up this hotel, on a picturesque cobbled street in the heart of Trastevere. The first-floor garden terrace is a great place to soak up the sun. Small pets are welcome. €€

AVENTINO AND TESTACCIO

Abitart
10–20 Via P. Matteucci
Tel: 06-454 3191
[p339, D4]
www.abitarthotel.com
A very modern hotel set in the heart of trendy Testaccio, and well positioned for the full-on nightlife that the area is famous for. The rooms are highly slick and contemporary, though some have a slightly bland, corporate feel. €€€

San Pio
19 Via di Santa Melania
Tel: 06-570 057
[p339, D3]
www.aventinohotels.com
The quiet residential area of the Aventino may not be the obvious choice as a base to explore the city, but it's well connected and very peaceful – ideal for those who want a break from the noisy chaos of the city centre. This hotel consists of three separate buildings which share the same attractive gardens. It has elegant, spacious rooms with antique furnishings and generous bathrooms with jacuzzis. €€€

Sant'Anselmo
2 Piazza Sant'Anselmo
Tel: 06-570 057
[p339, D3]
www.aventinohotels.com
Nestling in a peaceful garden on the leafy and exclusive Aventine Hill, this hotel has been lavishly redecorated. Each room has been given its own imaginative theme, and details such as four-poster beds, free-standing baths and frescoes make it a very special place to stay. The main drawback is its distance from the centre, although it's just a short walk from Testaccio and the Piramide metro stop. €€€–€€€€

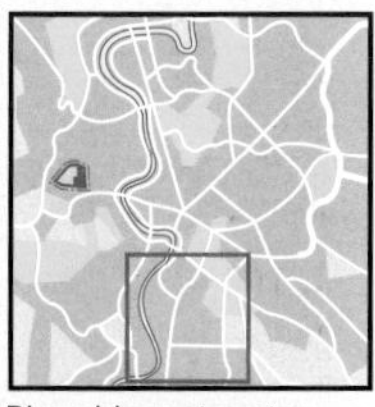

PRICE CATEGORIES

For a double room in high season:
€ = under €100
€€ = €100–180
€€€ = €180–260
€€€€ = €260–450
€€€€€ = over €450

TERMINI, MONTI AND ESQUILINO

Antica Locanda
84 Via del Boschetto
Tel: 06-484 894
[p336, A4]
www.antica-locanda.com
As the name suggests (*locanda* means inn), this is a cosy, wood-panelled wine bar with rooms to rent upstairs. The elegant rooms, named after famous composers and artists, are all individually furnished. Breakfast is served in the wine bar, and guests can use the roof terrace at any time of day. **€€€**

The Beehive
8 Via Marghera
Tel: 06-4470 4553
[p336, C3]
www.the-beehive.com
Rooms at this appealing budget option all have shared bathrooms, but are clean and stylishly decorated. Some impressive designer furnishings in the communal areas. There's a small restaurant, a yoga space and a patio. **€**

Capo d'Africa
54 Via Capo d'Africa
Tel: 06-772 801
[p340, B2]
www.hotelcapodafrica.com
This hotel's dramatic, palm-tree-lined entrance bodes well, and its 65 rooms are comfortable and contemporary. Views are delightful, especially from the stunning rooftop breakfast room, and the Colosseum is only a five-minute walk away. **€€€€**

Celio
35c Via dei Santissimi Quattro
Tel: 06-7049 5333
[p340, B2]
www.hotelcelio.com
This delightful, quirkily decorated hotel close to the Colosseum has twenty rooms and a lovely rooftop terrace. Frescoes and dramatic drapes throughout make it a great place to stay. **€€€€**

Des Artistes
20 Via Villafranca
Tel: 06-445 4365
[p336, C3]
www.hoteldesartistes.com
Quality of accommodation tends to dip around the station, but Des Artistes is an exception. Though its rooms are simple, they're comfortable and clean, and staff are friendly and helpful. The hotel also has dorm accommodation. **€€**

BELOW: the minimalist Radisson Blu es. Hotel.

Domus Sessoriana
10 Piazza Santa Croce in Gerusalemme
Tel: 06-706 151
[p341, D2]
www.domussessoriana.it
Attached to the church of Santa Croce in Gerusalemme, this hotel offers elegant, simple accommodation to a largely business clientele but don't let that dissuade you. There's a roof terrace with great views of San Giovanni in Laterano. **€€€**

Exedra
47 Piazza della Repubblica
Tel: 06-489 381
[p336, B3]
www.boscolohotels.com
Among the most opulent of the city's five-star hotels, the Exedra is chic and glamorous, with luxurious, no-expense-spared rooms. There's also a rooftop bar, restaurant, pool and a swanky spa. **€€€€€**

Forum
25–30 Via Tor de' Conti
Tel: 06-679 2446
[p340, A1]
www.hotelforumrome.com
This luxurious, old-fashioned hotel is ideally located for the Forum. Wonderful view from its roof-garden restaurant. **€€€–€€€€**

Hotel 47
47 Via Petroselli
Tel: 06-678 7816
[p339, D2]
www.47hotel.com
Near Piazza Venezia, this new-ish hotel is located on a street of imposing government offices. The Teatro di Marcello is at one end, and it leads out to the Temple of Vesta and the Bocca della Verità at the other. Set in an austere 1930s building, it has been tastefully converted and filled with repro furniture and contemporary artworks. The views are wonderful, as is the rooftop bar-restaurant. **€€€€–€€€€€**

Inn at the Roman Forum
30 Via degli Ibernesi
Tel: 06-6919 0970
[p340, A1]
www.theinnattheromanforum.com
This boutique hotel is another fairly new addition to the accommodation scene. Offering spacious, luxurious rooms with canopied beds, it's in a prime location and even has its own ancient Roman crypt, currently being excavated. **€€€€€**

Lancelot
47 Via Capo d'Africa
Tel: 06-7045 0615
[p340, B2] www.lancelothotel.com
This friendly, family-run

hotel has light, airy rooms and enjoys an enviable position, a few minutes' walk from the Colosseum. **€€**

Montreal
4 Via Carlo Alberto
Tel: 06-445 7797
[p336, B4]
www.hotelmontrealrome.com
Twenty-seven bright and spacious rooms. This is a popular mid-range option, so book ahead; check the website for off-season deals. **€€**

Nerva
3 Via Tor de' Conti
Tel: 06-678 1835
[p340, A1]
www.hotelnerva.com
The decor of this family-run hotel is nothing to get excited about, but it is quiet and well located on the border between the Imperial Fora and the hilly bohemian Monti district. **€€€**

Radisson Blu es. Hotel
171 Via Filippo Turati
Tel: 06-444 841
[p336, C4] www.radissonblu.com/eshotel-rome
This cutting-edge-design hotel is seriously minimalist: rooms are pure white with the odd splash of green. A spectacular decked rooftop terrace has a restaurant and a pool (in summer). Its location – right opposite the station – is convenient but far from picturesque. **€€€€**

St Regis Grand
3 Via V.E. Orlando
Tel: 06-47091
[p336, B3]
www.stregis.com/grandrome
Situated between the station and Via Veneto, it provides a taste of 19th-century *belle époque* grandeur. If you can't afford to stay here, at least try to drop in for high tea or cocktails. **€€€€€**

EXCURSIONS FROM ROME

Ostia Antica

Rodrigo De Vivar
18–19 Piazza della Rocca
Tel: 06-565 1939
www.rodrigodevivar.com
Near the excavations at Ostia Antica, and inside the medieval *borgo*, this upmarket country house hotel has 10 rooms and four suites, all luxuriously finished, with Persian carpets and Murano chandeliers. The hotel also organises activity days, with courses in everything from archery to restoration to painting. **€€€**

Tivoli

Hotel Adriano
194 Via di Villa Adriana
Tel: 0774-535 028
www.hoteladriano.it
Just outside the entrance to Hadrian's Villa, this pleasant hotel offers 10 rooms, of which three are suites; most requested is Suite 14, where Marguerite Yourcenar stayed when she wrote her classic novel *Memoirs of Hadrian*. There's a restaurant and, nearby, an array of facilities that can be used by guests, including a golf course, swimming pool and tennis court. **€€**

Grand Hotel Duca D'Este
330 Via Tiburtina Valeria
Tel: 0774-3833
www.ducadeste.com
The nearby thermal centre is the main attraction at this high-profile hotel complex. Designed for large groups, Duca D'Este offers spa services for a relaxing stay. There's a covered pool and an outdoor pool in the garden, as well as a sauna and massage room. **€€–€€€**

Castelli Romani

Hotel Flora
8 Viale Vittorio Veneto, Frascati
Tel: 06-941 6110
www.hotel-flora.it
The bright bedrooms and luxurious marble bathrooms at this hotel, built in the late 19th century and decorated in "Liberty" style, make it an appealing option if you're looking to stay in central Frascati. There's a pretty courtyard shaded by palm trees where you can take breakfast in warm weather. **€€**

Grand Hotel Villa Tuscolana
Via del Tuscolo km 1,500, Frascati
Tel: 06-942 900
www.villatuscolana.it
Just east of Frascati, this beautiful hillside villa has been lavishly restored and turned into a hotel with 110 rooms. The bedrooms are spacious and elegant, and the common areas – which include a restaurant (La Rufinella) and bar – impressively grand. Has an indoor pool. **€€€**

Il Cortile
9, Via Giulia, Nemi
Tel: 06-936 8147
Two quaint rooms with en suite bathroom, sharing a kitchenette in this B&B. Fresh breakfast delivered to your door every morning by the friendly owner, who is a mine of information on the area. **€**

Etruscan Towns

B&B Casa di Anna
5/6 Largo della Boccetta, Cerveteri
Tel: 338-750 8548
Right in the heart of the

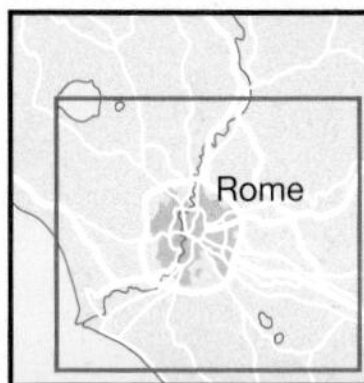

old town, this is a simple, no-frills B&B. Bedrooms are comfortable, though, with en suite bathrooms, and the breakfast is generous. Buses to the Necropolis are nearby. **€**

Viterbo Inn
17 Via San Luca, Viterbo
Tel: 0761-326 643
www.viterboinn.com
The 15 spacious rooms are organized on four floors, some with a fully-furnished kitchen. Great value for money considering the location, right in the medieval historic centre. **€**

PRICE CATEGORIES

For a double room in high season:
€ = under €100
€€ = €100–180
€€€ = €180–260
€€€€ = €260–450
€€€€€ = over €450

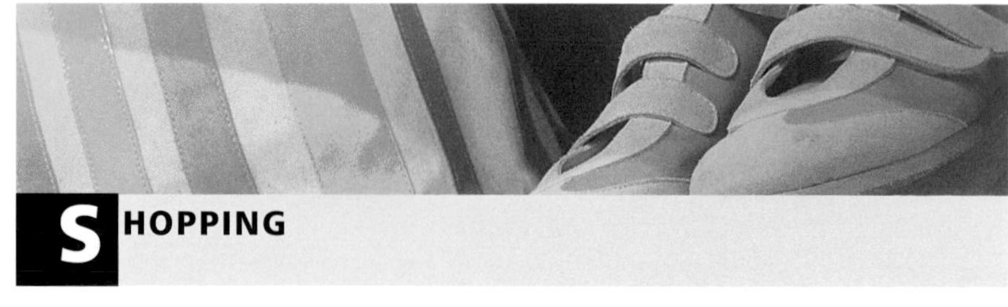

SHOPPING

BEST BUYS

Rome is the place for quality rather than bargains, so its best buys tend to be at the luxury end of the market, principally in the form of designer clothes and accessories, antiques and objets d'art. That said, careful shoppers may still come away with affordable buys: attractive books on art and architecture, classic leather shoes and bags, striking kitchenware, herbalists' concoctions, distinctive marbled notepaper, old prints, market bric-a-brac and a whole host of gourmet treats, all represent good value.

ABOVE: classic Italian style in an Alessi kettle.

WHAT TO BUY

Clothing

All the major designers and national retail chains are represented in Rome, and you don't have to be super-rich to kit yourself out in style. If Via Condotti and the Bulgari brigade are not in your budget, mid-range Italian labels including Liu Jo (188 Via Cola di Rienzo/137 Via del Corso), Stefanel (219 Via Cola di Rienzo/122 Via del Corso) and Carla G (121 Via del Babuino) offer high-quality styles ranging from chic to subdued, at prices that won't make you cringe. For reliable and reasonably priced staples, head to Benetton and sister-store Siseley, Class, or Spanish imports Zara and Mango. Peruse boutique originals and home-grown start-up collections along Via Governo Vecchio, Via del Boschetto and around Campo de' Fiori.

Shoes and Accessories

Before the introduction of the euro, a Fendi baguette or a pair of Prada shoes were the Italian shopping essentials. These days you're better off shopping in your home country first for designer bargains. For a great brand and price range, cruise the shops on Via Nazionale and Via Cola di Rienzo. Savvy shoe-shoppers should take advantage of the flashy, indie brands like Joseph Debach (19 Vicolo del Cinque) and trendy, upscale shoe shop Vic Matié (51 Via dei Giubbonari). For bags, Via Giubbonari (Campo de' Fiori) is lined with colourful boutiques, including Momento (Piazza Cairoli, end of the street) and Best Seller (No. 96). Aim for quality and originality in your adornments. "Made in Italy" is no longer a guarantee. In their quest to join ranks with the big guns, newer names on the Rome style scene, such as AVC and Casanita, are far more likely to sell you something that will last and impress.

Leather

Italian leather is still the best in the world, and you'll find it everywhere. Big leather vendors can be found on Via del Corso, Via Nazionale, and throughout the Tridente, whereas smaller, artisan leather goods are scattered throughout the city, and require a good eye to ascertain the quality. To get you started, check out Artigianato del Cuoio (90 Via Belsiana), where your own handbag designs are ready in under a week, and Claudio Sanò (67a Largo degli Osci), whose audacious hand-stitched bags are made on site.

Leather-bound notebooks and photo albums make gorgeous souvenirs. You can snatch them up at Cartoleria Pantheon and Papiro.

MONEY BACK?

As a general rule, it's next to impossible to return merchandise for a refund. While sales clerks are notoriously unrelenting, by law, unused items may be exchanged on site, but ask what the store's exchange policies are.

And More...

Rome is characterised by the olde-worlde values of artisan craftsmanship, artful design and good food, which define the shopping cityscape. Striking kitchenware abounds, from cute Alessi utensils and coffee services to elaborate appliances and hand-painted ceramics by Modigliani (24 Via Condotti). Stock up on top-of-the-line linens from Casa del Tessuto (64/66 Via del Statuto) and luxury bedding and fabrics from Fratelli Bassetti (73 Corso Vittorio Emanuele II).

Foodies will revel in the city's delis and speciality food shops. Castroni and Volpetti are mainstays for Italian and international delicacies, coffee and chocolate; wine and liqueurs are available at Trimani, Arcioni and many more around town.

WHERE TO BUY

Shopping Centres

Several shopping centres outside the city are good places to find last season's wares (mainly clothing) with discounts of up to 70 percent.

Castel Romano, south of EUR, has over 90 stores, including designer and mid-market brands such as Dolce & Gabbana, Versace, Calvin Klein and Diesel.
€ashion District in Valmontone southeast of Rome (trains leave hourly from Termini Station) has over 200 shops selling mostly mid-market brands.

For a mall within city limits, check out **Galleria Alberto Sordi** on Via del Corso. The arcade has been restored to its original grandeur after years of closure and neglect. Many new shops include Rome's first Zara, as well as a large Feltrinelli book and music store.

The new, large shopping centres are a bit out of the way but always worth the trek, especially on a rainy day. Check out Parco Leonardo and Parco da Vinci near Fiumicino airport, Porta di Roma at the end of Via Salaria, and Euroma 2 in EUR for hundreds of shops under the same roof.

Department Stores

Department stores are few and far between in Rome, but there are five main chains.
COIN, 7 Piazzale Appio (San Giovanni) and 73 Via Cola di Rienzo. Dependable, with some well-made and imaginative linen and household items.
La Rinascente, Piazza Fiume. The most elegant of the stores, with a vast range of goods, especially fashion for women and children.
Oviesse, 62 Viale Trastevere. Basic store for household goods, clothes and cosmetics.
Upim Piazza Santa Maria Maggiore. Economical store for household goods, cosmetics and children's clothes.
MAS (Piazza Vittorio) is an emporium of cheap and often tacky essentials. You'll have to get your hands dirty, but rare gems are known to reside within.

Fashion

Cult Couture

Those into serious shopping and couture names head to the Piazza di Spagna area and explore the high-fashion temples that are Via Condotti, Via Bocca di Leone and Via Borgognona. Ateliers succeed one another in dizzying fashion and prices to match. Here's a quick reference.

Dolce & Gabbana, 51–52 Via Condotti/D&G 93 Piazza di Spagna
Fendi, 419 Largo Goldoni
Gianfranco Ferrè, 7 Via Borgognona
Gianni Versace, 26 Bocca di Leone
Giorgio Armani, 77 Via Condotti/140 Via del Babuino. Armani Jeans: 137 Via Tomacelli
Gucci, 8 Via Condotti/7d Via Borgognona
Hogan, 110 Via del Babuino
Laura Biagiotti, 43 Via Borgognona
Max Mara, 28 Via Frattina
Prada, 90 Via Condotti
Roberto Cavalli, 25 Via Borgognona
Valentino, 15 Bocca di Leone.

Mid-Range Clothing

Nearby **Via del Corso** is far more budget-oriented. Although crass in parts, it holds some pearls for high-street fashion fanatics, such as Diesel (No. 186), H&M (No. 512), Miss Sixty (No. 486), Benetton (No. 288) and two Zara stores (Galleria Alberto Sordi and No. 129–35). Via del Corso ends (or begins) at Piazza del Popolo, but cross the river at Ponte

BELOW: Tad, the concept store on Via Del Babuino.

SIZE CHART

Women's dresses

Italian	UK	US
38	8	6
40	10	8
42	12	10
44	14	12

Men's shirts

Italian	UK	US
36	14	14
38	15	15
41	16	16
43	17	17

Women's shoes

Italian	UK	US
37	4	6
38	5	7½
39	6	8½
40	7	9

Men's shoes

Italian	UK	US
40	6½	7½
41	7	8
42	8	8½
43	9	9½

Margherita to **Via Cola di Rienzo** for more wallet-friendly shops, including many sister stores. There's Benetton (No. 193–209) and COIN department store (No. 173) as well as:

Blunauta, No. 303–309. Flowing designs in silk and cashmere.

Chopin, 38 Via Ottaviano. Colourful fashion items for women. In summer, grab skirts and dresses, in winter go for jumper dresses and wool suits.

Diesel, No. 247–248. Best-known for jeans and ultra-urban style.

Energie, No. 235. Skinny jeans and all things long and lean, in daring colours and prints. Great accessories, too.

Iron G, No. 50. Get club-ready and a bit extravagant at this twenty-something magnet.

Mango, No. 198. Spain's answer to Benetton and Gap has everything basic and trendy.

Chic Boutiques

For those in search of cool collections, one-of-a-kind styles and all-in-one concept stores, Rome is full of gems.

Angelo di Nepi, 28 Via Dei Giubbonari, sells colourful fitted jackets, wide linen trousers and beautiful dresses and scarves.

Carla G, 121 Via del Babuino, sells garments that are classy, well cut and very sassy.

Ethic, 11 Piazza B. Cairoli (end of Via dei Giubbonari) is one of many branches of a casualwear company that mixes styles, genres and fabrics with a penchant for the ethnic or unusual. Great looking, well priced pieces.

Gente, 277 Via Cola di Rienzo, carries fabulous designer clothes, accessories and shoes and lesser-known (but equally chic) brands.

Kristina Ti, 40 Via Mario de' Fiori, makes sexy and feminine dresses and bikinis.

Patrizia Pepe, 44 Via Frattina, is a Florentine designer who creates modern, feminine wear at user-friendly prices.

Maga Morgana, 27 and 98 Via del Governo Vecchio, specialises in Luciana Iannace's hand-knitted garments and old-fashioned dresses.

Momento, 9 Piazza Cairoli (Via dei Giubbonari). Choose from flowing boho dresses, original designs and enough shoes and bags to fill a million closets.

Nuyorica, 36–37 Piazza Pollarola. This boutique is also a shoe-lover's dream, and includes selections by Marni, Balenciaga, Rodolphe Menudier and Sigerson Morrison. Very hip, pretty pricey.

Bags, Shoes and Accessories

AVC, 88 Piazza di Spagna/141 Via Frattina/outlet: 66–68 Via Mastro Giorgio. Roman designer Adriana V. Campanile is up on the trends and far lower on the prices.

Boccanera, 36 Via Luca della Robbia (Testaccio). All the big Italian (and some foreign) brands under one roof: Hogan, Tod's, Prada and Dolce & Gabbana.

Borsalino, 72a Via di Campo Marzio. A time-honoured hat-maker.

Calzature Fausto Santini, 106 Via Santa Maria Maggiore. His main store is on Via Frattina, but this is where you get Santini's gems from past collections at half-price.

Casanita, 8 Via del Biscione. Upstairs resembles decade-old Gap designs for teenagers, but the shoes downstairs are a well-hidden wealth of comfort, style and adorable colours.

Coccinelle, 255 Via Cola di Rienzo. Luxuriously soft leather bags and pocketbooks in the colours of the season.

Fratelli Rossetti, 59A Via del Babuino. Another classic Italian footwear-maker, from Milan.

Furla, 22 Piazza di Spagna, and other branches around Rome, is Italy's mid-market answer to the bag dilemma, with a widely varied, constantly changing range of leather bags and accessories. Good quality, and pleasingly (almost) modest prices.

Geox, 3 Via Frattina. Comfortable, wearable and sexy shoes – a bit like Camper shoes.

Ibiz, 39 Via dei Chiavari. Handmade and wonderfully whimsical leather accessories of all sorts are made on site.

Mandarina Duck, 59 Via Due Macelli/272 Cola di Rienzo. Bolognese designer of pretty and functional bags and luggage.

TOP: Fratelli Rossetti for men.
ABOVE AND LEFT: Prada on Via Condotti.

Mencucci, 98 Via Cavour, dresses women from head to toe in highly selected shoes and garments.
Pollini, 22–24 Via Frattina. Classic shoes and handbags.
Sermoneta, 61 Piazza di Spagna. Gloves in a multitude of colours.
Tod's, 56a–57 Via Fontanella Borghese. Diego Della Valle's shoes and bags, sold here, have become cult items. *See also* **Tad** *(page 302).*

Vintage

Via Governo Vecchio is your first destination. Check out Abiti Usati (No. 35), Omero & Cecilia (No. 110) and Vestiti Usati Cinzia (No. 45). The **Micca Market** at the Micca Club lounge (7a Via Pietro Micca) is a veritable jumble sale starting every Sunday from 6pm onwards. **Pulp** (14 Via del Boschetto) is a small but treasure-packed second-hand shop in Monti. **People** (4 Piazza Teatro di Pompeo) is where the fashion-conscious head for original accessories.

Jewellery

Agau, 25 Via dei Serpenti, transforms 925 silver and semi-precious stones into elegant pieces of jewellery.
Buccellati, 31 Via Condotti. Famous Florentine jewellers, best-known for their elaborately worked silver pieces.
Bulgari, 10 Via Condotti. The supreme jeweller to royalty and the stars.
Giokeb, 79 Via della Lungaretta. A favourite for affordable baubles, the chunky gems – especially amber – and silver settings will blow your mind and not your wallet.
Ivano Langella, 73a Via di Ponte Sisto. Not your run-of-the-mill jeweller, Langella moulds chunks of silver, gold and bronze into unusual and stunning pendants, rings and necklaces.
Massimo Maria Melis, 57 Via dell'Orso. Custom-made jewellery, inspired by Roman and Etruscan artefacts.

Books

Almost Corner Bookshop, 45 Via del Moro. Australian-run, with well-chosen and reasonably priced titles.
Anglo-American Book Co, 102 Via della Vite. Novels, art books, travel tomes and a kids' section.
Bibli, 28 Via dei Fienaroli. Some English books, and a lovely café with an internet point. Serves brunch on Sundays.
Borri Books, Termini Station. A whole floor of English books inside the main train station.
The English Bookshop, 248 Via di Ripetta. A good range of travel, non-fiction and children's books. Also has a café.
Feltrinelli International, 84 Via V.E. Orlando. Large English-language section.
Libreria del Viaggiatore, 78 Via del Pellegrino. Travel books and maps.
Lion Bookshop, 33 Via dei Greci. The oldest English bookshop in Rome, with a wide assortment of titles and a coffee shop.
Open Door Bookshop, 23 Via della Lungaretta. Second-hand books in English.

Gifts

Via della Conciliazione, linking the Vatican with Castel Sant' Angelo, offers a wide range of religious artefacts including Vatican coins, statues, stamps, religious books and souvenirs. Similar objects are on sale around the Vatican itself and on Via dei Cestari, between the Pantheon and Largo Argentina.
Ai Monasteri, 72 Corso Rinascimento. Sells teas, honeys, liqueurs, ointments and potions made by monks from all over Italy.
Al Sogno, 53 Piazza Navona. Historic toy store specialising in soft toys of all shapes and sizes.
Cartoleria Pantheon, 15 Via della Rotonda. A well-stocked card store featuring hand-bound leather notebooks.
Città del Sole, 65 Via della Scrofa. A store for progressive parents and their progeny, crammed with educational toys, games and books.
Fabriano, 173 Via del Babuino. Quality writing paper, photo albums, wallets and travel

BARGAIN PICKS

Danielle and **Outlet**, Piazza Risorgimento. A great selection of all kinds of shoes at reasonable prices. The outlet sells overstock from Danielle at rock-bottom prices.
Lesley, 17A Via Bosi. Designer clothes and accessories worn once by models and slashed by up to 70%.
MAS, Piazza Vittorio (Esquilino). Definitely for the determined, this cheap and often tacky department store is worth a rummage.
Tessuti Camiceria, 92 Viale Mazzini (Prati). Handmade shirts and blouses in 100 percent cotton.

ABOVE: Roman deli.

diaries, plus a section with drawing products for children.

Mondadori Retail, 473 Via del Corso. A huge music shop with a good video and DVD selection, it also sells concert tickets and international magazines. Open until late.

Il Papiro, 5 Via del Pantheon. A stationery store featuring Florentine stationery, quill pens, and beautiful notebooks and albums.

Polvere di Tempo, 59 Via del Moro. Sells beautiful handmade copies of ancient time-measuring instruments, including sundials and sand clocks.

Profumum, 10 Via di Ripetta. Exclusive lines of perfumes inspired by the Italian flora and by life in Italy.

Tè e Teiere, 85 Via del Pellegrino. A tea-lover's haven in a coffee-oriented city, with expert staff to boot. The teas, pots and cups range from the modern and colourful to the traditional made out of bamboo and cast iron, and are sourced from all over the world.

OUTDONE YOURSELF?

Chances are your suitcase will be bursting at the seams. Luckily for you, baggage of all shapes, sizes and prices is on offer citywide. The budget luggage hub is conveniently located on **Via Nazionale** and around **Santa Maria Maggiore**, near Termini Station.

Diomedi, 99 Piazza San Bernardo. An old-fashioned shop selling exquisite beauty cases, suitcases and briefcases.

Segue, 160 Via Nazionale. The bag mecca by Benetton. This is the place for those hard and happy-coloured cases and matching carry-alls and carry-on bags.

Tedeschi Salvatore Paolo, 166 Via Nazionale. A fine selection of small and large suitcases in all price ranges. *See also* **Mandarina Duck** *on page 300.*

Food

Castroni, 196 Via Cola di Rienzo/55 Via Ottaviano. The hands-down favourite for Italian speciality items, international treats and amazing gifts. A tin of their roasted and ground espresso will not go unappreciated.

Innocenzi, 31 Via Natale del Grande. An old-fashioned treasure trove of a deli selling rice and grain out of big canvas sacks, many organic products, and ethnic foods from all over the world, as well as regional Italian delicacies.

Panella, 4 Largo Leopardi. A bread and pastry shop straight out of one's dreams.

Volpetti, 47 Via Marmorata. Probably the best deli in Rome.

Drink

Arcioni, 11–13 Via della Giuliana. Friendly and knowledgeable staff will help you find a bottle in your price range.

Constantini, 16 Piazza Cavour. Over 2,000 Italian wines to choose from.

Enoteca al Parlamento, 15 Via dei Prefetti. Hundreds of bottles in a mind-boggling selection.

Trimani, 20 Via Goito. Good selection of wines and tempting delicacies. One of Rome's oldest wine vendors.

Interior Design

Architettura D'Interni, 27–29 Via Bissolati. A striking store where interior design and architecture blend seamlessly.

DCube, 42 Via dei Crociferi. Sophisticated designer accessories and gadgets for the modern home.

Fattorini, 55 Via Arenula. A furniture showroom carrying the top names in Italian design, including the gorgeous FLOS lamps.

Spazio Sette, 7 Via dei Barbieri. One of Rome's premier furniture and home-furnishings stores.

Tad, 155a Via del Babuino. A so-called "concept store" with all the designer lifestyle must-haves: fashion, footwear, cosmetics, magazines, furniture. There's also a florist, hairdresser and a café.

Kitchenware

Bodum, 141 Via di San Francesco a Ripa. Teapots, coffee makers, cappuccino foaming tools and more by the celebrated Danish design brand. Functional and affordable, yet still stylish.

Cornucopia, 3 Piazza Rondanini. A fine collection of slick, modern Italian names in kitchenware and colourful appliances.

C.U.C.I.N.A. 65 Via Mario de' Fiori. Trendy, good-quality kitchenware with an appealing mix of prices.

Gusto, 7 Piazza Augusto Imperatore. Attached to the 'Gusto mega-restaurant *(see page 134)*, this is a delightful store with the most unusual and well-made cooking utensils and gadgets, as well as a range of cookery books and magazines.

Leone Limentani, 47 Via del Portico d'Ottavia. A wide variety of discounted ceramics, crystal, china and cutlery, and Alessi products, in a dusty and rambling warehouse.

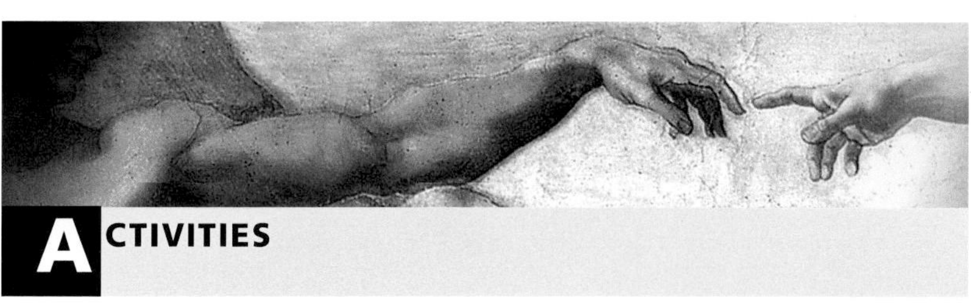

ACTIVITIES

THE ARTS, NIGHTLIFE, ANNUAL EVENTS, SPORT AND FESTIVALS

Romans know how to have fun – *La Dolce Vita*, the city's celebrated "good life", is still lived in the city. The best time for live music and cultural events is the summer, when classical ruins, Renaissance squares, villa gardens and parks play host to Estate Romana, an extravaganza of film, music, theatre, dance and much more. Rome's nightlife has never been as vibrant as it is today, and for sheer excitement and atmosphere you cannot beat an Italian football match at the Stadio Olimpico.

THE ARTS

Theatre

As plays are nearly always performed in Italian, an evening at the theatre is only recommended for fluent Italian-speakers. A notable exception are theatrical events related to the Roma Europa Festival *(see Festivals, page 308)* or some of the original-language performances put on at the ever-reliable **Teatro Argentina** (52 Largo Argentina, tel: 06-684 0001, www.teatrodiroma.net). However, in some cases it is worth attending a classical drama or play in translation, if the venue itself provides the drama – particularly summer events held outdoors, whether in amphitheatres, such as the one at **Ostia Antica** (Scavi di Ostia Antica, 117 Viale dei Romagnoli, tel: 06-5635 2003), or at other classical sites. Roman theatre embraces mainstream and contemporary, but the emphasis is on the tried and trusted Italian dramatists (such as Carlo Goldoni and Luigi Pirandello), musicals, or lighter, frothier stuff, often translated. However, the university theatres and smaller venues do stage experimental or fringe productions (known as "Teatro off"). One of the most interesting of these is the revamped **Teatro Palladium** (8 Piazza Bartolomeo Romano, tel: 06-5733 2768, www.teatro-palladium.it) which is attached to the University Roma 3 and puts on an interesting range of readings, films, dance and theatre events. The theatre season runs from October to early June, but there are numerous summer events linked to specific Roman festivals *(see* Roma Europa and *Estate Romana, page 309)*. Rome also has a last-minute theatre box office where unsold tickets can be bought on the same day for up to 50 percent off. The counter is located at 20 Via Bari (Piazza Salerno, tel: 06-4411 7799;

WHAT'S ON WHERE

For the most comprehensive listings of what's on in Rome, pick up *Roma C'è*, a weekly booklet that comes out on Wednesday and is available from news-stands. Listings are in Italian with an abbreviated section in English. The Thursday edition of the national daily *La Repubblica* carries a supplement called *TrovaRoma* that contains full listings for the upcoming week, and the fortnightly English magazine *Wanted in Rome* (available at news-stands) also has a listings section. The tourist information office and booths *(see page 317)* provide a multitude of leaflets, including the monthly guide *L'Evento* and a booklet called *Tourist's Passepartout*. Online, www.trovacinema.it lists all the films currently playing.

Tue–Sat 2–8pm, closed July and August; Policlinico metro stop line B).

The English Theatre of Rome (tel: 06-444 1375, www.rometheatre.com) has an interesting and varied programme of small-scale productions, with five English-language productions per season, usually put on at the intimate Teatro L'Arciliuto in the Centro Storico.

Opera and Ballet

The opera and ballet season runs from October to June at the Teatro dell'Opera, 1 Piazza Beniamino Gigli, tel: 06-4816 0255, www.operaroma.it. The ticket office is open Tue–Sat 9am–5pm, Sun 9am–1.30pm, but tickets can also be bought on its website and picked up at the opera house on the night of the performance. Ticket prices run from reasonable to exorbitant. The outdoor summer opera series (same number as above) has been held in a variety of venues in past years, including the Baths of Caracalla.

The best bet for international and contemporary dance is the **Teatro Olimpico** (17 Piazza Gentile da Fabriano, tel: 06-326 5991, www.teatroolimpico.it). Ticket office is open daily 11am–7pm.

BELOW: sculpture of Constantine's hand at the Museo Capitolino.

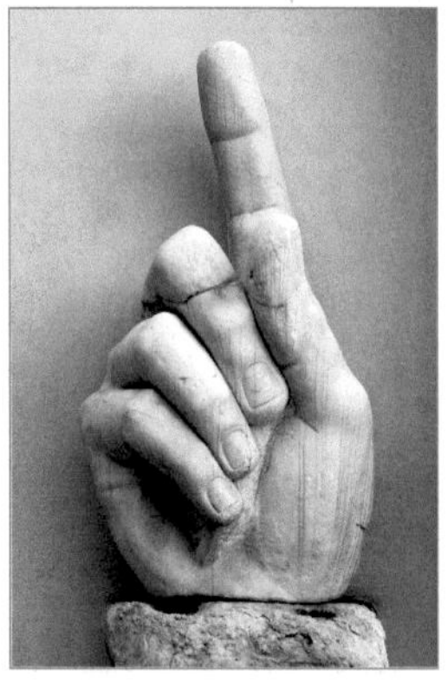

Classical Music

There is a wide range of venues for classical music. The season runs from October to June, but with special summer concerts there's something going on just about all year round.

The renowned, high-profile Accademia di Santa Cecilia (www.santacecilia.it), and its symphonic and chamber orchestras, hosts all its principal concerts from October to May at the new **Auditorium-Parco della Musica** (30 Viale Pietro de Coubertin, tel: 06-8024 1281, www.auditorium.com). Designed by Genoese architect Renzo Piano, it opened in December 2002 and features three concert halls with excellent acoustics. A 10-minute tram-ride from Piazzale Flaminio (just above Piazza del Popolo), the complex also features a large inner courtyard, which is used for outdoor concerts and events.

For more information, visit www.santacecilia.it or the Auditorium's website. There are many other venues for classical music, including churches and outdoor venues all over Rome in summer, many of them part of the Estate Romana series of events *(see Festivals, page 309)*. Some of the most atmospheric venues are the Terme di Caracalla, the Teatro di Marcello, the Fori Imperiali and the Terrazza del Pincio. Ask at a tourist information point for the monthly guide to cultural events, called *L'Evento*, or check the local press for more information on classical music events.

Museums and Galleries

The Roma Pass is an integrated ticket which costs €25, lasts three days and gives you free entrance to the first two museums or archaeological sites you visit (most major sites are included in the scheme; call 06-0608 or see www.romapass.it for details). The card also entitles you to reduced admission on any further sites you visit. Full access to the public transport system is included in the price. The pass is sold at all of the sites involved, at tourist information kiosks and at Fiumicino Airport's tourist information office in Terminal C.

A €7 Museum Card, valid for three days, is available and covers all the sites of the Museo Nazionale Romano. A €23.50 ticket (Roma Archeologia Card), valid for seven days, covers the sites of the Museo Nazionale Romano and the Colosseum, the Palatine, the Roman Forum, the Baths of Caracalla, the Tomb of Cecilia Metella and the Villa of the Quintili. They can be bought from any participating site.

Most museums are closed on Monday, though there are some exceptions. Important art exhibitions are usually open daily.

NIGHTLIFE

Roman nightlife tends to be fun rather than frenzied. Apart from a few privileged or exclusive clubs, the nightclub scene is far less adventurous than in Berlin, London or New York. In common with other capital cities, door policy determines whether you even get to cross the threshold of a club. If your look is not right you will either not get in or not fit in. As a general rule, however, in Rome it is safer to dress up rather than down, even if it makes rejection all the more humiliating.

You may be required to obtain temporary membership (a *tessera*, or membership card, should be available at the door). Entry price may include a free drink, but drinks are normally quite expensive. Groups of young men together are usually not welcome and, in some clubs, a man may be turned away unless accompanied by a woman.

Trastevere is still a reliable destination for Romans in search of a good time, while the slightly more alternative Testaccio is clubland central. A burgeoning gay, alternative and commercial scene is happening even further south in the industrial Ostiense quarter.

The historic quarters around Piazza Navona (around Via di Tor Millina), the Pantheon and Campo de' Fiori contain popular bars and clubs. The Via Veneto, scene of Fellini's *Dolce Vita*, is still home to certain elegant nightclubs and piano bars, which tend to be patronised by middle-aged, moneyed Americans.

Most nightclubs don't get going until midnight; most close Monday night, some on Sunday too. Several of the better ones are around Via di Monte Testaccio. Recently there's been an upsurge in so-called *discobar* and *ristodisco*, which as their names suggest mean bars and restaurants where there are also DJ sets and you can dance until late.

In summer, much young nightlife moves to the beach resorts south of the city. However, the glut of summer city festivals ensures that Rome remains lively. Apart from these, the best and most typical forms of Roman nightlife tend to be centred on a leisurely meal, a musical event or chatting and drinking at one of the many outdoor bars.

Nightclubs

Akab
69 Via di Monte Testaccio (Testaccio)
Tel: 06-5725 0585
www.akabcave.com
Ever-popular club with two floors and a terrace garden. The music is mainly commercial dance.

Alpheus
36 Via del Commercio (Testaccio)
Tel: 06-574 7826
www.alpheus.it
Everything from R&B and hip hop to house with live music nights that vary in genre from rock to Latin music.

Art Cafe
33 Viale del Galoppatoio (Villa Borghese)
Tel: 06-3600 6578

ABOVE: DJs often play bars and restaurants as well as clubs.

This slick, trendy club, which plays mainly commercial dance, attracts a well-heeled, party-loving crowd whose aim is to see and be seen.

Caruso
36 Via di Monte Testaccio (Testaccio)
Tel: 06-574 5019
www.carusocafe.com
Latin American music is the order of the day at this cosy club, which bursts with enthusiastic salsa-dancing couples most nights. There's a pleasant roof terrace for a breath of fresh air in the summer months.

Fake
64 Via di Monte Testaccio (Testaccio)
Tel: 06-4544 7627
Opened in 2005, this club has proved a success with the city's fashion crowd – thanks to its all-white, futuristic design, pop-art touches and mainly electronica music.

Goa
13 Via Libetta (Ostiense)
Tel: 333-847 4377
One of the city's most popular clubs. Music ranges from house to electronica.

La Maison
4 Vicolo dei Granari (Piazza Navona)
Tel: 06-683 3312
Very hip centrally located club with a 1970s-retro feel to the decor and ambience.

La Saponeria
20 Via degli Argonauti (Ostiense)
Tel: 06-574 6999
www.saponeriaclub.it
Industrial location with a retro 1970s design and music nights that range from hip hop to house.

Le Coppelle
52 Piazza delle Coppelle (Piazza Navona)
Tel: 349-740 4620
www.lecoppelle52americanbar.com
A so-called discobar with an enviably central location and a great line in cocktails. Outdoor seating on giant sofas in summer and a very cosmopolitan vibe.

Micca Club
7A Via Pietro Micca (Esquiline)
Tel: 06-8744 0079
www.miccaclub.com
The ex-oil cellar is now an alternative (and always crowded) dance club where DJs spin tunes from the 1950s and '60s. Weekly burlesque shows. Closed during the summer months.

Music Venues

Alexanderplatz
9 Via Ostia (Prati)
Tel: 06-5833 5781
www.alexanderplatz.it
When the big names come to town, they often come to this jazz club and restaurant, which runs the summer jazz series at the Villa Celimontana.

Beba do Samba
8 Via dei Messapi (San Lorenzo)
Tel: 328-575 0390
www.bebadosamba.it
Located in the student district of

San Lorenzo, this is a buzzy venue with live music (generally jazz or world) most nights.

Big Mama
18 Via San Francesco a Ripa (Trastevere)
Tel: 06-581 2551
www.bigmama.it
The blues club in Rome, but also hosts jazz and rock musicians.

Brancaleone
11 Via Levanna (Nomentana)
Tel: 06-8200 4382
www.brancaleone.it
One of the liveliest of Rome's *centri sociali*, attracting high-quality DJs and live acts.

Casa del Jazz
55 Viale di Porta Ardeatina (Aventine)
Tel: 06-704 731
www.casajazz.it
A classy villa and park hosting high-level jazz concerts nightly.

Circolo degli Artisti
42 Via Casilina Vecchia
Tel: 06-7030 5684
www.circoloartisti.it
Rock concerts take place once a week. See website for the full programme.

Palalottomattica
Piazzale dello Sport (EUR)
Tel: 199-128 800
Refurbished architectural landmark. Hosts indoor concerts.

The Place
27 Via Alberico II (Prati)
Tel: 06-6830 7137
www.theplace.it
This sophisticated club has a stage for live acts – mainly jazz bands (mostly Italian, some international).

Cinema

Virtually all films on general release are dubbed into Italian. For English-speaking cinema, try the following (films are marked VO – *versione originale*):

Alcazar, 14 Via Cardinale Merry del Val. Tel: 06-588 0099. The current film playing is shown in its original version on Monday.

Metropolitan, 7 Via del Corso. Tel: 06-320 0933. Multi-screen cinema with one screen devoted to original-version films.

ABOVE: at the Villa Borghese zoo.

Nuovo Olimpia, 16g Via in Lucina. Tel: 06-686 1068. Art-house movies are occasionally shown, as well as original-language films.

Warner Village Moderno, 45–46 Piazza della Repubblica. Tel: 06-477 7911. Frequent original-version films on one screen.

Children's Activities

Explora – Il Museo dei Bambini, 82 Via Flaminia; Tue–Sun 10am–5pm; visits by prior booking only on weekends, four slots daily; entrance fee; tel: 06-361 3776, www.mdbr.it. Rome's only children's museum. With four sections dedicated to humans, the environment, communications and society, there are plenty of signs and material in English. Kids can star in their own TV show and have fun with the interactive displays. There's also a restaurant.

Time Elevator, 20 Via SS Apostoli; daily screenings 11am–7.30pm; entrance fee; tel: 06-9774 6243, www.timeelevator.it. Touted as a multimedia experience that illustrates the history of Rome. You sit on a moving platform, wearing headphones, for a cinematic roller-coaster ride through history with various protagonists (such as Nero and Michelangelo) playing major parts, and a narrator to help with the chronology. Quite cheesy, but a fun introduction to the Eternal City. Memorable moments include watching Rome burn.

Museo Criminologico, 29 Via del Gonfalone; Tue–Sat 9am–1pm, Tue and Thur 2.30–6.30pm; entrance fee; tel: 06-6889 9442, www.museocriminologico.it. The Criminological Museum covers the history of the prison system in Italy, how criminal cases are solved and how criminals were punished over the centuries, but the part (older) children will enjoy best is the section with torture instruments and paintings depicting various and gruesome forms of punishment.

Capuchin Crypt, 27 Via Veneto; Fri–Wed 9am–noon and 3–6pm; tel: 06-487 1185; www.cappucciniviaveneto.it. Children are always impressed and amused by this chapel, festively decorated with artfully arranged bones and skulls of dead Capuchin monks and their family members. Not recommended for young children or the overly timorous.

Annual Events

Many festivals are linked to the Catholic Church. The tourist office *(see page 317)* can provide more details. Be aware that Romans throw firecrackers in the street when celebrating some occasions.

January

6 January: culmination of Christmas fair in Piazza Navona *(see December)*. Celebrating **Epiphany** (**Befana**), the traditional festival when good children receive presents and naughty children are given coal-shaped sweets.
17 January: **La Festa di Sant' Antonio Abate**. Blessing of

animals in the church of Sant'Eusebio all'Esquilino.

February

February/March: **Carnevale**. Roman children put on fancy dress and take to the streets, and clubs organise themed fancy-dress events, see www.carnevale.roma.it.

March

9 March: **Festa di Santa Francesca Romana**. Cars and mopeds are driven to the church of Santa Francesca Romana in the Foro Romano to be blessed by the patron saint of motorists.
La Festa della Primavera. The arrival of spring is marked by the decoration of the Spanish Steps with a sea of azaleas.
Maratona di Roma. The marathon takes place on the third or fourth Sunday in March. www.maratonadiroma.it.
Late March/early April: **Giornate FAI**. The Fondo Ambientale Italiano (Environmental Fund of Italy; www.fondoambiente.it) organises a weekend when usually closed churches, monuments and gardens can be visited.
March/April: Easter week is huge, from the big Mass on Palm Sunday and the distribution of palm fronds to the mass pilgrimages for **Holy Week** (**Settimana Santa**) and concerts all over the city. The Pope leads an outdoor **Mass at the Colosseum on Good Friday**, followed by a procession passing the Stations of the Cross. The week culminates on Easter morning with the Pope's Urbi et Orbi speech. Call the Vatican tourist office for more info *(see page 317)*.

April

21 April: **Il Natale di Roma**. Rome celebrates its legendary founding with fireworks, music and other events. Festivities are centred around the Campidoglio.
25 April: **La Festa della Liberazione**. Public holiday commemorating liberation of Italy by Allied forces at the end of World War II.
Late April or May: **Settimana della Cultura**. Cultural Week throughout Italy, when entrance is free to all state-run museums and historical sites, as well as many exhibitions, see www.beniculturali.it.

May

May Day is widely celebrated in Rome. A huge free concert is held in front of San Giovanni in Laterano.
Sporting Events – the Italian Open Tennis Championship is usually held in the first half of May, and the International Horse Show is at the end of the month in the Villa Borghese.

BELOW: Rome's marathon begins and ends in Via dei Fori Imperiali.

June

2 June: **Republic Day**. The Armed Forces parade on Via dei Fori Imperiali before the President and the state's most important personalities.
29 June: **San Pietro e San Paolo**. The founders of the Catholic Church are honoured with a public holiday. Special Masses are held in their basilicas.
Estate Romana begins in June *(see Festivals, page 309)*.

July

Summer Opera. Opera and ballet in the open air at the Baths of Caracalla (continues in August).
Festa de' Noantri. A street festival in Trastevere that runs for two weeks from mid-July.

August

5 August: **La Festa della Madonna della Neve**. Rose petals fall onto the congregation of Santa Maria Maggiore to commemorate the miraculous summer snowfall on this day in the year AD 352.

October

Symphonic music season begins at the Auditorium, www.auditorium.com.

November

2 November: **Giornata dei Defunti**, or Day of the Dead, when the Pope celebrates Mass at the Verano cemetery.

December

8 December: **Immacolata Concezione**. The Immaculate

ABOVE: Radisson Blu es. Hotel.

Conception of the Virgin is celebrated around the statue of the Madonna in Piazza di Spagna.
Mercatino di Natale a Piazza Navona. Christmas arts-and-crafts fair with stalls selling food. Opens the second week of December, lasts until January.
Christmas. Major shopping streets are beautifully decorated and *presepi* (Nativity scenes) set up in churches around the city.
31 December: **San Silvestro**: fireworks and free rock and pop concerts in Piazza del Popolo and other squares.

SPORT

Spectator Sports

You can find information on sporting events in two national papers devoted solely to sport: *Corriere dello Sport* and *Gazetta dello Sport* – easy enough to understand even if you speak no Italian. Many local sporting events are also listed in Rome editions of the daily papers.

Football

Sporting life in Rome revolves around football *(calcio)*. Rome's Olympic Stadium is home to both the local clubs, SS Lazio and AS Roma, who play there from September to May. For fixtures, ticket information and official team paraphernalia, go to the Lazio Point, 34 Via Farini (near Termini) or the AS Roma Store, 360 Piazza Colonna.

Major Events

The two major sporting events that take place in Rome during the year and attract international stars and audiences are:

Concorso Ippico Internazionale (International Horse Show) at Piazza Siena in the gardens of the Villa Borghese in May (ask at a tourist information point or log on to www.piazzadisiena.com).

The **Italian Tennis Open** (www.internazional ibnlditalia.it), held at the Foro Italico, takes place in late April/early May.

Participant Sports

Gyms

The sport Romans are most interested in is weight training at a local *palestra* (gym). The largest gym in the centre (which also has two Olympic indoor pools) is the **Roman Sport Center**, 33 Viale del Galoppatoio, tel: 06-320 1667, on the edge of Villa Borghese (access from the car park at the top of Via Veneto).

Farnese Fitness, 35 Vicolo delle Grotte, tel: 06-687 6931, near Campo de' Fiori, offers a decent range of classes in a 16th-century building.

Swimming

For a hot city, Rome is decidedly under-provided with swimming pools, and most that do exist are privately run. The few city council pools are booked up with slot systems that are incomprehensible and inaccessible even for many Romans. Some of the luxury hotels (especially those outside the historic centre) offer access to their pools. If you choose this option be prepared to pay for it.

Cavalieri Hilton Hotel, 101 Via Cadiolo (Monte Mario), tel: 06-35091 *(see page 292)*.

Hotel Parco dei Principi, 5 Via G. Frescobaldi, tel: 06-854 421. On the edge of the Villa Borghese, this pool is a tranquil oasis *(see page 290)*.

Radisson Blu es. Hotel, 171 Via Filippo Turati, tel: 06-444 841, www.radissonblu.com/eshotel-rome. A truly stunning rooftop pool with a unique view of Termini's train tracks and the city below *(see page 297)*.

Piscina delle Rose, 20 Viale America, tel: 06-5422 0333. Take the metro to EUR Palasport. An Olympic-sized outdoor pool with rose gardens nearby. Open May to September only.

Other possibilities for swimming are the beaches and the lakes. The lakes are more pleasant than the beaches closest to Rome. Swimming is possible in Lago di Bracciano and in some of the lakes of the Castelli Romani.

Tennis

Most tennis courts belong to private clubs and are open to members and their guests only. Check with your hotel or tourist office for clubs that allow non-members to play.

HOW TO GET TICKETS

Venues have ticket offices, phone booking lines and online booking possibilities. Failing that, the best agencies for tickets to all kinds of events are:
Hello Ticket
Tel: 06-4807 8400
Freephone: 800-907 080
www.helloticket.it (tickets can also be bought online and picked up at the venue beforehand).
Ricordi Mediastores
506 Via del Corso
Tel: 06-321 6860.
Orbis Servizi
37 Piazza Esquilino (behind Santa Maria Maggiore)
Tel: 06-474 4776.

FESTIVALS

Over the past few years the number of cultural events and festivals in Rome has almost tripled, and many new buildings and museums have helped this process. The two most established festivals, which nevertheless grow every year, are the RomaEuropa Festival and the Estate Romana.

The **RomaEuropa Festival** (www.romaeuropa.net) is a cutting-edge event which takes place every year from mid-September to at least mid-November and covers dance (usually modern), theatre, readings, cinema and music. Every year the festival has a different theme, and the performers are a highly interesting mix of well-established international performers and emerging or avant-garde troupes.

The **Estate Romana** (literally, Roman Summer, www.estateromana.comune.roma.it) is the umbrella name for the huge programme of events sponsored by the local council. Running from June to September, it sees some of the city's most attractive parks and piazzas become venues for rock, ethnic and jazz concerts, theatre performances (in Villa Ada, Villa Celimontana, at the Fori Imperiali and in Piazza del Popolo, to cite but a few), outdoor cinema (for example, in Piazza Vittorio Emanuele II and San Lorenzo), dance lessons and other cultural events such as readings, book fairs and gastronomic evenings. Check the local press and ask at the tourist information points for details, or log on to www.romeguide.it.

Rome's **International Photography Festival** (www.fotografiafestival.it) puts on a wide range of photographic shows in the most diverse settings.

The **Rome Film Fest** (www.romacinemafest.it) is the city's official movie event. It takes place every October at the Auditorium with world-premieres and celebrity guests.

Only the best international DJs take part in **Dissonanze** (www.dissonanze.it), a three-day electronic music festival taking place in May in the Palazzo dei Congressi (EUR).

SIGHTSEEING TOURS

Walking and sightseeing tours are organised by a number of travel agencies and tour guides, both licensed and unlicensed. The quality of what's on offer varies wildly. Recommended is **Enjoy Rome**, 8a Via Marghera, tel: 06-445 1843, www.enjoyrome.com, a friendly English-speaking office near the station that organises walking tours. They range from the Vatican to the Jewish Ghetto and Trastevere, and also offer a night tour of the ancient sites. Day trips to the ruins of Pompeii are organised in the summer months, and they also offer a free accommodation booking service. **Context:Rome** (tel: 06-9762 5204, www.contextrome.com) is a network of architects, historians and art historians who lead walking seminars for discerning travellers in order to share their love of the city, its history and culture. Taking one of these tours (which should be booked in advance) is a great way of making contact with people who really know the city inside out.

ABOVE: Vatican sightseers.

BELOW: visiting dance company Sasha Waltz and Guests perform *Impromptus*.

A–Z

AN ALPHABETICAL SUMMARY OF PRACTICAL INFORMATION

Admission Charges

Museum admission fees vary, but the major ones start at about €7 while the minor ones cost about €4. Most state or municipal museums offer free entrance to EU citizens under 18 or over 65. The entrance ticket to the Palatine can be used to visit the Colosseum and the Roman Forum. Entrance to the Pantheon and all basilicas and churches is free, as are the Vatican Museums on the last Sunday of the month (expect long queues).

Budgeting for Your Trip

Prices have rocketed in Rome in recent years, with many blaming the euro and lack of government control when it was introduced. Things have calmed down a bit, and some prices have normalised, but hotels and restaurants were two of the worst-hit sectors, and in some cases prices have doubled. Expect to pay at least €150 a night for a double room if you want to stay in the city centre somewhere decent. For a more elegant hotel the prices are well over €200 a night. The cost of eating out varies hugely; a three-course evening meal with wine costs about €40 a head, on average, at a decent restaurant in the Centro Storico, but it's also possible to pay as little as €15 if you're happy to settle for a no-frills meal (pizza being an ever-popular budget option). You will pay a bit less at lunchtime, or if you find a neighbourhood trattoria in the suburbs or something off the beaten track, but more if you are in blatant tourist territory or in a modern minimalist restaurant with a "creative" menu.

One thing that remains very cheap is public transport. A single tickets costs €1 and can be used for 75 minutes, and a number of passes are available. There are one-day, three-day and seven-day passes, called *Biglietto Integrato Giornaliero, Biglietto Turistico Integrato* and *Carta Integrata Settimanale*, which are good for unlimited metro, bus and local train or regional bus travel. They need to be validated only on first use. Month-long passes, *Abbonamento Mensile*, are also available. COTRAL, the regional bus company, offers a regional day-pass (BIRG), which

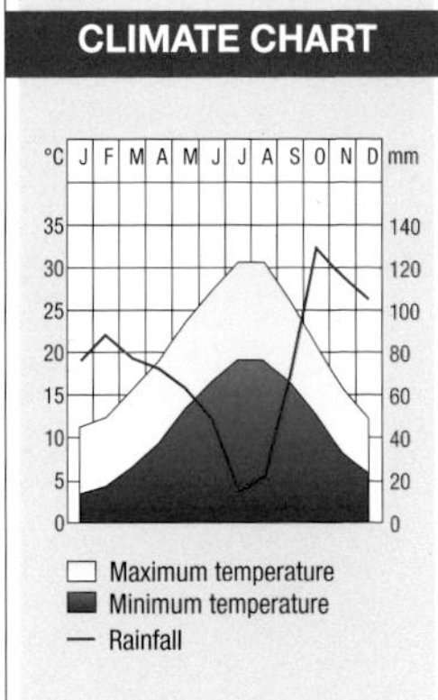

covers your round trip and in-city travel. Taxis are also cheaper than in most other capital cities, with a trip from the station to the centre (Piazza Navona) costing about €12–15 depending on the traffic; fares go up at night.

Climate

Despite some very unusual weather in the past few years (hail in July, heatwaves in May), Rome can still be said to have a classic Mediterranean climate: mild-ish winters and very hot, long summers. July and August are the hottest and most humid months, when it is advisable to stay indoors or in the shade in the middle of the day.

When to Visit

April, May, September and October are the best months to visit as the weather is usually sunny and warm but devoid of that heavy, airless quality. In August many Romans go on holiday (especially around the Feast of the Assumption on 15 August), but for the past few years the city council has put on an incredible range of world-class outdoor concerts and other cultural events from June to September, and the city is less deserted than it used to be.

What to Wear

Light summer clothes are suitable from spring to autumn. The Roman heat is sometimes alleviated by a light breeze which can produce cool evenings even in summer, so a cardigan or jacket is useful. Wear a hat in the summer if you burn easily. Sunglasses are essential.

In summer, the likelihood of rain is slight: sometimes there is no rainfall in Rome for more than three months. If it does rain, it will probably be a downpour in a thunderstorm. There is little point in preparing for this: just run for cover. At other times of the year, some form of waterproofing is worth considering, but not worth a lot of weight in your luggage. The most likely times for rain are autumn and spring.

In winter, warmer clothes are needed, including a heavy overcoat, as it can be very cold. Indoors, you may find the heating levels are below your expectations. In response to the climate, Roman building design has always concentrated on keeping heat out, rather than creating cosy interiors.

If visiting churches, and particularly St Peter's, remember that bare arms or shorts (on men or women) and short skirts are not acceptable, and you will be refused admittance. If wearing a short-sleeved or sleeveless garment, carry a light shirt/blouse or scarf with you.

Romans, like most Italians, consider clothes important. Most will dress smartly for an evening out, a restaurant meal or a visit to the theatre. Rome is accustomed to casually dressed tourists, but you may wish to follow local habits.

Dress codes for clubs and bars vary enormously and change with the seasons and fashions. In general, however, dress is still likely to be slightly more formal than would be expected in much of Northern Europe or the US.

Crime and Safety

The main problem tourists experience in Rome is petty crime: pickpocketing and bag-snatching, together with theft from parked cars. Reduce the possibility of theft by taking elementary precautions. Leave money and valuables, including airline tickets, in the hotel safe. Carry your camera out of sight and always be discreet with your money or wallet.

If you are carrying a handbag, keep it on the side away from the road, and when sitting in a café, place it firmly on your lap – one Roman speciality is the motorbike snatch. Backpacks, while convenient, make easy targets, so take them off or sling them under your arm in crowds. Always keep a separate record of credit card and cheque numbers just in case. A photocopy of your passport is also a useful precaution.

On the streets and especially near the main tourist attractions, keep an eye on beggars, particularly the small children who crowd around you with boxes in their hands. Take extra care on crowded buses and the metro, and on bus routes frequented by tourists, such as the No. 40 Express and the No. 64.

Put a car with a foreign number plate in a garage overnight. Take your radio out, even if your insurance company will replace it, because fixing a broken windscreen means wasted time and trouble. Don't leave any items visible in the car.

If you are unlucky enough to have something stolen, report the theft *(furto)* to the police as soon as possible: you will need the police report for any insurance claim and to replace stolen documents. For information on the nearest police station call the central station, the Questura Centrale, 15 Via San Vitale, tel: 06-46861. Report the loss of travellers' cheques or credit cards to your credit card company, and of passports to your consulate or embassy.

Customs

Visitors from EU countries are not obliged to declare goods imported into or exported from Italy if they are for personal use, up to the following limits: 800 cigarettes, 200 cigars or 1 kg of tobacco; 10 litres of spirits (over 22 percent alcohol) or 90 litres of fortified wine (under 22 percent alcohol).

For US citizens, the duty-free allowance is 200 cigarettes or 50 cigars; 1 litre of spirits or 2 litres of wine; one 50g bottle of perfume and duty-free gifts to the value of US$175.

Disabled Travellers

Rome is a difficult city for people with disabilities. Most churches, museums and archaeological sites have steps; streets and pavements are often uneven or cobbled, and pavements in the medieval centre are frequently too narrow for a wheelchair or have cars parked on the access ramps. However, things are improving, and the following attractions have installed ramps and lifts: the Vatican Museums, Galleria Doria Pamphilj, Castel Sant'Angelo, Palazzo Venezia, Palazzo delle Esposizioni, St Peter's, Galleria Borghese, Galleria Nazionale d'Arte Moderna and the Bioparco (zoo). Ask at the tourist information points for other sites with facilities for disabled people.

Some trains have access for the disabled, but you will need to call the railway at least 24 hours before travelling as assistance staff and equipment need to be booked in advance. Train timetables have a wheelchair symbol next to accessible trains. Seats at the front of city buses are reserved for the disabled, and many have designated wheelchair areas in the centre. The newest trams and buses all have large central doors and access ramps. On the metro, most of the central stations on line A are inaccessible, but all stations on line B have lifts, disabled toilets and designated parking spaces, except for Circo Massimo, Colosseo and Cavour. The metro website (www.atac.roma.it, follow the wheelchair symbol) has information on wheelchair-accessible stations.

Restaurants are usually helpful, but call in advance to ask about access. A number of hotels claim to offer access to travellers with disabilities, but check with the individual hotel – be as precise as possible about your needs and ask detailed questions.

For more details, contact Roma Per Tutti (tel: 06-5717 7094, www.romapertutti.it), an English-speaking information line.

DISABILITY SERVICE

A transport service for people with disabilities is available and costs €23 per ride for non-residents. Book in advance (toll-free telephone: 800 469 540), or visit www.atac.roma.it.

Electricity

Standard is 220 volts AC, 50 cycles. Sockets have either two or three round pins. For UK visitors, adaptors can be bought before you leave home, or at airports and main railway stations. Travellers from the US will need a transformer, though most laptops, phones and camcorders have it built in.

Embassies & Consulates

Consulates generally have answering machines on which you can leave a message in the event of a query or problem. If your passport is lost or stolen you will need to obtain a police report and have proof of your identity and suitable photos in order to get a new one.

Australia
5 Via Antonio Bosio
Tel: 06-852 721
www.italy.embassy.gov.au
Britain
80a Via XX Settembre
Tel: 06-4220 0001
www.britain.it
Canada
30 Via Zara
Tel: 06-854 441
www.canada.it
Ireland
3 Piazza Campitelli
Tel: 06-697 9121
www.ambasciata-irlanda.it
New Zealand
44 Via Clitunno
Tel: 06-853 7501
www.nzembassy.com/italy
South Africa
14 Via Tanaro
Tel: 06-852 541
www.sudafrica.it
United States of America
119a Via Veneto
Tel: 06-46741
www.usembassy.it
(Consulate: 121 Via Veneto, tel: 06-46741).

Gay & Lesbian Travellers

Rome has an active and vibrant gay community. For information on cultural events and news, contact:

Alibi, 40–44 Via di Monte Testaccio, tel: 06-574 3448, is a predominantly gay disco. Closed Mon–Wed.

Arci-Lesbica Roma, 15 Via Stefanini, tel: 06-418 0211, www.arcilesbica.it, is a group that runs a helpline and organises social get-togethers for lesbians.

Circolo di Cultura Mario Mieli, 2a Via Efeso, tel: 06-541 3985, www.mariomieli.org.

Coming Out, 8 Via San Giovanni in Laterano (near the Colosseum), tel: 06-700 9871, is a mainstay of the Roman gay

Emergency Numbers

Police	113
Carabinieri	112
Fire	115
Ambulance	118

scene – it is often as crowded on the pavement outside as inside.
Hangar, 69a Via in Selci (near Via Cavour), tel: 06-488 1397, is a well-established gay club. Closed Tuesday.
Luna e L'altra, 1a Via San Francesco di Sales (in Trastevere), tel: 06-6840 1727, is a women-only evening restaurant in the Casa Internazionale delle Donne (International House of Women; www.casainternazionaledelle donne.org). Closed Sunday.

Health & Medical Care

EU residents are entitled to the same medical treatment as an Italian citizen. Visitors will need to complete an EHIC form (see www.ehic.org.uk for information) before they go. This covers medical treatment and medicines, although it is still necessary to pay prescription charges and a percentage of the costs for medicines. Note that the EHIC does not give any cover for trip cancellations, nor does it provide repatriation in case of illness. For this, you will need to take out private insurance. US citizens are advised to take out private health insurance. Canadian citizens are also covered by a reciprocal arrangement between the Italian and Canadian governments.

If you are covered by a reciprocal scheme and need to visit a doctor while in Italy, take the EHIC card (if an EU resident) or proof of citizenship and residence (eg passport) to the local health office (Unità Sanitaria Locale), which will direct you to a doctor covered by the state system and supply the necessary paperwork. Not all doctors work in the state scheme, and those who do are often busy, so be prepared to

wait. A consultation with a private doctor may be quicker (and certainly requires less preparatory paperwork) but costs more, so private insurance is a good idea.

If you need emergency treatment, call 118 or tel: 06-5510 (Red Cross) for an ambulance or to get information on the nearest hospital with an emergency department *(pronto soccorso)*. The most central is **Ospedale Fatebenefratelli**, Isola Tiberina, tel: 06-68371. If your child is sick go to the **Ospedale Pediatrico Bambino Gesù**, 4 Piazza Sant'Onofrio, tel: 06-68591, on the Gianicolo hill.

Medical Services

The **International Medical Center** (tel: 06-488 2371) is a private referral service with English-speaking doctors who are on call for house visits 24 hours a day. The **Rome American Hospital** (69 Via Emilio Longoni, tel: 06-22551), 30–40 minutes' journey out of the town centre by taxi, has English-speaking doctors and dentists. The **George Eastman Hospital** (287 Viale Regina Elena, tel: 06-844 831) is Rome's only 24-hour dental hospital.

Chemists

Chemists *(farmacia)* can easily be identified by a green cross. Opening hours are usually Mon–Sat 8.30am–1pm and 4–8pm. A rotating system ensures there is always a chemist within walking distance which is open at night; a list outside every chemist indicates which it will be. Purchases at night carry a surcharge.

Some chemists are also open 24 hours a day. A couple of the most central are **Farmacia della Stazione**, 51 Piazza dei Cinquecento (corner of Via Cavour), tel: 06-488 0019, and **Farmacia Piram Omeopatia**, 228 Via Nazionale, tel: 06-488 0754.

Internet

Many of the city's green spaces are now wireless hotspots; you can surf the internet free in Villas Borghese, Pamphili, Ada and Torlonia (see www.romawireless.com for further information), as well as in many bars and cafés. There is no shortage of internet cafés:

Internet Train
12 Via dei Marrucini
Tel: 06-445 4953
This internet café in the student neighbourhood of San Lorenzo has two large rooms packed with computers and rates are fair.

Interpoint YX
106 Corso Vittorio Emanuele
Tel: 06-4542 9818
3 Piazza Sant'Andrea delle Valle
Tel: 06-9727 3136
Trained and helpful staff.

Lost Property

For property lost on public transport (except trains) contact the ATAC bus and tram network lost property office, tel: 800-43

1784. For objects lost on Metro A, tel: 06-487 4309 (9.30am–12.30pm Mon, Wed and Fri) and for things forgotten on Metro B, tel: 06-4695 8165 (7am–7pm Mon–Sat).

Left Luggage

The left-luggage office in Termini Station is below ground level (level –1) at the side of platform 24 (open daily 6am–midnight). Fiumicino Airport has 24-hour left-luggage facilities in the international terminals.

Maps

Free city maps are available from the main tourist information offices dotted around town *(see page 317)*. Free and comprehensive bus maps of the city centre are available from **ATAC** at 59 Via Volturno (Mon–Fri 9am–1pm, Tue and Thur also 2.30–5pm). Detailed transport maps of the city and outskirts called Roma Metro-Bus can be bought at any newsstand.

Most newsstands sell city maps, as do museum shops. At the latter ask for the Mondadori maps, available in various languages and very durable.

Media

Newspapers and Magazines

Most important European dailies are available on the day of publication from street kiosks, as is the *International Herald Tribune*.

The main Rome-based Italian newspapers are *La Repubblica* and *Il Messaggero*. Other Italian newspapers such as *Il Corriere della Sera* publish Rome editions with local news and entertainment listings. *La Stampa* offers serious economics coverage.

The best way to find out about what's on in Rome is *Roma C'è*, a comprehensive weekly guide to everything in the city, from museums and art exhibitions, to shopping, eating and films. It comes out on Wednesday and can be bought from any newsstand throughout the week. Listings are in Italian, but there is an abbreviated section in English.

Wanted in Rome, a fortnightly magazine in English, is another good source of information. The website (www.wantedinrome.com) is updated regularly.

Porta Portese (www.portaportese.com) comes out on Tuesday and Friday, with thousands of classified ads, including a large accommodation section.

The American Magazine (www.theamericanmag.com) is a monthly magazine on Italian cultural life, available from newsstands in the centre.

Television

Italy has six major networks (three owned by state broadcaster RAI and three by the Mediaset group owned by the Berlusconi family) and another two that are increasingly popular, MTV Italia and La7. MTV is the Italian version of the ever-popular US music channel, and La7 offers a worthy alternative to the other six channels, which are all connected in some way to former premier Silvio Berlusconi.

Most hotels also offer guests CNN, BBC World, and some French or German channels.

Radio

The three state-owned channels, RAI 1 (89.7 Mhz FM), RAI 2 (91.7 Mhz FM) and RAI 3 (93.7 Mhz FM), offer popular music, classical music, chat shows and news (RAI 3 is the most serious); see www.rai.it for a list of programmes.

The most popular music channels are Radio Capital (95.8 Mhz FM, www.capital.it) and Radio Deejay (101 Mhz FM, www.deejay.it).

Vatican Radio One-O-Five Live (105 Mhz FM, www.vaticanradio.org) offers news, commentary and spiritual programmes in English.

Money

The unit of currency in Italy is the euro (€), which is divided into 100 cents. There are €5, 10, 20, 50, 100, 200 and 500 notes, coins worth €1 and €2, and 1, 2, 5, 10, 20 and 50-cent coins.

Changing Money

You need your passport or identification card when changing money, which can be a slow operation. Not all banks will provide cash against a credit card, and some may refuse to cash travellers' cheques in certain currencies. On the whole, the larger banks (those with a national or international network) will be the best for tourist transactions.

Travellers' cheques are the safest way to carry money, but not the most economical, since banks charge a commission for cashing them, and shops and restaurants give unfavourable exchange rates if they accept them at all.

Credit Cards

Major credit cards are accepted by most hotels, shops and restaurants in Rome but are less easy to use in the countryside. Very few petrol stations accept travellers' cheques.

Automated cash dispensers (ATMs), called Bancomat, can be found throughout central Rome, and are linked with several international banking systems, including Cirrus. The transaction fee will depend on your home bank, but rates are generally the best. The daily withdrawal limit is €250.

Tipping

Service is not included in a restaurant bill unless noted on the menu. It is customary to leave a modest amount as a tip, but nothing like the 10–15 percent common in other countries. Romans usually leave between €1–5, depending on how satisfied they were with the service; tourists are expected to be slightly more generous.

By law, the old cover charge, called *pane e coperto* (bread and table linen), has been abolished, but still appears on many menus. Keep an eye out: in many cases it has turned into a charge for bread, which you may refuse if you wish.

When you take a taxi, just round the fare up to the nearest euro.

Opening Hours

Opening hours vary greatly, but in general shops open Mon–Sat 9am–1pm and 3.30–7.30pm. Many close on Monday morning. Recently, in the touristy areas, many shops have started opening on Sunday and through lunch. Hairdressers and barbers are open all day but closed on Monday. In general the small food shops are open 8am–1.30pm and 5.30–8pm, and closed Saturday afternoon in summer and Thursday afternoon the rest of the year. Many shops and restaurants close for two weeks in August.

Churches generally open 7am–7pm with a three-hour lunch break; the four main basilicas open 7am–7pm with no lunchtime closure.

Banks open Mon–Fri 8.30am–1.30pm and 2.45–4pm; a few in the city centre also open Saturday morning. Most currency exchange bureaux open until 7.30pm Mon–Sat, and even later in very touristy areas.

State and city museums are closed on Monday, but there are a few exceptions: the Colosseum, the Roman Forum and the Imperial Fora, the Vatican Museums and the Galleria Doria Pamphilj.

LOST CREDIT CARDS

American Express
Freephone: 800-914 912
Bank Americard
Freephone: 800-207 167
Diner's Club
Freephone: 800-864 064
Visa and Mastercard
Freephone: 800-819 014

Postal Services

Post offices are generally open Mon–Fri 8.30am–1pm; central post offices are generally open in the afternoon too (*see below*).

Stamps *(francobolli)* for postcards and standard-weight letters to most destinations can be bought at many tobacconists *(tabacchi)* and bars that sell tobacco products. Often you can buy stamps when you buy your postcards. You will only need a post office for more complicated transactions, such as sending a parcel, express letter or fax, or collecting Posta Restante.

Italian postboxes are red or yellow, but several blue boxes specifically for foreign letters have been set up in the centre. Postboxes have two slots, *per la città* (for Rome) and *tutte le altre destinazioni* (everywhere else). The Italian postal system has improved considerably in recent years and now runs a pretty efficient service. If posting valuables or important documents, send them registered *(raccommandata)*. If sending an urgent parcel ask for *posta celere*, a courier-style service that is slightly slower than those run by private companies, but far cheaper.

The Vatican runs its own postal service. When visiting St Peter's, buy Vatican-issued stamps for your postcards and post them immediately: they are only valid in the Vatican City's blue or yellow postboxes.

The main post office is in Piazza San Silvestro, just off Via del Corso (Mon–Sat 8am–7pm). The post office at Stazione Termini is also open Mon–Sat 8am–7pm. For more information

PUBLIC HOLIDAYS

Banks and most shops are closed on the following holidays, and banks may close early on the preceding day. Practically everything, including most monuments, is closed on New Year's Day.

New Year's Day *(Capodanno)*: 1 January
Epiphany *(Befana)*: 6 January
Pasqua *(Pasqua)*: variable, March–April
Easter Monday *(Pasquetta)*: variable, March–April
Liberation Day *(Anniversario della Liberazione)*: 25 April
May Day *(Festa del Lavoro)*: 1 May
Republic Day (Giorno della Repubblica): 2 June
Patron Saints of Rome *(San Pietro e San Paolo)*: 29 June
August Holiday *(Ferragosto)*: 15 August
All Saints' Day *(Ognissanti)*: 1 November
Immaculate Conception *(Immacolata Concezione)*: 8 December
Christmas Day *(Natale)*: 25 December
Boxing Day *(Santo Stefano)*: 26 December

visit www.poste.it or tel: 803 160, Mon–Sat 8am–8pm. There are many other post offices, so ask at your hotel or in a local bar for the nearest – *Dov'è l'ufficio postale più vicino?*

Religious Services

Anglican
All Saints' Anglican Church
153b Via del Babuino
Tel: 06-3600 1881
Sunday Eucharist: 8.30 and 10.30am

Catholic
Santa Susanna (American)
15 Via XX Settembre
Tel: 06-4201 4554
Sunday Masses: 9am and 10.30am (also 6pm Saturday).
San Silvestro (British)
1 Piazza S. Silvestro
Tel: 06-679 7775
Sunday Masses: 10am, 5.30pm.
St Patrick's (Irish)
60 Via Boncompagni
Tel: 06-420 3121
Sunday Mass: 10am

Episcopal
St Paul's within the Walls
58 Via Napoli
Tel: 06-488 3339
www.stpaulsrome.it
Sunday services: 8.30am and 10.30am

Islamic
Moschea di Roma (Centro Islamico)
Viale della Moschea (Parioli)
Tel: 06-808 2167

Jewish
Tempio Maggiore (Comunità Ebraica)
Lungotevere Cenci
Tel: 06-684 0061

Presbyterian
St Andrew's Church of Scotland
7 Via XX Settembre
Tel: 06-482 7627
Sunday service: 11am.

Student Travellers

The Centro Turistico Studentesco (CTS) is a chain of travel agents designed to meet the needs of young and student travellers. The main branch is at 16 Via Genova, tel: 06-462 0431, but its website (www.cts.it) lists the others. It can provide you with student discount cards, hostel membership and bookings, cheap flights and language courses.

Telephones

The mobile phone revolution has resulted in a considerable decrease in payphone demand, and the few phone booths left are bound to disappear soon. You'll have better chances of finding public telephones at the train station or at the airport. The newest phones take coins and even credit cards (although rates can be outrageously expensive), while the older ones only take telephone cards (schede telefoniche), available in several denominations from newsstands and tabacchi.

Additionally, there are a number of far cheaper international phonecards available from many newsstands, as well as call centres where you can make your call and pay later, particularly in the area around Stazione Termini. Currently the best for the UK and US are Europa and Eurocity.

Landlines in Rome have an 06 area code which you must use whether calling from within Rome, from outside Rome or from abroad. Numbers in Rome have four to eight digits. Toll-free

AN AUDIENCE WITH THE POPE

For many, the highlight of a visit to Rome is attending Mass in St Peter's, or even a Wednesday morning audience with the Pope. Mass is celebrated daily in St Peter's in several different languages. Confessions are heard in English and many other languages in all four main Roman basilicas: St Peter's, San Giovanni in Laterano, San Paolo fuori le Mura and Santa Maria Maggiore.

To attend an audience with the Pope, you need to write in advance to the Prefettura della Casa Pontificia, 00120 Città del Vaticano, tel: 06-6988 3273 (open Mon–Sat 9am–1.30pm), or fax them on 06-6988 5863. Specify the date you would like to attend and give a local phone number and address (your hotel) where tickets can be delivered. Alternatively, go to the *prefettura* offices in St Peter's Square (same hours as above) and get the tickets in person.

The general audiences are held either in St Peter's Square or in the Audience Room or, during the summer, at Castel Gandolfo, the Pope's summer residence in the Castelli Romani. There is no charge for attending an audience.

If you are in Rome for Christmas or Easter and want to attend Midnight Mass or Holy Week celebrations, ask the tourist information service for times and other information, as you may need tickets for some events.

numbers start with 800.

Mobile phone numbers begin with 3, for example 338, 340, 333, 348, and cost a lot more to call than landlines. If you bring your mobile phone with you, remember that if you are calling a local number you will need to dial the international access code as well as the country code before putting in the area code and subscriber number.

For a number outside Italy, first dial 00 (the international access code), then the country code, the area code (omitting the initial 0, if applicable) and then the subscriber number.

For international directory enquiries, tel: 892 412; for operator-assisted national and international calls, tel: 170.

Time Zone

Italy follows Central European Time (GMT+1). From the last Sunday in March to the last Sunday in September, clocks are advanced one hour (GMT+2). The following times apply in summer, when it is noon in Rome:

New York	6am
London	11am
Johannesburg	noon
Paris	noon
San Francisco	3am
Sydney	8pm.

Toilets

Bars are obliged by law to let you use their toilets. This doesn't mean that they will do so with good grace; if you don't consume something at the bar first they may throw you a look. However, if you ask politely you should not have any problems. In many cases bar toilets are locked and you will need to ask for the key *(chiave)* at the till; once inside you may find out that there is no soap or toilet paper. In the past few years public and modern toilets have been opened near most of the major sights and monuments, for which you have to pay a small fee.

Tourist Information

The main Rome Tourist Office (**APT**) is at 5 Via Parigi, tel: 06-488 991, but it's open to the public only Mon and Thur 9.30am–1pm, 2.30–4.30pm. The Hotel Reservation Service, in Stazione Termini opposite platform 24 (daily 7am–10pm), tel: 06-699 1000, www.hotelreservation.it, makes commission-free reservations.

PIT (*punto informativo turistico* or tourist information points) are open daily from 9am–7pm at:
Piazza Pia (Castel Sant'Angelo)
Piazza del Tempio della Pace (Via dei Fori Imperiali)
Piazza delle Cinque Lune (Piazza Navona)
Via Nazionale (Palazzo delle Esposizioni)
Piazza Sonnino (Trastevere)
Via dell'Olmata (Santa Maria Maggiore)
Via Marco Minghetti (Fontana di Trevi).

There is also an information point in Stazione Termini, in front of platform 24, which is open daily 8am–8.30pm.

The Vatican tourist office (Ufficio Pellegrini e Turisti) is in Braccio Carlo Magno, Piazza San Pietro (to the left of the basilica), tel: 06-6988 1662 (Mon–Sat 8.30am–6.30pm).

Useful Addresses

Italian Tourist Offices Abroad
Canada: 175 Bloor Street E, Suite 907, Toronto M4W 3R8, tel: 416-925 4882.
UK: 1 Princes Street, London W1B 8AY, tel: 020-7408 1254.
US: 630 5th Avenue, Suite 1565, New York, NY 10111, tel: 212-245 4822.

Travel Agents in Rome
American Express, 38 Piazza di Spagna, tel: 06-67641.

Airline Contacts
Air Canada, Fiumicino Airport, tel: 06-8351 4955.
Air France, 40 Via Sardegna, tel: 06-487 911.
Alitalia, 11 Via Bissolati, tel: 06-2222.
British Airways, Fiumicino Airport, tel: 06-6501 1575; call centre, tel: 199-712 266 (no office in the city).
Delta Airlines, 40 Via Sardegna, freephone: 848-780 376.

Visas and Passports

EU passport-holders do not require a visa; a valid passport or ID card is sufficient. Visitors from the US, Canada, Australia or New Zealand do not require visas for stays of up to three months; non-EU citizens need a full passport.

Nationals of most other countries do need a visa. This must be obtained in advance from the Italian Consulate. For addresses of embassies and consulates in Rome, see page 312.

Websites

www.turismoroma.it and www.060608.it (official Rome tourism sites)
www.comune.roma.it (Rome city council)
www.vatican.va (Vatican)
www.trenitalia.com (train information)
www.adr.it (airport information)
www.atac.roma.it (public transport)
www.trovacinema.it (cinema programmes for all Italy)
www.2night.it (regularly updated, hip nightlife and entertainment guide)
www.pierreci.it (art and culture).

LANGUAGE

UNDERSTANDING THE ITALIANS

Basic Rules

Here are a few basic rules of grammar and pronunciation: *c* before *e* or *i* is pronounced "ch" as in *ciao*. *Ch* before *i* or *e* is pronounced as "k", eg *la chiesa*. Likewise, *sci* or *sce* are pronounced as in "sheep" or "shed" respectively. *Gn* in Italian is rather like the sound in "onion", while *gl* is softened to resemble the sound in "bullion".

Nouns are either masculine (*il*, plural *i*) or feminine (*la*, plural *le*). Plurals of nouns are most often formed by changing an o to an i and an a to an e, e.g. *il panino, i panini; la chiesa, le chiese.*

Words are stressed on the penultimate syllable unless an accent indicates otherwise.

Italian has formal and informal words for "You". In the singular, *Tu* is informal while *Lei* is more polite. It is best to use the formal form unless invited to do otherwise.

Basic Phrases

Yes *Si*
No *No*
Thank you *Grazie*
Many thanks *Mille grazie/ tante grazie/molte grazie*
You're welcome *Prego*
All right/That's fine *Va bene*
Please *Per favore/per cortesia*
Excuse me (to get attention) *Scusi* (singular), *Scusate* (plural); **(to attract attention from a waiter)** *Senta!* **(in a crowd)** *Permesso;* **(sorry)** *Mi scusi*
Can I help you? (formal) *Posso aiutarla?*
Can you help me? (informal) *Può aiutarmi, per cortesia?*
Could you help me? (formal) *Potrebbe aiutarmi?*
Certainly *Ma, certo*
I need... *Ho bisogno di...*
I'm lost *Mi sono perso/a*
I'm sorry *Mi dispiace*
I don't know *Non lo so*
I don't understand *Non capisco*
Do you speak English/French? *Parla inglese/francese?*
Could you speak more slowly? *Può parlare più lentamente, per favore?*
Could you repeat that please? *Può ripetere, per piacere?*
here/there *qui/là*
yesterday/today/tomorrow *ieri/oggi/domani*
now/early/late *adesso/ presto/tardi*
What? *Quale/Come...?*
When/Why/Where? *Quando/ Perché/Dove?*
Where is the lavatory? *Dov'è il bagno?*

Greetings

Hello (good day) *Buon giorno*
Goodbye *Arrivederci*
Good afternoon/evening *Buona sera*
Goodnight *Buona notte*
Hello/Hi/Goodbye (familiar) *Ciao*
Mr/Mrs/Miss *Signor/Signora/ Signorina*
Pleased to meet you (formal) *Piacere di conoscerla*
I am English/American/ Irish/Scottish/Canadian/ Australian *Sono inglese/ americano(a)/ irlandese/ scozzese/canadese/ australiano(a)*
I'm here on holiday *Sono qui* in vacanza
Is it your first trip to Rome? *É il suo primo viaggio a Roma?*
Do you like it here? (formal) *Si trova bene qui?*
How are you (formal/informal)? *Come sta (come stai)?*
Fine, thanks *Bene, grazie*
See you later *A più tardi*
See you soon *A presto*
Take care (formal/informal) *Stia bene/Sta bene*
Do you like Italy/Florence/ Rome/Venice? *Le piace Italia/Firenze/Roma/Venezia?*
I like it a lot *Mi piace moltissimo*

Telephone Calls

I'd like to make a reverse-charge (collect) call *Vorrei fare una telefonata a carico del destinatario*

the area code *il prefisso telefonico*
May I use your telephone? *Posso usare il telefono?*
Hello (on the telephone) *Pronto*
My name's *Mi chiamo/Sono*
Could I speak to...? *Posso parlare con...?*
Sorry, he/she isn't in *Mi dispiace, è fuori*
Can he call you back? *Può richiamare?*
I'll try later *Riproverò piu tardi*
Can I leave a message? *Posso lasciare un messaggio?*
Please tell him I called *Gli dica, per favore, che ho telefonato*
Hold on *Un attimo, per favore*
a local call *una telefonata urbana*
Can you speak up please? *Può parlare più forte, per favore?*

In the Hotel

Do you have any vacant rooms? *Avete delle camere libere?*
I have a reservation *Ho fatto una prenotazione*
I'd like... *Vorrei...*
a single/double room *una camera singola/doppia*
a room with twin beds *una camera a due letti*
a room with a bath/shower *una camera con bagno/doccia*
for one night *per una notte*
for two nights *per due notti*
How much is it? *Quanto costa?*
On the first floor *Al primo piano*
Is breakfast included? *É compresa la prima colazione?*
Is everything included? *É tutto compreso?*
half/full board *mezza pensione/pensione completa*
It's expensive *E caro*
Do you have a room with a balcony/view of the sea? *C'è una camera con balcone/con vista mare?*
a room overlooking the park/the street/the back *una camera con vista sul parco/che dá sulla strada/sul retro*
Is it a quiet room? *É una stanza tranquilla?*
The room is too hot/cold/noisy/small *La camera è troppo calda/fredda/rumorosa/piccola*
We have one with a double bed *Ne abbiamo una doppia/matrimoniale*
Could you show me another room please? *Potrebbe mostrarmi un altra camera, per favore?*
Can I see the room? *Posso vedere la camera?*
What time does the hotel close? *A che ora chiude l'albergo?*
I'll take it *La prendo*
big/small *grande/piccola*
What time is breakfast? *A che ora è la prima colazione?*
Please give me a call at... *Mi può chiamare alle...*
Come in! *Avanti!*
Can I have the bill, please? *Posso avere il conto, per favore?*
Can you call me a taxi, please? *Può chiamarmi un taxi, per favore?*
dining room *la sala da pranzo*
key *la chiave*
lift *l'ascensore*
towel *un asciugamano*
toilet paper *la carta igienica*

At a Bar

I'd like... *Vorrei...*
coffee:
(small, strong and black) *un caffè espresso*; **(with hot, frothy milk)** *un cappuccino*; **(weak, served in tall glass)** *un caffè lungo*; **(with alcohol, probably brandy)** *un caffè corretto*
tea *un tè*
lemon tea *un tè al limone*
herbal tea *una tisana*
hot chocolate *una cioccolata calda*
(bottled) orange/lemon juice *un succo d'arancia/di limone*
orange squash *aranciata*
freshly squeezed orange/lemon juice *una spremuta di arancia/di limone*
mineral water (fizzy/still) *acqua minerale gassata/naturale*
with/without ice *con/senza ghiaccio*
red/white wine *vino rosso/bianco*
(draught) beer *una birra (alla spina)*
a bitter (Vermouth, etc) *un amaro*
milk *latte*
(half) a litre *un (mezzo) litro*
bottle *una bottiglia*
ice cream *un gelato*
cone *un cono*
pastry/brioche *una pasta*
sandwich *un tramezzino*
roll *un panino*
Anything else? *Desidera qualcos'altro?*
Cheers *Salute*

In a Restaurant

I'd like to book a table *Vorrei prenotare una tavola*
I have a reservation *Ho fatto una prenotazione*
lunch/supper *pranzo/cena*
we do not want a full meal *Non desideriamo un pasto completo*
Could we have another table? *Potremmo spostarci?*
I'm a vegetarian *Sono vegetariano/a*
Is there a vegetarian dish? *C'è un piatto vegetariano?*
May we have the menu? *Ci dia la carta*
wine list *la lista dei vini*
What would you recommend? *Che cosa ci consiglia?*
What would you like as a main course/dessert? *Che cosa prende di secondo/di dolce?*
What would you like to drink? *Che cosa desidera da bere?*
a carafe of red/white wine *una caraffa di vino rosso/bianco*
fixed-price menu *il menù a prezzo fisso*
dish of the day *il piatto del giorno*
home-made *fatto in casa*
VAT (sales tax) *IVA*
cover charge *il coperto/pane e coperto*
that's enough/no mor€ €hanks *basta così*
the bill, please *il conto per favore*
Is service included? *Il servizio è incluso?*
Where is the lavatory? *Dov'è il bagno?*
Keep the change *Va bene così*
I've enjoyed the meal *Mi è piaciuto molto*

Menu Decoder

Antipasti – Starters

antipasto misto **mixed hors d'oeuvres: cold cuts, cheeses, roast vegetables (ask for details)**
buffet freddo **cold buffet**
caponata **aubergine, olives, tomatoes**
insalata caprese **tomato and mozzarella salad**
insalata di mare **seafood salad**
insalata mista/verde **mixed/ green salad**
melanzane alla parmigiana **fried or baked aubergine with parmesan and tomato**
mortadella/salame **similar to salami**
pancetta **bacon**
proscuitto **ham**
peperonata **grilled peppers drenched in olive oil**

Primi – First Courses

gli asparagi **asparagus (in season)**
brodetto **fish soup**
brodo **broth**
crespolini **savoury pancakes**
gnocchi **potato and dough dumplings**
la minestra **soup**
il minestrone **thick vegetable soup**
pasta e fagioli **pasta and bean soup**
il prosciutto (cotto/crudo) **(cooked/cured) ham**
i supplì **rice croquettes**
i tartufi **truffles (fresh in season, otherwise bottled or vacuum-packed)**
la zuppa **soup**

Secondi – Main Courses

La Carne **Meat**
allo spiedo **on the spit**
arrosto **roast meat**
ai ferri **grilled without oil**
al forno **baked**
al girarrosto **spit-roasted**
alla griglia **grilled**
involtini **skewered veal, ham, etc**
stagionato **hung, well aged**
ben cotto **well done (steak)**
media cottura **medium**
al sangue **rare**
l'agnello **lamb**
la bresaola **dried salted beef**
la bistecca **steak**
il capriolo/cervo **venison**
il carpaccio **wafer-thin beef**
il cinghiale **wild boar**
il controfiletto **sirloin steak**
le cotolette **cutlets**
il fagiano **pheasant**
il fegato **liver**
il filetto **fillet**
la lepre **hare**
il maiale **pork**
il manzo **beef**
l'ossobuco **shin of veal**
il pollo **chicken**
le polpette **meatballs**
il polpettone **meat loaf**
la porchetta **roast suckling pig**
la salsiccia **sausage**
il saltimbocca (alla Romana) **veal escalopes with ham**
le scaloppine **escalopes**
lo stufato **braised, stewed**
il sugo **sauce**
la trippa **tripe**
il vitello **veal**

Frutti di Mare **Seafood**
affumicato **smoked**
alle brace **charcoal-grilled**
al ferro **grilled without oil**
fritto **fried**
alla griglia **grilled**
ripieno **stuffed**
al vapore **steamed**
acciughe **anchovies**
l'anguilla **eel**
l'aragosta **lobster**
il baccalà **dried salted cod**
i bianchetti **whitebait**
il branzino **sea bass**
i calamaretti **baby squid**
i calamari **squid**
la carpa **carp**
le cozze **mussels**
i crostacei **shellfish**
il fritto misto **mixed fried fish**
i gamberetti **shrimps**
i gamberi **prawns**
il granchio **crab**
il merluzzo **cod**
le ostriche **oysters**
il pesce **fish**
il pescespada **swordfish**
il polipo **octopus**
il risotto di mare **seafood risotto**
le sarde **sardines**
le seppie **cuttlefish**
la sogliola **sole**
surgelati **frozen**
il tonno **tuna**
la triglia **red mullet**
la trota **trout**
le vongole **clams**

I Legumi/La Verdura – Vegetables

a scelta **of your choice**
gli asparagi **asparagus**
la bietola **(similar to spinach)**
i carciofini **artichoke hearts**
il carciofo **artichoke**
le carote **carrots**
il cavolo **cabbage**
la cicoria **chicory**
la cipolla **onion**
i contorni **side dishes**
i fagioli **beans**
i fagiolini **French beans**
fave **broad beans**
il finocchio **fennel**
i funghi **mushrooms**
l'indivia **endive/chicory**
in*salata mista* **mixed salad**
in*salata verde* **green salad**
la melanzana **aubergine/ eggplant**
le patate **potatoes**
le patatine fritte **chips/fries**
i peperoni **peppers**
i piselli **peas**
i pomodori **tomatoes**
le primizie **spring vegetables**
il radicchio **red, bitter lettuce**
i ravanelli **radishes**
ripieno **stuffed**
rughetta **rocket**
spinaci **spinach**
la verdura **green vegetables**
la zucca **pumpkin/squash**
zucchini **courgettes**

La Frutta – Fruit

le albicocche **apricots**
le arance **oranges**
le banane **bananas**
le ciliege **cherries**
il cocomero **watermelon**
i fichi **figs**
le fragole **strawberries**
frutti di bosco **fruits of the forest**
i lamponi **raspberries**
la mela **apple**
la pera **pear**

la pesca **peach**
le uve **grapes**

I Dolci – Desserts

al carrello **desserts from the trolley**
la cassata **Sicilian ice cream with candied peel**
il dolce **dessert/sweet**
le fritelle **fritters**
un gelato (di lampone/limone) **(raspberry/lemon) ice cream**
una granita **water ice**
una macedonia di frutta **fruit salad**
un semifreddo **semi-frozen dessert (many types)**
il tartufo (nero) **(chocolate) ice-cream dessert**
il tiramisù **cold, creamy rum and coffee dessert**
la torta **cake/tart**
zabaglione **sweet dessert made with eggs and Marsala**
zuccotto **ice-cream liqueur**
la zuppa inglese **trifle**

Basic Foods

aceto **vinegar**
aglio **garlic**
burro **butter**
formaggio **cheese**
frittata **omelette**
grissini **bread sticks**
marmellata **jam**
olio **oil**
pane **bread**
pane integrale **wholemeal bread**
parmigiano **parmesan cheese**
pepe **pepper**
riso **rice**
sale **salt**
senape **mustard**
uova **eggs**
zucchero **sugar**

Sightseeing

abbazia (badia) **abbey**
basilica **church**
biblioteca **library**
castello **castle**
centro storico **old town/historic centre**
chiesa **church**
duomo/cattedrale **cathedral**
fiume **river**
giardino **garden**
lago **lake**
mercato **market**
monastero **monastery**
monumenti **monuments**
museo **museum**
parco **park**
pinacoteca **art gallery**
ponte **bridge**
ruderi **ruins**
scavi **excavations/archaeological site**
spiaggia **beach**
torre **tower**
ufficio turistico **tourist office**
il custode **custodian**
il sacristano **sacristan**
Aperto/a **Open**
Chiuso/a **Closed**
Chiuso per la festa/per ferie/per restauro **Closed for the festival/holidays/restoration**

At the Shops

What time do you open/close? *A che ora apre/chiude?*
Pull/Push (sign on doors) *Tirare/Spingere*
Entrance/Exit *Entrata/Uscita*
Can I help you? (formal) *Posso aiutarla?*
What would you like? *Che cosa desidera?*
I'm just looking *Sto soltanto guardando*
How much is this? *Quanto viene?*
Do you take credit cards? *Accettate le carte di credito?*
I'd like... *Vorrei...*
This one/that one *questo/quello*
Have you got...? *Avete...?*
We haven't got (any) *Non (ne) abbiamo*
Can I try it on? *Posso provare?*
the size (for clothes) *la taglia*
What size do you take? *Qual è la sua taglia?*
the size (for shoes) *il numero*
Is there/do you have...? *C'è (un/una)...?*
Yes, of course *Sì, certo*
No, we haven't (there isn't) *No, non c'è*
That's too expensive *È troppo caro*
Please write it down for me *Me lo scriva, per favore*
cheap *economico/a buon prezzo*
Do you have anything cheaper? *Ha niente che costa di meno?*
It's too small/big *È troppo piccolo/grande*
brown/blue/black *marrone/blu/nero*
green/red/white/yellow *verde/rosso/bianco/giallo*
pink/grey/gold/silver *rosa/grigio/oro/argento*
No thank you, I don't like it *Grazie, ma non è di mio gusto*
I'll take it/I'll leave it *Lo prendo/lo lascio*
This is faulty. May I have a replacement/refund? *C'è un difetto. Me lo potrebbe cambiare/rimborsare?*
Anything else? *Altro?*
The cash desk is over there *Si accomodi alla cassa*
Give me some of those *Mi dia alcuni di quelli lì*
(half) a kilo *un (mezzo) kilo*
100 grams *un etto*
200 grams *due etti*
more/less *più/meno*
with/without *con/senza*
a little *un pochino*

Types of Shops

antique dealer *l'antiquario*
bakery/cake shop *la panetteria/pasticceria*
bank *la banca*
bookshop *la libreria*
boutique/clothes shop *il negozio di moda*
butcher *la macelleria*
chemist *la farmacia*
delicatessen *la salumeria*
dry cleaner *la tintoria*
fishmonger *la pescheria*
florist *il fioraio*
food shop *l'alimentari*
greengrocer *l'ortolano/il fruttivendolo*
grocer *l'alimentari*
hairdresser *il parucchiere*
ice-cream parlour *la gelateria*
jeweller *il gioiellere*
leather shop *la pelletteria*
market *il mercato*
newsstand *l'edicola*
post office *l'ufficio postale*
shoe shop *il negozio di scarpe*
stationer *la cartoleria*
tobacconist *il tabaccaio*
travel agency *l'agenzia di viaggi*

Travelling

aeroplane *l'aereo*
airport *l'aeroporto*
arrivals/departures *arrivi/partenze*
boarding card *un biglietto di bordo*
boat *la barca*
bus *l'autobus/il pullman*
bus station *l'autostazione*
coach *il pullman*
couchette *la cucetta*
connection *la coincidenza*
ferry *il traghetto*
ferry terminal *la stazione marittima*
first/second class *la prima/seconda classe*
flight *il volo*
left-luggage office *il deposito bagagli*
platform *il binario*
port *il porto*
porter *il facchino*
railway station *ferrovia (la stazione ferroviaria)*
return ticket *un biglietto andata e ritorno*
single ticket *un biglietto solo andata*
sleeping car *la carrozza letti/il vagone letto*
smokers/non-smokers *fumatori/non-fumatori*
station *la stazione*
stop *la fermata*
ticket office *la biglietteria*
train *il treno*
WC *il gabinetto*

At the Station

(trains, buses and ferries)
Can you help me please? *Mi può aiutare, per favore?*
Where can I buy tickets? *Dove posso fare i biglietti?*
at the ticket office/at the counter *alla biglietteria/allo sportello*
What time does the train leave/arrive? *A che ora parte/arriva il treno?*
Can I book a seat? *Posso prenotare un posto?*
Are there any seats available? *Ci sono ancora posti liberi?*
Is this seat free/taken? *È libero/occupato questo posto?*
I'm afraid this is my seat *È il mio posto, mi dispiace*
You'll have to pay a supplement *Deve pagare un supplemento*
Do I have to change? *Devo cambiare?*
Where does it stop? *Dove si ferma?*
You need to change in Rome *Bisogna cambiare a Roma*
Which platform does the train leave from? *Da quale binario parte il treno?*
The train leaves from platform one *Il treno parte dal binario uno*
When is the next train/bus/ferry for Naples? *Quando parte il prossimo treno/pullman/traghetto per Napoli?*
How long does the crossing take? *Quanto dura la traversata?*
What time does the bus leave for Siena? *Quando parte l'autobus per Siena?*
How long will it take to get there? *Quanto tempo ci vuole per arrivare?*
Next stop, please *La prossima fermata per favore*
Is this the right stop? *È la fermata giusta?*
The train is late *Il treno è in ritardo*
Can you tell me where to get off? *Mi può dire dove devo scendere?*

Directions

left/right a sinistra/a destra
first left/second right *la prima a sinistra/la seconda a destra*
Turn to the left/right Gira a sinistra/destra
Go straight on *Va sempre diritto*
Go straight on until the traffic lights *Va sempre diritto fino al semaforo*
Is it far away/nearby? *È lontano/vicino?*
It's 5 minutes' walk *Cinque minuti a piedi*
It's 10 minutes by car *Dieci minuti con la macchina*
opposite/next to *di fronte/accanto a*
up/down *su/giù*
traffic lights *il semaforo*
junction *l'incrocio, il bivio*
building *il palazzo* (could be a palace or a block of flats)
Where is...? *Dov'è...?*
Where are...? *Dove sono...?*
Where is the nearest bank/petrol station/bus stop/hotel/garage? *Dov'è la banca/il benzinaio/la fermata di autobus/l'albergo/ l'officina più vicino?*
How do I get there? *Come si può andare?* (or: *Come faccio per arrivare a...?*)
How long does it take to get to...? *Quanto tempo ci vuole per andare a...?*
Can you show me where I am on the map? *Può indicarmi sulla cartina dove mi trovo?*
You're on the wrong road *Lei è sulla strada sbagliata*

Health

Is there a chemist nearby? *C'è una farmacia qui vicino?*
Which chemist is open at night? *Quale farmacia fa il turno di notte?*
I feel ill *Sto male/Mi sento male*
Where does it hurt? *Dove le fa male?*
It hurts here *Ho dolore qui*
I suffer from... *Soffro di...*
I have a headache *Ho mal di testa*
I have a sore throat *Ho mal di gola*
I have a stomach ache *Ho mal di pancia*
Have you got something for air sickness? *Ha/Avete qualcosa contro il mal d'aria?*
Have you got something for sea sickness? *Ha/Avete qualcosa contro il mal di mare?*
It's nothing serious *Non è niente di male*
Do I need a prescription? *Ci vuole la ricetta?*
antiseptic cream *la crema antisettica*
insect repellent *l'insettifugo*
sticking plaster *il cerotto*
sunburn *scottato del sole*
sunscreen *la crema antisolare*
tissues *i fazzoletti di carta*
toothpaste *il dentifricio*
upset-stomach pills *le pillole anti-coliche*

FURTHER READING

History and Society

The Early History of Rome, by Livy (Penguin Classics).
Daily Life in Ancient Rome, by Jérôme Carcopino (Penguin History, Yale US).
The Roman Emperors, by Michael Grant (Weidenfeld and Nicolson).
The Caesars, by Allan Massie (Secker & Warburg).
The Decline and Fall of the Roman Empire, by Edward Gibbon (Dent and Penguin).
A History of Rome, by Michael Grant (Faber & Faber).
Rome: Biography of a City, by Christopher Hibbert (Penguin).
The Italians, by Luigi Barzini (Penguin).
La Bella Figura: A Field Guide to the Italian Mind, by Beppe Severgnini (Broadway Books).
The Dark Heart of Italy, by Tobias Jones (Faber & Faber).
Rubicon: the Triumph and Tragedy of the Roman Republic, by Tom Holland (Abacus and Anchor).

Art and Literature

The Aeneid, by Virgil (Penguin).
Meditations, by Marcus Aurelius (Penguin).
Lives of the Artists, by Giorgio Vasari (Penguin).
The Life of Benvenuto Cellini, by Benvenuto Cellini (Macmillan).
Rome, by Emile Zola (The Echo Library).
Michelangelo and the Pope's Ceiling, by Ross King (Pimlico).
Portrait of a Lady, by Henry James (various).
The Woman of Rome and *Roman Tales*, by Alberto Moravia (Oxford University Press).
A Violent Life, by Pier Paolo Pasolini (Carcanet).
Fellini on Fellini, by Federico Fellini (Da Capo Press).
I Claudius, Claudius the God by Rupert Graves (Penguin).

Food and Wine

The Encyclopedia of Italian Wines, by Oz Clarke and Maureen Ashley (Prentice Hall and IBD).
Italian Food, by Elizabeth David (Penguin Cookery Library).
The Essentials of Classic Italian Cooking, by Marcella Hazan (Macmillan).
Jamie's Italy, by Jamie Oliver (Penguin).

FEEDBACK

We do our best to ensure the information in our books is as accurate and up-to-date as possible. However, some mistakes and omissions are inevitable and we are reliant on our readers to put us in the picture. We would welcome your feedback on any details related to your experiences using the book "on the road". The more details you can give us (particularly with regard to addresses, emails and telephone numbers), the better. We will acknowledge all contributions, and we'll offer an Insight Guide to the best letters received.

Please write to us at:
Insight Guides
PO Box 7910
London SE1 1WE
United Kingdom
Or send an email to:
insight@apaguide.co.uk

Famous Travellers

Pictures from Italy, by Charles Dickens (Penguin Classics).
Italian Journey, by Johann Wolfgang von Goethe, translated by W.H. Auden & Elizabeth Mayer (Pantheon Books and Penguin).
Italian Hours, by Henry James (Penguin Classics).
The Fountains of Rome and *A Traveller in Rome*, by Henry V. Morton (Methuen).
Byron in Italy, by Peter Quenell (Viking Press, New York).
The Grand Tour, by Christopher Hibbert (G.P. Putnam, New York).

Other Insight Guides

Insight Guide: Italy covers the whole country, with features on food and drink, culture and the arts. Other titles cover Northern Italy, Southern Italy, Florence, the Italian Lakes, Tuscany, Venice, Sicily and Sardinia.
Insight Smart Guides Smart Guide: Rome puts the city at your fingertips. The best of Rome is listed by district, with detailed maps to provide orientation. Rome A-Z lists over 400 amazing things to see and do, from architecture and bars to restaurants and shopping, and much more. Venice title also available.
Insight Step by Step Guides cover Florence, the Italian Lakes, Rome and Venice. These books provide a number of timed itineraries, with recommended stops for lunch. The walks are plotted on an accompanying pull-out map.
Insight Fleximaps combine clear, detailed cartography with essential travel information. Italian maps include Lake Garda & Verona, Milan, Rome, Sicily, Tuscany, Umbria and Venice.

Art and Photo Credits

c.20thC.Fox/Everett/Rex Features 45L
4Corners Images 9TR&BL
akg-images 33BR, 36TL, 43T
Alamy 146T, 180B, 187BR, 217B, 265, 270B
Alessi 298
The Art Archive 31CL, 34T, 37TL, 122T
Gaetano Barone 41C
The Bridgeman Art Library 10CR, 32R, 41TR, 102B, 105BR, 113C, 121T, 142BL&R, 157B, 162T, 164B, 186T
Casa Howard 13TL&TR
Cavalieri Hilton 147, 292
Cephas 13C
Corbis 10CL, 23, 24B, 25TL, 38(all), 39TL, 40C, 42BL, 43CL&BR, 45R, 49T, 52TL, 122B, 163TR, 193CR, 195B, 254T, 274T
darkensiva on Flickr 266B
Giovanna Dunmall 235BR
EPS/Rex Features 39TR
Mary Evans Picture Library 28B, 31TL, 33TL, 104C, 106TR
Roby Ferrari 277T
Fondazione MAXXI 196T
Fotolia 30B, 264, 269B
Getty Images 119B, 215B
Patrizia Giancotti 268TR, 270TL, 277BL
Frances Gransden/APA 8CR, 9CL, 82/3, 82/5, 106TL, 173T, 177T, 241TR, 256
John Heseltine 51TR, 251
Hotel Aleph 289
iStockphoto.com 108/109, 119T, 254B
Italian Cultural Institute 111C
Britta Jaschinski/APA 1, 3, 6T, 8B, 9C, 11(all), 19, 20(all), 21TR, 22TL&TR, 24TR, 25TR, 37B, 41TL, 47, 48B, 51B, 53TL, 56, 57, 59R, 62, 63, 64(all), 65R, 66T, 67TL&R, 69, 70CR&B, 71R, 81, 82/2, 82/3, 83/5, 88TR, 90CL&TR, 98T&B, 99B, 100, 102T&C, 108C, 110T, 111T, 112TI&TR, 113T&B, 117, 118L, 120T, 121C&B, 123(all), 125, 126C, 127B, 128B, 129T, 130T, 131C, 132T, 133T, 135, 138TR, 139BL, 141TR, 143T&C, 144, 155T&BL, 156CR&B, 157C, 158T, 160CR&BL, 162B, 163C, 164(all), 165(all), 169, 170C, 171B, 172BR, 176T, 178(all), 179TR, 181, 183(all), 187T, 191TL&TR, 193TL, 197(all), 201, 202CL, 203(all), 204T, 206CL, 207T, 208, 210, 211, 212R, 213(all), 214(all), 218, 219, 220, 221, 222L, 223C&B, 224T&BR, 226TL&B, 228, 229, 231(all), 232(all), 233B, 246/247, 250, 252(all), 253(all), 255(all), 257, 258(all), 259(all), 260(all), 261(all), 266T, 267(all), 268TL&B, 270TR, 271(all), 272, 275(all), 276B, 278(all), 279, 282(all), 283, 284T, 286, 287, 288, 291, 296, 300, 303, 304, 306, 308, 311, 313
The Kobal Collection 44T
Marka/Kay Reese&Associates 43C
Mockford&Bonetti/APA 8T, 10B, 12T, 48TL, 50TL, 58L, 83/2, 96, 99T, 101R, 127T, 155BR, 160BR, 164T, 172BL, 173B, 174T, 175T, 177L, 179B, 196B, 205CL&CR, 206BL&BR, 207B, 212L, 216(all), 222R, 233T&C, 234(all)
Cathy Muscat 120B, 160B, 172TL&CL, 182, 194B, 195T, 227, 307
Peter Namuth 36B
Gerd Pfeifer 269T
Pierluigi/Rex Features 44B
Pictures Colour Library 145
Andrea Pistolesi 126T
Raphaël Hotel 293
Mark Read/APA 7T
Roma Europa 309B
Alessandra Santarelli/APA 9CR, 12CL, 58R, 59L, 70TL&TR, 71L, 83/3, 83/4, 132B, 173C, 176B, 194C, 200, 235T&CL, 238, 240, 241TL&B, 242(all), 243(all), 299, 301(all), 302, 314
Scala Archives 8CL, 26, 27, 28T, 29L&R, 30TC&TR, 31TR, 32L, 33TR, 34B, 35(all), 36TR, 37TR, 39B, 40TL&BL, 41B, 42C&BR, 50/51, 52B, 53CL, 89T, 109TL&R, 126B, 128C, 130CL, 139CL, 140T, 141TC, 142TL, 156T, 159TL, 161C, 187BL, 192B, 202T, 204B, 205B, 224BL, 226TR, 239, 273, 274B, 276T, 277BR
Suasn Smart/APA 9TL&BR, 12B, 14/15, 16/17, 18, 21TL, 24TL, 42TL, 46, 48TR, 50CR, 53TR, 64TR, 65L, 66B, 67CL, 68, 76/77, 78/79, 80, 86, 87, 88B, 89B, 90B, 91, 97, 101L, 103B, 104B, 105BL&T, 106B, 107T&B, 111B, 112B, 116, 124, 128T, 129B, 130BR, 131T&B, 133B, 136, 137, 138TL, 139BR, 140B, 141B, 143B, 146L&BR, 152, 153T&B, 158B, 159B&TR, 167, 168, 170T&B, 171C, 174BL&R, 175B, 184, 185, 186B, 188T&B, 189T&B, 191B, 192C, 193B, 217TL&R, 225T&B, 236, 280, 284B, 285, 305, 309T, 317
Superstock 7B, 30TL
uitdragerij on Flickr 215C
Nika Vee 22B
Bill Wassman/APA 88TL, 98CR, 103T, 118R, 177R, 180CL, 316
zak mc on Flickr 163B

Photo Features

54/55: **The Bridgeman Art Library** 55BR; **Corbis** 54/55T, 55TR; **Mockford&Bonetti/APA** 54BR; **Scala** 54TL&BL, 55C.
60/61: **Alamy** 60T, 61CTL, CBL, CBR&BL; **Corbis** 61CTR; **Britta Jaschinski/APA** 60B; **Fondazione MAXXI** 61T.
72/73: **Alamy** 73CL; **Corbis** 73RB; **iStockphoto** 73RBT; **Britta Jaschinski/APA** 72/73T, 72BR; **Alessandra Santarelli/APA** 72CL, CR&BL, 73BL.
74/75: **Britta Jaschinski/APA** 74BL; **Alessandra Santarelli/APA** 74TL, 75TR&C; **Suasn Smart/APA** 74/75, 74CR&BR, 75BL
92/93: **Alamy** 93BC; **The Art Archive** 93CR; **Britta Jaschinski/APA** 92CR, 93BR; **Scala** 92CL, 93TR&BL; **Suasn Smart/APA** 92/93
94/95: **Alamy** 94T; **Cathy Muscat** 95CL; **Britta Jaschinski/APA** 94/95T, 94BR, 95CR; **Scala** 94BL, 95TR&B
114/115: **akg-images** 114/115, 114CL; **Britta Jaschinski/APA** 115CL&BL; **Scala** 114TL&BR, 115C; **Suasn Smart/APA** 115BR
148/149: all **Scala** except **Suasn Smart/APA** 148BR
150/151: all **Scala** except **The Bridgeman Art Library** 150/151T&B
198/199: all **Scala** except **Fotolia** 199TR
244/245: **The Art Archive** 244CR; **Corbis** 244TL&BL, 245TR; **Scala** 244/245T; **A. Tessore/Asia** 245CL; **Werner Forman Archive** 245BR
262/263: **Grandi Giardini Italiani Archives** 262/263T, 262TL, 263BR; **Britta Jaschinski/APA** 262BL, 263CR; **Alessandra Santarelli/APA** 262BR, 263CL.

Map Production: Apa Cartography Department

Production: Rebeka Ellam and Linton Donaldson

ROME STREET ATLAS

The key map shows the area of Rome covered by the atlas section. An index of street names and places of interest shown on the maps can be found on the following pages. For each entry there is a page number and grid reference.

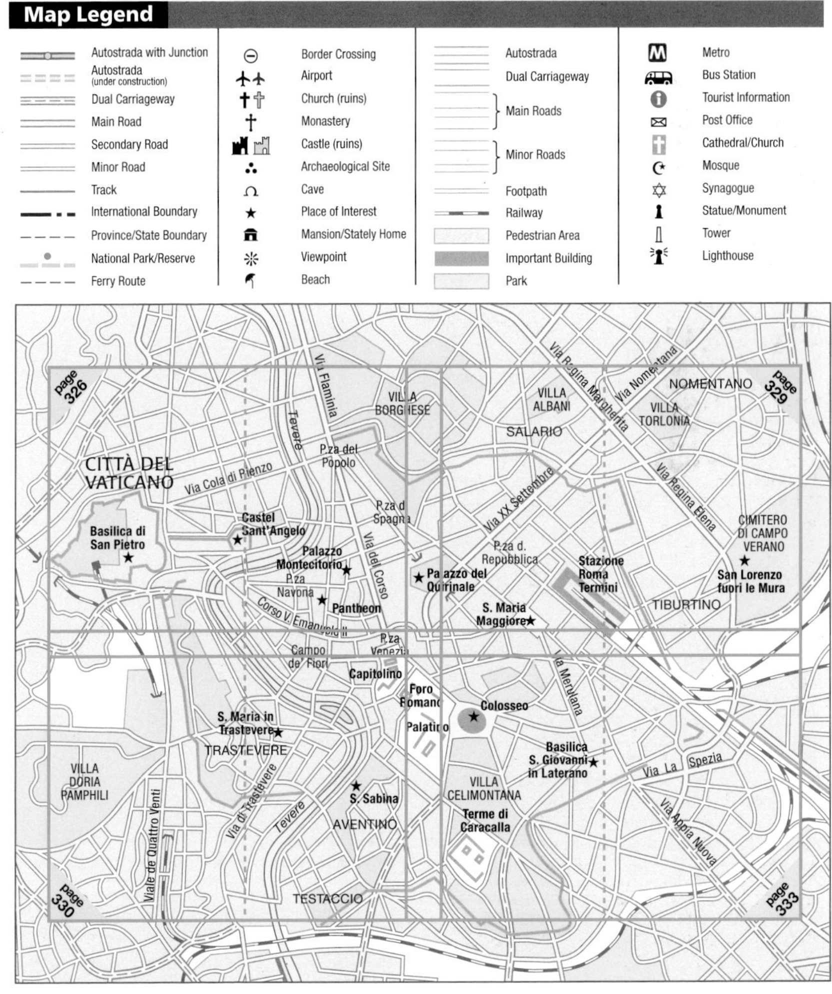

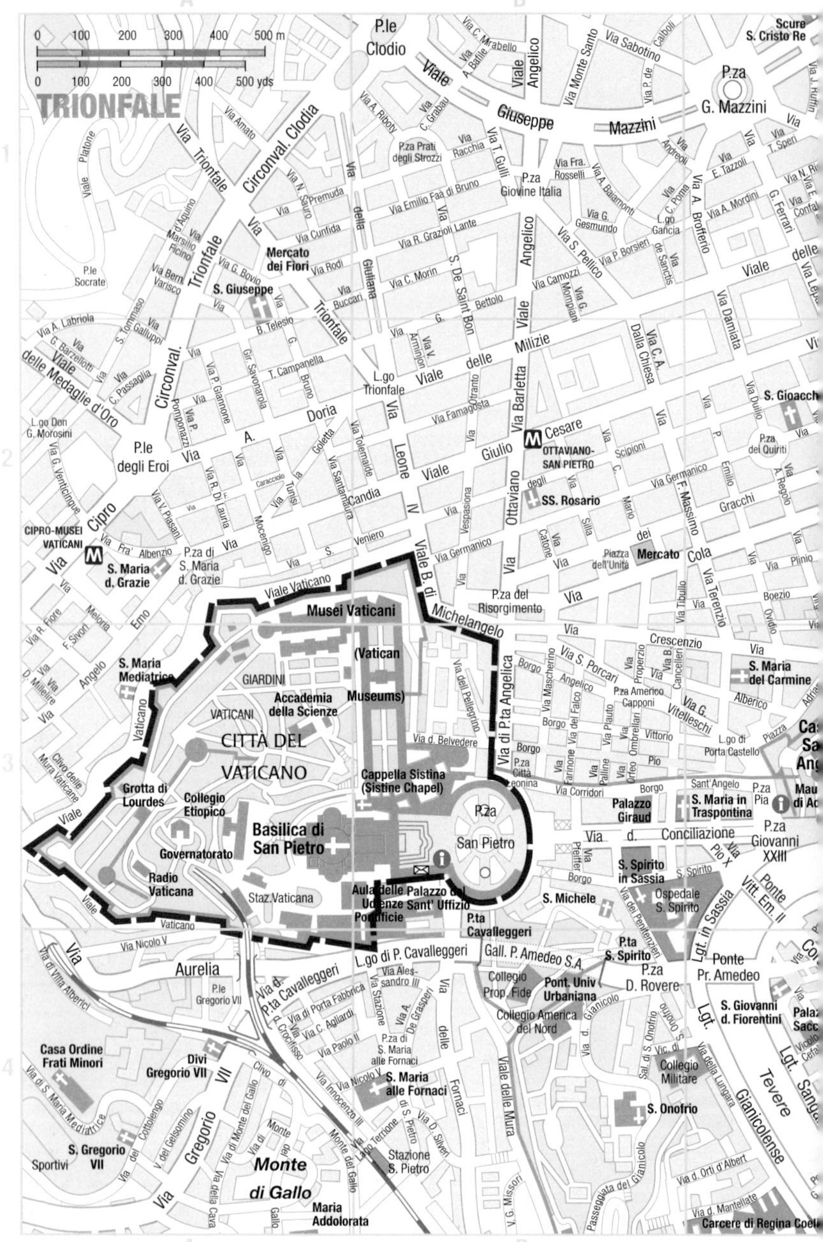
A
B
1
2
3
4
0 100 200 300 400 500 m
0 100 200 300 400 500 yds
TRIONFALE
P.le Clodio
Viale Giuseppe Mazzini
P.za G. Mazzini
Via Trionfale
Circonval. Clodia
Via della Giuliana
Viale Angelico
Via Sabotino
P.za Giovine Italia
Mercato dei Fiori
S. Giuseppe
P.le Socrate
Via A. Brofferio
Viale delle Milizie
L.go Trionfale
Viale delle Medaglie d'Oro
Circonval.
P.le degli Eroi
Via A. Doria
Via Leone IV
Viale Giulio Cesare
OTTAVIANO-SAN PIETRO
Via Ottaviano
SS. Rosario
Via Cipro
CIPRO-MUSEI VATICANI
S. Maria d. Grazie
P.za di S. Maria d. Grazie
Via Candia
Via Germanico
Via F. Massimo
Via Cola di Rienzo
Piazza dell'Unità
Mercato
P.za del Risorgimento
Viale Vaticano
Viale B. di Michelangelo
Musei Vaticani (Vatican Museums)
GIARDINI VATICANI
Accademia della Scienze
CITTÀ DEL VATICANO
S. Maria Mediatrice
Via Crescenzio
S. Maria del Carmine
Via di P.ta Angelica
Borgo Pio
Borgo Vittorio
Cappella Sistina (Sistine Chapel)
Grotta di Lourdes
Collegio Etiopico
Basilica di San Pietro
P.za San Pietro
Governatorato
Radio Vaticana
Staz. Vaticana
Aula delle Udienze Pontificie
Palazzo del Sant' Uffizio
P.ta Cavalleggeri
L.go di P. Cavalleggeri
Via d. Conciliazione
Palazzo Giraud
S. Maria in Traspontina
P.za Pia
P.za Giovanni XXIII
S. Spirito in Sassia
Ospedale S. Spirito
S. Michele
L.go di Porta Castello
Ponte Vitt. Em. II
P.ta S. Spirito
Gall. P. Amedeo S.A.
Collegio Prop. Fide
Pont. Univ. Urbaniana
Collegio America del Nord
P.za D. Rovere
Ponte Pr. Amedeo
Lgt. in Sassia
S. Giovanni d. Fiorentini
Via Aurelia
P.le Gregorio VII
Casa Ordine Frati Minori
Divi Gregorio VII
Via Gregorio VII
S. Gregorio VII
Sportivi
Monte di Gallo
Maria Addolorata
S. Maria alle Fornaci
Stazione S. Pietro
Viale delle Fornaci
Viale delle Mura
Collegio Militare
S. Onofrio
Passeggiata del Gianicolo
Lgt. Gianicolense
Tevere
Carcere di Regina Coeli

330

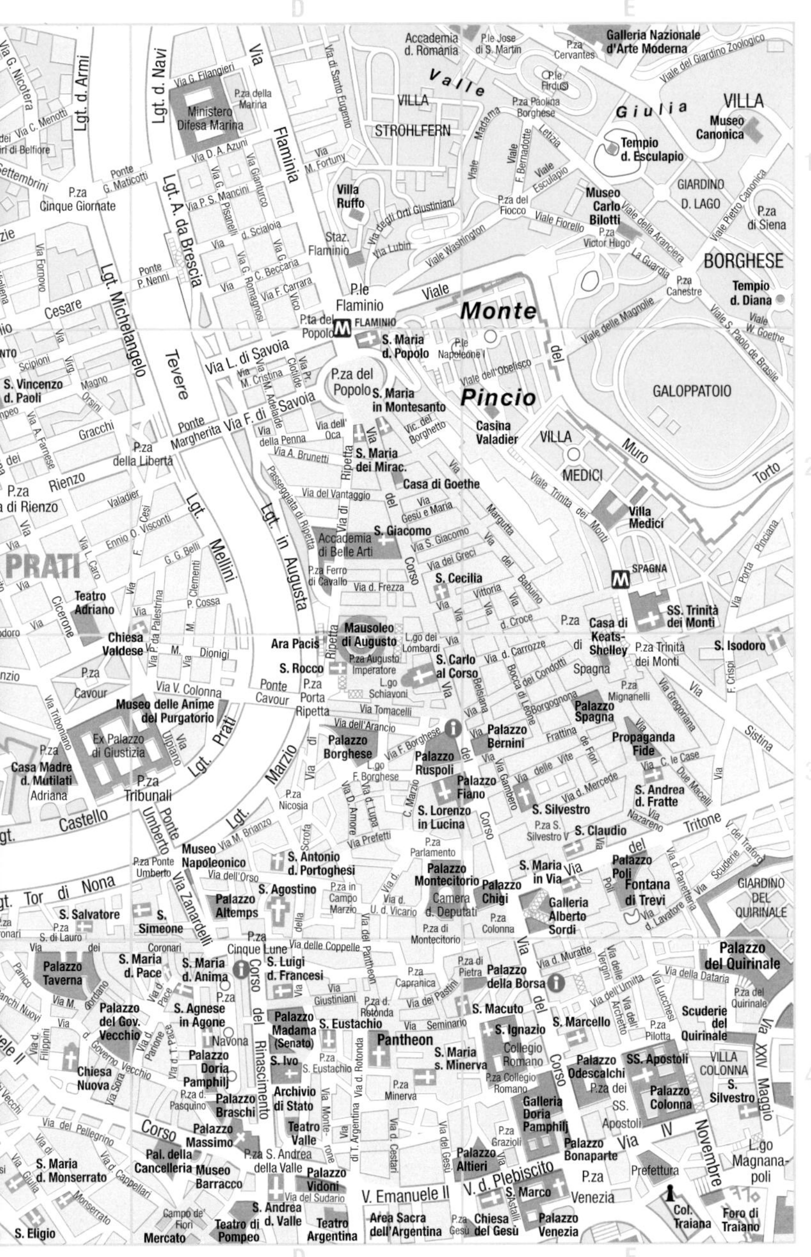

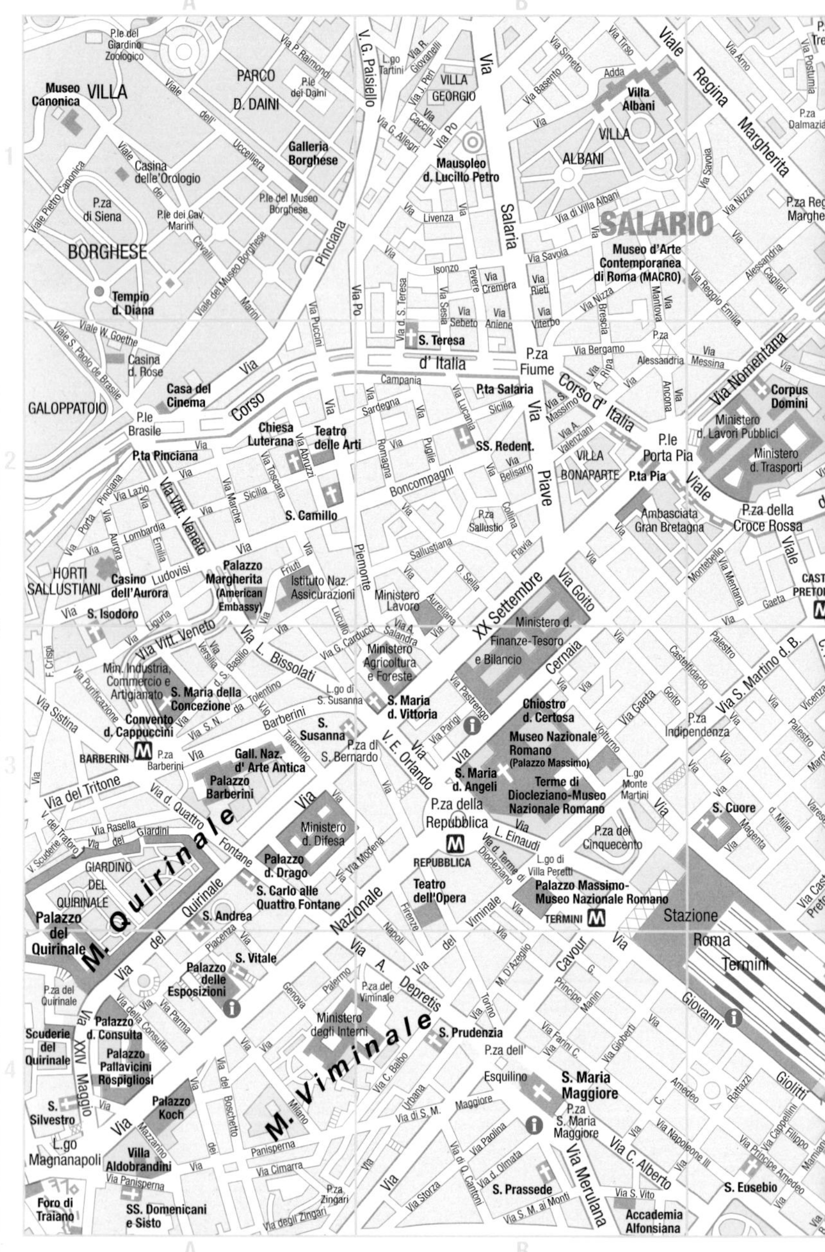
A
B
1
2
3
4
Museo Canonica
VILLA BORGHESE
PARCO D. DAINI
P.le dei Daini
P.le del Giardino Zoologico
Galleria Borghese
Casina dell'Orologio
P.za di Siena
P.le dei Cav. Marini
P.le del Museo Borghese
Tempio d. Diana
Casina d. Rose
Casa del Cinema
GALOPPATOIO
P.le Brasile
P.ta Pinciana
HORTI SALLUSTIANI
Casino dell'Aurora
S. Isodoro
Palazzo Margherita (American Embassy)
Chiesa Luterana
Teatro delle Arti
S. Camillo
Istituto Naz. Assicurazioni
Ministero Lavoro
Ministero Agricoltura e Foreste
S. Maria d. Vittoria
Min. Industria, Commercio e Artigianato
S. Maria della Concezione
Convento d. Cappuccini
BARBERINI
P.za Barberini
Gall. Naz. d'Arte Antica
Palazzo Barberini
S. Susanna
P.za di S. Bernardo
Ministero d. Difesa
Palazzo d. Drago
S. Carlo alle Quattro Fontane
GIARDINO DEL QUIRINALE
Palazzo del Quirinale
M. Quirinale
S. Andrea
S. Vitale
Palazzo delle Esposizioni
P.za del Quirinale
Scuderie del Quirinale
Palazzo d. Consulta
Palazzo Pallavicini Rospigliosi
S. Silvestro
Palazzo Koch
L.go Magnanapoli
Villa Aldobrandini
Foro di Traiano
SS. Domenicani e Sisto
M. Viminale
Ministero degli Interni
P.za del Viminale
S. Prudenzia
P.za dell' Esquilino
S. Maria Maggiore
P.za S. Maria Maggiore
S. Prassede
Accademia Alfonsiana
S. Eusebio
VILLA GEORGIO
Mausoleo d. Lucillo Petro
VILLA ALBANI
Villa Albani
SALARIO
Museo d'Arte Contemporanea di Roma (MACRO)
S. Teresa
P.za Fiume
P.ta Salaria
SS. Redent.
VILLA BONAPARTE
P.ta Pia
P.le Porta Pia
Ambasciata Gran Bretagna
Corpus Domini
Ministero d. Lavori Pubblici
Ministero d. Trasporti
P.za della Croce Rossa
Ministero d. Finanze-Tesoro e Bilancio
Chiostro d. Certosa
Museo Nazionale Romano (Palazzo Massimo)
S. Maria d. Angeli
Terme di Diocleziano-Museo Nazionale Romano
P.za della Repubblica
REPUBBLICA
Teatro dell'Opera
P.za del Cinquecento
Palazzo Massimo-Museo Nazionale Romano
TERMINI
Stazione Roma Termini
P.za Indipendenza
S. Cuore
L.go Monte Martini
L.go di Villa Peretti
Corso d'Italia
Via Salaria
Via Piave
Via Nomentana
Viale Regina Margherita
XX Settembre
Via Vitt. Veneto
Via del Tritone
Via Nazionale
Via A. Depretis
Via Cavour
Via Giovanni Giolitti
Via Merulana
Via C. Alberto
Via Napoleone III
Via Principe Amedeo
Via XXIV Maggio
Via Panisperna
Via degli Zingari
P.za Zingari
Via Pinciana
Via Po
V. G. Paisiello
Via L. Bissolati
V. E. Orlando
Via Barberini
Via d. Quattro Fontane
Via Sistina
Via Boncompagni
Via Goito
Via Gaeta
Via S. Martino d. B.

327

332

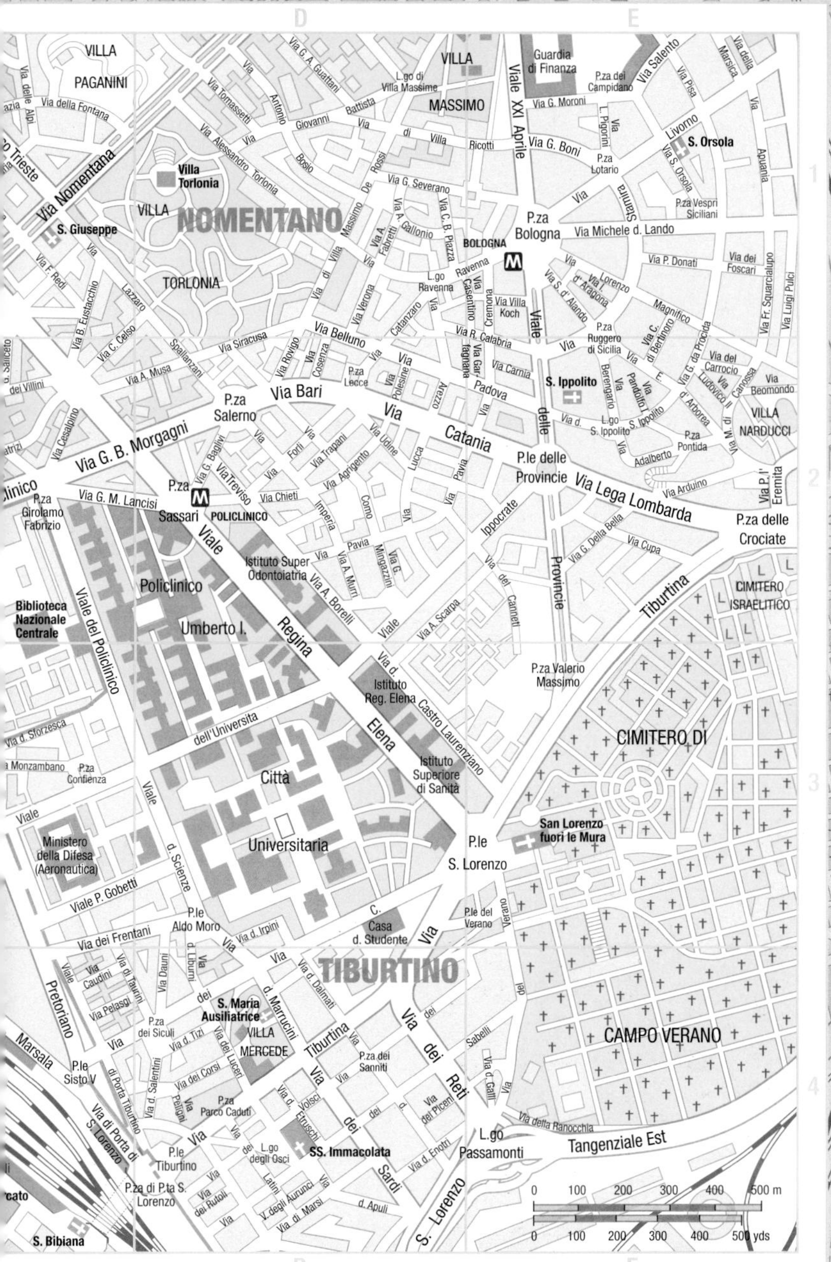
D
E
VILLA
PAGANINI
VILLA
MASSIMO
Guardia
di Finanza
Villa
Torlonia
NOMENTANO
VILLA
TORLONIA
S. Giuseppe
S. Orsola
Via Nomentana
Viale XXI Aprile
P.za
Bologna
BOLOGNA
Via Michele d. Lando
Via Belluno
Via Bari
P.za
Salerno
Via G. B. Morgagni
Via Catania
P.le delle
Provincie
Via Lega Lombarda
S. Ippolito
VILLA
NARDUCCI
P.za delle
Crociate
P.za
Sassari
POLICLINICO
Policlinico
Umberto I.
Biblioteca
Nazionale
Centrale
Viale del Policlinico
Viale Regina Elena
Istituto Super
Odontoiatria
Istituto
Reg. Elena
Istituto
Superiore
di Sanità
Via d. Castro Laurenziano
CIMITERO
ISRAELITICO
CIMITERO DI
CAMPO VERANO
San Lorenzo
fuori le Mura
P.le
S. Lorenzo
Città
Universitaria
Ministero
della Difesa
(Aeronautica)
Viale P. Gobetti
P.le
Aldo Moro
Via dei Frentani
Casa
d. Studente
TIBURTINO
S. Maria
Ausiliatrice
VILLA
MERCEDE
Via Tiburtina
Via dei Reti
Viale Pretoriano
P.le
Sisto V
P.le
Tiburtino
P.za di P.ta S.
Lorenzo
SS. Immacolata
L.go
Passamonti
Tangenziale Est
Via della Ranocchia
S. Bibiana
0 100 200 300 400 500 m
0 100 200 300 400 500 yds
1
2
3
4

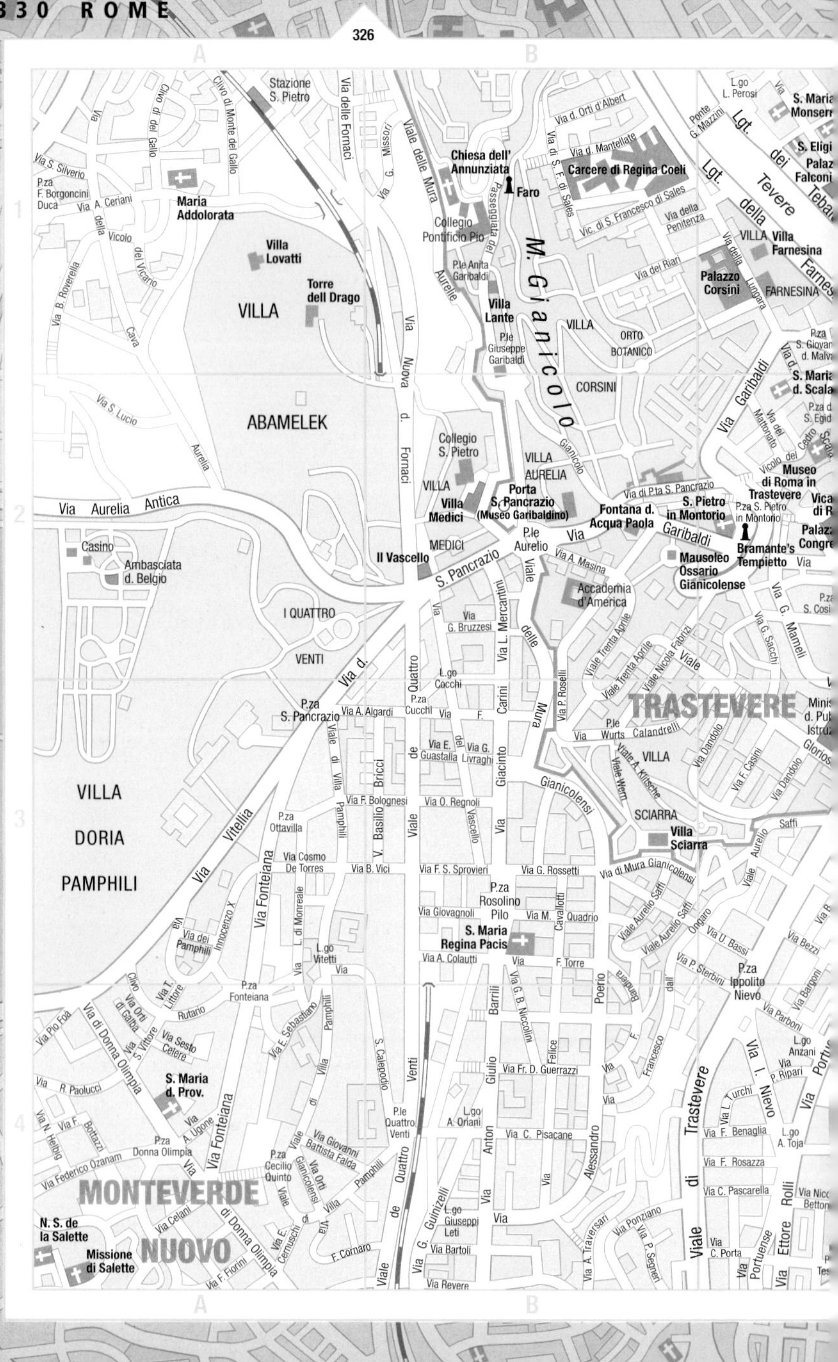

326

A B

1 2 3 4

Stazione S. Pietro
Via delle Fornaci
Viale delle Mura Aurelie
Chiesa dell' Annunziata
Faro
Carcere di Regina Coeli
S. Maria Monserr
S. Eligi
Palaz Falconi
Lgt. dei Tebaldi
Lgt. della Farnesina
Ponte G. Mazzini
L.go L. Perosi
Via d. Orti d'Alibert
Via d. Mantellate
Via di S. F. di Sales
Vic. di S. Francesco di Sales
Via della Penitenza
Via dei Riari
Via della Lungara
VILLA FARNESINA
Villa Farnesina
Palazzo Corsini
Via S. Silverio
P.za F. Borgoncini Duca
Via A. Ceriani
Vicolo del Vicario
Via B. Roverella
Civo di del Gallo
Clivo di Monte del Gallo
Maria Addolorata
Villa Lovatti
Torre dell Drago
VILLA ABAMELEK
Via G. Missori
Via Nuova d. Fornaci
Collegio Pontificio Pio
Passeggiata del Gianicolo
P.le Anita Garibaldi
M. Gianicolo
Villa Lante
P.le Giuseppe Garibaldi
VILLA CORSINI
ORTO BOTANICO
P.za S. Giovanni d. Malva
S. Maria d. Scala
P.za d. S. Egidio
Via del Mattonato
Vicolo del Cedro
Via Garibaldi
Via S. Lucio
Via Aurelia
Via Aurelia Antica
Collegio S. Pietro
VILLA AURELIA
VILLA MEDICI
Villa Medici
Porta S. Pancrazio (Museo Garibaldino)
Via di P.ta S. Pancrazio
Fontana d. Acqua Paola
S. Pietro in Montorio
P.za S. Pietro in Montorio
Bramante's Tempietto
Museo di Roma in Trastevere
Vicolo di R
Palazzo Congr
Casino
Ambasciata d. Belgio
Il Vascello
P.le Aurelio
Via A. Masina
Mausoleo Ossario Gianicolense
Accademia d'America
Via S. Pancrazio
VILLA I QUATTRO VENTI
Via G. Bruzzesi
Via L. Mercantini
Viale delle Mura Gianicolensi
Viale Trenta Aprile
Via Nicola Fabrizi
Via G. Sacchi
Via G. Mameli
P.za S. Cosimato
L.go Cocchi
P.za Cucchi
Via d. Quattro Venti
P.za S. Pancrazio
Via A. Algardi
Via F. Carini
Via P. Roselli
TRASTEVERE
Minis d. Pub Istruz
P.le Wurts
Via Calandrelli
VILLA SCIARRA
Viale A. Klitsche
Viale Wern
Via Dandolo
Via F. Casini
Glorioso
Viale di Villa Pamphili
V. Bricci
Via E. Guastalla
Via del Livraghi
Via G. Livraghi
Via Giacinto Carini
Via F. Bolognesi
Via O. Regnoli
Via Vascello
VILLA DORIA PAMPHILI
Via Vitellia
P.za Ottavilla
Via Basilio Bricci
Via Cosmo De Torres
Via B. Vici
Via F. S. Sprovieri
Via G. Rossetti
Villa Sciarra
Via di Mura Gianicolensi
Viale Aurelio Saffi
P.za Rosolino Pilo
Via Giovagnoli
Via M. Quadrio
Via Cavallotti
Via Fonteiana
Via Innocenzo X
Via dei Pamphili
Via L. di Monreale
L.go Vitetti
S. Maria Regina Pacis
Via A. Colautti
Via F. Torre
Via Ongaro
Via U. Bassi
Via Bezzi
Via P. Sterbini
P.za Ippolito Nievo
Via Bargoni
Via Parboni
Clivo Rutario
Via T. Littore
P.za Fonteiana
Via G. B. Niccolini
Via Barrili
Via Poerio
Via dall Bandiera
Via Francesco
Via Orti di Galba
Via S. Vittore
Via Sesto Celere
Via Pio Foà
Via di Donna Olimpia
Via E. Sebastiano
Via Pamphili
S. Calepodio
Via Felice
Via Fr. D. Guerrazzi
L.go Anzani
Via P. Ripari
Via I. Nievo
Via Portuense
Via R. Paolucci
S. Maria d. Prov.
Via F. Bottazzi
Via N. Heibig
Via A. Ugone
P.za Donna Olimpia
Via Federico Ozanam
P.le Quattro Venti
Via Giovanni Battista Falda
Via Orti Gianicolensi
P.za Cecilio Quinto
L.go A. Oriani
Via Anton Giulio Barrili
Via C. Pisacane
Via Alessandro Poerio
Viale di Trastevere
Via L. Turchi
Via F. Benaglia
L.go A. Toja
Via F. Rosazza
Via C. Pascarella
Via Nicola Bettoni
Via Ettore Rolli
MONTEVERDE NUOVO
N. S. de la Salette
Missione di Salette
Via Celani
Via di Donna Olimpia
Via E. Cermuschi
Via F. Cornaro
Viale de Quattro Venti
Via G. Guinizelli
L.go Giuseppi Leti
Via Bartoli
Via Revere
Via A. Traversari
Via Ponziano
Via P. Segneri
Via C. Porta
Via F. Fiorini

327

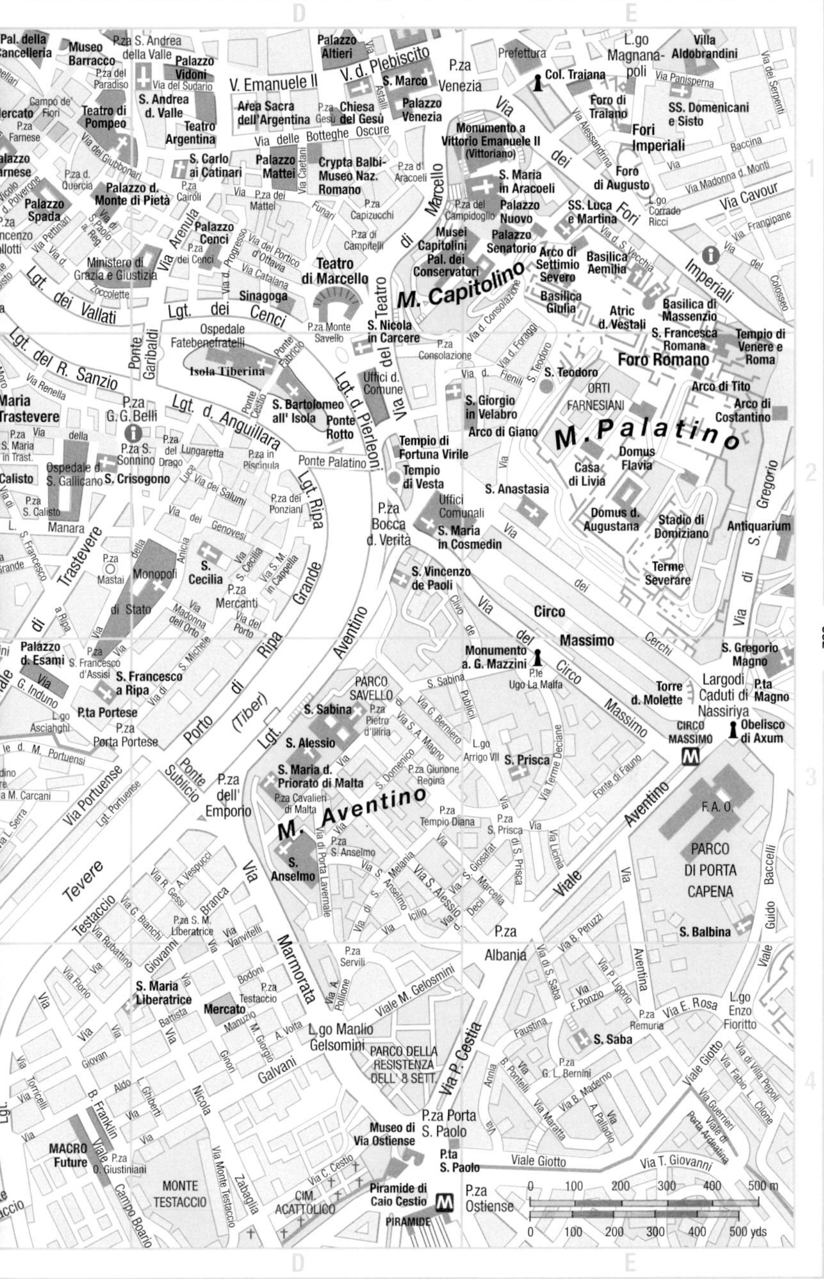

M. Capitolino
M. Palatino
M. Aventino
Foro Romano
Circo Massimo
Fori Imperiali
Teatro di Marcello
Isola Tiberina
Monumento a Vittorio Emanuele II (Vittoriano)
Musei Capitolini Pal. dei Conservatori
S. Maria in Cosmedin
Piramide di Caio Cestio
PARCO DI PORTA CAPENA
F. A. O.
MONTE TESTACCIO
PARCO SAVELLO
Tevere
Via dei Fori Imperiali
Via Cavour
Viale Aventino

332

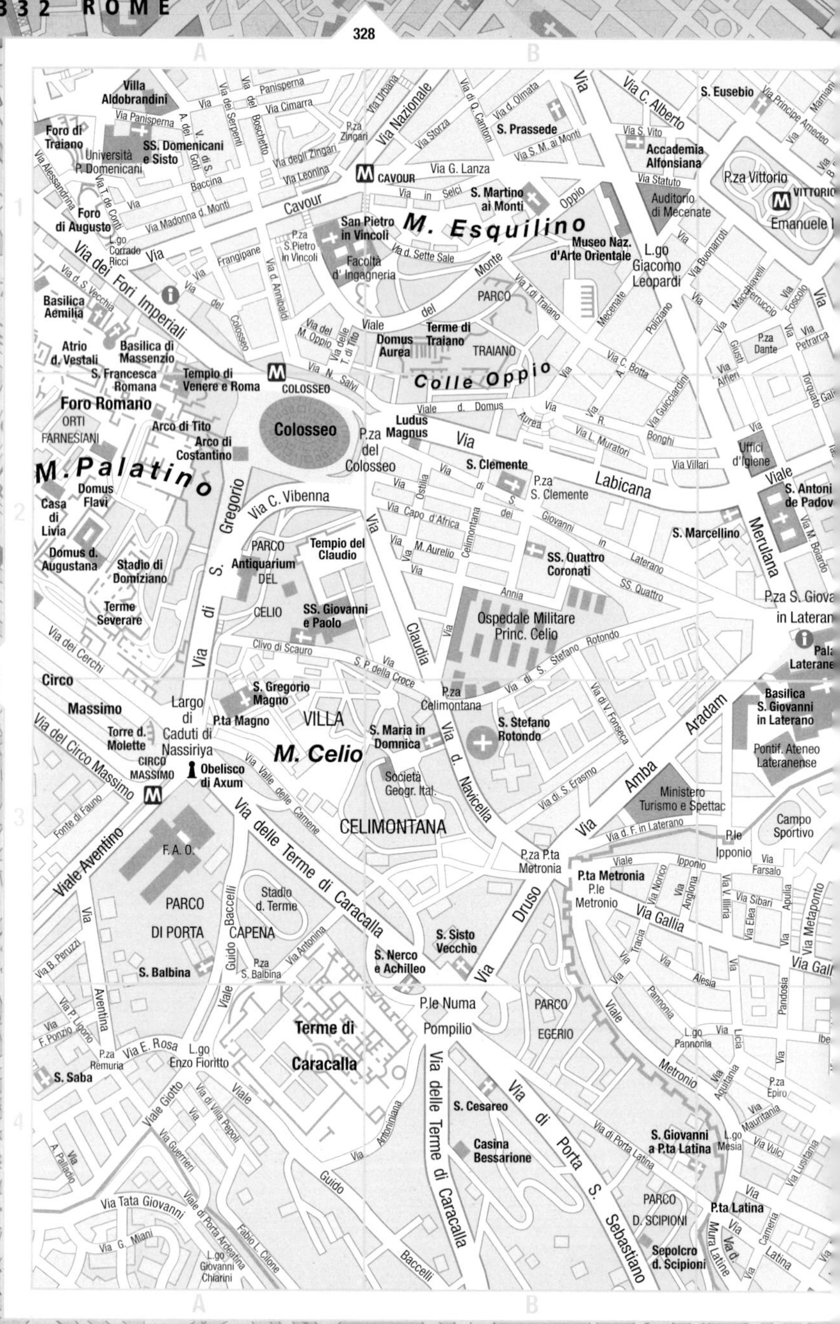

328

331

A B

1 2 3 4

Villa Aldobrandini
Foro di Traiano
Università P. Domenicani
SS. Domenicani e Sisto
Via Panisperna
Via dei Serpenti
Via del Boschetto
Via Cimarra
P.za Zingari
Via degli Zingari
Via Leonina
Via Urbana
Via Nazionale
Via di Q. Cantoni
Via Storza
Via d. Olmata
S. Prassede
Via S. M. ai Monti
Via C. Alberto
Via S. Vito
Accademia Alfonsiana
S. Eusebio
Via Principe Amedeo
Via Mamiani
P.za Vittorio Emanuele II
VITTORIO
Via Statuto
Auditorio di Mecenate
Via Alessandrina
Via T. de Conti
Via Baccina
Via Madonna d. Monti
Via Cavour
CAVOUR
Via G. Lanza
Via in Selci
S. Martino ai Monti
Oppio
Foro di Augusto
L.go Corrado Ricci
San Pietro in Vincoli
P.za S. Pietro in Vincoli
Via Frangipane
M. Esquilino
Museo Naz. d'Arte Orientale
L.go Giacomo Leopardi
Via Buonarroti
Via d. S. Vecchia
Via dei Fori Imperiali
Via del Colosseo
Via d. Annibaldi
Facoltà d' Ingagneria
Via d. Sette Sale
Monte
Via T. di Traiano
PARCO
Via Mecenate
Via Poliziano
Via Macchiavelli
Via Ferruccio
Via Foscolo
Basilica Aemilia
Atrio d. Vestali
Basilica di Massenzio
Via del M. Oppio
Via delle T. di Tito
Viale del
Domus Aurea
Terme di Traiano
TRAIANO
Colle Oppio
Via C. Botta
Via A.
Via Guicciardini
Via Giusti
Via Alfieri
P.za Dante
Via Petrarca
Via Torquato
S. Francesca Romana
Tempio di Venere e Roma
COLOSSEO
Via N. Salvi
Foro Romano
ORTI FARNESIANI
Arco di Tito
Arco di Costantino
Colosseo
P.za del Colosseo
Ludus Magnus
Viale d. Domus Aurea
Via R. Bonghi
Via L. Muratori
Via Villari
Uffici d'Igiene
M. Palatino
Domus Flavi
Casa di Livia
Via di S. Gregorio
Via C. Vibenna
Via Ostilia
Via Capo d'Africa
S. Clemente
P.za S. Clemente
Via di S. Giovanni in Laterano
Via Labicana
Viale Manzoni
S. Antonio da Padova
S. Marcellino
Via Merulana
Via M. Boiardo
Domus d. Augustana
Stadio di Domiziano
PARCO DEL CELIO
Antiquarium
Tempio del Claudio
Via M. Aurelio
Via Celimontana
SS. Quattro Coronati
Via SS. Quattro
Via Annia
P.za S. Giovanni in Laterano
Terme Severare
SS. Giovanni e Paolo
Via Claudia
Ospedale Militare Princ. Celio
Via dei Cerchi
Clivo di Scauro
Via S. P. della Croce
Via di S. Stefano Rotondo
Palazzo Laterano
Circo Massimo
Largo di Caduti di Nassiriya
S. Gregorio Magno
P.ta Magno
VILLA
P.za Celimontana
Via di V. Fonseca
Via Amba Aradam
Basilica S. Giovanni in Laterano
Via del Circo Massimo
Torre d. Molette
CIRCO MASSIMO
Obelisco di Axum
M. Celio
S. Maria in Domnica
Via d. Navicella
S. Stefano Rotondo
Pontif. Ateneo Lateranense
Fonte di Fauno
Viale Aventino
Via Valle delle Camene
Società Geogr. Ital.
CELIMONTANA
Via di S. Erasmo
Ministero Turismo e Spettac
Campo Sportivo
F. A. O.
Via delle Terme di Caracalla
Via d. F. in Laterano
P.le Ipponio
P.za P.ta Metronia
Viale Ipponio
P.ta Metronia
P.le Metronio
Via Farsalo
Via Norico
Via Angiona
Via V. Illiria
Via Sibari
Via Apulia
Via Metaponto
PARCO DI PORTA CAPENA
Via Baccelli
Stadio d. Terme
Via Druso
Via Gallia
Via Elea
Via Aventina
Via B. Peruzzi
Via Antonina
S. Nerco e Achilleo
S. Sisto Vecchio
Via Tracia
Via Alesia
S. Balbina
P.za S. Balbina
Viale Guido
P.le Numa Pompilio
PARCO EGERIO
Via Pannonia
Viale Metronio
Via Pandosia
Via P. Ligorio
Via F. Ponzio
Terme di Caracalla
L.go Pannonia
Via Licia
P.za Remuria
Via E. Rosa
L.go Enzo Fioritto
S. Saba
Via di Porta S. Sebastiano
Via Aquitania
P.za Epiro
Viale Giotto
Via di Villa Pepoli
Via Antoniniana
S. Cesareo
Casina Bessarione
Via Mauritania
Via di Porta Latina
S. Giovanni a P.ta Latina
L.go Mesia
Via Vulci
Via Lusitania
Via A. Palladio
Via Guerrieri
Guido
PARCO D. SCIPIONI
P.ta Latina
Via Latina
Via Camena
Via Tata Giovanni
Viale di Porta Ardeatina
Fabio L. Cilone
Via G. Miani
L.go Giovanni Chiarini
Baccelli
Sepolcro d. Scipioni
Mura Latine
Via d.

329

D
E
D
E
1
2
3
4
0 100 200 300 400 500 m
0 100 200 300 400 500 yds
P.le Tiburtino
P.za di P.ta S. Lorenzo
S. Bibiana
Via S. Lorenzo
Via d. Scalo
Sopraelevata
Via Ottavio Piccolomini
Via Caprara
Via Prenestina
P.za Prenestina
P.za di Porta Maggiore
P.ta Maggiore
Via di Porta Maggiore
Giovanni Giolitti
Pr. Eugenio
Manzoni
Villa Altieri
Acquedotto Neroniano
VILLA WOLKONSKI
P.za di S. Croce in Gerusalemme
S. Croce in Gerusalemme
Anfiteatro Castrense
Viale Castrense
Via Casilina
Via L' Aquila
P.za del Pigneto
Via del Pigneto
P.za Lodi
Via Alghero
Viale Carlo Felice
P.za Porta S. Giovanni
L.go Brindisi
P.le Appio
P.ta Asinaria
P.ta S. Giovanni
S. GIOVANNI
Via La Spezia
P.za Camerino
SS. Immacolata
SS. Fabiano
P.za di Villa Fiorelli
P.za Castroreale
Via Taranto
P.za Lugo
S. Maria d. Orto
Via Appia Nuova
P.za dei Re di Roma
RE DI ROMA
L.go Vercelli
L.go Frassinetti
P.za Asti
P.za Ragusa
P.za Tuscolo
Via Etruria
Ognissanti
PONTE LUNGO
Staz. Roma Tuscolana F.S.
Via Gela
Via Tuscolana
P.za di Ponte Lungo
P.za Finocchiaro Aprile
Istituto Antoniano di Roma
Circonvallazione Appia
Via Cappadocia
P.za Camillo Re
Via F. Camillo
TUSCOLANO
P.za Zama
P.za Armenia
Via Britannia
Via Acaia
Via Albenga
Via Ivrea
Via Soluntо
Via Magna Grecia
L.go Magna Grecia
P.za Tarquinia
P.za Imola
P.za Sulmona
Via Monza
Via Aosta
Via Nola
Via Eleniana
Via Teramo
P.za Caballini
P.le Labicano
Via Casilina Vecchia
Via Montepulciano
Via Enna
P.za S. Donà di Piave
L.go Don Orione
Via Cerveteri
Via Pomezia
Via Albalonga
Via Vercelli
Via Sermide
Via C. Monferrato
Via Pordenone
Via d. Rogazionisti
Via S. Remo
Via Matera
Via Pinerolo
Via Casoria
Via Orvieto
Via Foligno
Via Savona
Via Voghera
Via Pistoia
Via Spoleto
Via Terni
Via Portoferraio
Via Volterra
Via Fermo
Via SS. F. e Venanzio
Via Crema
Via Pescara
Via Chioggia
Via Cittaduc
Via Portogruaro
Via Verbania
Via Alba
Via Saluzzo
Via Modica
Via Noto
Via Adria
Via Assisi
Via Gubbio
Via Amelia
Via Veturia
Via Targ.
Via Prisco
Via Niso
Via Siria
Via Vescia
Via Satrico
Via Concordia
Via Sinuessa
Via Dacia
Via Cutilia
Via Imera
Via Ferento
Via Domodossola
Via Tortona
Via Susa
Via Ceneda
Via Astura
Via Soana
Via Gabi
Via Cuma
Via Suessola
Via Lavinio
Via Ardea
Via Fregene
Via Faleria
Via Veio
Via Fidene
Via Sannio
Via Amiterno
Via Urbino
Via Cesena
Via Rimini
Via Vibo Valentia
Via Gerace
Via Nicastro
Via Biella
Via Bobbio
Via Acqui
Via Mondovi
Via Cividale del Friuli
Via Gallipoli
Via P. Tola
P. Paruta
Via Acireale
Via Caltagirone
Via Mistretta
Via Lanusei
Via Nuoro
Via Ozieri
Via Alcamo
Via Oristano
Via Melfi
Via Avezzano
Via S. Castulo
Via Tuscolana
Via Mirandola
Via Orti Variani
Via Sondrio
Via Pesaro
Via A. Perugia
Via Piceno
Via Macerata
Via Casilina
Vic. del Pigneto
Via P. R. Mellis
Via Grosseto
Via Fivizzano
Via Campobasso
Via Caltanissetta
Circonval.
Via R. Montecuccoli
Via Marsigli
Via dei Rutoli
Viad. Equi
Via dei Sabelli
V. degli Aurunci
Via Marsi
d. Apuli
Via d. Campani
Via de Lucani
L.go E. Talamo
Via degli Anamari
Via dei Bruzi
Via di Porta Labicana
Via Caroli
Via P. Umberto
Via Bixio
Via Verde
Via Bailila
Via Carlo Emanuele I
Via di S. Croce in Gerusalemme
L. Luzzatti
Statilia
Via S. Quintino
MANZONI
Via G. B. Piatti
Via Sessoriana
Savoia
Biancamano
Ludovico di Savoia
Umberto
Via C. Rosso
Emanuele Filiberto
Via Ceneda
Via Casilina
P.le Appio

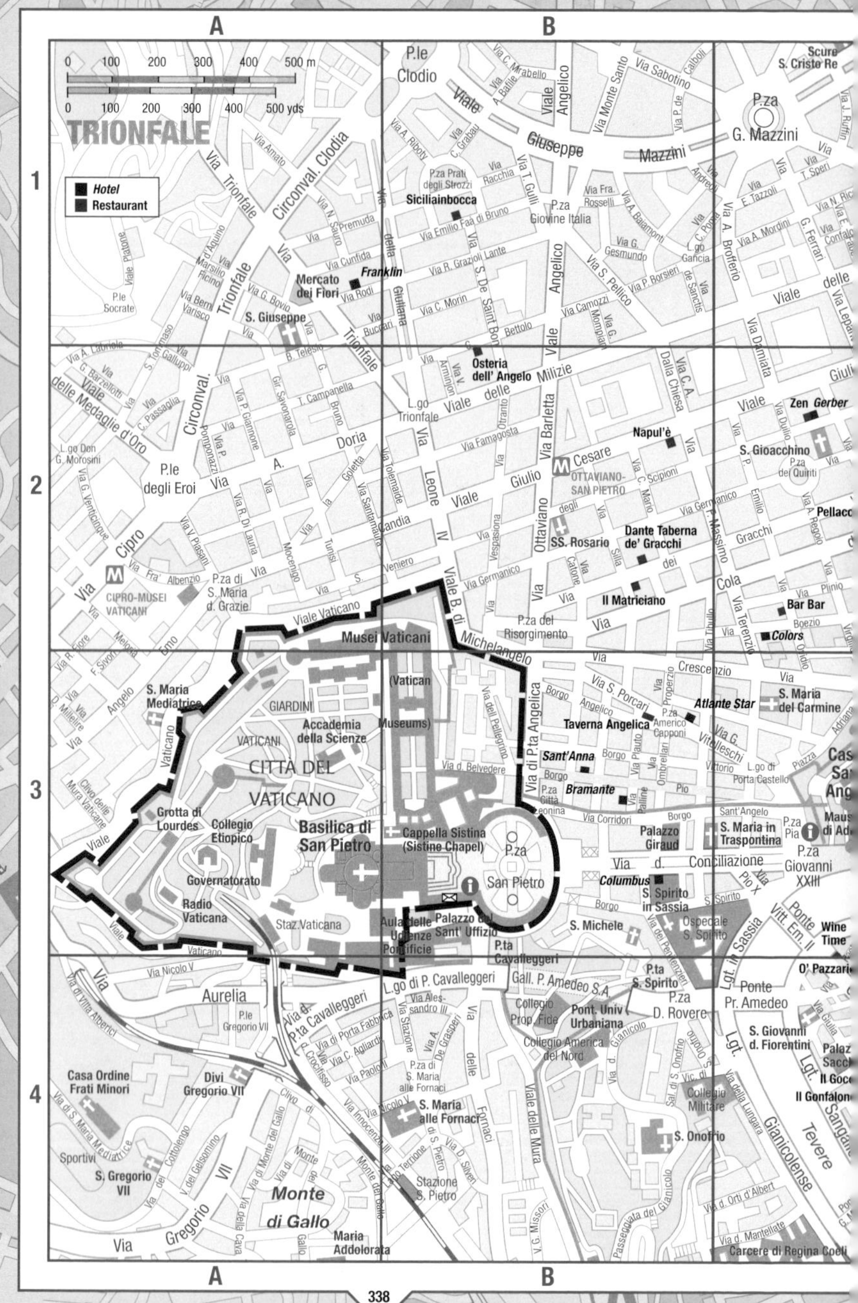
A
B
1
2
3
4
0 100 200 300 400 500 m
0 100 200 300 400 500 yds
TRIONFALE
Hotel
Restaurant
P.le Clodio
Viale Giuseppe Mazzini
P.za G. Mazzini
Scure S. Cristo Re
Via Trionfale
Circonval. Clodia
Siciliainbocca
P.za Prati degli Strozzi
P.za Giovine Italia
Mercato dei Fiori
Franklin
S. Giuseppe
P.le Socrate
Osteria dell' Angelo
Viale delle Milizie
Viale delle Medaglie d'Oro
Circonval. Trionfale
L.go Trionfale
Via Leone IV
Via Andrea Doria
P.le degli Eroi
Viale Giulio Cesare
Napul'è
OTTAVIANO-SAN PIETRO
Zen
Gerber
S. Gioacchino
P.za dei Quiriti
Pellacc
SS. Rosario
Dante Taberna de' Gracchi
Il Matriciano
Via Cola di Rienzo
Bar Bar
Colors
Via Cipro
CIPRO-MUSEI VATICANI
P.za di S. Maria d. Grazie
Viale Vaticano
Musei Vaticani
Viale B. di Michelangelo
P.za del Risorgimento
Via Crescenzio
S. Maria Mediatrice
GIARDINI VATICANI
(Vatican Museums)
Accademia della Scienze
CITTÀ DEL VATICANO
Atlante Star
S. Maria del Carmine
Taverna Angelica
Sant'Anna
Bramante
Via di P.ta Angelica
Borgo Pio
L.go di Porta Castello
Grotta di Lourdes
Collegio Etiopico
Basilica di San Pietro
Cappella Sistina (Sistine Chapel)
P.za San Pietro
Palazzo Giraud
S. Maria in Traspontina
P.za Pia
P.za Giovanni XXIII
Via d. Conciliazione
Governatorato
Radio Vaticana
Columbus
S. Spirito in Sassia
Staz. Vaticana
Aula delle Udienze Pontificie
Palazzo del Sant' Uffizio
S. Michele
Ospedale S. Spirito
Wine Time
P.ta Cavalleggeri
O' Pazzari
Via Aurelia
L.go di P. Cavalleggeri
Gall. P. Amedeo S.A.
Collegio Prop. Fide
Pont. Univ. Urbaniana
P.ta S. Spirito
P.za D. Rovere
Ponte Pr. Amedeo
Collegio America del Nord
S. Giovanni d. Fiorentini
Il Goc
Il Gonfalone
Casa Ordine Frati Minori
Divi Gregorio VII
S. Maria alle Fornaci
Collegio Militare
S. Onofrio
S. Gregorio VII
Monte di Gallo
Stazione S. Pietro
Viale delle Mura
Via Gregorio VII
Maria Addolorata
Lgt. Gianicolense
Tevere
Carcere di Regina Coeli
A
B

338

D
E
1
2
3
4
336
Accademia d. Romania
P.le Jose di S. Martin
P.za Cervantes
Galleria Nazionale d'Arte Moderna
Viale del Giardino Zoologico
Valle Giulia
VILLA
Museo Canonica
Tempio d. Esculapio
VILLA STROHLFERN
P.za Paolina Borghese
P.le Firdusi
Via Flaminia
Lgt. d. Navi
Lgt. d. Armi
Ministero Difesa Marina
P.za della Marina
Setembrini
P.za Cinque Giornate
Villa Ruffo
Viale Washington
Staz. Flaminio
Museo Carlo Bilotti
GIARDINO D. LAGO
P.za di Siena
BORGHESE
Tempio d. Diana
P.za Canestre
P.le Flaminio
Monte
Pincio
P.ta del Popolo
FLAMINIO
S. Maria d. Popolo
P.za del Popolo
Farnese
S. Vincenzo d. Paoli
Dal Bolognese
Canova
De Russie
Rosati
Casina Valadier
VILLA MEDICI
GALOPPATOIO
Viale delle Magnolie
Muro Torto
PizzaRé
Valadier
Locarno
Buccone
Café Notegen
Il Margutta RistorArte
Villa Medici
Hotel Art
Ciampini al Café du Jardin
Splendide Royal
PRATI
Lgt. Michelangelo
Tevere
Ponte Margherita
P.za della Libertà
P.za di Rienzo
Lgt. Mellini
Lgt. in Augusta
Accademia di Belle Arti
S. Giacomo
Gran Caffè La Caffettiera
Porto Maltese
SPAGNA
La Terrazza dell'Eden
Eden
Dei Mellini
S. Cecilia
Otello alla Concordia
Recafé
'Gusto
L'Osteria
Taverna Ripetta
Teatro Adriano
Enoteca Antica di Via della Croce
Al 34
SS. Trinità dei Monti
Hassler
Scalinata di Spagna
S. Isodoro
Mausoleo di Augusto
Ara Pacis
Pensione Panda
Hotel San Carlo
Antico Caffè Greco
Inn at the Spanish Steps
S. Rocco
P.za Augusto Imperatore
La Lumiere di Piazza di Spagna
Portrait Suites
Nino
Gregoriana
Modigliani
P.za Cavour
Museo delle Anime del Purgatorio
La Baguette
Palazzo Spagna
Casa Howard
D'Inghilterra
Palazzo Borghese
Matricianella
Palazzo Bernini
Suisse
Ex Palazzo di Giustizia
Casa Madre d. Mutilati
P.za Tribunali
Fontanella Borghese
Palazzo Fiano
S. Andrea d. Fratte
S. Silvestro
S. Lorenzo in Lucina
S. Claudio
Il Gelato di San Crispino
Al Presidente
Hostaria dell'Orso
Due Torri
Da Gino
News Café
S. Maria in Via
Le Tamerici
Il Convivio Troiani
Ricccioli Café
Maccheroni
Palazzo Montecitorio
Palazzo Chigi
Giolitti
Galleria Alberto Sordi
Vineria Il Chianti
GIARDINO DEL QUIRINALE
S. Salvatore
S. Simeone
L'Osteria di Memmo
Il Bacaro
Le Coppelle
Nazionale
Fontana di Trevi
Fontana
Relais Palazzo Taverna
Raphael
Jonathan's Angels
Fortunato al Pantheon
Osteria dell'Ingegno
Regno
Palazzo del Quirinale
Zio Ciro
La Rosetta
Tazza D'Oro
La Caffettiera
1 Clemente alla Maddalena
2 La Cantina di Ninco Nanco
Abruzzi
Sole al Pantheon
Il Fico
Da Tonino
Caffè Novecento
Teatro Pace 33
Cremeria Monteforte
Pantheon
S. Maria s. Minerva
S. Ignazio
S. Marcello
Scuderie del Quirinale
Da Baffetto
Cul de Sac
S. Ivo
Santa Chiara
Palazzo Odescalchi
SS. Apostoli
VILLA COLONNA
Da Luigi
Antica Trattoria Polese
Terra di Siena
Navona
Casa Bleve
Grand Hotel de la Minerve
Galleria Doria Pamphilj
Palazzo Colonna
S. Silvestro
Palazzo Massimo
Vecchia Locanda
Hosteria del Pesce
Palazzo Bonaparte
Lot 87
Ditirambo
Palazzo Altieri
Via IV Novembre
Via XXIV Maggio
L.go Magnanapoli
S. Maria d. Monserrato
Sciam
Della Lunetta
Palazzo Vidoni
C. V. Emanuele II
V. d. Plebiscito
S. Marco
P.za Venezia
Prefettura
Campo de' Fiori
Teatro di Pompeo
Renato e Luisa
Il Centrale Ristotheatre
Col. Traiana
Foro di Traiano
Der Pallaro
Sole
Pomezia
Barrett
Palazzo Venezia
Mercato
Rinascimento
Corso
Via del Corso

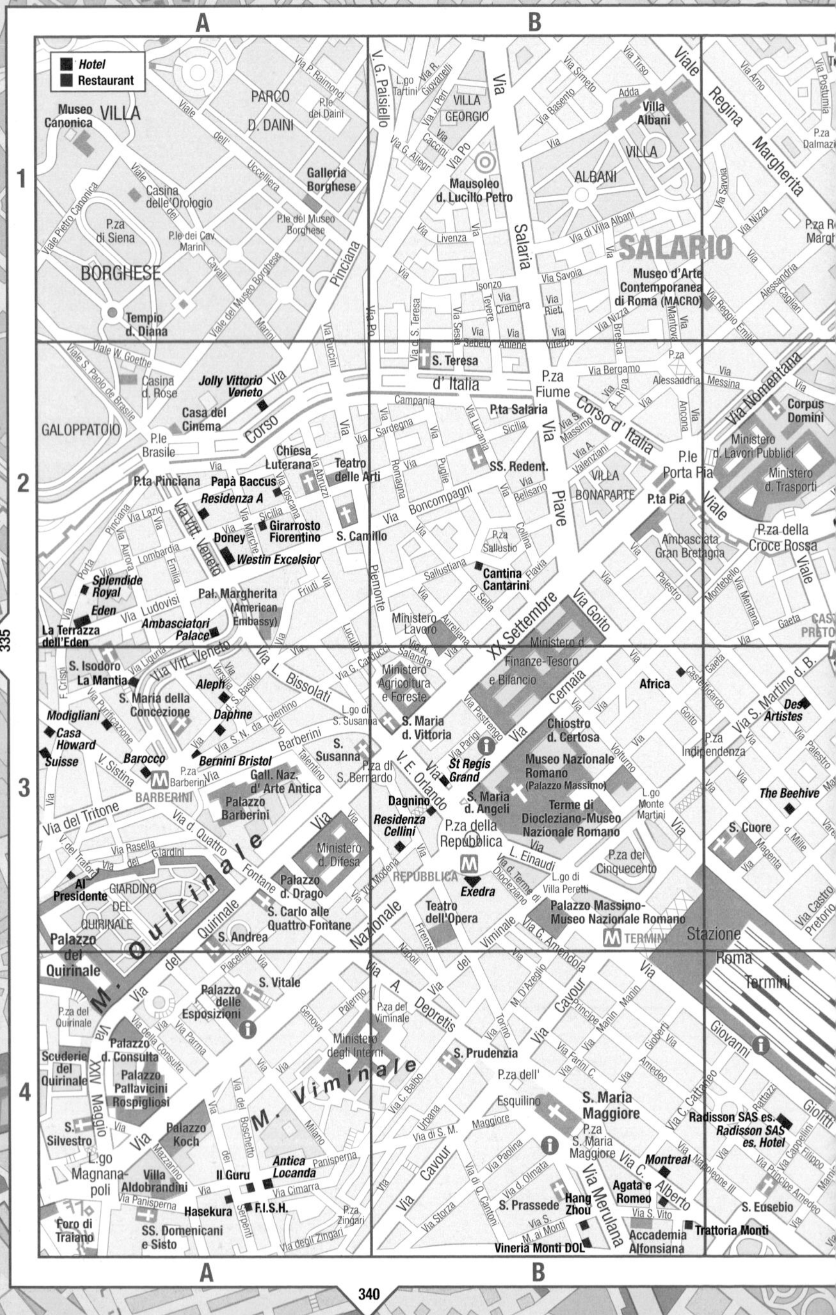
A
B
1
2
3
4
Hotel
Restaurant
Museo Canonica
VILLA BORGHESE
PARCO D. DAINI
P.le dei Daini
Via P. Raimondi
Viale dell' Uccelliera
Galleria Borghese
Casina delle Orologio
P.za di Siena
P.le dei Cav. Marini
P.le del Museo Borghese
Viale Pietro Canonica
Viale dei Cavalli Marini
Viale del Museo Borghese
Tempio d. Diana
Via Pinciana
V. G. Paisiello
L.go Tartini
Via R. Giovanelli
Via J. Peri
VILLA GEORGIO
Via Caccini
Via G. Allegri
Via Po
Mausoleo d. Lucillo Petro
Via Livenza
Via Salaria
Via Simeto
Via Tirso
Via Basento
Via Adda
Villa Albani
VILLA ALBANI
Viale Regina Margherita
Via Arno
Via Postumia
P.za Dalmazia
Via Savoia
Via Nizza
Via di Villa Albani
SALARIO
Museo d'Arte Contemporanea di Roma (MACRO)
Via Reggio Emilia
Via Alessandria
Via Cagliari
Via Isonzo
Via Tevere
Via Cremera
Via Rieti
Via Sebeto
Via Aniene
Via Viterbo
Via Brescia
Via Mantova
Via d. S. Teresa
Via Sesia
Via Puccini
S. Teresa
Corso d' Italia
P.za Fiume
Via Bergamo
Via Messina
Via Nomentana
Corpus Domini
Viale W. Goethe
Viale S. Paolo de Brasile
Casina d. Rose
Jolly Vittorio Veneto
Casa del Cinema
GALOPPATOIO
P.le Brasile
Via Campania
P.ta Salaria
Via Sardegna
Via Sicilia
Via Lucania
Via S. Massimo
Via A. Valenziani
Via A. Ripa
Corso d' Italia
Ministero d. Lavori Pubblici
Ministero d. Trasporti
P.le Porta Pia
VILLA BONAPARTE
P.ta Pia
Chiesa Luterana
Teatro delle Arti
P.ta Pinciana
Papà Baccus
Residenza A
Via Abruzzi
Via Toscana
Via Romagna
Via Puglie
SS. Redent.
Via Belisario
Via Piave
Via Lazio
Via Aurora
Via Vitt. Veneto
Via Sicilia
Via Marche
Doney
Girarrosto Fiorentino
S. Camillo
Via Boncompagni
Via Lombardia
Via Emilia
Westin Excelsior
P.za Sallustio
Via Collina
Ambasciata Gran Bretagna
P.za della Croce Rossa
Via Porta Pinciana
Splendide Royal
Eden
La Terrazza dell'Eden
Via Ludovisi
Ambasciatori Palace
Pal. Margherita (American Embassy)
Via Friuli
Via Piemonte
Via Sallustiana
Cantina Cantarini
Via Flavia
Via Palestro
Via Montebello
Via Mentana
Via Gaeta
Ministero Lavoro
Via Aureliana
Via XX Settembre
Via Goito
Ministero d. Finanze-Tesoro e Bilancio
Via Liguria
S. Isodoro
La Mantia
F. Crispi
Via Veneto
Aleph
S. Maria della Concezione
Via Purificazione
Daphne
Modigliani
Casa Howard
Suisse
Barocco
P.za Barberini
BARBERINI
Bernini Bristol
Via S. N. da Tolentino
Via L. Bissolati
Via G. Carducci
Via A. Salandra
Ministero Agricoltura e Foreste
L.go di S. Susanna
S. Maria d. Vittoria
Via Cernaia
Chiostro d. Certosa
Africa
Via Castelfidardo
Via S. Martino d. B.
Des Artistes
P.za Indipendenza
Via Barberini
S. Susanna
P.za di S. Bernardo
Gall. Naz. d' Arte Antica
Palazzo Barberini
Via V. E. Orlando
Via Parigi
St Regis Grand
Museo Nazionale Romano (Palazzo Massimo)
Via Volturno
L.go Monte Martini
The Beehive
Via del Tritone
V. Sistina
Via d. Quattro Fontane
Dagnino
Residenza Cellini
S. Maria d. Angeli
Terme di Diocleziano-Museo Nazionale Romano
S. Cuore
Via Magenta
Via d. Mille
Via Rasella
Via dei Giardini
Ministero d. Difesa
P.za della Repubblica
L. Einaudi
P.za dei Cinquecento
Al Presidente
GIARDINO DEL QUIRINALE
Via Quirinale
Palazzo d. Drago
REPUBBLICA
Exedra
Via Modena
Via d. Terme di Diocleziano
L.go di Villa Peretti
S. Carlo alle Quattro Fontane
Via Nazionale
Teatro dell'Opera
Via Firenze
Palazzo Massimo-Museo Nazionale Romano
TERMINI
Stazione Roma Termini
Via Castro Pretorio
Palazzo del Quirinale
M. Quirinale
S. Andrea
Via Napoli
Via del Viminale
Via G. Amendola
Via Piacenza
S. Vitale
Palazzo delle Esposizioni
Via Genova
Via Palermo
P.za del Viminale
Via A. Depretis
Via M. D'Azeglio
Via Cavour
Via Principe
Via Manin
Via Giovanni Giolitti
P.za del Quirinale
Via della Consulta
Via Parma
Palazzo d. Consulta
Ministero degli Interni
M. Viminale
Via Torino
S. Prudenzia
Via Farini
Via Gioberti
Via Amedeo
Scuderie del Quirinale
Palazzo Pallavicini Rospigliosi
Via XXIV Maggio
Via C. Balbo
P.za dell' Esquilino
S. Maria Maggiore
P.za S. Maria Maggiore
Via C. Cattaneo
Via Rattazzi
Radisson SAS es.
Radisson SAS es. Hotel
S. Silvestro
Palazzo Koch
Via del Boschetto
Via Milano
Via Urbana
Via di S. M. Maggiore
Via Paolina
Via Cappellini
Via Filippo Turati
L.go Magnanapoli
Villa Aldobrandini
Via Mazzarino
Via dei Serpenti
Il Guru
Antica Locanda
Via Panisperna
Via Cimarra
Via Carlo Alberto
Montreal
Via Napoleone III
Via Principe Amedeo
Hasekura
F.I.S.H.
Via d. Olmata
Via di Q. Cantoni
Via Merulana
S. Prassede
Hang Zhou
Agata e Romeo
S. Eusebio
Via S. Vito
Foro di Traiano
SS. Domenicani e Sisto
P.za Zingari
Via degli Zingari
Via Storza
Via S. M. ai Monti
Vineria Monti DOL
Accademia Alfonsiana
Trattoria Monti
335
340

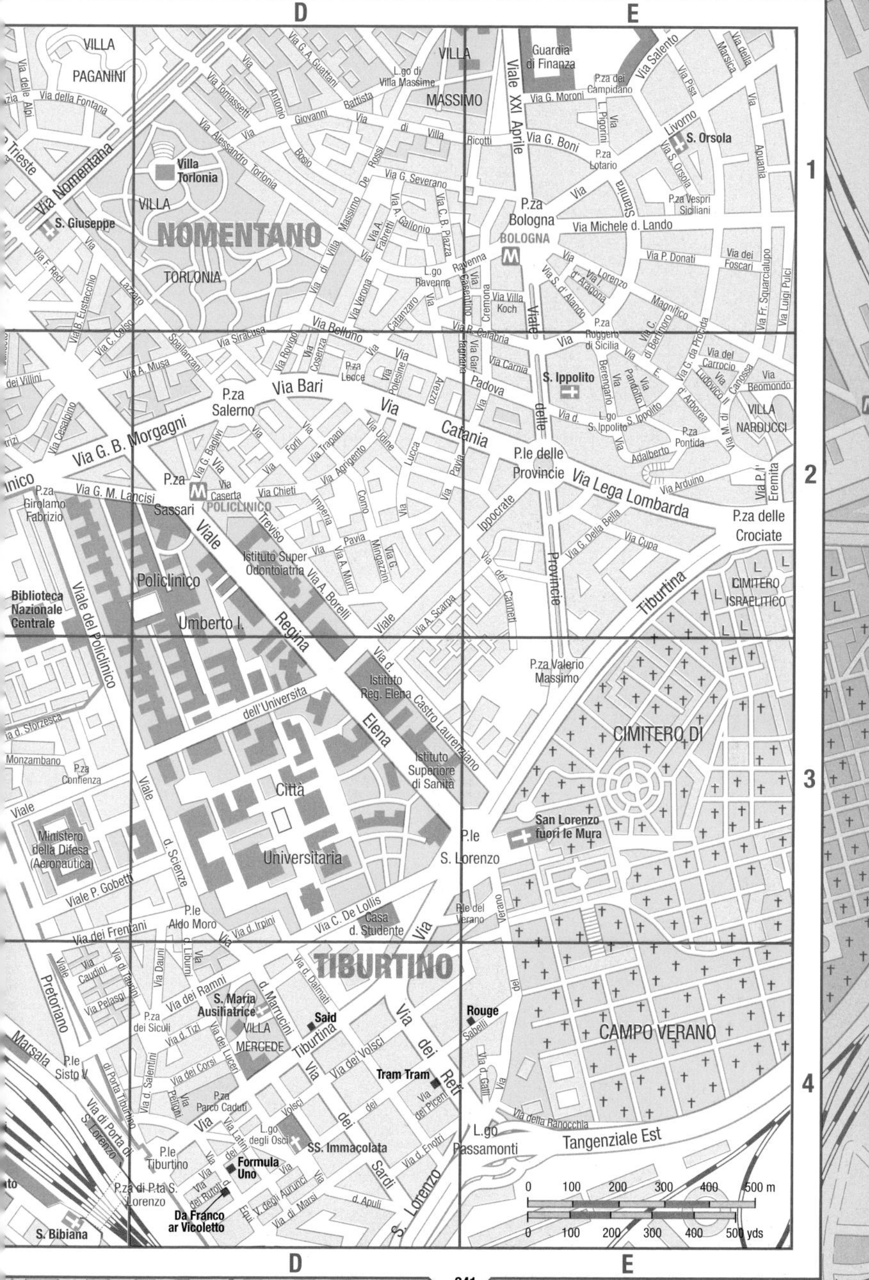
D
E
1
2
3
4
NOMENTANO
TIBURTINO
VILLA PAGANINI
VILLA TORLONIA
Villa Torlonia
VILLA MASSIMO
Guardia di Finanza
S. Orsola
S. Giuseppe
P.za Bologna
BOLOGNA
S. Ippolito
VILLA NARDUCCI
P.le delle Provincie
Via Lega Lombarda
P.za delle Crociate
CIMITERO ISRAELITICO
POLICLINICO
Policlinico Umberto I.
Biblioteca Nazionale Centrale
Istituto Super Odontoiatria
Istituto Reg. Elena
Istituto Superiore di Sanità
CIMITERO DI CAMPO VERANO
San Lorenzo fuori le Mura
Città Universitaria
Ministero della Difesa (Aeronautica)
Casa d. Studente
P.le Aldo Moro
S. Maria Ausiliatrice
VILLA MERCEDE
Said
Rouge
Tram Tram
SS. Immacolata
Formula Uno
Da Franco ar Vicoletto
S. Bibiana
P.le Tiburtino
P.le Sisto V
L.go Passamonti
Tangenziale Est
Viale Regina Elena
Via Tiburtina
Via Nomentana
Viale XXI Aprile
Via Catania
Via Bari
Via G. B. Morgagni
Viale del Policlinico
0 100 200 300 400 500 m
0 100 200 300 400 500 yds

341

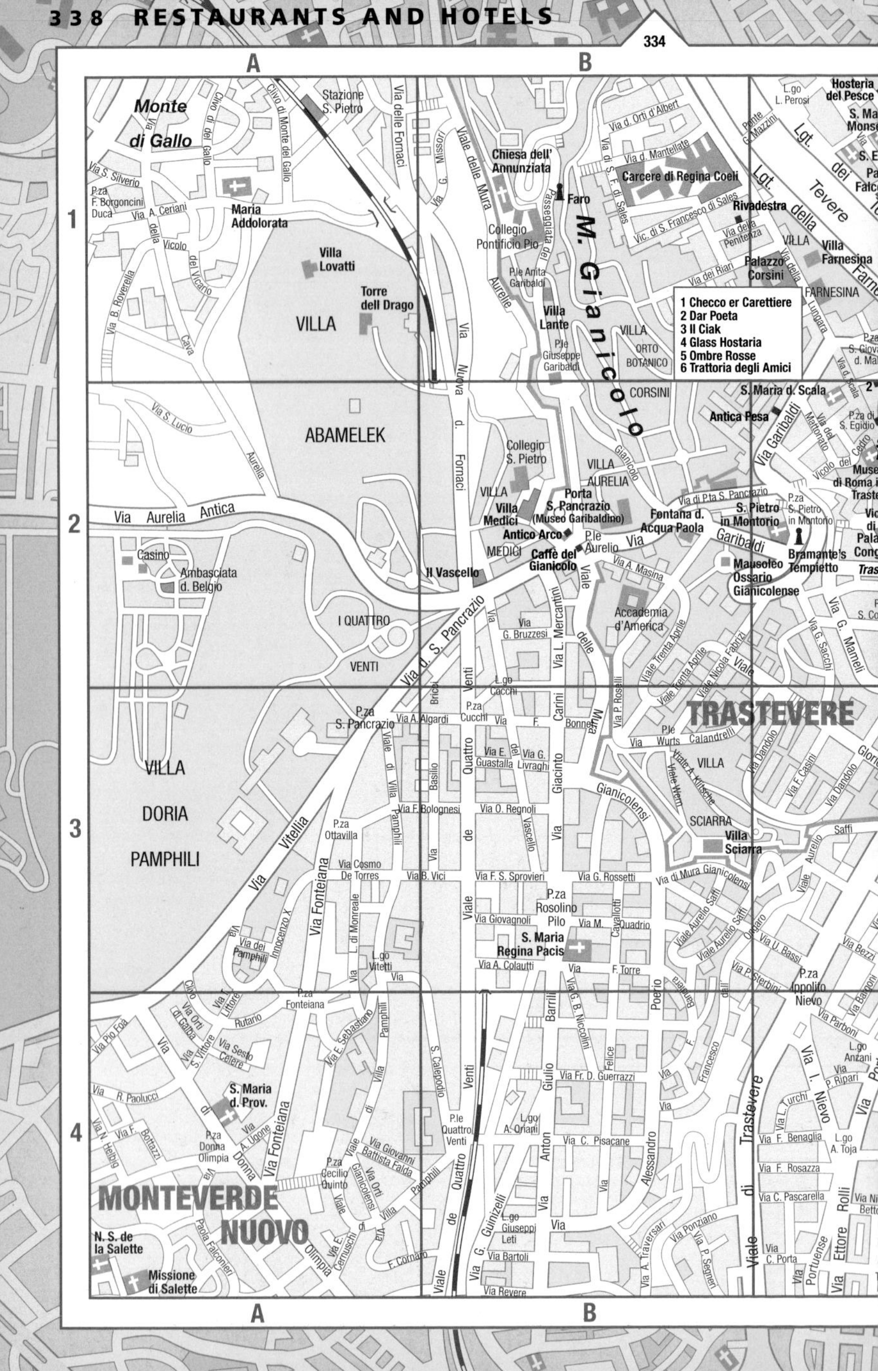
334
A
B
1
2
3
4
1 Checco er Carettiere
2 Dar Poeta
3 Il Ciak
4 Glass Hostaria
5 Ombre Rosse
6 Trattoria degli Amici
Monte di Gallo
Stazione S. Pietro
Maria Addolorata
Villa Lovatti
Torre dell Drago
VILLA
ABAMELEK
Chiesa dell' Annunziata
Faro
Collegio Pontificio Pio
Carcere di Regina Coeli
Rivadestra
Palazzo Corsini
Villa Farnesina
FARNESINA
Hosteria del Pesce
M. Gianicolo
Villa Lante
P.le Giuseppe Garibaldi
P.le Anita Garibaldi
VILLA
ORTO BOTANICO
CORSINI
S. Maria d. Scala
Antica Pesa
Collegio S. Pietro
VILLA AURELIA
VILLA
Villa Medici
MEDICI
Porta S. Pancrazio (Museo Garibaldino)
Antico Arco
Caffè del Gianicolo
P.le Aurelio
Fontana d. Acqua Paola
S. Pietro in Montorio
Bramante's Tempietto
Mausoleo Ossario Gianicolense
Il Vascello
Casino
Ambasciata d. Belgio
I QUATTRO VENTI
Accademia d'America
Via Aurelia Antica
Via Garibaldi
Via d. S. Pancrazio
Viale di Trastevere
Via Nuova d. Fornaci
Viale delle Mura Aurelie
P.za S. Pancrazio
TRASTEVERE
VILLA SCIARRA
Villa Sciarra
VILLA DORIA PAMPHILI
Via Vitellia
Via Fonteiana
P.za Rosolino Pilo
S. Maria Regina Pacis
Viale dei Quattro Venti
Via Giacinto Carini
Viale di Villa Pamphili
P.za Ippolito Nievo
Via Alessandro Poerio
Via Anton Giulio Barrili
S. Maria d. Prov.
P.za Donna Olimpia
Via Donna Olimpia
P.le Quattro Venti
MONTEVERDE NUOVO
N. S. de la Salette
Missione di Salette
Via Ettore Rolli
Via Portuense

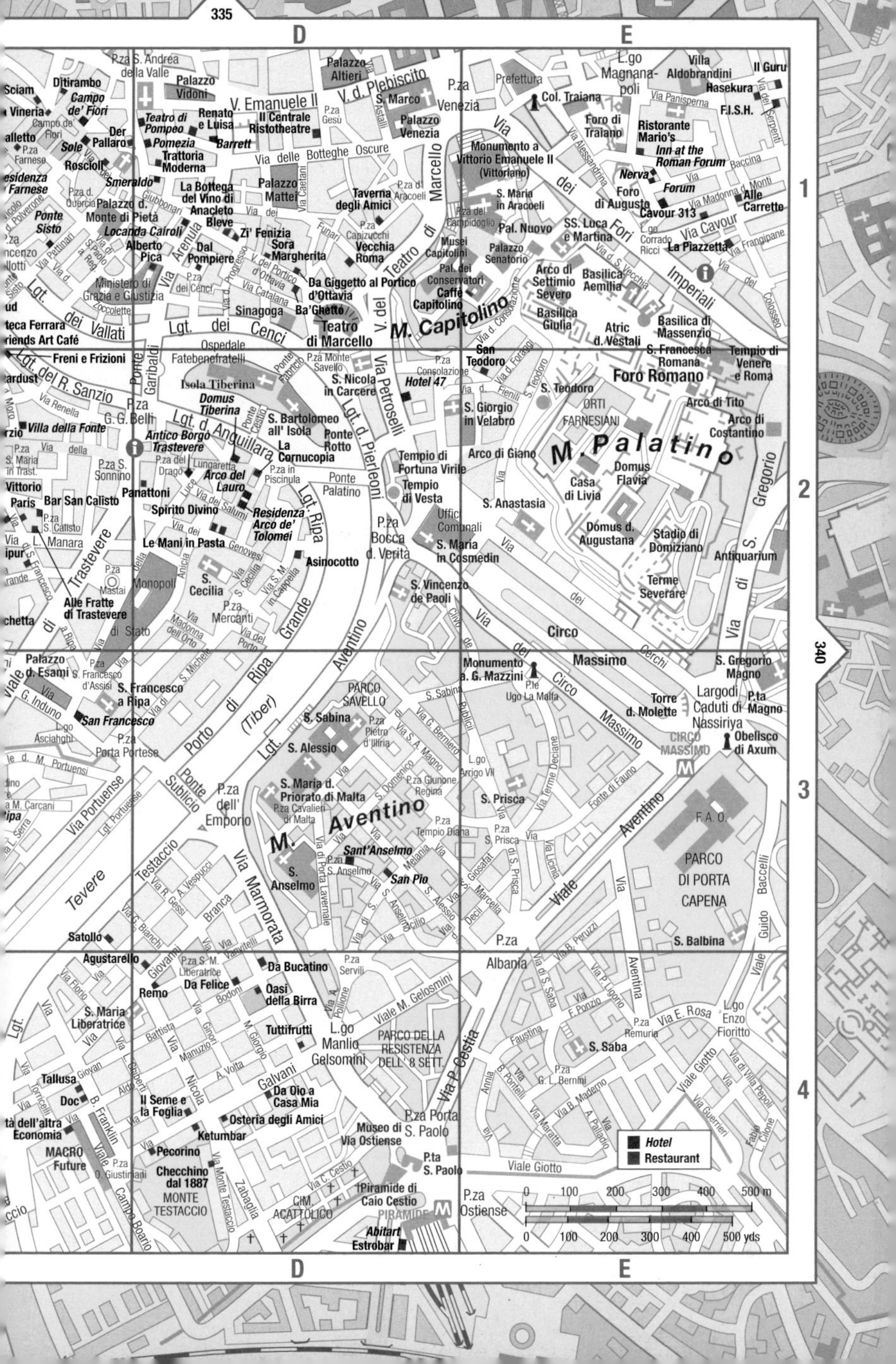

335

D E

Ditirambo
Campo de' Fiori
Der Pallaro
Sole
Roscioli
Smeraldo
Residenza Farnese
Palazzo d. Monte di Pietà
Ponte Sisto
Locanda Cairoli
Alberto Pica
Teatro di Pompeo
Pomezia
Renato e Luisa
Barrett
Trattoria Moderna
Il Centrale Ristotheatre
La Bottega del Vino di Anacleto Bleve
Zi' Fenizia
Sora Margherita
Dal Pompiere
Da Giggetto al Portico d'Ottavia
Ba'Ghetto
Taverna degli Amici
Vecchia Roma
Palazzo Mattei
Palazzo Altieri
S. Marco
Palazzo Venezia
Monumento a Vittorio Emanuele II (Vittoriano)
S. Maria in Aracoeli
Pal. Nuovo
Musei Capitolini
Palazzo Senatorio
Pal. dei Conservatori
Caffè Capitolino
M. Capitolino
Teatro di Marcello
Sinagoga
Col. Traiana
Foro di Traiano
Ristorante Mario's
Inn at the Roman Forum
Nerva
Forum
Foro di Augusto
Cavour 313
Alle Carrette
La Piazzetta
Hasekura
F.I.S.H.
Il Guru
Villa Aldobrandini
SS. Luca e Martina
Arco di Settimio Severo
Basilica Aemilia
Basilica Giulia
Atric d. Vestali
Basilica di Massenzio
S. Francesca Romana
Tempio di Venere e Roma
Foro Romano
Arco di Tito
Arco di Costantino
M. Palatino
Orti Farnesiani
Domus Flavia
Casa di Livia
Domus d. Augustana
Stadio di Domiziano
Antiquarium
Terme Severare
Circo Massimo
Freni e Frizioni
Isola Tiberina
Domus Tiberina
S. Bartolomeo all' Isola
Villa della Fonte
Antico Borgo Trastevere
Arco del Lauro
La Cornucopia
Panattoni
Bar San Calisto
Paris
Vittorio
Spirito Divino
Residenza Arco de' Tolomei
Le Mani in Pasta
Asinocotto
S. Cecilia
Alle Fratte di Trastevere
S. Nicola in Carcere
Hotel 47
San Teodoro
S. Teodoro
S. Giorgio in Velabro
Arco di Giano
Tempio di Fortuna Virile
Tempio di Vesta
S. Anastasia
S. Maria in Cosmedin
S. Vincenzo de Paoli
Monumento a. G. Mazzini
S. Gregorio Magno
Torre d. Molette
Largo Caduti di Nassiriya
Obelisco di Axum
Palazzo d. Esami
S. Francesco a Ripa
San Francesco
Parco Savello
S. Sabina
S. Alessio
S. Maria d. Priorato di Malta
M. Aventino
S. Anselmo
Sant'Anselmo
San Pio
S. Prisca
F.A.O.
Parco di Porta Capena
S. Balbina
Satollo
Agustarello
Da Bucatino
Da Felice
Remo
Oasi della Birra
S. Maria Liberatrice
Tuttifrutti
Parco della Resistenza dell' 8 Sett.
S. Saba
Tallusa
Doc
Il Seme e la Foglia
Osteria degli Amici
Da Oio a Casa Mia
Città dell'altra Economia
MACRO Future
Ketumbar
Pecorino
Checchino dal 1887
Monte Testaccio
Museo di Via Ostiense
P.ta S. Paolo
Piramide di Caio Cestio
Cim. Acattolico
Abitart
Estrobar

1 2 3 4

Hotel
Restaurant

0 100 200 300 400 500 m
0 100 200 300 400 500 yds

340

D E

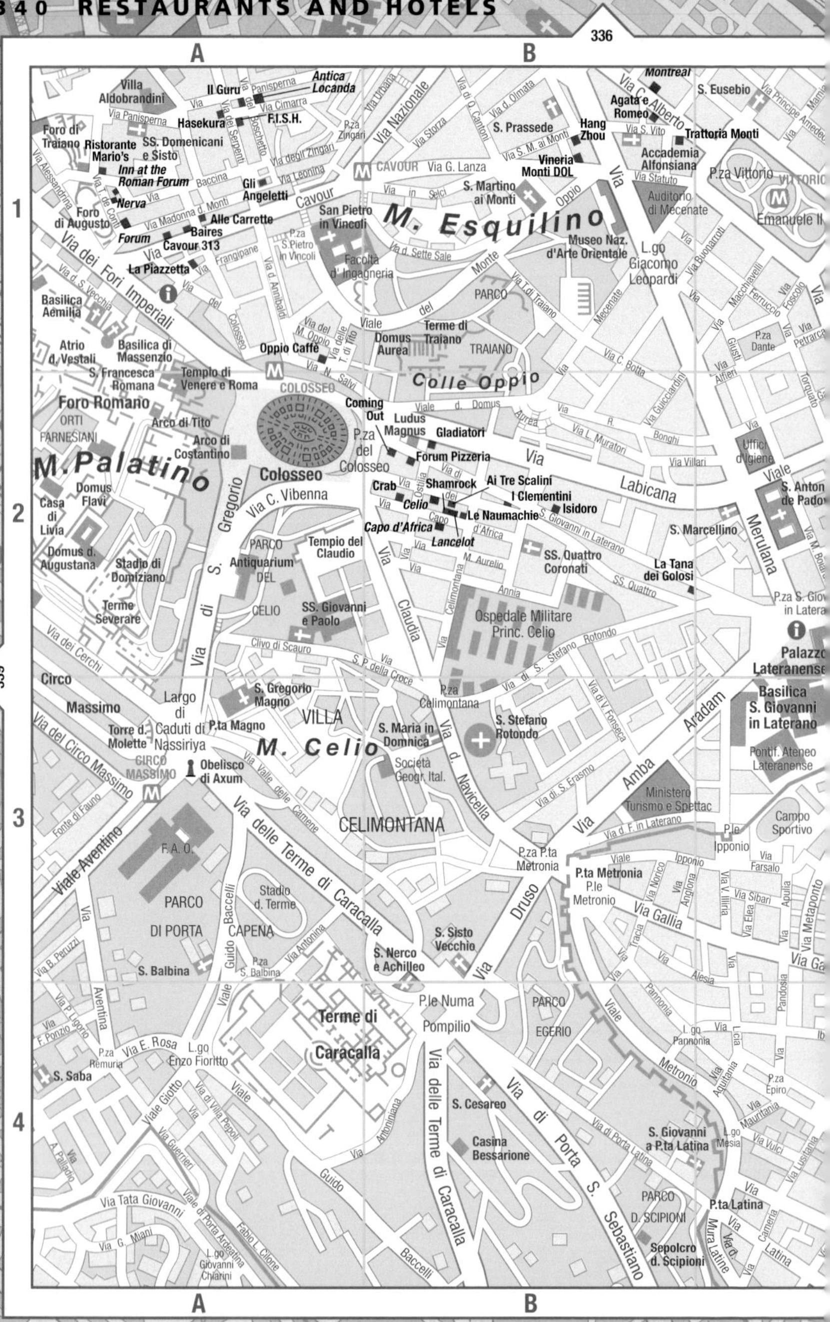
336
339
A
B
1
2
3
4
Villa Aldobrandini
Il Guru
Antica Locanda
Via Panisperna
Via Cimarra
F.I.S.H.
Hasekura
Via dei Serpenti
Boschetto
P.za Zingari
Via degli Zingari
Foro di Traiano
Ristorante Mario's
SS. Domenicani e Sisto
Inn at the Roman Forum
Baccina
Gli Angeletti
Via Leonina
Via Alessandrina
Nerva
Foro di Augusto
Via Madonna d. Monti
Alle Carrette
Baires
Forum
Cavour 313
Cavour
Frangipane
La Piazzetta
San Pietro in Vincoli
P.za S. Pietro in Vincoli
Via dei Fori Imperiali
Via d. S. Vecchia
Basilica Aemilia
Atrio d. Vestali
Basilica di Massenzio
S. Francesca Romana
Tempio di Venere e Roma
Foro Romano
Orti Farnesiani
Arco di Tito
Arco di Costantino
M. Palatino
Colosseo
Casa di Livia
Domus Flavi
Domus d. Augustana
Stadio di Domiziano
Terme Severare
Via dei Cerchi
Circo Massimo
Largo di Caduti di Nassiriya
Torre d. Molette
Via del Circo Massimo
Obelisco di Axum
Fonte di Fauno
Viale Aventino
F.A.O.
Parco di Porta Capena
S. Balbina
P.za S. Balbina
Via B. Peruzzi
Aventina
Via P. Ligorio
F. Ponzio
P.za Remuria
Via E. Rosa
L.go Enzo Fioritto
S. Saba
Viale Giotto
Via di Villa Pepoli
Via Guerrieri
A. Palladio
Via Tata Giovanni
Viale di Porta Ardeatina
Via G. Miani
Fabio L. Cilone
L.go Giovanni Chiarini
Via Nazionale
Via Urbana
Via Storza
Via di Q. Cantoni
Via d. Olmata
S. Prassede
Via S. M. ai Monti
Cavour
Via G. Lanza
Via in Selci
S. Martino ai Monti
Vineria
Monti DOL
Hang Zhou
M. Esquilino
Facoltà d' Ingegneria
Via d. Sette Sale
Via d. Annibaldi
Via del Colosseo
Via del M. Oppio
Via delle T. di Tito
Oppio Caffè
Via N. Salvi
Viale del Monte Oppio
Domus Aurea
Terme di Traiano
Parco Traiano
Colle Oppio
Via T. di Traiano
Museo Naz. d'Arte Orientale
Montreal
Via C. Alberto
Agata e Romeo
S. Eusebio
Via Principe Amedeo
Trattoria Monti
Via S. Vito
Accademia Alfonsiana
Via Statuto
Auditorio di Mecenate
P.za Vittorio
Vittorio Emanuele II
L.go Giacomo Leopardi
Via Mecenate
Via Buonarroti
Via Macchiavelli
Via Ferruccio
Via Foscolo
P.za Dante
Via Petrarca
Via Giusti
Via Alfieri
Torquato
Via C. Botta
Via Guicciardini
Via Aurea
Viale d. Domus
Via R. Bonghi
Via L. Muratori
Via Villari
Ufficio d'Igiene
Coming Out
Ludus Magnus
Gladiatori
P.za del Colosseo
Forum Pizzeria
Via Labicana
Via C. Vibenna
Via di S. Gregorio
Crab
Via Ostilia
Shamrock
Ai Tre Scalini
I Clementini
Isidoro
Celio
Le Naumachie
Capo d'Africa
Lancelot
Via S. Giovanni in Laterano
S. Marcellino
Merulana
Viale S. Antonio de Padova
Via M. Boiardo
Tempio del Claudio
Parco del Celio
Antiquarium
Via Claudia
M. Aurelio
SS. Quattro Coronati
La Tana dei Golosi
Via SS. Quattro
Annia
P.za S. Giovanni in Laterano
Via Celimontana
Ospedale Militare Princ. Celio
SS. Giovanni e Paolo
Clivo di Scauro
Via S. Stefano Rotondo
Palazzo Lateranense
Via S. P. della Croce
S. Gregorio Magno
P.ta Magno
Villa Celimontana
M. Celio
P.za Celimontana
Via d. Navicella
S. Stefano Rotondo
Via di V. Fonseca
Basilica S. Giovanni in Laterano
Pontif. Ateneo Lateranense
S. Maria in Domnica
Società Geogr. Ital.
Via Valle delle Camene
Via di S. Erasmo
Via Amba Aradam
Ministero Turismo e Spettac
Via delle Terme di Caracalla
Stadio d. Terme
P.za P.ta Metronia
Via d. F. in Laterano
P.le Ipponio
Campo Sportivo
Via Farsala
P.ta Metronia
P.le Metronio
Viale Ipponio
Via Norico
Via Angiona
Via V. Illiria
Via Sibari
Via Elea
Apulia
Via Metaponto
Via Gallia
Via Tracia
Via Druso
S. Sisto Vecchio
Via Antonina
S. Nerco e Achilleo
Viale Guido Baccelli
P.le Numa Pompilio
Terme di Caracalla
Parco Egerio
Viale Pannonia
Via Alesia
Pandosia
Via Ga
L.go Pannonia
Via Lucia
Viale Metronio
Via Aquitania
P.za Epiro
Via Mauritania
Via Vulci
Via Lusitania
L.go Mesia
S. Giovanni a P.ta Latina
Via delle Terme di Caracalla
Via di Porta S. Sebastiano
Via di Porta Latina
S. Cesareo
Casina Bessarione
Parco d. Scipioni
Sepolcro d. Scipioni
P.ta Latina
Via Latina
Via Camelia
Mura Latine
Via Antoniniana
Guido Baccelli

337

D E

0 100 200 300 400 500 m

0 100 200 300 400 500 yds

Hotel
Restaurant

1 2 3 4

P.le Tiburtino
Formula Uno
Arancia Blu
P.za di P.ta S. Lorenzo
Da Franco ar Vicoletto
S. Bibiana
Il Palazzo del Freddo di Giovanni Fassi
P.za Prenestina
P.za di Porta Maggiore
P.ta Maggiore
Hostaria degli Artisti
Villa Altieri
Acquedotto Neroniano
Villa Wolkonski
P.za di S. Croce in Gerusalemme
Domus Sessoriana
S. Croce in Gerusalemme
Anfiteatro Castrense
P.za Porta S. Giovanni
L.go Brindisi
P.le Appio
P.ta Asinaria
P.ta S. Giovanni
S. Giovanni
SS. Immacolata
P.za Caballini
P.za del Pigneto
P.za Lodi
P.za Camerino
P.za Castroreale
SS. Fabiano
P.za di Villa Fiorelli
P.za Lugo
S. Maria d. Orto
P.za dei Re di Roma
Re di Roma
L.go Vercelli
L.go Frassinetti
P.za Asti
P.za Ragusa
Staz. Roma-Tuscolana F.S.
P.za S. Donà di Piave
Ognissanti
Ponte Lungo
L.go Don Orione
P.za di Ponte Lungo
P.za Finocchiaro Aprile
P.za Camillo Re
Istituto Antoniano di Roma
P.za Tuscolo
P.za Armenia
P.za Zama
P.za Tarquinia
L.go Magna Grecia
P.za Sulmona
P.za Imola
Tuscolano

Via Prenestina
Via Casilina
Viale Castrense
Via La Spezia
Via Appia Nuova
Via Tuscolana
Via Etruria
Circonvallazione Appia
Sopraelevata
Via d. Scalo S. Lorenzo
Via di Porta Maggiore
Viale Carlo Felice
Via Giovanni Giolitti
Via L'Aquila
Via del Pigneto

D E

STREET INDEX

D

E

F

G

H–K

L

Q

R

S

T

U

V

W–Z

General Index

A page reference in **bold** indicates the main entry in the book.

D

E

F

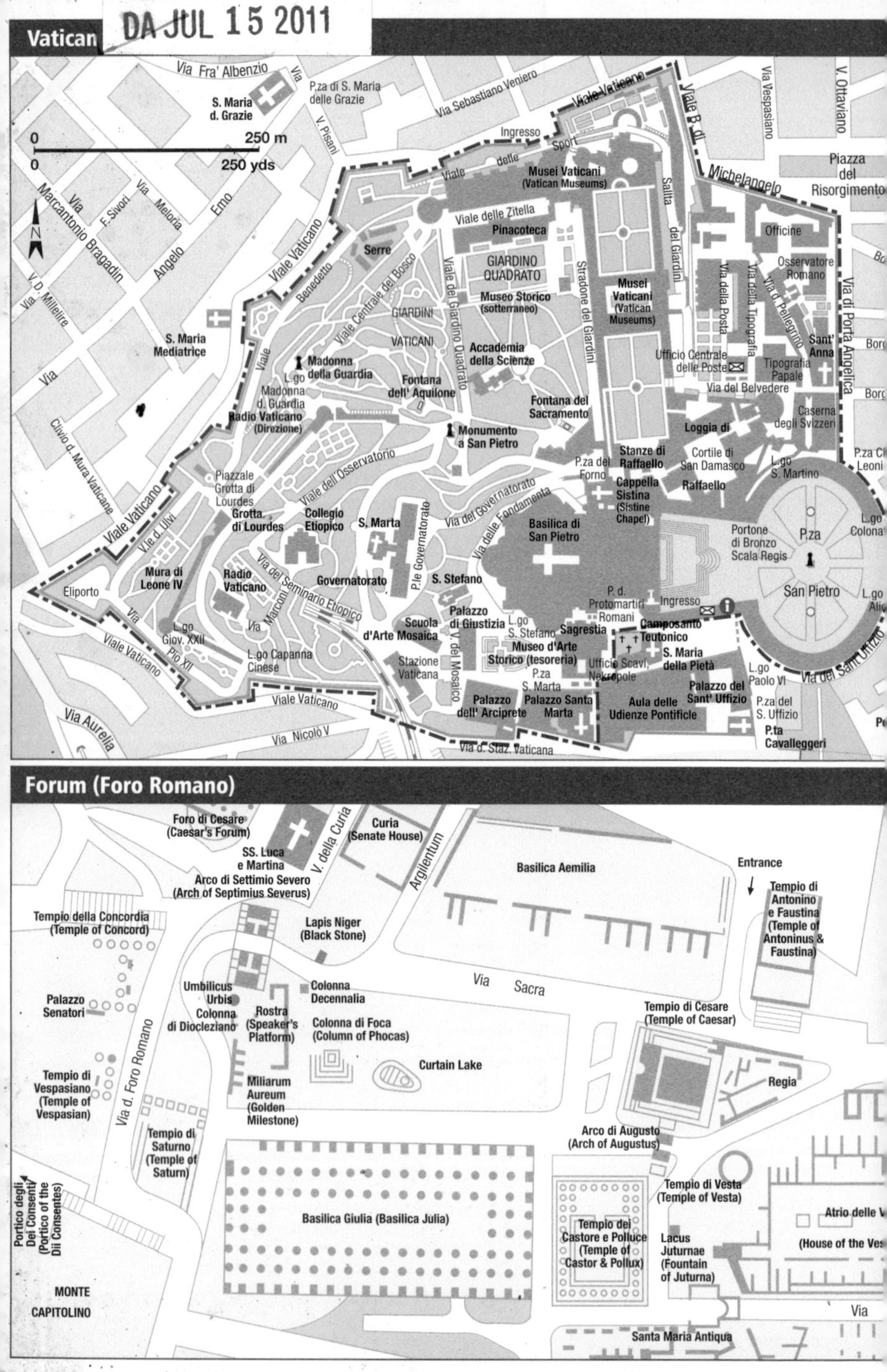

Vatican
DA JUL 15 2011
Via Fra' Albenzio
P.za di S. Maria delle Grazie
S. Maria d. Grazie
V. Pisani
Via Sebastiano Veniero
Viale Vaticano
Viale B. di Michelangelo
Via Vespasiano
V. Ottaviano
Piazza del Risorgimento
0 250 m
0 250 yds
Via Marcantonio Bragadin
F. Sivori
Via Meloria
Emo
Angelo
V.D. Millelire
Via
Ingresso
Viale delle Sport
Musei Vaticani (Vatican Museums)
Viale delle Zitella
Pinacoteca
GIARDINO QUADRATO
Museo Storico (sotterraneo)
Serre
Benedetto
Viale Centrale del Bosco
GIARDINI VATICANI
Viale del Giardino Quadrato
Stradone dei Giardini
Salita dei Giardini
Musei Vaticani (Vatican Museums)
Via della Posta
Via della Tipografia
Via d. Pellegrino
Officine
Osservatore Romano
Via di Porta Angelica
Sant' Anna
Tipografia Papale
Ufficio Centrale delle Poste
Via del Belvedere
Caserna degli Svizzeri
S. Maria Mediatrice
Viale
Madonna della Guardia
L.go Madonna d. Guardia
Fontana dell' Aquilone
Accademia della Scienze
Fontana del Sacramento
Radio Vaticano (Direzione)
Monumento a San Pietro
Loggia di Raffaello
Cortile di San Damasco
L.go S. Martino
P.za Città Leoni
Clivio d. Mura Vaticane
Piazzale Grotta di Lourdes
Grotta di Lourdes
Viale dell' Osservatorio
Collegio Etiopico
S. Marta
P.le Governatorato
Via del Governatorato
Via delle Fondamenta
P.za del Forno
Stanze di Raffaello
Cappella Sistina (Sistine Chapel)
Basilica di San Pietro
Portone di Bronzo Scala Regis
P.za San Pietro
L.go Colonna
Viale Vaticano
V.le d. Ulivi
Mura di Leone IV
Eliporto
Radio Vaticano
Via del Seminario Etiopico
Via Marconi
Governatorato
S. Stefano
P. d. Protomartiri Romani
Ingresso
Camposanto Teutonico
L.go Alicorni
Via
L.go Giov. XXIII
Pio XII
Via
L.go Capanna Cinese
Scuola d'Arte Mosaica
Palazzo di Giustizia
L.go S. Stefano
Sagrestia
Museo d'Arte Storico (tesoreria)
Ufficio Scavi, Nekropole
S. Maria della Pietà
Via del Sant' Uffizio
Stazione Vaticana
V. del Mosaico
P.za S. Marta
L.go Paolo VI
Palazzo del Sant' Uffizio
Viale Vaticano
Via Aurelia
Palazzo dell' Arciprete
Palazzo Santa Marta
Aula delle Udienze Pontificie
P.za del S. Uffizio
P.ta Cavalleggeri
Via Nicolò V
Via d. Staz. Vaticana
Forum (Foro Romano)
Foro di Cesare (Caesar's Forum)
SS. Luca e Martina
V. della Curia
Curia (Senate House)
Argilentum
Basilica Aemilia
Entrance
Arco di Settimio Severo (Arch of Septimius Severus)
Tempio di Antonino e Faustina (Temple of Antoninus & Faustina)
Tempio della Concordia (Temple of Concord)
Lapis Niger (Black Stone)
Via Sacra
Palazzo Senatori
Umbilicus Urbis
Colonna di Diocleziano
Colonna Decennalia
Rostra (Speaker's Platform)
Colonna di Foca (Column of Phocas)
Tempio di Cesare (Temple of Caesar)
Curtain Lake
Regia
Tempio di Vespasiano (Temple of Vespasian)
Via d. Foro Romano
Miliarum Aureum (Golden Milestone)
Tempio di Saturno (Temple of Saturn)
Arco di Augusto (Arch of Augustus)
Portico degli Dei Consenti (Portico of the Dii Consentes)
Basilica Giulia (Basilica Julia)
Tempio dei Castore e Polluce (Temple of Castor & Pollux)
Tempio di Vesta (Temple of Vesta)
Lacus Juturnae (Fountain of Juturna)
MONTE CAPITOLINO
Santa Maria Antiqua
Via